Windows XP®

in 10 Simple Steps or Less

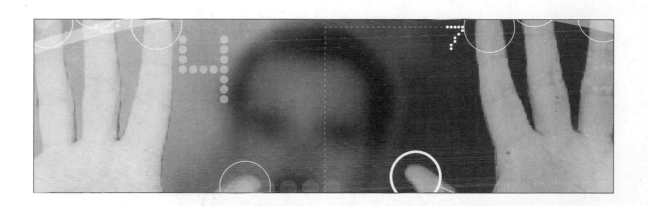

Bill Hatfield and Bradley L. Jones

Wiley Publishing, Inc.

Windows XP® in 10 Simple Steps or Less

Published by
Wiley Publishing, Inc.
10475 Crosspoint Boulevard
Indianapolis, IN 46256
www.wiley.com

Copyright © 2004 by Wiley Publishing, Inc., Indianapolis, Indiana

Published simultaneously in Canada

ISBN: 0-7645-4236-2

Manufactured in the United States of America

10 9 8 7 6 5 4 3 2 1

1O/QY/RQ/QU/IN

This book is dedicated to Zoe Rose Hatfield, born Friday, December 20, 2002.

Zoe, your sweet smile and quick laugh have lit up your mother's and my life ever since we brought you home a few short months ago. And there's nothing in the world I love more than holding you in my arms as you fall asleep at night.

I can already see the personality of an independent, loving, playful little girl emerging. I can't wait to see the kind of girl, and woman, you'll grow up to be!

—Bill Hatfield

For the love of my life, my wife, Melissa.

—Bradley Jones

Credits

Acquisitions Editor
Sharon Cox

Development Editor
Chandani Thapa

Production Editor
Vincent Kunkemueller

Technical Editor
Lee Musick

Copy Editor
Joanne Slike

Editorial Manager
Kathryn A. Malm

Vice President & Executive Group Publisher
Richard Swadley

Vice President and Executive Publisher
Bob Ipsen

Vice President and Publisher
Joseph B. Wikert

Executive Editorial Director
Mary Bednarek

Project Coordinator
Nancee Reeves

Graphics and Production Specialists
Beth Brooks, LeAndra Hosier, Lynsey Osborn,
Heather Pope

Quality Control Technician
Laura Albert

Proofreading and Indexing
Tom Dinse, Sossity R. Smith

About the Authors

Bill Hatfield is the bestselling author of books on a variety of subjects including *ASP.NET For Dummies* and *Active Server Pages For Dummies* (Wiley). He is also the Editor of *Hardcore Visual Studio .NET* and *Hardcore Delphi*, two technical journals from Pinnacle for professional software developers. He's an independent corporate trainer and works from his home in Indianapolis, Indiana, where he and his wife have been blessed with two great kids — Bryce (`BryceHatfield.com`) and Zoe (`ZoeHatfield.com`).

Bradley Jones oversees a number of high-profile Web sites within the internet.com division of Jupiter Media. This has included sites such as HTMLGoodies.com and Javascripts.com, as well as more technical sites like CodeGuru, Developer.com, and Gamelan. Bradley, an internationally best-selling author, has written a number of books for people who are interested in learning about computers and technology. These include writing Sams *Teach Yourself C# in 21 Days* and *Even You Can Soup Up and Fix PCs*.

Acknowledgments

First, we want to thank Sharon Cox for inviting us into the process of writing this book and for her guidance along the way. When pulling together a book, there are dozens of people involved in the process. While it is impossible to thank them all, in addition to Sharon Cox, we would also like to acknowledge the work of several others. They are a part of the team who worked together to make this the best possible book for you.

Foremost, we would like to thank Lee Musick, who diligently went through every step in every task of this book to ensure that you were getting the most accurate information available.

We'd also like to acknowledge Chandani Thapa, Joanne Slike, and Vince Kunkemueller. They helped construct this book, and they ensured that the project came together into a complete package. Their help and feedback made this a better book.

We would also like to thank you, the reader, for choosing this book over the many other Windows XP books that you could have chosen.

Finally, Bradley would like to thank his wife, Melissa, who read through the book to make sure that it was written in a way that the average person could understand what was being presented. Her reviews helped to hone the material so that even a person using a computer for the first time would find value in this book.

Contents

About the Authors   v

Acknowledgments   vii

Introduction   xix

Part 1: Understanding Windows XP Basics   **1**

Task 1: Starting Up and Logging In   2

Task 2: Logging Off and Shutting Down   4

Task 3: Activating Windows   6

Task 4: Enabling Fast Switching between Users   8

Task 5: Setting Your Computer's Clock and Time Zone   10

Task 6: Setting the Clock Automatically   12

Task 7: Adjusting Your Computer's Volume   14

Task 8: Automatically Turning the Monitor Off   16

Task 9: Locking and Unlocking the Computer   18

Task 10: Locking Your Computer with a Screen Saver   20

Task 11: Getting Help   22

Task 12: Customizing Help Screens   24

Task 13: Setting Search Options for Help   26

Task 14: Creating a Help and Support Favorites List   28

Task 15: Using the Knowledge Base   30

Task 16: Getting Basic Information about Your System   32

Task 17: Automatically Keeping Windows Up-to-Date   34

Task 18: Manually Updating Windows XP   36

Task 19: Installing New Software   38

Task 20: Removing Application Software   40

Part 2: Working with Folders and Files   **43**

Task 21: Accessing My Computer   44

Task 22: Navigating What's on the Hard Drive   46

Task 23: Creating, Renaming, and Deleting Files and Folders   48

Task 24: Creating Copies of Files and Folders   50

Task 25: Moving a File or Folder · 52

Task 26: Using Different Folder Views · 54

Task 27: Customizing the Details Folder View · 56

Task 28: Settings Options on All Folders · 58

Task 29: Customizing Windows Explorer · 60

Task 30: Recovering Deleted Files · 62

Task 31: Setting Recycle Bin Options · 64

Task 32: Searching for Files or Folders · 66

Task 33: Setting File Properties · 68

Task 34: Creating a Shortcut · 70

Task 35: Copying Files to a CD-ROM · 72

Task 36: Saving Space by Compressing a Drive · 74

Task 37: Creating a Zip File · 76

Task 38: Accessing and Adding to a Zip File · 78

Task 39: Extracting All Items from a Zip File · 80

Part 3: Personalizing Windows XP · **83**

Task 40: Choosing a Theme · 84

Task 41: Setting the Screen Colors and Resolution · 86

Task 42: Choosing a Desktop Background Image · 88

Task 43: Setting or Changing a Screen Saver · 90

Task 44: Choosing or Changing an Appearance · 92

Task 45: Assigning Sounds to Events · 94

Task 46: Creating a New Theme · 96

Task 47: Customizing Your Taskbar · 98

Task 48: Customizing the Quick Launch Toolbar · 100

Task 49: Customizing the Start Menu · 102

Task 50: Adding Shortcuts to Your Desktop · 104

Task 51: Arranging Your Desktop Items · 106

Task 52: Picking a Program's Icon to Display · 108

Task 53: Placing Standard Items and Icons on the Desktop · 110

Task 54: Putting Web Pages on Your Desktop · 112

Task 55: Customizing Mouse Options · 114

Task 56: Customizing the Mouse Pointers · 116

Task 57: Setting Keyboard Options · 118

Task 58: Automatically Starting a Program at Startup · 120

Task 59: Changing Regional Settings · 122

Task 60: Changing Number and Currency Formatting · 124

Part 4: Graphics and Digital Photography — 127

Task 61: Copying Pictures from Your Camera to Your Hard Drive — 128
Task 62: Using a Scanner to Capture Photographs — 130
Task 63: Capturing a Picture of Your Screen — 132
Task 64: Creating Your Own Icons in Paint — 134
Task 65: Drawing Pictures in Paint — 136
Task 66: Organizing Your Pictures into Folders and Photo Albums — 138
Task 67: Storing and Retrieving Information about Your Pictures — 140
Task 68: Viewing, Zooming, and Reorienting Your Pictures — 142
Task 69: Resizing a Picture — 144
Task 70: Cropping a Picture — 146
Task 71: Adding Notes and Drawings to a Picture — 148
Task 72: Converting a Picture's File Type — 150
Task 73: Printing a Picture — 152
Task 74: Ordering Prints of Your Pictures Online — 154
Task 75: Putting Your Pictures on the Web — 156
Task 76: Creating a Screen Saver with Your Own Pictures — 158

Part 5: Working with Digital Music — 161

Task 77: Upgrading Windows Media Player — 162
Task 78: Playing Music CDs — 164
Task 79: Copying Music from a CD to Your Hard Drive — 166
Task 80: Identifying Your Album Name, Artist, and Tracks — 168
Task 81: Finding and Playing Music in Your Media Library — 170
Task 82: Searching for Music to Add to Your Media Library — 172
Task 83: Adding and Viewing Song Lyrics — 174
Task 84: Creating and Listening to a Playlist — 176
Task 85: Downloading Music from the Internet — 178
Task 86: Tuning In to Internet Radio — 180
Task 87: Copying Music to a Portable Music Player — 182
Task 88: Creating Your Own Audio CD — 184
Task 89: Duplicating an Audio CD — 186
Task 90: Making Windows Media Player Beautiful with Skins — 188

Part 6: Working with Digital Movies — 191

Task 91: Upgrading Windows Movie Maker — 192
Task 92: Playing a Movie on DVD — 194
Task 93: Playing a Video File — 196
Task 94: Creating and Deleting Collections in Windows Movie Maker — 198

Task 95: Importing Clips and Other Items into Your Collections in   200
        Windows Movie Maker

Task 96: Making Movies   202

Task 97: Capturing Video from Your Camcorder   204

Task 98: Capturing a Photograph from a Video   206

Task 99: Capturing Live Video   208

Task 100: Splitting and Combining Video Clips   210

Task 101: Trimming a Video Clip   212

Task 102: Adding Transitions between Your Video Clips   214

Task 103: Adding Video Effects to Your Clips   216

Task 104: Adding Titles and Credits to Your Movie   218

Task 105: Adding Photographs to a Movie   220

Task 106: Adding Background Music and Sound Effects to a Movie   222

Task 107: Adding Narration to a Movie   224

Task 108: Saving a Movie to View on Your Computer   226

Task 109: Sending a Movie via Email   228

Part 7: Working with Notepad   **231**

Task 110: Creating a New Document Using Notepad   232

Task 111: Saving a Document from Notepad   234

Task 112: Changing the Page Setup in Notepad   236

Task 113: Creating Headers and Footers on a Notepad Document   238

Task 114: Changing the Font in Notepad   240

Task 115: Printing a Document in Notepad   242

Task 116: Finding and Replacing Text in Notepad   244

Task 117: Creating a Log File with Notepad   246

Task 118: Creating a Web Page in Notepad   248

Part 8: Working with WordPad   **251**

Task 119: Creating a New Document in WordPad   252

Task 120: Saving a Document in WordPad   254

Task 121: Changing the Page Setup in WordPad   256

Task 122: Using WordPad's Print Preview   258

Task 123: Printing from WordPad   260

Task 124: Changing Font Characteristics in WordPad   262

Task 125: Formatting Paragraph Margins in WordPad   264

Task 126: Adding Lists to a WordPad Document   266

Task 127: Searching and Replacing Text in WordPad   268

Task 128: Inserting a Picture into a WordPad Document   270

Task 129: Adding an Object to a WordPad Document   272

Task 130: Changing Object Properties in a Document   274

Task 131: Sending a WordPad Document to Someone Else   276
Task 132: Setting Options in WordPad   278

Part 9: Getting Connected to the Internet   281
Task 133: Creating an MSN Account to Access the Internet Using a Modem   282
Task 134: Connecting to the Internet with a Modem Using Another ISP   284
Task 135: Connecting to the Internet with a Broadband Cable or DSL Line   286
Task 136: Connecting to the Internet with a LAN and a Router   288
Task 137: Connecting to a Virtual Private Network   290

Part 10: Surfing the Web with Microsoft Internet Explorer   293
Task 138: Using Internet Explorer for the First Time   294
Task 139: Going to a Site's Address with Microsoft Internet Explorer   296
Task 140: Searching the Web   298
Task 141: Saving a Web Page   300
Task 142: Emailing Web Pages   302
Task 143: Printing Web Pages   304
Task 144: Downloading Files from the Web   306
Task 145: Copying and Saving Images from the Web   308
Task 146: Keeping a Favorites List of Sites   310
Task 147: Organizing Your Favorites List of Sites   312
Task 148: Customizing the Links Bar   314
Task 149: Checking Your History in Internet Explorer   316
Task 150: Clearing and Customizing History Features   318
Task 151: Deleting Temporary Internet Files   320
Task 152: Setting Your Home Page   322
Task 153: Customizing Internet Explorer's Support Programs   324
Task 154: Customizing Internet Explorer's Tools and More   326
Task 155: Choosing Privacy Settings   328
Task 156: Choosing Security Settings   330
Task 157: Restricting Objectionable Materials   332

Part 11: Interacting with Email   335
Task 158: Setting Up Your Email   336
Task 159: Retrieving and Viewing Email Messages   338
Task 160: Opening and Saving Received Attachments   340
Task 161: Creating and Sending Email   342
Task 162: Forwarding or Replying to a Message   344
Task 163: Sending a Picture or File as an Attachment   346
Task 164: Using Stationery   348
Task 165: Creating Your Own Stationery   350

Task 166: Creating and Using a Signature   352
Task 167: Organizing Your Inbox   354
Task 168: Filing Your Email into Folders   356
Task 169: Finding a Message   358
Task 170: Using Your Address Book   360
Task 171: Creating Your Own Virtual Business Card   362
Task 172: Sending Virtual Business Cards   364
Task 173: Adding Virtual Business Cards to Your Address Book   366
Task 174: Using Message Rules to Kill Spam and Do Other Cool Stuff   368

Part 12: Discussing with Newsgroups   **371**
Task 175: Connecting to a Newsgroup Server   372
Task 176: Searching for and Subscribing to Newsgroups   374
Task 177: Reading Newsgroup Messages   376
Task 178: Posting a New Message to a Newsgroup   378
Task 179: Replying to a Newsgroup Message   380
Task 180: Downloading Newsgroup Message Attachments   382
Task 181: Downloading Multipart Newsgroup Message Attachments   384
Task 182: Searching for Messages in a Newsgroup   386

Part 13: Exploring Windows Messenger   **389**
Task 183: Creating a Passport Account   390
Task 184: Adding and Deleting Contacts   392
Task 185: Carrying On a Conversation   394
Task 186: Changing Your Look in Windows Messenger   396
Task 187: Sending a File or a Picture   398
Task 188: Receiving a File or a Picture   400
Task 189: Configuring Your Audio and Video in Windows Messenger   402
Task 190: Adding Voice and Video to Your Conversation   404

Part 14: Exploring the Other Accessories   **407**
Task 191: Using the Basic Calculator   408
Task 192: Using the Scientific Calculator   410
Task 193: Performing Statistical Calculations   412
Task 194: Converting Numbers   414
Task 195: Configuring Your Computer to Send Faxes   416
Task 196: Sending a Fax   418
Task 197: Recording Sounds: The Sound Recorder   420
Task 198: Mixing and Modifying Sounds   422

Part 15: Accessibility Features   425

Task 199: Changing the Windows Font Size   426

Task 200: Using the Magnifier   428

Task 201: Using the Narrator   430

Task 202: Using the On-Screen Keyboard   432

Task 203: Selecting the On-Screen Keyboard Layout   434

Task 204: Setting Usability Feature Options   436

Task 205: Setting Usability Feature Options with the Accessibility Wizard   438

Task 206: Using and Setting StickyKeys   440

Task 207: Using and Setting FilterKeys   442

Part 16: Working with User Accounts   445

Task 208: Setting Up a Guest Account   446

Task 209: Creating New User Accounts   448

Task 210: Deleting a User Account   450

Task 211: Changing a User's Account Name   452

Task 212: Changing the Icon on a User Account   454

Task 213: Changing a User's Account Type   456

Task 214: Adding a Password to a User Account   458

Task 215: Changing a User Account's Password   460

Task 216: Removing a Password from a User Account   462

Part 17: Configuring Your Hardware   465

Task 217: Checking Your Hardware's Status   466

Task 218: Customizing Speaker Settings   468

Task 219: Installing a Printer   470

Task 220: Using a Removable Storage Device   472

Task 221: Installing a Game Controller   474

Task 222: Setting Up Two Monitors   476

Task 223: Uninstalling a Device   478

Part 18: Creating a Simple Network (LAN)   481

Task 224: Setting Up Your Own Network   482

Task 225: Configuring Your Computers for the Network   484

Task 226: Sharing a Printer   486

Task 227: Accessing a Shared Printer   488

Task 228: Sharing Files   490

Task 229: Accessing Shared Files   492

Task 230: Assigning a Drive Letter to a Shared Folder   494

Part 19: Taking Windows XP on the Road   **497**

Task 231: Conserving Power   498

Task 232: Putting Your Computer to Sleep: Hibernating   500

Task 233: Creating Multiple Dial-Up Connections   502

Task 234: Taking Files with You: Identifying Offline Files   504

Task 235: Using Offline Files and Resynchronizing   506

Task 236: Creating and Using a Briefcase   508

Part 20: Maintenance and Optimization   **511**

Task 237: Checking Your Hard Drive for Errors   512

Task 238: Defragmenting Your Hard Drive   514

Task 239: Cleaning Up Your Hard Drive and Making Room   516

Task 240: Adding and Removing Windows Components   518

Task 241: Removing an Application   520

Task 242: Cleaning Up Your Desktop   522

Task 243: The Ultimate Undo: System Restore   524

Task 244: Creating a Restore Point   526

Task 245: Configuring System Restore   528

Task 246: Backing Up Your Files   530

Task 247: Restoring Files from a Backup   532

Task 248: Updating Your System with the Latest Patches and Add-Ons   534

Part 21: Troubleshooting   **537**

Task 249: Getting Detailed Information about Your Computer   538

Task 250: Getting Older Programs to Run in Windows XP   540

Task 251: Closing a Program That Stops Responding   542

Task 252: Finding Lost Files   544

Task 253: Fixing the Screen When It Doesn't Look Right   546

Task 254: Configuring Your System for Remote Access   548

Task 255: Using Remote Desktop   550

Task 256: Asking for Remote Assistance   552

Task 257: Providing Remote Assistance   554

Task 258: Updating Your Video Driver   556

Task 259: Reporting Errors to Microsoft   558

Task 260: Fine-Tuning Your System's Performance   560

Task 261: My Computer's Still Too Slow!   562

Index   **565**

Introduction

Welcome to *Windows XP in 10 Simple Steps or Less*, a quick-reference designed to help you do exactly what you want in Windows XP, without a lot of reading! All you have to do is flip the book open to the table of contents, find what you want to do and turn to the page — where you'll find the illustrated steps you need to quickly get the job done *in ten simple steps or less!*

This book is written for anyone who uses Windows XP. You don't need any special knowledge or training. You will need access to a computer running a copy of Microsoft Windows XP Home Edition or Microsoft Windows XP Professional Edition. This book will help you regardless of the version of Windows XP you are using.

Why Do You Need This Book?

While Microsoft has continued to strive to make Windows easier to use, in reality it is still a complex set of programs that are not always intuitive. In today's fast-paced world, there are times when you need to know how to get something done and how to do it quickly and easily.

If you simply want a book to help you figure out how to accomplish a task — or to find out if a task can be accomplished — in Windows XP, then, again, this book is for you. If you want to learn all about the key features and programs within Windows XP, this book is also for you.

In addition to the concise steps and figures provided to accomplish specific tasks, we've also included numerous tips, tricks, and techniques in the margins to point out additional capabilities or to show you how to get things done faster the next time.

How This Book Is Organized

This book is organized into various parts that are described in the following.

Part 1: Understanding Windows XP Basics

Learn how to start using Windows XP effectively. You'll find out how to correctly start and exit Windows XP. You'll set the clock's time, adjust the computer's volume, lock and unlock the system, and more. You'll even discover how to access the various types of help available in Windows XP.

Part 2: Working with Files and Folders

Chances are, you will be working with files and documents on your computer. In fact, your computer can create, modify, delete, and move files and documents. In this second part, you will master the many features of Windows XP that help you in manipulating files and documents stored on your computer.

Part 3: Personalizing Windows XP

Everyone has his or her own likes and dislikes. Fortunately, Windows XP allows you to customize its look, feel, and even many of its operations based on your tastes. You'll learn to set the colors, choose a theme, change settings, start programs automatically, and more. If you want to personalize something in Windows XP, this is the place to begin.

Part 4: Graphics and Digital Photography

Now that you've bought that digital camera, what do you do with it? Many exciting and informative answers can be found in this part. You might start off by copying the pictures from your camera to your computer's hard drive. From there you might want to crop them, resize them, and organize them. Of course, pictures are no fun unless you share them with others, so you'll also learn how to view them on your screen, put them on a Web site, print them on your printer, or even send them off for professional picture processing. Finally, you'll also find out how to do other helpful things with graphic files on your computer such as scanning photographs, capturing a picture of your screen, making icons, converting a picture's file type, and even creating your own pictures.

Part 5: Working with Digital Music

Wouldn't it be nice if you could organize your collection of CDs just like you organize files on your hard drive? And wouldn't it be cool if you could search your collection for just the right music to match your mood? With Windows XP it's all possible. You'll find out how to copy songs from your CD to your hard drive, how to organize and play your music, and how to search your hard drive for exactly the right tune. You'll also find out how to (legally) download songs from the Internet and how to tune in to radio stations from all over the world. For those times when you're away from the computer, you'll discover how you can create your own CDs with your own mix of music or download songs to your portable digital music player.

Part 6: Working with Digital Movies

With Windows XP you can edit your own home videos with many of the same capabilities used by digital video professionals. After you capture the video from your camcorder, you can organize your clips into libraries. Then you can start putting your clips together as you like along with titles, credits, transitions, and even a few special effects. Finish your work with a musical score and a few sound effects.

Part 7: Working with Notepad

Notepad is a simple but powerful program, included with Windows XP, that allows you to create, edit, or view text documents. In this part you will learn the key steps to using Notepad.

Part 8: Working with WordPad

Whereas Notepad is designed to create and edit simple text documents, WordPad is a more sophisticated program that creates, edits, or views formatted documents. With WordPad you can add special layouts, fonts, colors, pictures, and much more. In this part you will discover all the important features available in WordPad.

Part 9: Getting Connected to the Internet

Everyone says how easy it is to surf the Web. But getting to that point is not always as easy as it should be. Whether you are interested in cable modems, DSL lines, or a simple dial-up connection, you'll find the steps you need to get wired here.

Part 10: Surfing the Web with Microsoft Internet Explorer

Windows XP includes Microsoft's Internet Explorer Web browser. Discover all the ins and outs of using this tool to surf Web pages and a whole lot more. Want to find out where your browser has been lately? Want to keep other people from finding out where you've been lately? You'll find these and many other tips and tricks in this part.

Part 11: Interacting with Email

Email is right up there with Web browsing as one of the most important capabilities offered by the Internet. At any given moment, thousands of email messages are jetting across the world over the Internet. Email allows people to stay in touch in ways they never would have before. Find out how to get connected to your email account and how to retrieve and send messages. You can even customize your messages with beautiful stationery and a personalized signature.

Part 12: Discussing with Newsgroups

A newsgroup isn't a place where you go to get news. It is more like a discussion forum. Each newsgroup has a topic. Anyone can go and read messages that others have posted on the particular topic and then post a message of their own to respond to one of the other posts, to make a statement, or to ask a question. These worldwide discussion forums are a great place to learn from and share with others who are interested in the same things you are interested in. Here you'll find out how to get connected to a newsgroup server, how to search for a newsgroup, how to read messages, and how to post your own messages.

Part 13: Exploring Windows Messenger

You can think of Windows Messenger as your buddy list. You add friends to your Windows Messenger list and it lets you know who's online right now and who's not. Then if you want to talk to one of your buddies, just double-click their name and you can start a live, text conversation. Find out how to add friends to your list, start conversations, send files or pictures, and even have voice or video conversations.

Part 14: Exploring the Other Accessories

A number of secondary programs are included with Windows XP that you might find useful. Within this part you will learn to work with the calculator, the sound mixer, and the fax programs that are all a part of the Windows XP accessories.

Part 15: Accessibility Features

Windows XP includes a number of features to help people who have disabilities. In this part, you will learn to use these accessibility features.

Part 16: Working with User Accounts

If more than one person is going to be using your computer, or if you want to create more than one custom setup, then you will need to work with User Accounts. User Accounts let you set up separate areas that can be customized for each user of your computer. In this part, you will learn to create these accounts, as well as how to change settings within the accounts.

Part 17: Configuring Your Hardware

Just bought a new joystick, printer, or external hard drive and don't know what to do next? This part will show you the steps you need to take to get Windows XP to recognize and customize itself to work correctly with these and other devices.

Part 18: Creating a Simple Network (LAN)

If you have more than one computer in the house and you've wondered how you could share files between them or use the printer on one computer from another computer, then you should consider setting up a simple network. The tasks in this part show you what hardware you need, how to set it up, and how to get Windows XP to recognize the other computers on your network.

Part 19: Taking Windows XP on the Road

Windows XP is a great desktop operating system. But it's also a great laptop operating system. Discover all the cool features that make being a road warrior a breeze, including power conservation, juggling multiple dial-up connections, and transferring files back and forth with your main computer.

Part 20: Maintenance and Optimization

Maintenance is not often fun and exciting, but as with your car, computer maintenance is necessary to keep things running smoothly. In this part, you'll explore everything from checking your hard disk for errors, defragmenting the hard disk, cleaning things up and making more room, restoring your computer when things go bad, and performing backup and recovery operations.

Part 21: Troubleshooting

There are a number of common problems you may encounter when using Windows XP. In this part, you will find step-by-step solutions for some of the more common problems. In addition, you'll learn the steps for getting or giving help using remote assistance and remote desktop.

What You'll Need

To use this book, the only thing you need is a PC running Microsoft Windows XP. You can be using any version of Microsoft Windows XP, including Microsoft Windows XP Professional Edition or Microsoft Windows XP Home Edition.

Conventions Used in This Book

As you go through this book, you will find a few unique elements. We'll describe those elements here so that you'll understand them when you see them.

Text You Type and Text on the Screen

Whenever you are asked to type in text, the text you are to type appears in bold like this:

Type in this address: **101 E. Washington**.

When we are referring to URLs or other text you'll see on the screen, we'll use a monospace font, like this:

Check out `www.msn.com`.

Icons

A number of special icons appear in the margins of each task to provide additional information you might find helpful.

note

The Note icon is used to provide additional information or help in working with Windows XP.

tip

The Tip icon is used to point out an interesting idea or technique that will save you time, effort, money, or all three.

caution

The Caution icon is used to alert you to potential problems that you might run into when working with Windows XP.

cross-reference

Although this book is divided into tasks to make it easy to find exactly what you're looking for, few tasks really stand completely alone. The Cross-Reference icon provides us the opportunity to point out other tasks in the book you might want to look at if you're interested in this task.

Contacting the Authors

We welcome your questions, comments, and constructive criticism regarding the book. You can contact Bill at billhatfield@edgequest.com and Brad at Brad@TeachYourselfCSharp.com or brad@jones123.com.

Part 1: Understanding Windows XP Basics

Task 1:   Starting Up and Logging In

Task 2:   Logging Off and Shutting Down

Task 3:   Activating Windows

Task 4:   Enabling Fast Switching between Users

Task 5:   Setting Your Computer's Clock and Time Zone

Task 6:   Setting the Clock Automatically

Task 7:   Adjusting Your Computer's Volume

Task 8:   Automatically Turning the Monitor Off

Task 9:   Locking and Unlocking the Computer

Task 10: Locking Your Computer with a Screen Saver

Task 11: Getting Help

Task 12: Customizing Help Screens

Task 13: Setting Search Options for Help

Task 14: Creating a Help and Support Favorites List

Task 15: Using the Knowledge Base

Task 16: Getting Basic Information about Your System

Task 17: Automatically Keeping Windows Up-to-Date

Task 18: Manually Updating Windows XP

Task 19: Installing New Software

Task 20: Removing Application Software

Starting Up and Logging In

When Windows XP is installed, it requires that an account be set up for at least one user. If you are using Windows XP Home Edition, and you only set up one account without a password, when you turn on your computer, you are taken directly to the desktop. If you are using Windows XP Professional or Windows XP Home and have a password, when you turn on the computer, you are taken to the login screen where the user account can be selected. You can create an account for each person that will be using the computer, or you can create multiple accounts for yourself. Additionally, each of these profiles can be customized.

To use the login screen, do the following steps:

1. Turn on your computer, if it isn't on already. The computer runs through its startup procedures. If your computer only has one user account and that account does not have a password, you may be taken directly to the Windows XP desktop. If this is not the case, continue with the following steps.

2. A welcome screen, as shown in Figure 1-1, appears. Your screen will have different usernames than in Figure 1-1. Additionally, your screen may have a different number of user account icons and names.

Figure 1-1: The Windows XP Welcome screen.

3. On this screen select your account by clicking the appropriate square graphics (icon) or username.

4. If you don't have a password on your account, you are taken to the desktop. If the user profile you selected has a password associated with it, an entry box appears (see Figure 1-2). In this case, click the

cross-reference

Task 212 shows you how to customize your user graphic (also called an icon).

note

If your computer is on a network, logging in may be slightly different. You may be presented with a dialog window that requests your ID and password.

entry box and type your password into it. Your password is case-sensitive.

Figure 1-2: The password prompt.

5. If you have forgotten your password, select the Help icon for a hint. The password hint appears (see Figure 1-3).

The arrow icon

Figure 1-3: The password hint.

6. After typing in your password, click the arrow icon or press Enter on your keyboard.

7. If you entered the password correctly, you are taken to the desktop. If you entered the password incorrectly, a help message appears next to the entry box, as shown in Figure 1-4.

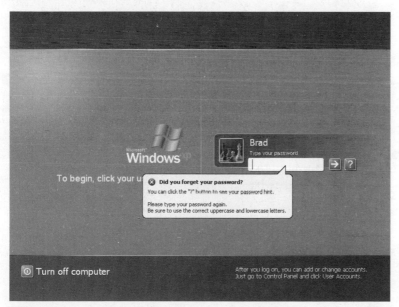

Figure 1-4: The error message for entering a wrong password.

8. Once you enter the password successfully, the Windows XP desktop is displayed.

Task 2

Logging Off and Shutting Down

While some people choose to leave their computer running, there are times when you will want to turn your computer off. Even if you choose to leave your computer on, you may find that it makes sense to log off. Logging off is the process of closing the desktop and returning to the Windows login screen.

The following steps walk you through logging off and turning off your computer:

1. Click the Start button.

2. Determine if you will leave the computer on or turn the computer off. If you want to leave the computer on, select the Log Off button. This takes you to the Windows Welcome screen (see Figure 2-1).

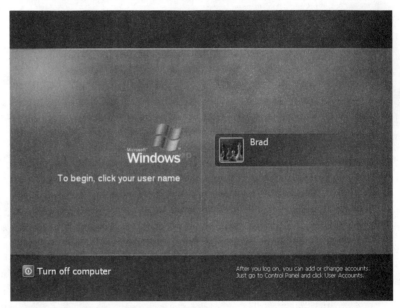

Figure 2-1: The Windows Welcome screen.

3. If you've decided to turn the computer off, choose the Turn Off Computer button. The window in Figure 2-2 appears. When this dialog box is displayed, you cannot do anything more in Windows XP.

---

caution

Before turning the power off on your computer, you should first save any documents, end any programs, and shut down Windows XP. Otherwise, changes to documents and program settings may be lost.

note

Figure 2-1 shows the standard login screen. If you are on a network or have changed your login settings, you may see a dialog box instead of the standard Welcome screen shown in the figure.

cross-reference

Task 209 shows you how to create a new account profile.

note

Logging off closes all of the programs you have running and stops everything. In Windows XP you can switch to a different user account and profile without logging off of your account — thus without ending all your programs. This is called *fast switching* and is shown in Task 4.

caution

You should always check to make sure your files are saved before starting the turn off or log off process.

Figure 2-2: The Turn Off Computer dialog box.

4. If you need to go back to Windows, you click the Cancel button.

5. If you want to turn off the computer, select the Turn Off button. This causes Windows XP to shut down safely. Some computers will even turn the power off. Others will shut down Windows XP and display a screen that says it is safe to turn off your computer. Once you see such a screen, you can safely press your computer's power button.

6. If you want to simply turn your computer off and then back on, choose the Restart button. This causes the computer to go through the process of turning off, logging off, shutting down, and then immediately starting back up. You will generally not do this unless you have installed new software that asks you to restart your machine.

7. Select the Stand By button if you are using a notebook computer or if you are interested in saving power, but don't want to completely turn off your computer.

8. If available, select the Hibernate button if you want to completely turn your computer off, yet have it ready to start up relatively fast. If you don't see a Hibernate button, press the Shift key when the Turn Off Computer dialog is displayed. If the hibernate function is supported by your computer, pressing the Shift key changes the Stand By button text to "Hibernate." You can then click this button to hibernate the computer.

Task 2

tip

If you are using a notebook computer on battery power, you should choose Hibernate rather than Stand By. Stand By will continue to use your battery's power.

note

Hibernation mode makes a copy of what is in the computer's memory and writes it to the hard drive. When you restart the computer, Windows XP reads this written information right back into memory and picks up where it left off.

cross-reference

See Part 19 for more on working with notebook computers and Windows XP.

note

When you select Stand By, the computer goes into a low-power state that appears as though the computer is turned off, even though it isn't completely off. The benefit of this mode is that the computer will restart relatively fast.

note

Hibernate is similar to Stand By in that the computer will be able to start up relatively fast. Instead of going into low-power mode, the computer will copy what is currently in memory and then turn completely off.

cross-reference
See Task 1 for starting
Windows XP.

note
Activating windows does not
require any personal information from you.

caution
If your system has not been
activated, you will not be able
to run Windows XP after the
grace period expires. This grace
period is 30 days from the day
it is installed.

note
When you click on the Activate
icon in the notification bar on
the bottom right of your screen,
the activation process begins
and the icon is removed from
the notification bar once the
activation is completed.

tip
If you want to know how many
days you have left to activate
your copy of Windows XP, just
hold the mouse pointer over
the Notification icon. A pop-up
tip appears providing the information.

Task 3

Activating Windows

If you installed or updated Windows XP on your machine, you will need to activate it. Activation requires letting Microsoft know about your copy of Windows so it can be verified as a legal copy. If your machine came with Windows XP preinstalled, you most likely will not need to activate your copy. If you do need to activate your copy, a message is displayed daily in your notification bar, if not more often. You'll also have an Activation icon in your notification area.

1. Click on the Activation icon in the notification bar. Alternatively, you can click the Start button and then choose All Programs⇨ Accessories⇨System Tools⇨Activate Windows. Either action starts the installation process and presents the window in Figure 3-1.

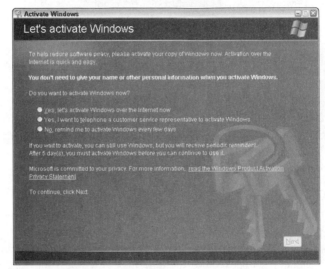

Figure 3-1: The activation window.

2. Select the way you will activate your copy of Windows XP. The easiest method is over the Internet with an Internet connection, or you can call a Microsoft representative. Select the option you will use.

3. Press the Next button. This takes you to additional instructions based on the option you selected in Step 2.

4. Follow the instructions on the screen.

   If you chose to call a representative, an ID is generated and you are presented with information to use when calling Microsoft. Follow the information on your activation window (as shown in Figure 3-2). This will determine the number you should call as well.

5. If you choose to activate using the Internet, you are presented a screen asking if you would also like to register your copy of Windows XP in addition to activating it. If you do not register, your activation will process. If you choose to register, the registration screen appears (see Figure 3-3).

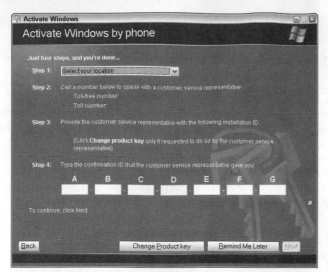

Figure 3-2: The activation window for calling a representative.

6. Fill in the registration information or press the Skip button. Windows XP then attempts to connect to the Internet. If the connection fails, Windows XP provides you with questions to help connect. If the connection succeeds, the activation process occurs. Once activation is completed, a confirmation message appears, stating that you have successfully activated your copy of Windows.

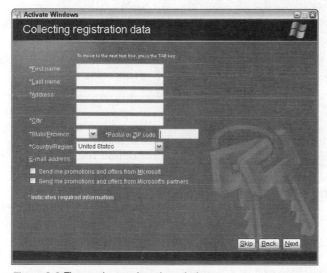

Figure 3-3: The product registration window.

7. Close the window.

caution

There is a limited number of times that you can activate your copy of Windows. You should only need to activate it once. If you need to reinstall Windows XP on your machine, you will need to reactivate the copy.

note

Activation is a process from Microsoft to ensure that copies of Windows XP are not stolen or shared. The basic licensing agreement limits the number of machines (usually to one) that a copy of Windows XP can be installed on.

caution

If you choose to do an Internet activation, Windows XP attempts to find a connection. If a connection is not found, you are prompted to use a modem or other source to connect to the Internet. If you are not connected to the Internet, you will have to call a Microsoft representative.

Task 4

Enabling Fast Switching between Users

Task 209 shows how to set up multiple users on Windows XP. Each user can have his or her own account that contains individual settings, documents, and other files. For example, a family could have an account for the parents and a separate account for a child.

Windows XP can be set up to switch between these different accounts. Although Windows XP can be set up to force you to log out before switching to a different account, it can also be set up for fast switching, which allows you to switch between accounts without stopping and turning off all programs. This allows you to switch between different users' accounts much quicker. The following steps show you how to confirm that fast switching is turned on:

1. Click the Start menu and then select Control Panel.

2. Double-click User Accounts to see the User Accounts window (see Figure 4-1).

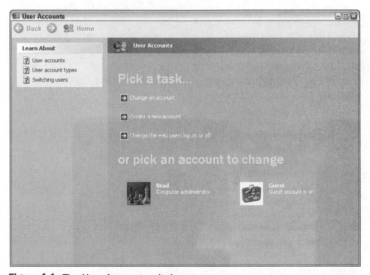

Figure 4-1: The User Accounts window.

3. Click on Change The Way Users Log On or Off. This changes the User Accounts window to the one in Figure 4-2.

4. To enable fast switching, check the box next to Use Fast User Switching. If you instead remove the check, fast user switching is turned off.

5. Click the Apply Options button to save any changes. You are returned to the primary User Accounts window. You can close this window. If you checked the box indicated, the fast switching option is set on, and you can now switch users without closing all the programs:

cross-reference

Task 1 provides the details of logging in to Windows XP.

cross-reference

Task 209 shows you how to add a new user account.

caution

If more than one person or account is logged in to Windows XP, you will not be able to change the fast switching options. You must log out any other users.

cross-reference

For you to change the fast switching option, your account must be set up as an administrator. Task 213 shows you how to change a user's account type.

Task **4**

a. Click Start, then click the Log Off button. The Log Off dialog box appears (see Figure 4-3).

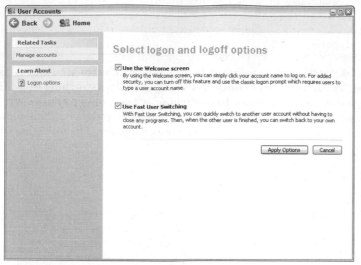

Figure 4-2: The User Accounts window.

Figure 4-3: The Log Off dialog box with fast switching turned on.

Note that if you have fast switching turned off, you are presented with the Log Off dialog box in Figure 4-4.

Figure 4-4: The Log Off dialog box with fast switching turned off.

b. Click on the Switch User button to be shown the Welcome screen or Login dialog box.

c. Click on the icon or username for the user account you want to switch to.

Setting Your Computer's Clock and Time Zone

Your computer has a clock that keeps the date and time. Additionally, this clock can keep track of daylight saving time and more. Some computers' clocks run a little fast or a little slow. As such, after a while you may need to adjust the clock. If your computer is connected to the Internet, you can have it automatically update the time on a regular basis (see Task 6). By default, the clock is displayed on the right-hand corner of the taskbar, as shown in Figure 5-1.

Figure 5-1: The time on the taskbar.

cross-reference

To have your computer auto-matically correct the time, see Task 6.

1. To change the time, use the Date and Time Properties dialog box. You can access this dialog in one of two ways. The quick way is to double-click on the time in the taskbar. If the time is not displayed in the taskbar, you can display this dialog by selecting the Control Panel option on the Start menu (Select Start, then Control Panel). Once you've displayed the Control Panel, select Date and Time. The Date and Time dialog appears (see Figure 5-2).

Figure 5-2: The Date and Time Properties dialog box.

note

If you enter in a single number, such as 7, into one of the values, a leading zero is automatically added.

2. To set the date, start by setting the year. You can do this by either clicking on the up and down arrows to increase and decrease the date, or by selecting the year and typing in a new one.

   You can then select the month by using the drop-down list. The calendar of days changes according to the year and month you select. Leap years are also considered in the displays of days. You can pick the day by clicking on it.

3. The time is displayed as both an analog clock and with numbers. You can change the time using the numbers. To change the time, select the part of the time you wish to change, either the hours, minutes, seconds, or whether it is P.M. or A.M. Select this by clicking on the numbers.

4. Once a portion of the time is selected, click the up and down arrows or type in a new number to change that portion of the time.

5. Switch from A.M. to P.M. or P.M. to A.M. by clicking on the current value and then clicking the up or down arrow.

6. Once you are done setting values, click the Apply button to apply the new date and time to the system.

7. If you want to adjust the time zone, select the Time Zone tab at the top of the dialog. A display similar to Figure 5-3 appears.

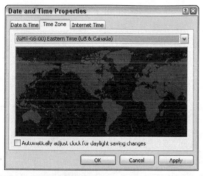

Figure 5-3: The Time Zone setting.

8. Select your time zone from the drop-down box. If the time zone you select includes daylight saving time, a check box is displayed as shown in Figure 5-3. Check the box to observe daylight saving time. Uncheck the box to ignore daylight saving time. If your time zone selection does not include daylight saving time, the check box is not displayed.

9. Select Apply to set the new time zone on your computer.

10. Select OK to close the dialog.

note

Only valid values will be accepted. For example, you can't enter a number greater than 59 in the minutes or seconds field.

note

The computer's clock is used to mark files with the date and time when they are created or saved. Because of this, you'll want to keep the clock as accurate as possible.

note

The world display in Figure 5-3 will center the time zone you select on the map.

Task 6

Setting the Clock Automatically

Task 5 showed you how to set your clock manually. You can also configure your computer to automatically adjust your computer's clock to make sure it is always accurate.

caution

If you are not connected to the Internet, you will not be able to automatically update the time.

cross-reference

To set the time manually to the current time — or to any other time — see Task 5.

1. Access the Date and Time Properties dialog by double-clicking on the time in the taskbar. If the time is not displayed in the taskbar, you can display this dialog by selecting the Control Panel option on the Start menu (select Start, then Control Panel). Once you've displayed the Control Panel, select Date and Time. The Date and Time dialog shown in Figure 6-1 appears.

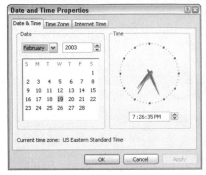

Figure 6-1: The Date and Time Properties dialog box.

2. Select the Internet Time tab. The dialog in Figure 6-2 appears.

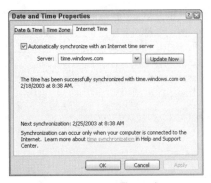

Figure 6-2: The Internet Time tab.

3. If the Automatically Synchronize With An Internet Time Server check box is not selected, the information on the screen will be protected ("grayed out" and cannot be modified). Make sure the check box is selected.

4. Click the Update Now button to update the current time immediately. The computer accesses the Internet site listed in the Server box. By default, this is time.windows.com. If you would prefer to get the time from a government site, or if the site is busy, you can change this to time.nist.gov.

5. Leave the Automatically Synchronize With An Internet Time Server check box checked if you want to have the time on your computer updated once a week. Otherwise, uncheck the box. The dialog tells you the next time it will update the time.

6. Windows XP provides a couple of Web sites for synchronizing your computer's time. You can also type in a different server name in the Server box. If you are unsure of sites for getting the time, it is best to not change the value. If you do enter an invalid site and then press the Update Now button, the error message shown in Figure 6-3 appears. You can then use the drop-down box to select a correct site.

Figure 6-3: www.Jones123.com is an invalid site for obtaining the time.

7. Select OK to exit the dialog.

note

If the Automatically Synchronize with an Internet Time Server box is not checked, you will not be able to click the Update Now button.

caution

The date will also be updated automatically.

note

If you are running a firewall, you may be prevented from using the automatic update. In this case, you should manually update the date and time as shown in Task 5.

Adjusting Your Computer's Volume

Many computers ship with fancy keyboards with lots of extra buttons. Some computers also include volume controls on the computer's keyboard that change the system's volume. You can also change the volume directly within Windows XP. If your computer has stereo speakers, you can even change the volume on each speaker independently. You can get to the advanced volume control by selecting Start, then All Programs➪Accessories➪Entertainment➪Volume Control. To access more options for volume, including adding a quick-access button on your taskbar, use the following steps:

1. Select the Control Panel from the Start menu.

2. Double-click on Sounds, Speech, and Audio Devices. The Sounds, Speech, and Audio Devices window appears (see Figure 7-1).

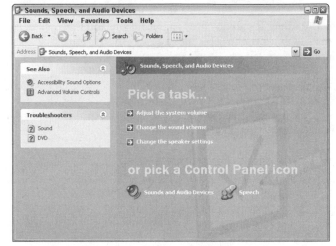

Figure 7-1: The Sounds, Speech, and Audio Devices window.

3. Select Adjust the system volume by clicking on it. The Sounds and Audio Devices Properties dialog appears (see Figure 7-2).

4. Drag the slider in the Device Volume section to change the volume. Moving toward Low decreases the volume; moving toward High increases the volume. You can also click anywhere on the volume scale. The volume slider moves to where you click, and a tone sounds at the selected volume level.

5. If you want more control over the volume, you can select the Advanced button in the Device Volume area. This displays the Volume Control dialog box in Figure 7-3. Here you can adjust various volumes within your system.

cross-reference

To learn about more specific settings related to volume and speakers, see Task 218.

caution

If your computer has speakers with volume controls on them, be aware that this volume control is generally independent of the volume setting in Windows XP. The volume you set on the speaker will generally be the maximum volume that Windows XP is able to set.

note

If you'd like to turn the volume completely off, you should check the Mute box.

Figure 7-2: The Sounds and Audio Devices Properties dialog box.

6. When you are satisfied with the volume level, click OK to save and exit the dialog. If you want to remain on the Sounds and Audio Devices Properties dialog, click the Apply button to save your settings.

7. To make it easier and faster to change the volume, you can add a volume control to your notification area (the area on the right side of the taskbar). To do this, check the box next to the Place Volume icon in the taskbar. This results in a Speaker icon appearing.

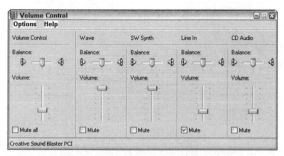

Figure 7-3: The Volume Control dialog box.

8. Left-click the Speaker icon in the notification area. The slider control in Figure 7-4 appears. You can move the slider to immediately change the computer's volume. You can also right-click the Speaker icon to quickly access the Sound and Audio Devices Properties dialog (Adjust Audio Properties) and the Volume Control dialog.

Figure 7-4: The notification bar volume control.

cross-reference

To learn how to assign sounds to different actions in Windows XP, see Task 45.

tip

Windows XP has a number of preset defaults for volume. You can select the appropriate one for your computer's speaker configuration using the Advanced Audio Properties dialog, which is available from the Advanced button in the Speaker settings.

note

If your computer has a sound card, the Volume Control dialog displays the name of the card at the bottom. Figure 7-3 shows a system with a Creative Sound Blaster PCI card.

note

You can adjust the volume of your speakers independently by selecting the Speaker Volume button in the Speaker Settings area of the Sounds and Audio Devices Properties dialog.

Automatically Turning the Monitor Off

Y ou can customize Windows in a number of ways. One feature that you can set is to turn the monitor off automatically if the computer is unused for a fixed amount of time. While a screen saver can be used, you will often find that at times it is better to have your computer screen simply turn off. There are a number of reasons to do this. The obvious reason is to conserve energy. You may also want the monitor to turn off simply to reduce the light coming from it when the computer is not in use.

cross-reference

Setting up and selecting a screen saver is shown in Task 43.

tip

You can also get to the Display Properties dialog by selecting the Control Panel on the Start menu. Then choose Appearance and Themes. Finally, pick the Display option in the Control Panel icons near the bottom of the window. As you can see, it is much simpler to just right-click on the desktop and select Properties!

note

You will see that you can automatically turn the hard drive off in the same way that the monitor can be turned off. Most hard drives operate minimally when not in use, so it is often not as important to automatically turn them off unless you are using a notebook computer with a battery.

1. Right-click on an open area of your desktop and click Properties from the menu. The Display Properties dialog box appears.

2. Select the Screen Saver tab. The dialog box in Figure 8-1 appears.

Figure 8-1: The Display Properties dialog box.

3. Click the Power button in the Monitor power section. The Power Options Properties dialog appears (see Figure 8-2).

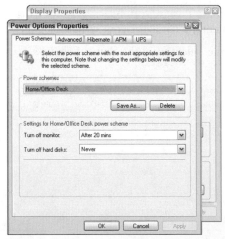

Figure 8-2: The Power Options Properties dialog box.

4. Select the amount of time that you would like to wait until the monitor turns off. You select this from the drop-down list next to the Turn Off Monitor: Text. You are given a limited number of choices, ranging from one minute to never, as shown in Figure 8-3.

Figure 8-3: The time choices for automatically turning off the monitor.

5. Once you've made your selection, click Apply to save your choice and remain on this dialog.

6. You may want to set up different scenarios for managing when your monitor will turn off. For example, if you are watching a streaming video on the Internet or if you are giving an automated presentation on your computer, you may want the monitor to remain on even though you are not pressing keys or using the mouse. At other times you may want the monitor to turn off after 20 minutes. You can set up multiple scenarios and save them with names. These scenarios are called *schemes*. A number of schemes for different power options already exist. Additionally, you can add new ones.

7. To save your settings as a new scheme, select the Save As... button in the Power schemes pane on the Power Options Properties dialog. A box pops up where you can enter a name for your scheme.

8. To change to a different scheme, select from the Power Schemes drop-down list.

9. When you are done selecting and saving schemes or with changing the time for the monitor to turn off, select OK to exit the Power Options Properties dialog.

tip

Having your monitor automatically turn off can help to keep sensitive information from being seen by someone who might be walking by when you are away from your computer.

note

This task is showing you how to turn off the monitor automatically. If your hardware does not support this feature, your monitor will actually go blank (black). Windows XP will not be sending a signal to the monitor, so energy will still be conserved.

tip

If you are doing a presentation, you may want to change the power setting to Never. You can change the setting back to a shorter time after you're finished with the presentation.

note

You can also delete a power scheme by selecting the Delete button when one is chosen in the Power schemes drop-down list. Once deleted, the scheme is gone. You can re-create it, but you can't get it back!

Locking and Unlocking the Computer

If you are worried about others getting onto your computer, you may want to lock Windows XP to keep them out. Locking the computer requires that a password be entered before anyone can start using it again. There are two ways to set up a password and lock your computer. One is to use a screen saver with a password. This is covered in Task 10. The other is to force your computer to lock immediately.

Making the changes in this task also requires that you enter a password when you first turn on your computer. In fact, your Welcome screen will change to a dialog that requires a username and password to be entered. Note that if you or another user doesn't have a password, you can leave that information blank.

cross-reference

For most people, a screen saver password is a better option than fully locking the computer. See Task 10 for setting a password using a screen saver.

caution

A person with administrator-level access can use his or her own password to get back into the computer. Only non-administrator-level people will be locked off the computer. See Task 213 for changing a user's account type.

1. Go to the User Accounts window. Do this by selecting Start, then Control Panel. From the Control Panel select User Accounts.

2. On the User Accounts window select User Accounts. A new dialog window opens.

3. Choose the task Change the Way Users Log On or Off. The window in Figure 9-1 appears.

Figure 9-1: The User Account window for changing logon and logoff options.

caution

Making the changes in this task will impact how you get into and out of Windows XP.
You can always change the settings back if you don't like the differences.

4. If the box next to Use the Welcome Screen is checked, uncheck it. This will also protect and uncheck the Use Fast User Switching box (if it was selected). If the Use the Welcome Screen box was not checked, skip this step.

5. Click the Apply Options button. You will now find that when you log off of your computer, you are given a dialog box for logging in instead of the normal Welcome screen. If you are using Windows XP Home Edition with only one account, you will now have a login dialog when you start your computer. If you want the normal Welcome screen returned (or in XP if you want to skip the sign-on process), simply repeat Steps 1 through 4 and check the Use the Welcome screen box instead of unchecking it.

6. If you are at the User Accounts window, close it by clicking the Windows close button (the small × in the top-right corner).

   Your computer is now set up to where you can immediately lock it.

7. Press the Ctrl, Alt, and Delete keys all at the same time. The Windows Security dialog appears. If you are shown the Windows Task Manager dialog instead, make sure you followed Steps 1 through 6.

   If you don't have a Lock Computer button, you can change your settings to present the Lock Computer button by following Steps 8 and 9.

8. Add or change a password by selecting the Change Password... button. The password for locking the computer can be the same password that you use to log in to Windows from the Welcome screen. If you already have a password, you can skip this step. If not, be aware that you will need to use this same password when you log in to Windows XP.

9. Click the Lock Computer... button to lock the computer. The Unlock Computer dialog appears (see Figure 9-2).

Figure 9-2: The Unlock Computer dialog.

Entering the correct password returns you to Windows.

Task 9

tip
To keep others locked off the computer, you should make sure their accounts are not set as administrators. For example, parents can be administrators and kids can be regular users. This allows you to lock the kids off the computer.

caution
If you don't use a password for logging in to Windows XP, a password will not be needed to get back into Windows XP when you lock it.

cross-reference
To set or change a password on a user account, see Task 215.

Locking Your Computer with a Screen Saver

Almost everyone uses a screen saver on his or her computer. There are several reasons for using a screen saver. Originally screen savers were used to prevent images from burning into the monitor's screen. With current hardware, this is really not an issue.

The other reason many people use a screen saver is to hide the information being displayed on their computer when they are away. If you are concerned with people getting onto your computer when you are away from it, you may also want to do more than just hide the information with a screen saver. You may also want to lock the computer. Task 9 shows you one way to lock your computer with a password. Another is to add a password to your screen saver.

1. Go to the Screen Saver tab on the Display Properties dialog.

    a. Right-click on the background of your desktop where there are no windows being displayed. This presents a pop-up menu.

    b. Select Properties. The Display Properties dialog appears. Select the Screen Saver tab. The dialog box in Figure 10-1 appears.

Figure 10-1: The Screen Saver tab in the Display Properties dialog box.

cross-reference

See Task 215 to learn how to change your password. Task 216 shows how to remove a password.

caution

Even though you may select this option, a prompt will be displayed only if you have a password associated with your user account. See Task 214 for setting a password if you don't have one.

note

Using the Preview button to see the screen saver does not require you to enter a password to get back to Windows. The password is only required when the screen saver has been activated because of waiting.

caution

If your account does not have a password associated with it, selecting the On Resume, Password Protect option will not cause a prompt for a password.

As an alternative to right-clicking on the desktop, you can also get to the Screen Saver tab on the Displays Properties dialog by going through the Control Panel.

  a. Select Start, then Control Panel.

  b. On the Control Panel, select Appearance and Themes. This presents you with the appearance and theme tasks.

  c. Select Choose a Screen Saver. The Displays Properties dialog is displayed with the Screen Saver tab selected.

2. Select the box next to On Resume, Password Protect. This sets the screen saver to prompt for a password. If you want to turn off the password, unselect this box.

3. Click Apply to save any changes to your settings. Click the OK button to save any changes and to close the dialog. Select Cancel to leave without saving any additional changes.

When returning from the screen saver after it is displayed, you will need to enter your password, if you have one set. Figure 10-2 shows the dialog box for entering your password.

Figure 10-2: The screen saver password dialog box in Windows XP Professional.

cross-reference

Task 43 shows you how to customize a screen saver in a number of ways.

caution

Passwords should not be simple words that are easy to guess, such as names and special days.

tip

A good password will often contain both characters and numbers.

Task **11**

Getting Help

When something goes wrong, when you run into a problem, or when you need to know how to do something, what do you do? First, of course, you should turn to this book. Another solution is to turn to Windows XP itself for help. Windows XP has a robust help system and support center that can solve nearly all of the issues that come up. To use the help and support system, you need to launch the Help and Support Center window.

1. From the Start menu, select Help and Support. The Help and Support Center window appears (see Figure 11-1). From this window you can select help in a number of different formats and for a number of different issues.

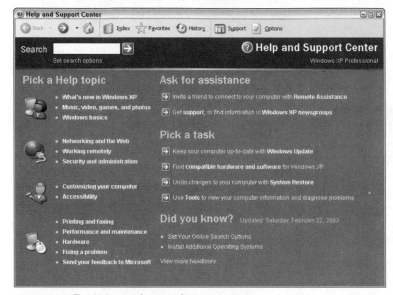

Figure 11-1: The Help and Support Center window.

2. Select by clicking on any topic on this page that interests you or that may solve your problem.

3. You can search for help and support on a specific word or set of words by first entering the word in the Search entry box.

4. Press the Enter key or click the arrow button to start searching. The results are displayed in a results box, as shown in Figure 11-2.

   The search results are displayed in different groupings. The Suggested Topics are considered the best results for your search criteria. The Full-Text Search Matches are search results that contained the specific words that you entered into the search box. In Windows XP Home Edition, the Full-Text Search Matches are only provided if no Suggested Topics were found. The third area is Microsoft Knowledge Base results, which contains help topics found on the Microsoft Knowledge Base Web site. Results are only provided in this section if you are connected to the Internet.

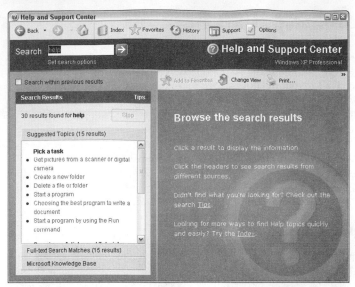

Figure 11-2: The Search Results screen.

5. Click on the title bar of each section to list the results. Click on the specific result to see detailed help. The detailed help is displayed on the right side of the window.

6. You can also search for a word by looking in the help index. From the Help and Support Center window (or nearly any other Help window), select the Index button from the toolbar at the top of the screen. The Index in Figure 11-3 appears.

7. Search the index or scroll through it. Double-clicking on a topic selects it. You can also single-click the Display button. The detailed help is displayed on the right side of the window.

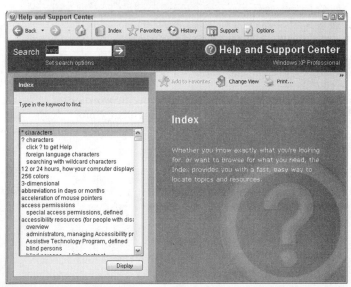

Figure 11-3: The help index.

tip

It is amazing what you can learn by jumping into the Windows XP help system. Taking a few minutes every now and then to simply look through some of the help topics can lead to lots of interesting discoveries of tips and tricks. It can be like turning to a random task in this book!

note

Help and troubleshooting are two different things. Help is information on a topic or process. Troubleshooting is an attempt to resolve an actual problem or issue.

cross-reference

See Tasks 249 through 261 for a number of tasks that focus on troubleshooting specific hardware and software issues you may run into.

tip

When searching, enter specific search words rather than sentences.

Customizing Help Screens

One of the best features in Windows XP is the help and support features. As you learn to use Windows XP, you may find that you consult the help and support pages a number of times. If so, there are a number of settings that you can change to customize the icons and text. To set these options, use the following steps:

1. Select Help and Support from the Start menu. This displays the Help and Support window.

2. Click on the Options icon near the top-right side of the window. The Help and Support Center Options window appears (see Figure 12-1).

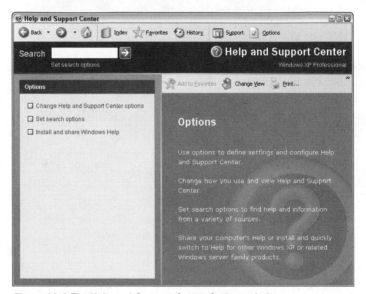

Figure 12-1:The Help and Support Center Options window.

3. Click on Change Help and Support Center Options. This changes the display on the right side of the window to the options shown in Figure 12-2.

4. Check the Show Favorites on the navigation bar if you want the Favorites icon displayed on the toolbar within the Windows Help and Support system. Uncheck this if you want the Favorites icon removed.

5. Check the Show History on the navigation bar if you want the History icon displayed on the toolbar within the Windows Help and Support system. Uncheck this if you want the History icon removed.

cross-reference

If you don't know how to get help in Windows XP, see Task 11.

note

The Favorites option allows you to create a list of help, search, and other topics that you can quickly jump to by clicking on them in the list. Task 14 shows you how to create and use a Help and Support Favorites list.

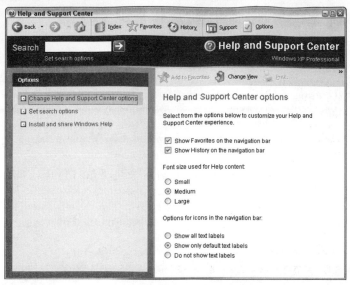

Figure 12-2: The primary Help and Support Center options.

6. Select the size for the font you would like used in the Windows help system. Your options are Small, Medium, and Large.
7. Select the display option for the icons in the navigation bar. You can choose to show text labels for all icons in the toolbar, to show no labels in the toolbar, or to show only default text labels. Figures 12-3 to 12-5 show the toolbar with each of these options.

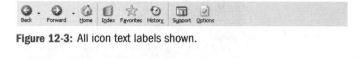

Figure 12-3: All icon text labels shown.

Figure 12-4: No icon text labels shown.

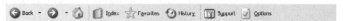

Figure 12-5: Default icon text labels shown.

8. Close the Help and Support Center window. Your selections take place the moment you make them. When you have completed your selections, you can close the Help and Support Center window.

Task 12

tip

You can turn on text labels for all of the icons if you are not familiar with all of the standard icons used in Windows XP. If you are familiar with all of the icons, you can turn off the text labels to make more room.

note

Clicking the History icon on the toolbar presents you with a list of help and support pages that you have recently visited.

cross-reference

To learn how to customize the results you get from searching within the Windows XP help and support system, see Task 13.

Setting Search Options for Help

Windows has a robust help and support system that you can use to find answers to questions and issues you have regarding Windows XP and many of the programs installed on it. In Task 11 you learn how to use Help in Windows XP. In this task you learn to customize a number of features for searching the Windows XP Help system. This includes options such as setting the maximum number of items displayed in search results, how search phrases are treated, and more. The following steps walk you through customizing your search options:

1. Select Help and Support from the Start menu. This displays the Help and Support window.

2. Click on the Options icon near the top-right side of the window. The Help and Support Center Options window appears, as shown in Figure 13-1.

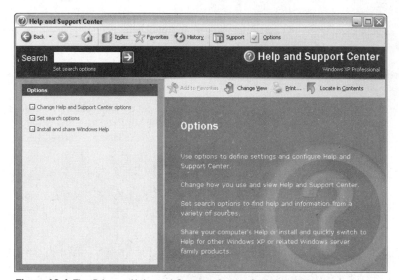

Figure 13-1: The Primary Help and Support Center Options window.

3. Click on Set Search Options. The display on the right side of the window changes to the search options, as shown in Figure 13-2.

4. Change the number in the box if you want more (or fewer) results to be displayed when searching. While the default value is 15, you can change this to any number you like. More results can be returned if the number is set higher.

5. Check the box next to Turn On Search Highlight if you want to have the words you are searching for highlighted in the results returned. This is checked by default.

6. Check the box next to Suggested Topics if you want to have suggested topics returned when you search. Suggested topics may not have the exact search word or words you entered for your search. Rather, they are help documents that may be related.

cross-reference

You learn how to search the Windows XP help files in Task 11.

note

Once you set the search option settings, they are in effect for all help and support searches until you change them again.

note

You check or uncheck a box by clicking on it.

note

The number of results set in Step 4 is the maximum number of items that will be displayed. If there are fewer matches found in the help system, then only those items are displayed.

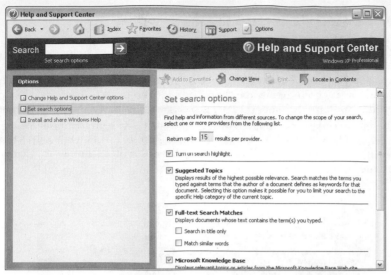

Figure 13-2: The Search Options window.

7. Check the box next to Full-Text Search Matches if you want Windows XP to search for the specific words you entered into the search box. When this option is checked, you can also select two additional options:

   a. Check the Search in Title Only option if you want to just check titles for the words you entered. If you check this option, the search will not look at the information within the help documents for your keywords. This almost always results in fewer finds.

   b. Check the Match Similar Words option if you want help to find similar words to the ones you entered. This almost always results in additional results being found.

8. Check the Microsoft Knowledge Base if you are connected to the Internet. This option searches the Microsoft Knowledge Base Web site for information related to your search terms. When you have selected this option, you are given a number of additional options that you can set:

   a. Select the name of a product. By default, All Microsoft Products is selected; however, you can change this option if you want to only check for information related to a specific product.

   b. Select the Search For: option if you are searching for more than one word. Among your choices, you can set this option to look for the exact phrase you entered or you can set it to look for any or all of the words you entered.

   c. Check the box next to Search in Title Only if you want to just search the titles on the Microsoft Knowledge Base Web site. You will generally get more results if you don't check this box.

note

The suggested topic search looks for documents that are related by checking keywords that are included with each help document. Windows XP attempts to present the most relevant results based on the search words you enter.

tip

You should not turn off searching for suggested topics. There is a chance you will find search results in the suggested topics that you wouldn't find in just a full-text search.

tip

If you are not connected to the Internet, you should uncheck the Microsoft Knowledge Base to turn it off.

cross-reference

Learn more about using the Knowledge Base in Task 15.

Creating a Help and Support Favorites List

If you find that there is a help page you want to remember, or if there is a help page that you go to often, you should add it to your list of Favorites. You can also add search results and other pages to your list of Favorites. You can then keep this list of Favorites just a click away. A Favorites icon can be included on the Help and Support Center toolbar (see Task 13). When you select the Favorites icon, you are presented with the list of Favorites similar to what is presented in Figure 14-1.

cross-reference

The Favorites icon is on the Help and Support window toolbar by default; however, it can be turned off. To turn it on, see Task 12 on customizing your help windows.

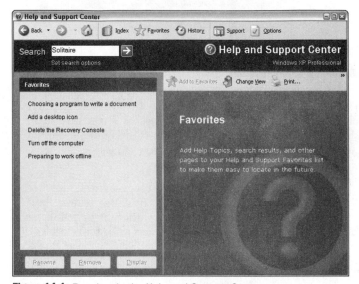

Figure 14-1: Favorites in the Help and Support Center.

To add items to Favorites, use the following steps:

1. Locate a topic within the Help and Support Center. This can be any page within the help system. Task 11 shows how to use Help.

   On the help pages displayed, an Add to Favorites icon will be included. Figure 14-2 shows the result of searching for "Pinball" and then selecting the result that was listed. You can also see that there is an Add to Favorites icon right above the information on playing with Windows games.

2. Click the Add to Favorites icon. The item is added to your Help and Support Favorites list and a message appears, confirming that the item was added (see Figure 14-3).

3. Click OK on the message. Your new favorite item has been added.

caution

The Favorites list in Help and Support is a separate list from the Favorites list in other programs such as Microsoft Internet Explorer.

tip

Adding items to the Help and Support Favorites list will make the items easy to find in the future!

note

To remove an item from the Favorites list, click the item to select it, and then click the Remove button.

Figure 14-2: Results for "Pinball" in the Help and Support Center.

Figure 14-3: The confirmation message for adding a favorite item.

4. Click on the Favorites icon at the top of the page, and note that the new item has been added to the Favorites list. Figure 14-4 shows the Favorites list from Figure 14-1 after following these steps and adding the search results from "Pinball."

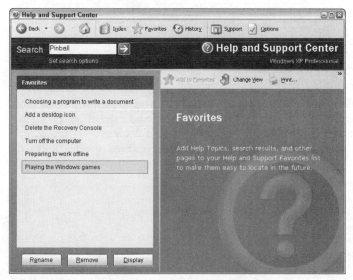

Figure 14-4: An updated Help and Support Favorites list.

tip

Remove items out of your Favorites list if you don't need to remember or go to them any more. This keeps your list from getting so big that it isn't very useful.

tip

You can rename items in your Help and Support Favorites list. Click the item to select it in the list. Then click the Rename button at the bottom of the list. This places the cursor in the name and allows you to make changes.

cross-reference

See Task 146 to learn how to save your favorite Web pages in Microsoft Internet Explorer.

Using the Knowledge Base

Windows XP Help and Support includes access to the Microsoft Knowledge Base. If you are connected to the Internet, then when you use the Help and Support system, Windows XP not only looks on your machine for help, but it also queries the Microsoft Knowledge Base Web site. This site includes additional information, tips, tricks, tutorials, and more. Additionally, it includes information on specific Microsoft products. The information in over 250,000 articles is made available when you do searches and other help requests.

1. Select Help and Support from the Start menu. This displays the Help and Support window.

2. Enter a word or group of words into the Search Box and press Enter or click the button to start searching. The search results page appears. Figure 15-1 shows the search result page after the term **Games** is entered.

Figure 15-1: The search results for "Games."

3. Click the Microsoft Knowledge Base heading to show the search results that were found in the Knowledge Base. If you are not connected to the Internet, a warning similar to the one displayed in Figure 15-2 appears.

cross-reference

For more information on searching, see Task 11 for getting help and Task 13 for setting the search options.

caution

If you are not connected to the Internet, you cannot access the Knowledge Base information.

cross-reference

You can add Knowledge Base articles to your Favorites list by right-clicking on the title of the article and selecting Add to Favorites.

cross-reference

To increase the maximum number of search results that can be displayed in the Knowledge Base section, see Task 13 on setting search options.

note

On the primary Help and Support window there is a section called Did You Know? Like the Knowledge Base, this section features articles from the Internet.

Task 15

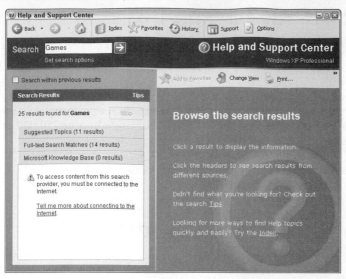

Figure 15-2: Error trying to access Microsoft Knowledge Base when not connected to the Internet.

If you are connected, the top articles found in the Knowledge Base appear. The results will vary depending on what search terms you use.

4. Click on the title of the article you want to read. This displays the article on the right side of the Help and Support Center window, as shown in Figure 15-3.

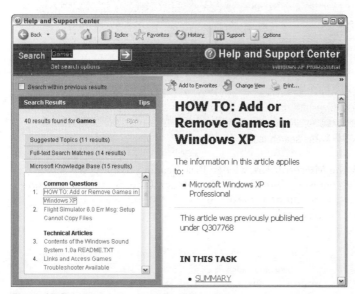

Figure 15-3: A displayed Knowledge Base article.

tip
You can set options to force the Knowledge Base to only look for help on a specific product. By default, it looks for articles on all Microsoft products. To change this to an individual product, you can change a search option. Task 13 covers changing search options.

Getting Basic Information about Your System

Do you know the basic information about your system? For example, do you know the speed of your processor? How much memory does your computer have? What type of processor is being used? You can find all of this information in fewer than 10 steps.

cross-reference

See Tasks 217 to 223 to learn about installing different hardware on your computer.

1. Select My Computer from the Start menu. The My Computer window appears (see Figure 16-1). Some of what is displayed in the main portion of your window will most likely be different from what is in Figure 16-1.

   Within this window, you can see your computer's hard drive(s) and other storage devices. You'll also be able to see some — but not all — connected devices that are on your machine. In Figure 16-1, you can see that my computer has a 3 1/2-inch floppy drive, a regular CD drive, a separate CD-RW drive, and an Intel PC camera all hooked to it.

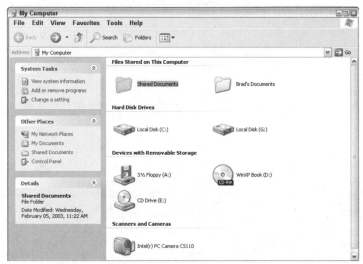

Figure 16-1: The My Computer window.

note

Your computer may have multiple hard disk drives listed even though only a single hard drive is in your computer. A single hard drive can be broken into different pieces, which are each given a different letter. Windows looks at each of these pieces as separate "logical" drives even though they are on the same physical drive. One of the benefits of creating these "logical" drives is that it allows you to separate documents and files stored on your computer.

tip

If your computer is running slow, you can look at the processor speed and memory. If your memory is 128MB or less, adding more memory may help your computer run better.

2. Select the View System Information system task from the left side of the My Computer dialog window. This displays the General tab in the System Properties dialog box similar to Figure 16-2. From this dialog, you can see a number of key pieces of information about your computer:

   - *The version of Windows you are running.* The computer from Figure 16-2 is running Microsoft Windows XP Professional Version 2002.

   - *The name and company that registered the copy of Windows.* The computer from Figure 16-2 was registered to Brad Jones with a company name of "Windows XP in 10 Steps or Less." As you can see, there are a limited number of characters for the company name.

   - *The registration number.* This is the unique number for your copy of Windows. This number was determined based on the registration key entered when Windows was installed.

- *The processor type and speed*. The computer in Figure 16-2 has an Intel Pentium II processor that runs at 400 MHz. Your computer may have a different processor and most likely a faster speed.

- *The amount of RAM*. The computer in Figure 16-2 has 512MB of RAM, which is quite a bit for a home computer. RAM is the amount of memory your computer has available. Windows XP Home or Professional requires 128MB of RAM or higher.

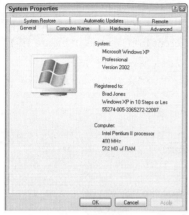

Figure 16-2: The System Properties dialog box.

3. Select the Hardware tab in the System Properties dialog box for more advanced and specific information on your computer.

4. In the middle of this dialog click the Device Manger button to display the Device Manager, shown in Figure 16-3.

5. You can right-click on items in this list and select Properties from the pop-up menu to get more detailed information. Be cautious, however. If you make changes to any values, you can cause Windows XP to no longer be able to recognize a device on your computer.

Figure 16-3: The Device Manager.

cross-reference

To see what printers you have installed on your computer, follow the first few steps in Task 219.

note

You can expand the information in the Device Manager by clicking the plus signs. If there is a dash next to the item, the item is already expanded. If there is neither a plus sign nor a dash, you cannot expand that item any farther.

caution

Changes made in the properties dialogs in the Device Manager impact how Windows XP sees your computer's hardware. A wrong change can cause Windows XP to no longer recognize a piece of hardware.

Automatically Keeping Windows Up-to-Date

W indows XP is not perfect. As people continue to use it in new and unique ways, they find problems and issues. Microsoft works hard to address these issues in a timely manner. Many of these problems can be resolved by providing an update to Windows XP. If you have a connection to the Internet, you can apply any updates automatically or manually. In this task you learn the steps to configure Windows XP to automatically retrieve and install these updates. You also learn how to set checkpoints so you can be alerted before retrieving, downloading, or installing any updates.

To set up Windows XP to allow for automatic updates, use the following steps:

1. Select the Control Panel by clicking on it on the Start menu.

2. Select Performance and Maintenance by clicking on it in the Control Panel. The Performance and Maintenance window appears (see Figure 17-1).

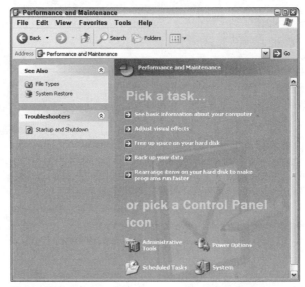

Figure 17-1: The Performance and Maintenance dialog window.

3. Click the System icon near the bottom of the window. The System Properties dialog appears.

4. Select the Automatic Updates tab. The dialog in Figure 17-2 appears.

---

note

The figures in this task are from Windows XP Professional. If you are using Windows XP Home Edition, you may have slightly different options.

cross-reference

If you want more control over the updates to Windows XP, you can find and install updates manually. Task 18 shows how to do a manual update.

caution

When doing updates, you may have to restart your computer. You should save any files and documents, as well as close any open programs, before doing an update.

note

A *patch* is an update to an existing program. It is usually a program that is run to update the program.

note

A *service release* is a group of patches rolled into a single program so that you can do all the updates at once rather than install a bunch of individual programs.

note

If you are not connected to the Internet, you will not be able to do these automatic updates. Windows XP uses the Internet to check for available updates.

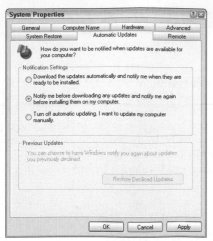

Figure 17-2: The Automatic Updates information in the System Properties dialog.

5. Select the option you'd like implemented for notifying and applying updates from the Notification Settings pane:

   • Select the first option to automatically download any updates and wait. Once they are downloaded, an icon is placed in your notification area. You can then decide when to install the updates by clicking on the icon when you are ready.

   • Select the second option if you want to be automatically notified when updates are available, as well as when they have been downloaded to update. This option allows you to have the most control, while still allowing you to be automatically informed.

   • Select the third option if you don't want to be notified or have automatic updates occur.

6. Click the Apply button to update your settings. You can close the window.

When an update is available, then if you have selected to be notified, an icon will be placed in the notification area. To proceed with the installations, you click on the icon in the notification Window and follow the instructions. If you selected automatic downloads and automatic updates, you won't need to do anything.

note

Many updates are for security. If your computer is connected to the Internet, it is often good to go ahead and let the security patches install.

caution

If your computer is on a network domain, you may not be able to do the automatic updates. It will depend on your network settings.

note

To set up the automatic updates, you must have administrator access for Windows XP. In Windows XP Home Edition, you must be logged on as the administrator. See Task 213 for viewing and changing an account's access rights.

cross-reference

If you want to install a specific update, you can use the manual installation process as shown in Task 18.

tip

You can get to the System Properties dialog quicker by clicking Start, then right-clicking on System, and selecting Properties from the menu that pops up.

Manually Updating Windows XP

As stated in Task 17, Windows XP is not perfect. As people continue to use it in new and unique ways, problems and issues are found. Many of these problems can be resolved by providing an update to Windows XP. If you have a connection to the Internet, you can list, select, and apply any updates that you would like. The process is outlined in the following steps:

1. Click the Start menu, then select Control Panel.

2. Click on the Windows Update link in the See Also box on the left side of the Control Panel window. This launches the Web page displayed in Figure 18-1.

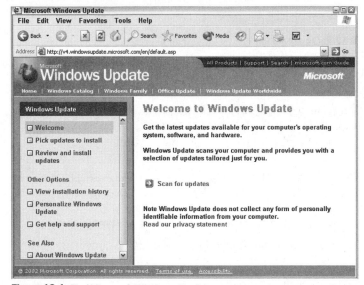

Figure 18-1: The Microsoft Windows Update page.

3. Click the Scan for Updates link on this page. The computer then uses the Internet to find updates. A status of this search is displayed on the right side of the window. When the scan is complete, you are presented with an updated window similar to Figure 18-2 that indicates the search is completed. This gives you a summary of any updates found and allows you to review and add others.

4. Click on Review and Install Updates from either the left side of the window or the right. This lists the critical updates that you should install. You can remove any updates by scrolling through the list and clicking the Remove button.

5. Add any additional updates. Critical Updates and Services Packs list the items that are considered critical. You can also add additional updates that are not considered critical. In Figure 18-2, you see two other categories: Windows XP Updates and Driver Updates. Click on these links to see the list of items. You can then click the Add button to add them to the list of updates to install. Once you have selected all the items you want to update, you can continue.

cross-reference

See Task 17 if you would prefer to have Windows XP install updates automatically. Task 17 also shows you how to turn off automatic updates.

caution

When doing updates, you may have to restart your computer. Before doing an update, you should save any files and documents, as well as close any open programs.

caution

If you are asked to reboot (restart) your computer, you should do so. If you do not, the update process may not have been completely updated. This may result in having your computer do unpredictable things until you do reboot.

note

The Review and Install Updates list contains all updates from any of the subcategories that may be listed. The numbers in the subcategories don't total to the number for the Review and Install Updates list because some updates fall into multiple categories.

cross-reference

To apply updates, you must have administrator access for Windows XP. In Windows XP Home Edition, you must be logged on as the administrator. See Task 213 for changing an account's access rights.

Task **18**

6. Click the Review and Install Updates link on the left side of the page. This presents you with information similar to what is in Figure 18-3, with the items you had selected listed.

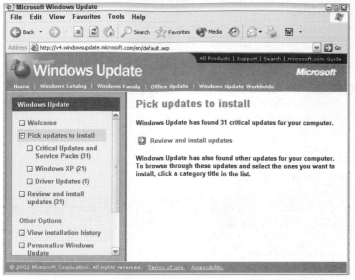

Figure 18-2: The Microsoft Windows Update page with found updates.

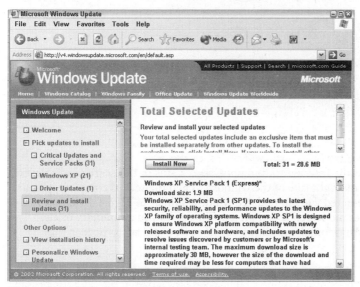

Figure 18-3: Total Selected Updates window.

7. Click the Install Now button. Depending on what is being updated, you may be prompted to accept licensing agreements, to reboot your computer, or to enter additional information. What occurs depends on what updates are being installed. When everything is completed, a page appears, saying that installation is complete. You can close this window or you can choose to view the installation history.

Installing New Software

Invariably you will want to install new software onto your computer. While many programs come with installation routines built in, you should consider following the steps when installing a new application. Before starting the installation process, you should close any unnecessary programs and save any files. Many software programs have you restart your computer as a part of the installation process. This restart can cause any unsaved changes to open files and documents to be lost. As such, it is best to save and close everything before starting a new program installation.

1. Close any unnecessary programs and save any important files.

2. Select Control Panel on the Start menu.

3. Click on Add or Remove Programs. A window appears that lists programs that have been installed on your computer. Figure 19-1 shows a computer that has only had Microsoft Office installed. This window tells you the amount of space used by each program, as well as how often you use the program. Only programs that are designed to register with Windows are displayed in this list.

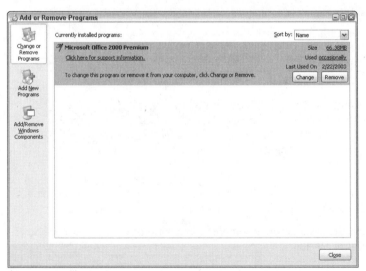

Figure 19-1: The Add or Remove Programs list of currently installed software.

4. In the Control Panel, click the Add New Programs icon on the left side of the window. This changes the options in the window to allow you to install new programs from a CD or diskette, as shown in Figure 19-2.

5. If you are installing from a CD or diskette, click the CD or Floppy button or press Alt+F. A wizard appears that will walk you through starting the installation of new software. Figure 19-3 shows the initial screen of the wizard.

note

You may need to disable any antivirus software that is running before you can install some software.

cross-reference

To learn how to correctly uninstall programs, see Task 20.

cross-reference

Windows XP includes a number of programs and features that can be installed. To learn how to add Windows XP components that may not have been installed already, see Task 240.

note

Not every program installed on your computer will be listed on the Add or Remove Programs window. Programs that are a part of Microsoft Windows XP, such as Notepad, Internet Explorer, and Solitaire will not be listed. Programs you install without using the Add or Remove Programs procedure shown in this task also may not be displayed.

note

Many programs that come on diskettes or CDs include an AutoRun feature that automatically starts the installation process when you insert them.

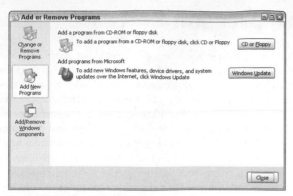

Figure 19-2: The Add New Programs options.

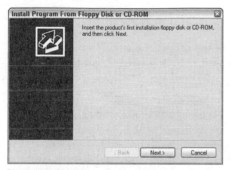

Figure 19-3: The Install Program Wizard.

6. Follow the steps in the Install Program from Floppy Disk or
CD-ROM Wizard, starting with the first step of inserting the CD or
floppy disk into your computer. The wizard launches any installation
programs associated with the program you are installing if they
haven't already started. During the installation you may be asked to
restart your computer. If prompted, be aware that you may not be
able to *correctly* run the program you are installing until you do
restart your computer.

When the installation is complete, you should see the message shown
in Figure 19-4.

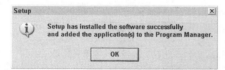

Figure 19-4: The completion message.

7. Press OK. You are done installing and can close the Add or Remove
Programs window.

Task 19

cross-reference

Programs are installed onto
your hard drive. If you don't
have enough free space on
your hard drive, you may not be
able to install a program. See
Task 239 to learn how to clean
up unused files.

tip

When possible, it is best to use
the procedures in this task
when installing software.

cross-reference

Some older programs may have
trouble running in Windows XP.
For help, see Task 250.

Task 20

Removing Application Software

When you find that you are no longer interested in using a program, you may want to remove it from your system. Additionally, there are times when you want to clear older programs off your computer's hard drive to make more room for other stuff. One thing to keep in mind is that you should never go to the hard drive and simply delete the program files. Instead, you should go through the following steps.

Before starting the process to uninstall software, you should close any unnecessary programs and save any files. Many software programs have you restart your computer as a part of uninstalling. This restart can cause any unsaved changes to open files and documents to be lost. As such, it is best to save and close everything before starting a new program installation.

1. Close any unnecessary programs and save any important files.

2. Check the Start menu to see if the program contains an uninstall routine. If an uninstall program has been provided that is compatible with Windows, it should be listed on the Start menu.

3. Select Start menu, click All Programs, and then follow the menus to the program you want to uninstall. For example, you can see in Figure 20-1 that Microsoft Age of Empires II has an uninstall program provided on the menu. If an uninstall program is provided, click on it and follow its instructions. If an uninstall program isn't provided, follow the remaining steps in this task.

Figure 20-1: Checking the programs menu for an uninstall program.

note

You may need to disable any antivirus software that is running before you can install some software.

cross-reference

Old programs that are not being used can be removed from your computer. Task 241 shows you how to uninstall an application.

cross-reference

There is a different, yet similar, process for removing Windows XP components. See Task 240 for more information.

caution

To uninstall a program, you should follow the steps in this task. You should never simply delete the files from your hard drive. This may leave files in other locations. Additionally, Windows XP often stores information about a program that will also need to be removed.

cross-reference

If you are not sure about the impact of uninstalling a program, you should consider backing up your hard drive before proceeding. Task 246 shows you how to do a backup.

4. Select the Control Panel on the Start menu.

5. In the Control Panel, click on Add or Remove Programs.

   The Change or Remove Programs information is displayed. This is a list of programs that have been installed on your computer and registered with Windows XP. This window tells you the amount of space used by each program, as well as how often you use the program. Only programs that are designed to register with Windows will be displayed in this list. Figure 20-2 shows the Change or Remove Programs window with two installed programs.

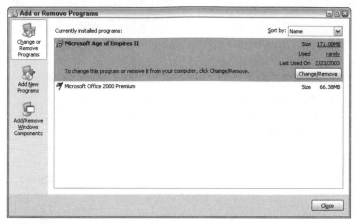

Figure 20-2: The Add or Remove Programs window.

6. Click on the name of the software product you want to uninstall. This displays additional information about that program. For example, in Figure 20-2, you can see the last day that Age of Empires II was used. Additionally, you see the amount of disk space it uses and how often it is used. To see the detailed information on other products, click on their name.

7. Click the Change/Remove button beside the software product you want to uninstall. This launches the uninstall program specific to the software you are removing. Follow the instructions on the screen to remove the software. When you have completed the instructions, you should be returned to the Change or Remove Programs window. The program you uninstalled should no longer be listed.

8. If your program was not listed in the Change or Remove Programs window, check with the help files or documentation provided with the software for instructions specific to that software.

note

Windows XP reports usage in three categories: rarely, occasionally, and frequently.

caution

The amount of space that is estimated in the Change or Remove Programs list is only an estimate and can be wrong. In general, if it is wrong, it is low. This measurement includes the files in the folder and subfolders that the software was installed into.

Part 2: Working with Folders and Files

Task 21: Accessing My Computer

Task 22: Navigating What's on the Hard Drive

Task 23: Creating, Renaming, and Deleting Files and Folders

Task 24: Creating Copies of Files and Folders

Task 25: Moving a File or Folder

Task 26: Using Different Folder Views

Task 27: Customizing the Details Folder View

Task 28: Settings Options on All Folders

Task 29: Customizing Windows Explorer

Task 30: Recovering Deleted Files

Task 31: Setting Recycle Bin Options

Task 32: Searching for Files or Folders

Task 33: Setting File Properties

Task 34: Creating a Shortcut

Task 35: Copying Files to a CD-ROM

Task 36: Saving Space by Compressing a Drive

Task 37: Creating a Zip File

Task 38: Accessing and Adding to a Zip File

Task 39: Extracting All Items from a Zip File

Accessing My Computer

On Microsoft Windows XP, you can use My Computer to navigate around your computer. This program provides you with a starting point for accessing system information, adding or removing programs, and changing settings. The overall function of My Computer is to provide you information and access to your computer. The following steps show you how to obtain basic information about your computer via My Computer:

1. Select the Start menu. The Start menu appears (see Figure 21-1).

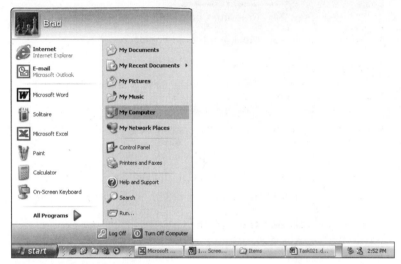

Figure 21-1: The Start menu.

2. Select My Computer. The My Computer dialog window appears (see Figure 21-2). The actual information shown in the right side on your monitor will be different from what is shown in Figure 21-2; however, the areas presented will be the same.

   As you can see from the figure, the right side of the My Computer dialog window presents you with key areas for the files stored on your computer, as well as information on the hard drives and other devices.

3. Double-click on the name of an item on the right side of the My Computer window to open it. If you double-click on a document folder, you are presented with the documents and folders that are stored in that folder. The same result happens if you select one of the other folders in the My Documents window of your computer.

4. Click on the Back button in the upper-left part of the window if you double-clicked on a document folder. This returns you to the My Computer window's original information.

5. Double-click a Hard Disk Drive, preferably one labeled Local Disk. In Figure 21-2, this would be Local Disk (C:). This causes the files and folders stored on your local drive to be displayed.

cross-reference

Task 22 shows you an alternate way to navigate the files on your computer.

note

The My Computer dialog window provides you an easy way to see all the devices that are on your computer, as well as how full they are. For example, you can see that the computer in Figure 21-2 has a local hard drive, a floppy drive, a DVD drive, and a removable disk. You can also see that the hard drive is barely used, with 38.7 out of 41.9GB still free.

tip

Many of the features you can get to from My Computer are covered in the other tasks in this book.

cross-reference

Many of the options you can find in My Computer can also be found in the Control Panel. For example, you can add or remove programs (see Tasks 19 and 20). The system task Change a Setting actually takes you to the Control Panel.

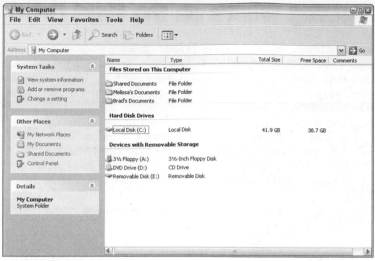

Figure 21-2: The My Computer dialog window.

6. Click on the Back button to return to the My Computer window's original information.

7. Click on the View system information option on the left side of the My Computer dialog window. The System Tasks provide links to do various things. In the case of viewing system information, this presents the dialog in Figure 21-3. This dialog contains information about your system that you may find useful, such as listing your processor, the amount of memory, and the version of Windows you are running.

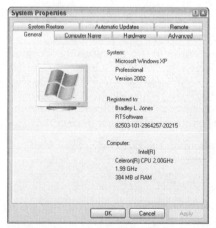

Figure 21-3: The System Properties dialog window.

8. Click the OK button in the System Properties dialog window to close it.

9. Select File⇨Close to close the My Computer dialog window.

tip

If you don't know how much memory your computer has, or what the processor speed is, you can find this out in Step 7 of this task.

tip

You can also close the My Computer dialog window by clicking on the close button (the " × " button on the top right of the title bar).

Navigating What's on the Hard Drive

You can navigate the documents and folders that are stored on your computer's hard drive. Windows XP includes a program, called Windows Explorer, which you can use to navigate through the files, drives, documents, and folders on your computer. The following steps walk you through some of the uses of Windows Explorer:

cross-reference

My Computer is a special link that uses Windows Explorer. My Computer is covered in Task 21.

tip

You can also get to Windows Explorer by right-clicking on the Start button and then selecting Explore from the pop-up menu.

1. Open Windows Explorer. From the Start menu, select All Programs⇨ Accessories⇨Windows Explorer. Figure 22-1 shows Windows Explorer when it is first opened. Note that the files and folders displayed may be different depending on what is on your computer.

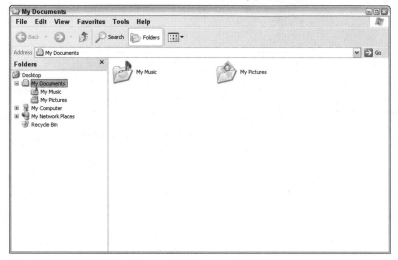

Figure 22-1: Windows Explorer.

cross-reference

You can copy, paste, delete, and move files within Windows Explorer. Other tasks in this part show you how to do all of these.

tip

A folder may contain subfolders if there is a plus sign next to it in the Folder pane on the left side of the Windows Explorer window. Clicking on the item displays its contents in the right pane of the window. Additionally, it causes any subfolders to be displayed in the Folders pane.

2. Click on the Folders icon in the toolbar if it is not already selected (see Figure 22-2 if you are not sure which icon to select). Clicking this icon shows the folders that are on your computer. It also shows the drives, desktop, and other key areas. This information is shown in the left pane.

Back Forward Up   Selected for Folder view

Figure 22-2: Navigation icons in Windows Explorer.

3. Click on the name of a drive, folder, or other location in the left pane of the Windows Explorer window. This selects the item and shows its contents in the right side. Figure 22-3 shows the result of clicking on the My Pictures folder located in the My Documents folder.

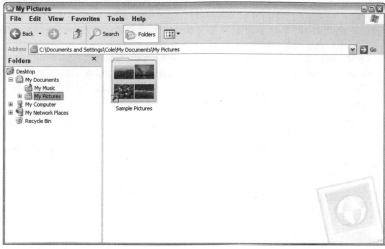

Figure 22-3: The selected My Pictures folder in Windows Explorer.

4. Double-click a folder or drive in the right pane. This selects and opens the folder. The contents of the folder are displayed. Additionally, the folder is selected in the left pane.

5. Click on the Up icon to move to the folder above the current folder. Figure 22-2 shows where the Up icon is located. Looking at the left pane, notice that the folders and drives are organized in a hierarchical manner. If you are at the base folder, the Up icon will not be selectable.

6. Click the Back icon to return to the previous item displayed in Windows Explorer. For example, if you start in the My Documents folder, then click the My Pictures folder, you will see the items in the My Pictures folder. You could then select the Back button to return to the My Documents folder. When you get to the folder you started in, the Back button is disabled.

7. Click the Forward button to go to a folder that had been previously selected. This can only be selected if you've used the Back button. If you have not used the Back button, the Forward button is disabled.

note

Clicking on the plus sign next to an item in the Folder pane displays any subfolders and changes the plus sign to a dash. Clicking the dash hides the subfolders and changes the dash to a plus sign. Clicking on either the plus or dash does not cause the contents of the right pane to change, because an item was not actually selected.

cross-reference

The way the items in the right pane are displayed can be changed. Task 26 shows how to change this presentation.

note

If you unselect the Folder icon in the toolbar, the folder pane is replaced with a view that provides common options, as well as links to some of the key places on your computer. This includes links to My Documents, Shared Documents, and My Computer. Clicking on these other places opens them in Windows Explorer.

note

Double-clicking on an item in the right pane of Windows Explorer selects and opens that item.

tip

You can go to other key locations on your computer by selecting the View⇨Go To menu option. The Go To menu contains a number of key locations you can select.

Task 23

Creating, Renaming, and Deleting Files and Folders

Task 22 showed you how to navigate on your computer. One reason for navigating is to organize files and folders. This can include adding new files and folders, as well as renaming or deleting them. Following are the steps involved with each of these processes:

1. Open Windows Explorer or one of the common folder areas such as My Documents, and navigate to the place where you want to create, rename, or delete a file or folder.
2. Make a new folder by using the following steps:
   a. Click on the Make a New Folder text in the File and Folder Tasks options. This creates a new folder, as shown in Figure 23-1.

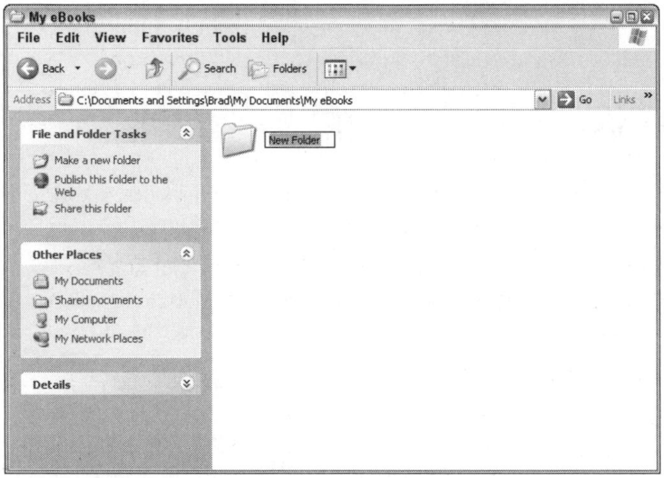

Figure 23-1: Creating a new folder.

   b. Type the name for the new folder into the highlighted box, and then press Enter.

3. Create a new file or document in the current folder by using the following steps:
   a. Select File⇨New from the Explorer menu. This displays a menu that contains the types of documents and files you can create.
   b. Select the file type you want to create. A file is added to the current folder with the name highlighted.

cross-reference

See Task 26 if you need help displaying the Explorer bar in the left pane as shown in Figure 23-1.

note

If the filename includes an extension, you must keep the extension the same. The extension helps identify the type of file. For example, a text document generally has a .txt extension.

tip

You can also right-click on an open area of the main Explorer window to get a pop-up menu of options. Selecting New displays the list of items that you can add, including new folders and new files.

c. Type in the new name for the file. Make sure to keep the extension of the file the same. The extension is the part of the name at the end. It is generally a period followed by three characters.

d. Press the Enter key to accept the new name. If you change the extension, or leave it off, the warning in Figure 23-2 appears. You need to select the No button and re-enter the filename with the extension.

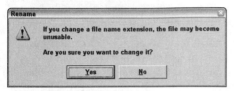

Figure 23-2: Warning for changing a file extension.

4. Rename an existing file or folder by using the following steps:

a. Click on the item you want to rename to select it. Once selected, click on Rename This File or Rename This Document in the File and Folder Tasks options, or simply press the F2 key. This places a box around the filename or folder name and allows you to make changes.

b. Type the new name, remembering to keep the extension the same.

c. Press the Enter key to save the new name. If you change the extension on a filename, you will be given the warning message in Figure 23-2.

5. Delete an existing file or folder using the following steps:

a. Click on the item you want to delete to select it. Once selected, click on Delete This File or Delete This Folder in the File and Folder Tasks options or simply press the Delete (Del) key. If you are using the default Windows options, you will be prompted with a message similar to Figure 23-3 asking if you are sure you want to delete the file or folder.

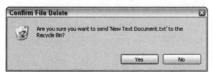

Figure 23-3: Warning for deleting a folder or file.

b. Click Yes to remove the file or folder. This moves the file to the Recycle Bin.

tip

When a file is deleted, it is placed in the Recycle Bin (see Task 30). To completely delete a file and thus bypass the Recycle Bin, hold the Shift key when selecting to delete the file.

note

Although you can add an extension to a folder's name, they generally already have one.

cross-reference

For more on deleting or recovering deleted files, see Tasks 30 and 31 about the Recycle Bin.

tip

You can move more than one file at a time. To select multiple files, click on each while holding down the Ctrl key. Each file you select by clicking on it will be highlighted. You can deselect a file by clicking on it a second time while still holding down the Ctrl key. You can also use the Shift key to select multiple files.

Task **24**

Creating Copies of Files and Folders

When you want to share a file with a friend or if you want to create a backup of a file, the easiest solution is to copy the file. Copying files and folders makes duplicates that are completely separate from the original. You can copy files and documents within the same folder, to another folder, or even to another drive. The following steps walk you through copying files and folders:

1. Locate the file or folder you want to copy. Use Windows Explorer or one of the common folder areas to find the file.

2. Click on the file or folder to select it. You can also select multiple files to copy all at the same time. Select multiple files by holding down the Ctrl key while clicking on the folder or filenames in the right pane of Windows Explorer. Figure 24-1 shows a file selected in the My Documents folder.

Figure 24-1: A file selected in the Explorer window.

3. Make sure that you see the File and Folder Tasks in the left Windows Explorer pane as shown in Figure 24-1. If you don't see these tasks, click on the Folders icon in the toolbar.

4. Select Copy This File, Copy This Folder, or Copy the Selected Items from the File and Folder Tasks options. Which text you have to select depends on whether you have selected a file, a folder, or more than one item, respectively. The dialog in Figure 24-2 appears.

cross-reference

If you need help navigating folders and files, see Task 22.

cross-reference

If you want to access the same file from two different folders, you can use shortcuts instead of creating a copy. Shortcuts are covered in more detail in Task 34.

cross-reference

If you copied items to the same directory where the original files are located, they will be named differently than the original items. You will want to rename these to something more appropriate. See Task 23 to learn how to rename files.

Figure 24-2: The Copy Items dialog window.

5. Select the location where you want to copy the item(s). If you want to place the item into a new folder, then

   a. Select the existing folder that will hold your new folder.

   b. Click the Make New Folder button. This adds a new folder item into the list in the dialog as shown in Figure 24-3.

Figure 24-3: Adding a new folder into the Copy Items dialog window.

   c. Type the name for your new folder and press Enter.

   d. Select the new folder as the location where you will copy the item(s).

6. Click the Copy button. The item(s) is copied to the new location and you are returned to the original folder.

Task 24

tip

You can copy more than one item at a time. To select multiple files and folders, click on each while holding down the Ctrl key. Each item you select by clicking on it will be highlighted. You can unselect an item by clicking on it a second time while still holding down the Ctrl key. You can also use the Shift key to select multiple files or folders.

note

If you change your mind after doing a copy, you can undo the copy by selecting Edit⇨ Undo Move in the Windows Explorer menu options or by pressing Ctrl+Z. You can do this immediately after you do a copy.

cross-reference

Task 25 shows you how to move files instead of copying them.

tip

An advanced way to copy a file is to right-click on the original file and select Copy from the pop-up menu. You can then right-click on an open area in the folder where you want to place the copy and select Paste from the pop-up menu. This copies and then pastes the file into the location you choose.

Task 25

Moving a File or Folder

As you save more and more documents and other files on your computer, you will eventually want to move some of them to new locations. You may want to move them to an existing folder or to a new folder. There may even be times when you want to move your folders. The following steps walk you through moving a file or folder from one location to another:

1. Locate the file or folder you want to move. Use Windows Explorer or one of the common folder areas to find the item.

2. Click on the file or folder to select it. Figure 25-1 shows a file selected in the My Documents folder.

Figure 25-1: A file selected in the Explorer window.

3. Make sure that you see the File and Folder Tasks in the left Explorer pane as shown in Figure 25-1. If you don't, click the Folders icon in the toolbar.

4. Select Move This File, Move This Folder, or Move the Selected Items from the File and Folder Tasks options. The dialog in Figure 25-2 appears.

cross-reference

If you need help navigating folders and files, see Task 22.

tip

You can also move files and folders by left-clicking on them in Windows Explorer and then dragging them to the new location. When you release the mouse, a pop-up menu is displayed that allows you to choose to Move Here to move the item.

tip

You can move more than one file or folder at a time. To select multiple items, click on each while holding down the Ctrl key. Each file or folder you select by clicking on it will be highlighted. You can unselect an item by clicking on it a second time while still holding down the Ctrl key. You can also use the Shift key to select multiple items.

Figure 25-2: The Move Items dialog window.

5. Select the location to where you want to move the file or folder. If you want to place the item into a new folder, then

   a. Select the folder that will contain your new folder.

   b. Click the Make New Folder button. This adds a new folder item into the list in the dialog as shown in Figure 25-3.

Figure 25-3: Adding a new folder into the Move Items dialog window.

   c. Type the name for your new folder and press Enter.

   d. Select the new folder as the location where you will move the file.

6. Click the Move button. The file or folder is moved to the new location and you are returned to the original folder.

note

If you change your mind after doing a move, you can undo the move by selecting Edit⇨ Undo Move in the Windows Explorer menu options or by pressing Ctrl+Z. You can do this immediately after you do a move.

cross-reference

Task 24 shows you how to copy files instead of moving them.

cross-reference

You can move a file to a compressed or zipped file as well as to a different drive. Task 36 shows you how to use compressed drives. Tasks 37 to 39 show you how to work with zip files.

Using Different Folder Views

Windows XP lets you change a number of settings for viewing folders and drives on your computer. These settings can be applied when you are viewing folders and files in Windows Explorer, as well as when you are viewing items in other windows such as the My Documents window. In this task, you learn how to select a different view for the current folder. You also step through the different views available. You can learn to retain these settings, as well as to make other customizations to your folders in the other tasks.

cross-reference

See Task 22 for more information on opening and navigating in Windows Explorer.

tip

You can also access Windows Explorer by right-clicking on the Start button and selecting Explore from the pop-up menu.

cross-reference

See Task 28 to learn how to apply the selected view to all the folders on your computer.

cross-reference

See Tasks 27, 28, and 29 to learn how to set other folder options.

1. Open Windows Explorer. On the Start menu, select All Programs⇨ Accessories⇨Windows Explorer.

2. Navigate to the folder or drive that you want to view.

3. Select View⇨Thumbnail. This changes the view to Thumbnail. Alternatively, you can click on the Views button in the toolbar and select Thumbnail. Your items are now displayed in the same manner as those in Figure 26-1. As you can see, the Thumbnail view gives you a small picture of what is stored in each item along with the item's name.

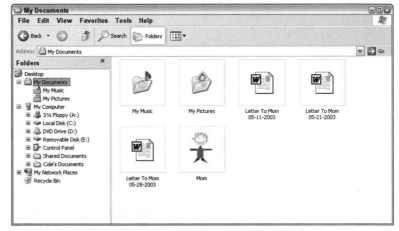

Figure 26-1: The Thumbnail view.

4. Select View⇨Tiles. This changes the view to Tiles. Alternatively, you can click on the Views button in the toolbar and select Tiles. Your items are now displayed in the same manner as those in Figure 26-2. The Tiles view provides you with details about each item, along with showing you an icon.

Figure 26-2: The Tiles view.

5. Select View⇨Icons. This changes the view to icons. Alternatively, you can click on the Views button in the toolbar and select Icons. Unlike the Tiles view, you only get the icon and the filename; however, more items can be displayed as shown in Figure 26-3.

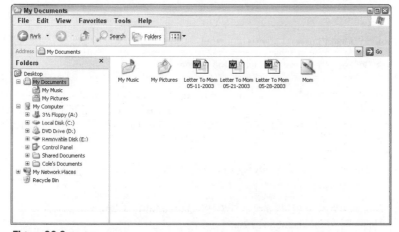

Figure 26-3: The Icons view.

6. Select View⇨List. This changes the view to List. Alternatively, you can click on the Views button in the toolbar and select List. In the List view just the filenames are displayed without icons. If you have a lot of files, this allows you to list the most items within the viewable area of the window.

7. Select View⇨Details. This changes the view to Details. Alternatively, you can click on the Views button in the toolbar and select Details. Your items are now displayed with detailed information. This view allows you to display the most information about the items.

note

When you select the View menu or click on the Views button, you are shown the available views. The current view has a dot next to it.

note

An additional view called Filmstrip is available in the My Pictures folder. The Filmstrip view allows you to look at and manipulate pictures in the folder. For example, you can rotate a picture.

cross-reference

In Task 27 you learn how to customize the Details view to display other types of information about the items.

Task 27

Customizing the Details Folder View

I n Task 26 you learn how to select different views for looking at items that are stored on your computer. One view that you can further customize is the Details view. Figure 27-1 shows a list of items displayed using Windows Explorer in the Details view.

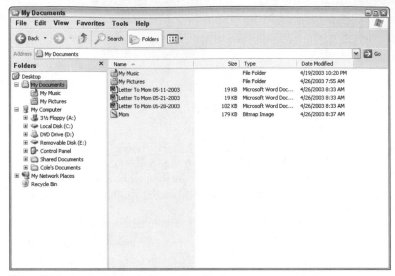

Figure 27-1: Windows Explorer in the Details view.

By default, the Details view presents you with the name of each of the items, along with the file size, the type of file it is, and the date it was last modified. You can change the display to include additional values for each item. The following steps show you how to change what is displayed in this view:

1. Open Windows Explorer. On the Start menu, select All Programs⇨ Accessories⇨Windows Explorer.

2. Navigate to the folder or drive that you want to view.

3. Make sure you are in Details view by selecting View⇨Details from the Windows Explorer menu.

4. Select View⇨Choose Details from the menu. The dialog in Figure 27-2 appears.

5. Select the items that you would like to have displayed in the Details view by clicking on the associated check box. If you don't want something displayed, uncheck the box. Alternatively, you can select an item by clicking on its name and then clicking on the Show button. If an item is already selected, you can unselect it by clicking on the name followed by clicking on the Hide button.

6. Place the items in the order you want them to appear. You can click on a Details item to select it. You can then use the Move Up and Move Down buttons to change the order in which the items display.

cross-reference

Task 26 shows you several alternate views you can use with Windows Explorer. The Details view, however, can be customized to change the values that are displayed.

tip

You can also access Windows Explorer by right-clicking on the Start button and selecting Explore from the pop-up menu.

note

The Name item cannot be removed or hidden from the Detail view.

cross-reference

Tasks 28 and 29 show you other ways to customize Windows Explorer options, including how to apply your selections for the Details to all of the folders on your computer.

note

If an item is checked in the Details pane of the Choose Details dialog, then when it is selected, the Show button is disabled. If it is not checked, the Hide button is disabled. This is to help you know what can and can't be done.

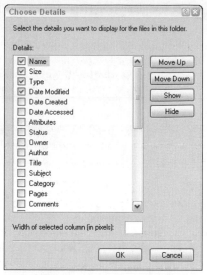

Figure 27-2: The Choose Details dialog.

7. Set the widths for each item by entering a value in the Width of Selection Columns (in pixels) box.

8. Click the OK button to apply the changes.

You can also select items to be displayed in the Details view by right-clicking on the labels above the Details information. This presents the pop-up menu in Figure 27-3. Simply click on an item you want displayed. A check appears next to the item in the menu, and the item is displayed. Clicking on an item that is already displayed causes the check mark to be removed and the item to be hidden. If the item you want is not in the pop-up list of items, you can select the More option.

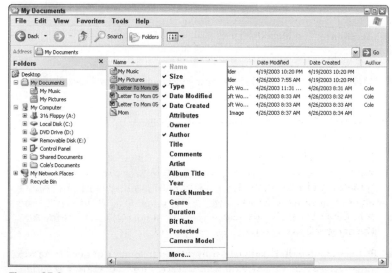

Figure 27-3: The Details pop-up menu.

---

tip

You can also change the order in which details are displayed in the Details view by dragging the column heading right or left to the new location. For example, you can click and hold your mouse on the Size heading and drag it to the right.

---

tip

If you click on the heading of a column, it sorts the column by that value. For example, clicking on the Name heading sorts the items listed by their names. Clicking on the heading a second time reverses the order, but the column still remains sorted.

---

note

While you could select to display every type of information for the Details view, this would not be practical. Some values don't apply to all files; plus if you selected them all, you'd have to do a lot of horizontal scrolling to see the values. It is better to select only the information you are interested in seeing.

---

tip

You can change the width of a column in the Detail view by using the mouse. Place the mouse cursor on the line between two cursor headers, then right-click and drag the line to resize the column.

Task 28

Settings Options on All Folders

You can set a number of options for viewing items on your hard drive, including the type of view, whether you have to click once or twice to open an item, whether additional details and links are provided, and whether folders open in the current window or in a new window. A few of these settings can be set once and they apply to everything,

In Task 26 you learn how to change the view you see when looking at the files in folders on your computer. The view determines what you see and how it is displayed. You can customize or select your preferred view and then apply it to all of your folders.

The following steps show you how to set some of the global options for viewing files and folders. Once these options are set, they can impact all of your folders. Before doing Step 8 of the following, you should make sure that the current folder is set to the View options that you want to use as the defaults for all your folders.

1. Open Windows Explorer. On the Start menu, select All Programs⇨ Accessories⇨Windows Explorer.

2. Select Tools⇨Folder Options from the menus. The Folder Options dialog window appears (see in Figure 28-1).

Figure 28-1: The Folder Options dialog window.

3. Select the General tab if it is not already selected. The General tab, shown in Figure 28-1, allows you to customize several options that impact all of your folders.

4. Turn on or off the Explorer pane. The Explorer pane is the left side of Windows Explorer. If you select Show Common Tasks in Folders, you are given the Explorer pane. If you select Use Windows Classic Folders, the Explorer pane is turned off. Figure 28-2 shows the difference between the two.

5. Determine whether you want to navigate from one folder to the next in the same window or if you want each folder to open in a separate window. If you select Open Each Folder in the Same Window, then

when you click on a folder, its contents replace the current window's contents. If you select Open Each Folder in Its Own Window, each time you display a different folder, it opens and displays its contents in a new window.

Showing common task   Classic view

Figure 28-2: Showing common tasks versus using classic folders.

6. Select whether you want to have your Windows folders act like Web pages or whether you would prefer them to act like standard windows. You can have your folders act more like Web pages by selecting Single-Click to Open an Item.

7. Click the Apply button to apply these settings to all your windows.

8. Click the View tab. The Folder Views options, as well as the advanced options for folders, appear (see Figure 28-3).

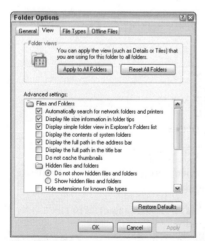

Figure 28-3: The View tab of the Folder Options dialog window.

9. Click the Apply to All Folders button. This applies the view settings from the current folder to all of your folders.

10. Click the OK button to close the Folder Options dialog window.

tip

If you make global settings and find that things don't operate as you want, you can always go to the Folder Options and select the Restore Defaults buttons on the General and View tabs.

note

Click the Reset All Folders button on the View tab of the Folder Options dialog if you want to restore the default settings for all of your folders. Note that this will not change any toolbar settings you may have changed.

cross-reference

See Task 26 to learn how to set the view for browsing your computer's files and folders. It is the settings you make in Task 26 that are applied when you do Step 10.

Task **29** **Customizing Windows Explorer**

I n addition to customizing the manner in which folders are formatted and displayed (see Tasks 26 through 28), you can also customize the Windows Explorer program itself. This includes changing items such as toolbars and status bars, as well as determining what is shown in the Explorer pane on the left side of Windows Explorer. The following steps walk you through many of the key customizations you may find useful:

1. Open Windows Explorer. On the Start menu, select All Programs⇨ Accessories⇨Windows Explorer.

2. Select the toolbars you want displayed. You can use three different toolbars in Windows Explorer: Standard Buttons bar, Address bar, and Links bar. These are selected from the View⇨Toolbars menu. If you select it again, the toolbar is hidden. The three different toolbars are identified in Figure 29-1.

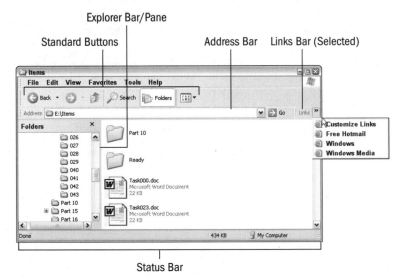

Figure 29-1: Windows Explorer.

3. Customize the Standard toolbar. You can change the icons that are on the Standard toolbar, as well as whether text is displayed with them:

    a. Select View⇨Toolbars⇨Customize. This displays the Customize Toolbar dialog, as shown in Figure 29-2.

    b. Click on an icon in the list of Available Toolbar Buttons.

    c. Click the Add button to add this to the toolbar.

    d. Click on the icon in the Current Toolbar Buttons list.

    e. Use the Move Up and Move Down button to move the icon to the location you want it in the toolbar.

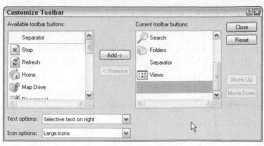

Figure 29-2: The Customize Toolbar dialog.

   f. Repeat these steps for each button you want added.

   g. Customize the overall toolbar icons by choosing from the Text Options and Icon Options drop-down lists.

   h. Click the Close button when you have made all of your changes.

4. Add or remove the status bar. Figure 29-1 shows the status bar that can also be displayed or removed from Windows Explorer. To add this, select View⇨Status Bar from the menus. To remove the status bar, select the option again.

5. Pick the Explorer bar you want to display. You can click the Folders icon in the Standard Buttons toolbar to display the Folders view, as shown in Figure 29-1. Deselecting this icon displays the Common areas in the Explorer pane. You can also select a number of other options to display in this pane. These options can be found by selecting View⇨Explorer Bar from the menus. The options include Search, Favorites, Media, History, and Folders.

6. Turn on or off the Tip of the Day. A tip area can be displayed by selecting View⇨Explorer Bar⇨Tip of the Day. Figure 29-3 shows the Tip of the Day in Windows Explorer.

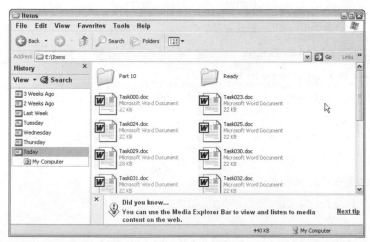

Figure 29-3: Windows Explorer with the Tip of the Day and with the History Explorer bar.

Task 29

note

Separators can be added to the Standard toolbar in order to group different icons. A separator appears as a vertical line in the toolbar. These are added in the same way that icons are added.

note

A check mark appears next to the toolbar and status bar menu options when they are active.

note

You can remove items from the Standard toolbar by selecting them and using the Remove button.

tip

To reset your Standard Buttons toolbar back to the original icons, you can click the Reset button in the Customize Toolbar dialog (see Step 3).

note

You can use the History Explorer bar to see where you have been. This keeps track of documents and files on your computer, as well as Web pages. (See Figure 29-3.)

Recovering Deleted Files

When you delete a document, folder, or other file in Windows XP, it is actually placed in the Recycle Bin. The Recycle Bin is generally represented as a trash can on your desktop. If you need to recover a document or other file that you have deleted, you can pull it out of the Recycle Bin. The steps that follow will help you recover a deleted file from the Recycle Bin.

This is, of course, provided that the file was lost because you deleted it, and it assumes you've not emptied the trash can since the time the item was removed. If you overwrite a document or file, Windows XP may not be able to help you.

1. Right-click on the Recycle Bin icon on your desktop.

2. Select Explore from the pop-up menu. This displays the contents of the Recycle Bin in a Windows Explorer window. Figure 30-1 is an example of the opened Recycle Bin.

Figure 30-1: Exploring the Recycle Bin.

3. Find the item you want to restore in the items listed.

4. Right-click on the item. A pop-up menu appears.

cross-reference

The way files are displayed in the Recycle Bin depends on your settings for Windows Explorer. See Tasks 26 through 30 to learn how to change the display.

cross-reference

See Task 31 to learn how to customize the Recycle Bin settings, including a setting that deletes files instead of placing them in the Recycle Bin — thus making them unrecoverable using Windows XP.

note

The trash can icon on the desktop shows papers sticking out of it if items have been deleted. When you empty the Recycle Bin, the trash can appears empty.

tip

You can also open the Recycle Bin by double-clicking on its icon on the desktop.

note

Just like choosing Explore, choosing Open from the Recycle Bin also displays the list of items that have been deleted. In Explorer, however, the folders are displayed in the Explorer bar on the left side of the window. This makes it easier to navigate on your computer. See Task 22 for more on navigating.

5. Click Restore to restore the item to its original location. Alternatively, you can click Properties to display information about the file you have selected. Figure 30-2 shows the Properties window of a deleted bitmap image. As you can see, it is possible to restore the item by clicking on the Restore button in the Properties dialog window too.

Figure 30-2: Properties for a deleted item.

6. Close the Recycle Bin window by selecting File⇨Close or by clicking the Close button.

Note that if you have emptied the Recycle Bin or if you have deleted files directly from the Recycle Bin, those files are *not* recoverable. You empty the Recycle Bin by right-clicking on it and selecting Empty Recycle Bin from the pop-up menu. Again, if you do this, the files are not recoverable. Because they are not recoverable, a warning message like the one in Figure 30-3 appears before the Recycle Bin permanently removes the files.

Figure 30-3: Warning message when emptying the Recycle Bin.

Setting Recycle Bin Options

When you delete a document, folder, or other file in Windows XP, it is actually placed in the Recycle Bin. Task 30 shows you how to recover files from the Recycle Bin and thus restore them to your system. You can, however, change the settings in the Recycle Bin to determine if files are recoverable, as well as how much room can be used to help make files recoverable. To set these and other Recycle Bin options, use the following steps. Be aware that you must have an administrator-type account to make these changes. If you try to make these changes without having an administrator account type, you will get the error message in Figure 31-1.

cross-reference

See Task 30 to understand how to restore files from the Recycle Bin.

Figure 31-1: The error message for not having the right access.

1. Right-click on the Recycle Bin icon on your desktop.

2. Select Properties from the pop-up menu. The Global tab in the Recycle Bin Properties dialog window appears (see Figure 31-2).

caution

If you remove the check mark from the Display Delete Confirmation Dialog check box, you will not receive any type of message when you delete a file. Leave this option checked to get a confirmation message and to avoid deleting an item by mistake.

Figure 31-2: The Recycle Bin Properties window.

3. Select whether you want to have a single set of settings that apply to all of the drives on your computer or whether you would like each drive to have its own settings. If you have only one drive, the end

note

If a file is deleted from the Recycle Bin, then it is gone. Some third-party programs are available that may be able to restore the file; however, these will generally only work if you have not written any new files to the hard drive since the time you deleted the file.

result of either selection will be the same. If unsure, select Use One Setting for All Drives.

4. If you choose to configure each drive independently, select the tab in the Recycle Bin Properties for the drive you want to configure. Figure 31-3 shows the Local Disk (C:) tab selected after choosing Configure drives independently on the Global tab. As you can see, the settings are similar to those in the Global tab.

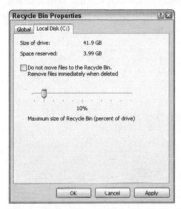

Figure 31-3: A Local Disk tab in the Recycle Bin Properties window.

5. Select the check box titled Do Not Move Files to the Recycle Bin, if you want to permanently delete files instead of placing them in the Recycle Bin.

6. Set the amount of disk space you would like used for deleted files. In Figure 31-2 and 31-3 you can see that 10% of the hard drive is set aside to hold deleted files. If you want to be able to recover more files, increase this amount by moving the slider. If you don't have a lot of disk space to spare, you can decrease this amount. If you decrease the amount, when a file that is too big to fit in the Recycle Bin is deleted, you will be warned that it will be permanently deleted rather than placed in the Recycle Bin. Figure 31-4 shows this warning.

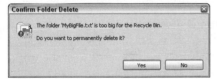

Figure 31-4: The warning message for not having enough room in the Recycle Bin.

tip

The tabs for the drives on your computer include information about how much disk space a drive has and how much is actually reserved.

caution

If you select the Do Not Move Files to the Recycle Bin option, you will not be able to recover deleted files using Windows XP. It is recommended that you do not select this option.

tip

If you need to save disk space, set a lower value for the maximum value of the Recycle Bin. If you have a lot of unused disk space, you can increase this value to keep deleted files around longer.

Task 32

Searching for Files or Folders

As you create more files and folders on your computer, it becomes more likely that you will lose track of where some are stored. Windows XP enables you to easily search for files and folders. You can search using a number of criteria, including the filename, the size, the date it was created, and more. You can also set up a search to look in a single folder, across a drive, or across your entire computer. The following steps walk you through searching for a file or folder:

1. Select the Search option from the Start menu.

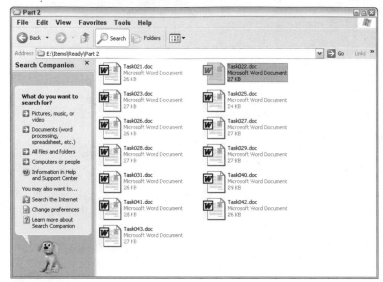

Figure 32-1: The Search Companion.

2. Select an option for what you want to find. There are special search options to help you find pictures, music, or videos, as well as documents such as word processor and spreadsheet files. You can use the All Files and Folders option to search for any file or folder on your computer, including pictures, music, videos, word processor documents, and spreadsheets.

    Each of the three options has similar prompts for finding your files or folders. Selecting All Files and Folders changes the Search Companion to the dialog in Figure 32-2.

3. Fill in all or part of the filename, as well as a word or phrase that is in the file. You don't have to enter both of these.

4. Select where you want to search by selecting a value in the Look In drop-down list. By default, Windows XP generally looks in the current folder. You can change this value to search a different folder, drive, your entire computer (select My Computer), a drive such as a disk drive, or even network drives if you are on a network.

note

Windows Explorer, My Computer, and several other programs include a Search icon in their toolbar, as well as an option on their menu that also brings up the Search Companion that is shown in the left pane of Figure 32-1.

note

You can always use the All Files or Folders search option; however, if you know you are looking for a picture, music file, video, document, or spreadsheet, you can use the specialized searches as well.

note

If you don't fill in search information, your search may find everything on your hard drive! Entering all or even part of the filename generally provides the best search results.

Task 32

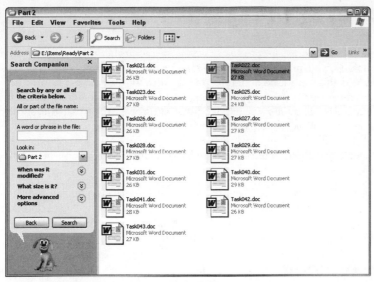

Figure 32-2: Searching for all files and folders.

5. If you want, you can enter advanced options for your search. To enter advanced options, click on the advanced items to expand them.

6. Click the Search button. The search begins and you are shown a status of the search. When the search is complete, the results — if any — are shown as illustrated in Figure 32-3.

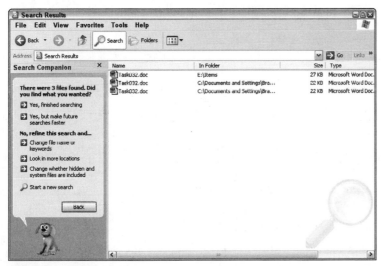

Figure 32-3: Search results.

7. Click Start a New Search if you want to do a new search; otherwise, you can pick options to refine the search.

8. Click Yes, Finished Searching if you found what you were searching for.

tip

Pressing Ctrl+E brings up the Search Companion in Windows Explorer's left pane.

tip

You don't have to fill out all of the entry boxes and prompts in the search forms. You only need to fill out enough to help identify what you are trying to find. If you get too many results, you can always refine your search.

tip

You can indicate whether the search should include subfolders. This is done in the advanced options (see Figure 32-3).

tip

You can search for a specific type of file. This is set in the Type of File drop-down list in the advanced options (see Figure 32-3).

cross-reference

Tasks 13 and 14 show you how to search the help files. Searching the help files differs from searching to find files and folders.

Task **33**

Setting File Properties

Windows XP allows you to see as well as set a number of properties on your files. This includes being able to change the properties so that the file can only be read and cannot be updated. You can also hide a file so it cannot be seen by the average user. Other properties that can be set include descriptive information about a file. The following steps walk you through the process of setting properties on a file:

1. Locate the file in Windows Explorer, My Computer, or another Explorer window.

2. Select File⇨Properties from the menu. Alternatively, you can right-click on the item and select Properties from the pop-up menu that is displayed. The Properties window is displayed. Figure 33-1 is the Properties window for a picture file called `Bball 001.jpg`.

Figure 33-1: The Properties window for a file.

As you can see from Figure 33-1, the Properties tag includes a lot of information about a file. It shows the type of file and the size of the file, as well as how much disk space it is taking and when the file was created and modified last.

3. Select the Read-Only attribute value if you don't want anyone to be able to make changes to this file.

4. Select the Hidden attribute if you want this file to be hidden on your hard drive.

5. Click the Advanced button to see additional attributes you can set. Figure 33-2 shows the Advanced Attributes dialog window. Click OK

in the Advanced Attributes dialog to return to the standard Properties dialog window.

Figure 33-2: The Advanced Attributes options.

6. Click the Apply button to apply any changes in the attributes.

7. Click the Summary tab to select the Summary information. Most files allow you to enter summary information about the file. This includes a title, subject, author, categories, keywords, and comments. Some files may have additional items you can enter, while others may protect some of these values. Figure 33-3 shows the simple Summary tab.

Figure 33-3: The simple Summary file properties.

8. Enter any summary information you would like associated with this file. You can provide any information you want to associate. For example, for a picture file you could add information on when and where the picture was taken.

9. Click the OK button to save the changes and exit the Properties window.

cross-reference

Users with administrator account types can set their computer to show hidden files. Limited account users should not be able to see hidden files. Task 221 shows how to set the account types.

caution

Not all files allow you to enter summary information. Primarily, you can enter summary information for files you create, such as documents, music files, icons, movies, and more. Program files and other files created by others may not have an option for you to add summary information.

note

The Summary tab may include an Advanced button. The information presented in the advanced summary area is specific to the type of file you are reviewing. For example, a Microsoft Word file may include information such as number of characters, words, and pages, while a picture file may display information such as width, height, and resolution.

Creating a Shortcut

In Tasks 24 and 25 you can learn how to copy and move files. One other option exists in Windows XP for accessing a file from a different location: creating a shortcut. A shortcut allows you to get to a single file from multiple locations on your computer. For example, you can have an important file stored in your My Documents folder. If this is a file you access all the time, you may want to get to it from your desktop as well. By placing a shortcut to the document on the desktop, you can use it to get to the document quicker.

cross-reference

Task 21 shows you how to access My Computer. Task 22 shows you how to navigate the folders on your computer.

1. Navigate to the folder or location where you want to place the shortcut. You can use My Computer or Windows Explorer to get to the folder. You can also go to the desktop.

2. Right-click on an open area within the folder, or on an open area of the desktop if placing a shortcut on the desktop. The pop-up menu in Figure 34-1 appears.

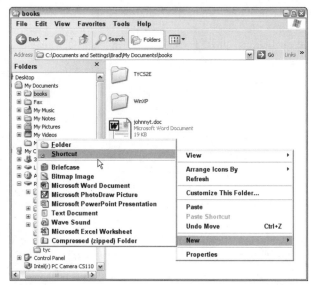

Figure 34-1: Selecting to create a new shortcut.

cross-reference

See Tasks 24 and 25 for more on copying and moving files. You can copy and move shortcuts just like other files. The shortcut will still point to the original file after you copy or move it.

3. Select New⇨Shortcut from the pop-up menu. This starts the Create Shortcut Wizard with the dialog window presented in Figure 34-2.

4. Enter the item you want to create a shortcut to. You can click the Browse button to look for the item. Clicking the Browse button presents a dialog as shown in Figure 34-3. You can click on the plus signs to expand the folders.

5. Click on the item you want to create the shortcut to, then click OK. This places the name of the item and its location into the dialog window for you.

tip

Shortcut icons have a small arrow at the bottom-left corner to show that they are pointing to a different file.

Figure 34-2: The Create Shortcut Wizard.

6. Click Next in the Create Shortcut Wizard. The dialog window in Figure 34-3 appears. Enter the name you want given to the shortcut. The default name will be the same as the item you are linking to.

Figure 34-3: Browsing for an item to create a shortcut to.

7. Click Finish to create your shortcut.

Figure 34-4: Naming your shortcut.

note

You can create a shortcut in the same folder for an item by right-clicking and selecting Create Shortcut from the pop-up menu. You will then need to move the shortcut to the desired location.

cross-reference

You can find out what a shortcut really points to by looking at its properties. You can access the properties by right-clicking and selecting Properties from the pop-up menu. See Task 33 for more on file properties.

note

Deleting a shortcut does not delete the file that the shortcut points to.

Task **35**

Copying Files to a CD-ROM

Copying files to a writable CD is done a little differently than copying files to another folder. Windows XP helps you organize your files and then writes them all at once to a CD. This feature also allows you to easily write the same files to more than one CD. The following steps walk you through copying files to a CD:

1. Open Windows Explorer or My Computer and navigate to the location of the folder or files you want to copy to the CD.

2. Select the folder or files by clicking on them. You can select multiple files by holding down the Ctrl key while selecting the files.

3. Select the Copy link in the File and Folder Tasks of Windows Explorer. This link copies the selected files or folders. The Copy Items dialog window appears, similar to what is shown in Figure 35-1.

Figure 35-1: The Copy Items dialog window.

4. Select the CD drive that you are copying the files to, and press the OK button. The files are copied to a temporary area.

5. Open My Computer, and select the CD drive. The files that are ready to be written are displayed as shown in Figure 35-2.

note

This task assumes you have a writable CD drive that can create CDs. These drives are generally referred to as CD-R or CD-RW drives.

cross-reference

While a CD can store a lot of files, if you are storing pictures, you may want to compress them before copying them to the CD to save space. See Task 37 to learn how to create zip files that can be copied to a CD.

cross-reference

You can copy music to a CD using the Media Player. See Task 87 for more on using the Media Player.

caution

It is up to you to make sure you don't copy too much onto the CD. Otherwise, you may get an error. A standard CD can hold approximately 650MB. Some CDs can hold more.

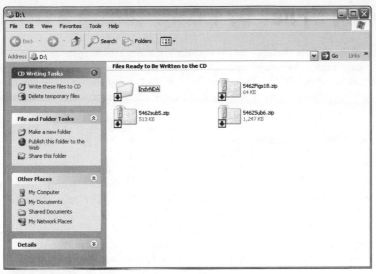

Figure 35-2: Files ready to be copied to a CD.

6. From the CD Writing options, select Write These Files to CD. This starts the CD Writing Wizard, as shown in Figure 35-3.

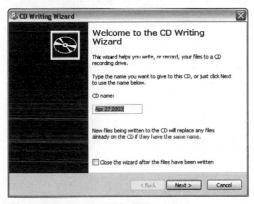

Figure 35-3: The CD Writing Wizard.

7. Fill in the information requested by the wizard. The wizard takes care of copying the files to the CD. A status bar is displayed as the files are copied. When the wizard has completed, you are presented with a Completing page. You can choose to write another CD by checking the box, or you can click the Finish button to end the copying.

Saving Space by Compressing a Drive

Task **36**

Windows XP comes with two features that allow you to save disk space when placing information on your computer's hard drive. One of these methods is described in Task 37. The other method involves compressing — or shrinking — items that are placed on your hard drive. Windows XP can do this compression automatically. When you use a compressed file, Windows XP automatically uncompresses the file for you. When you save the file, Windows XP again compresses the file automatically.

For compression to work, you have to identify what you want compressed. It will not work automatically until you turn it on. Additionally, compression will only work if your hard drive is set up as an NTFS drive. The following steps show you how to verify if a hard drive is NTFS:

1. Click on My Computer in the Start menu. This displays the My Computer dialog window (see Task 21 for more on My Computer).

2. Right-click on the hard drive you want to verify. Most likely this will be Local Disk (C:). A pop-up menu appears.

3. Select Properties. This displays a dialog window similar to Figure 36-1, with information about your hard drive, including an entry for File System. If File System is NTFS, you can use compression. Otherwise, you can't use compression, but you can still use zipped files.

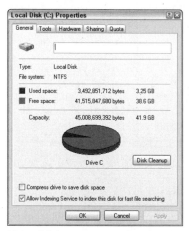

Figure 36-1: Hard drive properties.

4. Close the dialog and My Computer windows.

Task **36**

If your hard drive is NTFS, you can compress the entire hard drive, individual folders, or individual files. The following steps walk you through turning on compression.

1. Follow Steps 1 through 3 in the preceding list. This takes you to the Properties dialog window for the hard drive you want to compress.

2. Check the Compress Drive to Save Disk Space option at the bottom of the dialog window.

3. Click the Apply button. The dialog shown in Figure 36-2 appears. You can see that this dialog window tells you what you are doing: compress.

Figure 36-2: Confirmation dialog window.

4. Select to compress documents and files in just the base (root) folder, or select to compress everything on the hard drive (Apply Changes to C:\, Subfolders and Files).

5. Click the OK button. Compression is applied to the selection you made. If you selected to compress everything, you may see errors as shown in Figure 36-3. This is a result of a file or document that can't be compressed. It is recommended that you press the Ignore button or the Ignore All button on these. Often these are files that are in use.

Figure 36-3: Files that can't currently be compressed.

6. Click OK on the local disk Properties dialog window.

7. Close the My Computer dialog window.

Creating a Zip File

Zip files are compressed files. You can store documents, pictures, folders, and more in a zip file. When the files, documents, or folders are placed into the zip file, they are also compressed. Using zip files, you can lower the amount of disk space needed to store one or more other files. Using programs like Windows Explorer, you can also access zip files, as well as the files stored within them.

Zip files can be copied to diskettes, to writable CDs, to the Internet, and more. You can share them with others who are using Windows XP or even with people using another operating system. While Microsoft Windows XP can directly work with zip files, you should be aware that older versions of Windows cannot. Rather, people using other operating systems will need to install a zip program such as PKZIP. Once installed, they will be able to access the items in a zip file.

The following steps show you how to create a zip file:

1. Select My Computer from the Start menu. This displays the My Computer dialog window that lists the main folders and drives on your computer.

2. Double-click the drive or folder where you want to create the compressed zip file. This opens the folder or drive.

3. Continue to click into folders until you get to the location where you want to place the zip file.

4. Select File⇨New⇨Compress (zipped) file from the menus as shown in Figure 37-1.

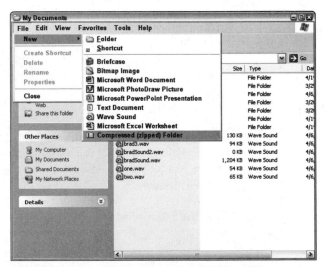

Figure 37-1: Selecting the menu option for a zipped file.

cross-reference

Unlike the compressed files covered in Task 36, you cannot make changes to a file stored in a zip file. Rather, you must unzip (uncompress) the files, make the changes, and then add them back into the zip file. You can view documents and files stored in a zip file.

cross-reference

See Tasks 38 and 39 to learn how to pull files out of a zip file.

tip

Zippers will appear on the icons for compressed zipped files.

tip

Instead of using the menu, you can right-click an open area in the list of files and folders. This displays a pop-up menu. From the pop-up menu, you can select New⇨Compress (zipped) file.

caution

You can run some programs directly from a zip file; however, you cannot run all of them. If a program uses additional files, you need to unzip all of the files before you can run the program. Task 39 shows you how to extract files.

This creates a new zip file as shown in Figure 37-2. You'll see that the default name of `New Compressed (zipped) Folder.zip` is used and that the name is highlighted right after you edited it.

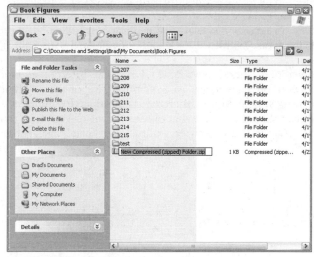

Figure 37-2: The new zip file.

5. Type in a new name for the zip file. Include .zip as the extension. If you don't include the .zip as part of the name, you will get a warning message as shown in Figure 37-3. At this point, you have created the new zip file and have given it a name. You can treat this file like a normal Windows XP folder.

Figure 37-3: A warning message for changing the file extension.

You can add documents, files, and folders to a zip file in the same way you add items to a regular folder. This includes dragging and dropping items into the zip file. See Task 23 for more on adding files to a folder.

tip

You can also create zip files within Windows Explorer in the same manner as shown in this task.

caution

If you install a different compression program, such as PKZIP, it replaces Windows XP's compression option on some menus.

Task 38

Accessing and Adding to a Zip File

cross-reference

Task 37 shows you how to create a zip file. Task 39 shows you how to extract all the files from a zip file at once.

tip

You can't change an item within a zip file. You can, however, extract the item, make the change, and then copy the updated item back into the zip file.

note

You can select multiple files and extract or delete them all at once.

Zip files can contain compressed files, documents, and folders. A single zip file can contain as many items as you want. You can access the items within the zip file to view them, and you can extract items from a zip file to use them. Newer versions of files or other items can be copied into a zip file, or you can add completely new files, documents, or folders. The following steps walk you through some of the ways for accessing a zip file to add or update items and to extract individual files:

1. Open My Computer or Windows Explorer and navigate to the zip file you want to access.

2. Double-click on the name of the zip file. This opens the file and displays its contents in a new window. The contents are displayed just as the contents of any folder would be displayed. Figure 38-1 shows the contents of a zipped file that contains a folder and three pictures.

Figure 38-1: An opened zip file.

3. Click on the file you want to manipulate, then do one of the following steps:

   a. Drag the file you want to extract from the zip folder to a different folder. Using the left mouse button creates an uncompressed copy of the file at the new location. Using the right mouse button to drag the file causes a pop-up menu to be displayed when you drop the file. You can then select from the pop-up menu to move or copy the file. The resulting file is uncompressed. If you extract a file that has a password, you are prompted with a dialog similar to Figure 38-2 asking for you to enter the password.

Figure 38-2: Prompt for entering a password to extract a file.

b. Right-click on the file and select Delete from the pop-up menu. This deletes the file from the zip folder. Before permanently deleting the file, you are prompted with a message as shown in Figure 38-3, asking if you are sure you want to delete the file.

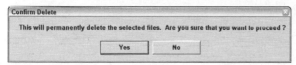

Figure 38-3: Message confirming you want to delete a file from a zip file.

4. Update a file in a zip file by dragging and dropping a new copy onto the zip file or into the opened zip file folder. If the file exists in the zip file, you are asked to confirm that you want to update the file with a message similar to the one in Figure 38-4. Select the appropriate answer from the prompt.

Figure 38-4: Message confirming you want to overwrite an existing item in a zip file.

cross-reference

Compressed files differ from zipped files in that you can treat a compressed file like a normal folder in Windows XP. You can update and save changes directly in the compressed folder. With a zip file, you cannot do the updates directly in the zipped folder. Compressed files are described in Task 36.

tip

You can add a password to a zip file by selecting File⇨ Add a Password... from the Explorer menu when the zip file is selected or opened.

Extracting All Items from a Zip File

Zipped files are compressed folders that can contain files, documents, and other folders. While you can view what is in a zip file, if you want to change any of those items, you need to extract the item out of the zip. Extracting the files uncompresses them to another location on your computer.

You may want to extract the items from a zip file that you downloaded from the Internet or that you received from someone else. Regardless of where the zip file came from, you can extract the items using the following steps:

1. Use My Computer or Windows Explorer to locate the zip file you want to extract files from.

2. Click on the zip filename to select it. Don't double-click, only single-click to highlight the filename.

3. Select File⮫Extract All from the menus. The Extraction Wizard appears (see Figure 39-1).

Figure 39-1: The Extraction Wizard.

4. Click the Next button. This takes you to the next page of the Extraction Wizard, as shown in Figure 39-2.

5. Enter a folder name (directory) in which to place the extracted files. The default name will be the same as the zip file, and the folder will be placed in the current location.

6. Click the Next button. If the zip file has a password associated with it, or if any of the items have a password, a dialog is displayed, as shown in Figure 39-3. Enter the password into this dialog and click OK.

cross-reference

See Task 32 for more information on finding a file if you need help.

cross-reference

See Task 38 for extracting individual items from a zip file.

tip

As an alternative to using the File menu option, you can right-click on the name of the zip file. This displays a pop-up menu with an option to Extract All.

note

While you can run some programs without extracting them from a zip file, if the program requires more than one program to run, then you must extract it. This task shows you how to extract the files.

cross-reference

See Task 37 for creating a zip file.

tip

You can use the Browse button if you would like to search the hard drive for a different location to place the extracted files.

Figure 39-2: The Extraction Wizard destination selection.

The files are extracted and placed at the location entered in the wizard. The indicator at the bottom of the page in Figure 39-2 shows you the status of the files being extracted. When all the files are extracted, you are presented with the Extraction Complete page of the wizard, as shown in Figure 39-4.

Figure 39-3: The prompt for the password.

7. Select or unselect the Show Extracted Files option. If this option is selected, when you finish the wizard, Windows Explorer is opened, displaying the folder (directory) containing your extracted files.

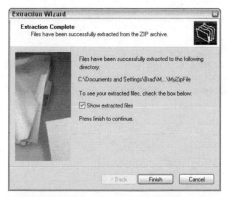

Figure 39-4: The Extraction Wizard extraction complete page.

8. Click the Finish button. If you selected the Show Extracted Files option, a Windows Explorer window opens as described in the previous step. If you did not select Show Extracted Files, the wizard ends and your files are simply extracted to the location you indicated without any display.

tip

Rather than copy a zip file from a diskette or CD, you can extract files directly from the zip file on those media to your hard drive.

cross-reference

Zip files can be password-protected. See Task 38 for additional information on using passwords with zip files.

caution

Before extracting and using files from a zip file, make sure you know where the zip file came from. Some zip files attached to emails or that you can download from the Internet could contain virus programs.

caution

Be careful extracting files from a zip file on a diskette or CD-ROM. These media may not have enough room to hold the extracted files or may be write-protected (meaning you may not be able to write the extracted files to them).

Part 3: Personalizing Windows XP

Task 40: Choosing a Theme

Task 41: Setting the Screen Colors and Resolution

Task 42: Choosing a Desktop Background Image

Task 43: Setting or Changing a Screen Saver

Task 44: Choosing or Changing an Appearance

Task 45: Assigning Sounds to Events

Task 46: Creating a New Theme

Task 47: Customizing Your Taskbar

Task 48: Customizing the Quick Launch Toolbar

Task 49: Customizing the Start Menu

Task 50: Adding Shortcuts to Your Desktop

Task 51: Arranging Your Desktop Items

Task 52: Picking a Program's Icon to Display

Task 53: Placing Standard Items and Icons on the Desktop

Task 54: Putting Web Pages on Your Desktop

Task 55: Customizing Mouse Options

Task 56: Customizing the Mouse Pointers

Task 57: Setting Keyboard Options

Task 58: Automatically Starting a Program at Startup

Task 59: Changing Regional Settings

Task 60: Changing Number and Currency Formatting

Task **40**

Choosing a Theme

Windows XP allows you to customize its look and feel. If more than one person is using the computer, or if you have more than one account, you can set each account to use a different theme. When you apply a new theme, a number of features may be modified on your desktop. Table 40-1 lists the items that may change with a theme.

Table 40-1: Key Features That Can Be Changed within a Theme

Area	Customizable Features
Display	The desktop background, color, and position of the background; the icons associated with desktop programs; the screen saver
Windows	The border and overall appearance, the buttons, the color scheme, the size, color, and style for fonts
Pointers	The pointers used
Sounds	The different sounds used for events

Windows XP comes with a couple of themes already available: the Windows XP theme and the Classic Windows theme. You can select a theme using the following steps:

1. Select Control Panel from the Start menu.

2. Select Appearance and Themes from the categories listed in the Control Panel. The Appearances and Themes window appears.

3. Select the Change the Computer's Theme task. The Display Properties dialog window appears (see Figure 40-1).

Figure 40-1: The Themes tab in the Display Properties dialog window.

cross-reference

Changing the theme will not change everything. For example, the Start menu changes the look you choose in your theme; however, it retains its layout. To change its layout, see Task 49.

tip

You can copy and rename a theme by clicking on the Save As button in the Themes tab of the Display Properties dialog window. You will be prompted to enter a new name.

note

If you make changes to the appearance or other theme features, then a custom theme will automatically be created.

4. Select a value from the Theme: drop-down list. There are a number of different values you can select:

- *Windows XP.* This is the default theme for Windows XP. It has the big icons, bold colors, and rounded windows.

- *Windows Classic.* This is a theme that provides a look and feel similar to older versions of Windows. It has squared windows and more subtle colors and fonts. Figure 40-2 shows the result of selecting this theme.

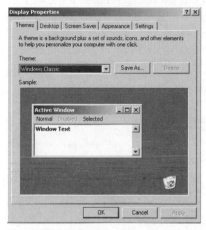

Figure 40-2: The Windows Classic theme's desktop.

- *More Themes Online.* This is a link to the Internet. The default page for this link is the Microsoft Plus! Pack Web page. The Microsoft Plus! Pack, which is an additional product that Microsoft sells, contains several themes you can install.

- *Browse.* This allows you to search your current computer for theme files. When you create a custom theme, you can save it anywhere on your computer. If you select this option, you are automatically taken to a window that you can use to find and select a theme file.

5. Click the Apply button. You are presented with a "Please wait" message while the new theme is applied. This message may be displayed for a few seconds to a minute depending on the complexity of the theme being applied. Once this message disappears, your new theme is used.

6. Click the OK button to close the Display Properties dialog window.

tip

You can use a shortcut to get to the Themes tab by clicking the right mouse button on an empty place on the desktop. Select Properties from the menu that is displayed. This presents the Display Properties dialog window. Select the Themes tab.

cross-reference

You can learn to create and save your own personalized theme in Task 46.

tip

If you have not created or copied any themes to your computer, then you will probably not want to use the Browse option in the Theme list.

note

For the Windows Classic theme, the default background does not have an image.

note

You can remove themes from your computer when you are no longer going to use them. Do this by clicking the Delete button on the Themes tab in the Display Properties dialog window.

caution

The Microsoft Plus! pack contains a number of very cool themes you can use; however, it is a separate product you must buy. Additionally, to use all the theme features, you may be required to have a video card with at least 32MB of memory.

Task 41

Setting the Screen Colors and Resolution

tip

If you increase the size of your resolution, everything on the desktop will look smaller.

tip

There is a shortcut to getting to the Desktop tab in the Display Properties dialog window. Instead of Steps 1 through 3, you can right-click on an open area of your desktop. On the menu, select Properties to show the Display Properties dialog window. You can then click on the Settings tab.

cross-reference

If an image you want to display on your background is larger or smaller than your screen, you can either change the screen resolution or you can stretch the image. Task 42 shows you how to add and stretch an image on the background of your desktop.

note

The resolution is the number of pixels horizontally and vertically that is used to display information. Standard resolutions are 640 across by 480 vertically, 800 across by 600 vertically, and 1,024 across by 768 vertically. A number of additional resolutions can be used as well.

note

How high the resolution is that you can set in Windows XP depends on how much memory your graphics or video card has, as well as what is the largest resolution your monitor can support. The number of supported colors is also determined by these factors.

If you'd like everything to be smaller so you can get more on your screens, or if you would like everything on your screen to be larger so it is easier to read, you can change the resolution that is used to display Windows XP. In basic terms, the *resolution* is the number of dots of color that can be displayed vertically and horizontally on your screen. The more dots you display, the smaller things will generally be; however, the more things you can display.

In addition to the resolution, you may want to change the color depth. The *color depth* is the number of colors that are supported. The more colors your monitor can display, the more realistic the images displayed can look.

1. From the Start menu, select Control Panel.

2. Select Appearance and Theme.

3. Select Change the Screen Resolution. The Settings tab in the Display Properties dialog window appears (see Figure 41-1).

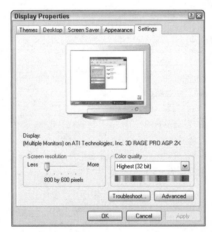

Figure 41-1: The Settings tab in the Display Properties dialog window.

4. Click on and drag the slider control in the Screen Resolution area. Alternatively, you can click on the area between Less and More. As you move the slider toward Less, you will see a lower screen resolution. As you move it toward More, you increase the resolution. The resolutions you can see depend on your computer. Select the resolution you want.

   As you change the resolution, you will see that the sample screen changes as well. In Figure 41-1, the resolution was set at 800×600. In Figure 41-2, the resolution is set at 1600×1200. As you can see, the sample dialog is much smaller on screen with higher resolution.

5. Select the drop-down list in the Color Quality area. This lists the different color resolutions you have available. You should see a list similar to the one shown in Figure 41-3.

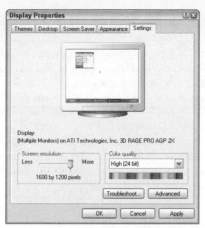

Figure 41-2: Settings for a higher resolution.

note

Resolution and color depth are often dependent on each other. Often you will have a lower number of colors available at the higher resolutions. This is because the higher settings of either color or resolution require more video memory to support.

6. Click the Apply button to try the settings. Your screen may go black for a few seconds before the new resolution is applied. If you have never used the resolution before, a message like the one in Figure 41-4 appears, asking if you'd like to keep the settings.

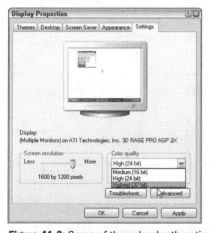

Figure 41-3: Some of the color depth options.

7. Click OK on the message to keep the settings. Click No or just wait a few seconds to return to the previous settings.

Figure 41-4: The prompt for keeping the settings.

8. Click OK in the Display Properties dialog window to close it.

cross-reference

When you change the resolution, the icons on your desk may be moved. You can move them to new locations as well by following the steps in Task 51.

tip

If you have a very large monitor, you may want to set your resolution higher.

Choosing a Desktop Background Image

The most noticeable way to customize Windows XP is to change the background image on your desktop. You can use nearly any picture you like. You can use one of the many pictures that comes with Windows XP, you can download an image from the Internet, you can create a picture of your own, you can pull a picture from a digital camera, or you can load in a picture from somewhere else. You can even use a picture of your family members or of your pet. If you prefer a clean desktop, you can turn off the background image altogether and display a simple solid color.

1. From the Start menu, select Control Panel.

2. Select Appearance and Theme.

3. Select Change the Desktop Background. The Desktop tab in the Display Properties dialog window appears (see Figure 42-1).

Figure 42-1: The Desktop settings.

4. Select the background image from the Background: scroll box. If you click on a background name in the scroll window, the small screen presents a sample of what the image will look like. In Figure 42-1, you see the Bliss background images displayed. Figure 42-2 shows the result of clicking on the Azul image in the preview window.

5. Click the Browse button if you prefer to use an image of your own. This takes you to a Browse window that allows you to search your computer for pictures. When you have found an image you want to use, click on the image name and then on the Open button. This returns you to the Display Property dialog window with your image displayed.

cross-reference

Tasks 61 through 76 give you lots of tips on working with graphics and images. You can learn how to import images from a digital camera, how to scan an image, how to create a picture, and more.

cross-reference

You can make your desktop active. This includes adding a Web page, stock ticker, or other features. Task 54 presents one of the customizations you can do on your screen.

cross-reference

For more on finding files, see Task 22 about navigating what is on your hard drive or Task 32 for searching for a file.

cross-reference

The My Pictures Slideshow screen saver displays pictures from your My Pictures folder as a slide show. Task 43 shows you how to set a screen saver.

cross-reference

Lots of pictures are available on the Internet. Task 144 presents you with information on finding and downloading images from a Web site.

cross-reference

If you choose to remove the background image, you will have a background that is a solid color. By default this is white. You can learn to change the color of the background in Task 44 on changing or setting appearances.

Figure 42-2: The Desktop settings with a background being previewed.

6. Once you have decided on an image to display on your background, you may then select a position. You have three options for positions: Center, Tile, or Stretch. Figure 42-3 illustrates each of these options using the Zapotec background image that comes with Windows XP.

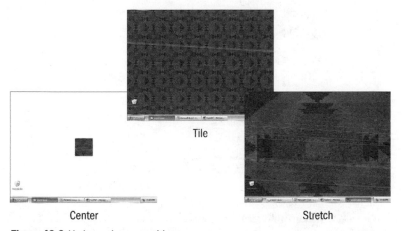

Center   Stretch

Figure 42-3: Various picture positions.

As you can see, the Center option centers the graphic, the Tile option repeats the graphic in order to fill the screen, and the Stretch option stretches the graphic to fill the screen.

7. Click the Apply button to place the image on your background.

8. Click OK to close the Display Properties dialog window.

Setting or Changing a Screen Saver

Screen savers are a great way to customize your system. In the past, a screen saver was used to prevent images from being burned into your computer's monitor; however, with today's technology that is rarely a problem. Most people use a screen saver to simply hide what is on their screen if they are away from their computer. Windows XP gives you several options for setting and using screen savers. Additionally, they provide you with a number of screen savers to use. To set or change your screen saver, use the following steps:

1. Go to the Screen Saver tab on the Display Properties dialog:

   a. Right-click on the background of your desktop where no windows are being displayed. A pop-up menu appears.

   b. Select Properties. The Displays Properties dialog appears. Selecting the Screen Saver tab results in the dialog in Figure 43-1.

Figure 43-1: The Screen Saver tab in the Display Properties dialog.

   c. Select Start, then Control Panel.

   d. On the Control Panel, select Appearance and Themes. The appearance and theme tasks appear.

   e. Select Choose a Screen Saver. The Displays Properties dialog is displayed with the Screen Saver tab selected.

2. Click the drop-down list in the Screen Saver section of the window. This presents you with the list of available screen savers, as shown in Figure 43-2.

3. Click on the name of the screen saver you are interested in viewing or using. The small display changes to show a preview of the newly selected screen saver.

4. Click the Settings button to see if the screen saver can be configured. If not, a warning is displayed.

tip

As an alternative to right-clicking on the desktop, you can also get to the Screen Saver tab on the Display Properties dialog by going through the Control Panel.

note

The picture on the Screen Saver tab of the Display Properties dialog window shows you a preview of the current screen saver. You can also select the Preview button to see the screen saver in action.

tip

Selecting (None) as the screen saver turns off the screen saver.

Figure 43-2: The selection of available screen savers.

If available, make the change to the settings and then press OK to save them. Settings can include changes to a number of features including:

- The speed of the screen saver

- Colors

- Text

- Number of things happening

- Size of graphics

- Locations

The exact settings depend on the specific screen saver. For example, the settings for the Marquee screen saver allow you to pick a text color, the background color for the screen, the text to display, the speed at which the text scrolls, and the format and font of the text. It also allows you to choose whether the text scrolls across the middle or at random places (see Figure 43-3). By changing these settings, you can tweak the screen saver to behave the way you want.

Figure 43-3: The Marquee screen saver setup dialog.

5. Select the Apply button to immediately set the screen saver and your settings. Select OK to save the screen saver and close the Display Properties dialog. Select Cancel to leave the screen without saving any further changes.

cross-reference

Task 10 shows you how to password-protect your system using a screen saver.

tip

The screen saver will be displayed after your computer is inactive for a period of time. You can change the amount of time that the screen saver waits by adjusting the time in the Wait: box.

note

The My Picture Slide show screen saver looks for images in your My Pictures folder as a screen saver slide show.

note

If you install a theme onto your computer, be aware that it may also install and change your screen saver.

caution

If you use the Preview button, any movement of the mouse will end the preview.

Choosing or Changing an Appearance

Windows XP lets you customize the appearance of a number of desktop items. This includes changing the overall color scheme, the button style, and basic font size. To make changes:

1. Select Control Panel from the Start menu.

2. Select Appearance and Theme.

3. Click the Display icon. You are presented with the Display Properties dialog window.

4. Select the Appearance tab to display the Appearance options. Figure 44-1 shows the options in this tab.

Figure 44-1: The Appearance tab in the Display Properties dialog window.

5. Select the type of buttons and windows you'd like displayed. You can pick either Windows XP style or Windows Classic style from the Windows and buttons drop-down list. Figure 44-1 shows a sample of the Windows XP style. Figure 44-2 shows a Windows Classic sample.

6. Select the color scheme you'd like to use from the Color Scheme drop-down list. The list contains different values depending on what you selected in Step 5.

cross-reference

To change the overall look and feel for the pages, you can select a theme. Task 40 shows you how to select a theme.

cross-reference

You can save a number of these settings as part of a theme. See Task 46 for creating a new theme.

note

If you change an appearance setting, it causes your current theme to be changed. Your current theme will, however, be renamed.

note

The available color schemes depend on what you select for Windows and buttons. You will generally have more options for the Windows Classic Style than for the Windows XP style.

Figure 44-2: The Windows Classic style.

7. Select the font size you would like to use. Select this from the Font Size drop-down list. Again, you can see a preview of your selection in the top portion of the window.

8. Set any effects you want by clicking the Effects button. This presents you with a number of additional options you can select that will impact the appearance of your windows. Figure 44-3 presents the Effects dialog window. When you are done selecting effects options, click the OK button to close the window.

Figure 44-3: The Effects dialog window.

9. Click Apply to save your changes.

10. Click OK to exit the Display Properties dialog window.

note

Check the first box on the Effects window if you want to have a transition occur when menus and ToolTips are opened and closed. Once selected, you can pick a transition from the drop-down list. Uncheck this if you don't want transitions.

tip

If you use a higher resolution, you might want to use large icons so that they are easier to see.

tip

If your system is slow, you should uncheck a couple of the effects options. This includes unchecking (turning off) the option to use transitions for menus and ToolTips, the option for using shadows, and the option for showing windows contents while dragging.

Task 45

Assigning Sounds to Events

One way to customize Windows XP is through the use of sounds. In Windows XP you can assign different sounds to different events that can occur. You can set a sound when you start Windows, when you log off, when you open or close a window, and for lots of other events. To see the events and assign sounds to them, use the steps that follow. Once you've assigned the various sounds, you can save them as a sound scheme. You can actually set up a number of different sound schemes.

1. Select the Control Panel from the Start menu.

2. Select Sounds, Speech, and Audio Devices. The Sounds, Speech, and Audio Devices window appears (see Figure 45-1).

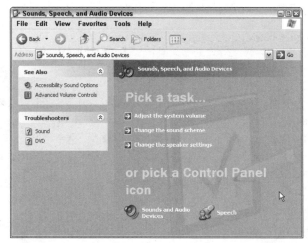

Figure 45-1: The Sounds, Speech, and Audio Device Control Panel window.

3. Select Change the Sound Scheme from the tasks. The Sound tab in the Sounds and Audio Devices Properties dialog window appears (see Figure 45-2).

4. In the Program Events list, select a program event to which you would like to assign a sound. Be aware that this is a scrollable list, so there are a large number of items you can choose from.

cross-reference

If your computer has a microphone, you can use the Sound Recorder to record your own sounds. To learn how to record sounds, see Task 197.

note

Sounds are generally stored in "wave" files. Wave files have the extension .wav.

tip

If an event has a speaker icon next to it, you are replacing an existing sound. If there is no icon, you are adding a new sound.

note

Within the Program events list, you will find a number of events you can assign sounds to, including events for specific programs you have installed. These events are listed after the program name. For example, you can find Windows Explorer listed along with four different sound events you can assign within it.

Figure 45-2: The Sounds and Audio Devices Properties dialog window.

5. Select the sound to assign to the event selected in Step 4. Do this either by selecting a sound from the Sounds drop-down list or by clicking the Browse button and searching for a sound file on your machine.

6. Listen to your sound if you want. You can play the selected sound by clicking the Play button next to the Sounds drop-down list.

7. Repeat Steps 4 though 6 until you've set all the sounds you want to set.

8. Click the Apply button to apply the sounds.

9. Determine if you want to save the group of sounds currently assigned to Windows XP as a scheme. If you do, then click the Save As button under the Sound Scheme drop-down list. This presents you with a prompt, shown in Figure 45-3, in which to enter a scheme name.

Figure 45-3: The Save Scheme As prompt.

Enter the name for your scheme and press Enter or click OK.

10. Click the OK button to close the dialog window.

cross-reference

Your sound selections can be saved as a part of a Windows XP theme. You can learn more about themes in Tasks 40 and 46.

tip

You can use the same scheme name again. This updates the current scheme with your changes.

Creating a New Theme

Within Windows XP, you can change the sounds associated to different events. You can change your background image. You can change the colors associated with your windows. You can change the color, size, and style of font. Once you have all the settings the way you want, you can then save them as a group. This group is a theme.

You can create multiple themes that have different settings. This allows you to customize the look and feel of your copy of Windows XP. The following steps walk you through the process of creating and saving a theme:

1. Customize your Windows appearance to how you want it to be in your theme. Some of the customizations are as follows:

   - Set the background as shown in Task 42.

   - Set the screen saver as shown in Task 43.

   - Set the window appearances as shown in Task 44.

   - Set the event sounds as shown in Task 45.

   - Customize standard items and their icons as shown in Task 53.

   - Set the mouse pointer as shown in Task 55.

2. Select Control Panel from the Start menu.

3. Select the Appearance and Themes category. The Appearance and Themes dialog window appears (see Figure 46-1).

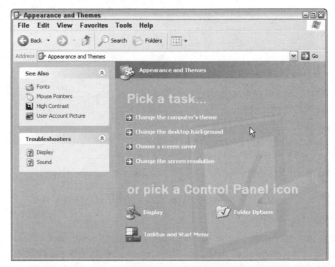

Figure 46-1: The Appearance and Themes dialog window.

4. Make any additional changes to your Windows XP settings by selecting the various tasks and options on the Appearance and Themes dialog window.

tip

You should name your theme something that describes its overall look or base it on something you can easily remember.

note

A theme is a group of settings that you can save under a single name. This includes the background image, assigned sounds, icons, mouse pointers, and the screen saver.

cross-reference

Task 42 presents step-by-step details for changing the background.

cross-reference

Task 43 provides step-by-step details for setting a screen saver.

5. Select Change the Computer's Theme from the list of tasks. This presents the Display Properties dialog window with the Theme tab selected, as shown in Figure 46-2.

Figure 46-2: The Theme tab in the Display Properties dialog window.

6. Click the Save As button. The standard Save As dialog from Windows XP appears (see Figure 46-3). Notice that the file type (Save as Type value) is defaulted to Theme.

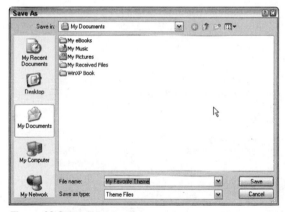

Figure 46-3: The Save As dialog.

7. Enter a filename for your theme. You can change the folder where you want to save the theme.

8. Click the Save button to finalize the saving of your theme. You are taken back to the Display Properties dialog window. Click the OK button to close the dialog window.

tip

You can share your theme with others or copy it to another machine. You can do this by sharing or copying the theme file you save in Step 7. Be aware, however, that if your theme includes a background image, screen saver, icon, or sound that is not a standard item in Windows XP, you will need to share or copy that as well.

tip

You can create themes that all center on a single topic — that have a theme! For example, you could create a Neon theme that uses neon colors in the background, icons, and screen saver.

tip

You can also purchase themes for Windows XP. The Microsoft Plus! Pack contains several themes such as nature or space. These themes include icons, sounds, background images, and screen savers.

tip

You can update or change a theme by using the same name of the existing theme.

Customizing Your Taskbar

The taskbar is the area at the bottom of your screen. It includes the Start button, a Quick Launch area, links to the currently running programs, and the system tray. It can also include the date and time. The items actually shown on the taskbar and how the taskbar displays them can be changed. In this task, you learn how to customize the taskbar to make it more useful to you. Figure 47-1 shows you the areas on the taskbar.

cross-reference

In addition to the taskbar, you can also customize the Start menu. Task 49 shows you how to make changes to the Start menu.

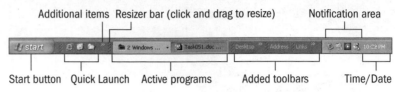

Figure 47-1: The areas of the taskbar.

1. Right-click in any area of the taskbar that is empty. The menu in Figure 47-2 appears.

Figure 47-2: The pop-up menu from the taskbar.

2. Select Properties from the menu. The Taskbar and Start Menu Properties dialog window appears (see Figure 47-3). The Taskbar tab should be selected.

tip

Your taskbar does not have to be at the bottom of your screen. You can place the taskbar at the top or on either side of your screen by clicking on an empty area with the left mouse button and then dragging the taskbar to the side of the screen where you want it displayed. Hold the mouse button down while dragging the taskbar.

note

You can change if and when the items within the notification area are hidden. Use the Customize button on the Taskbar and Start Menu Properties dialog window (see Step 4). This only applies when you are hiding inactive icons on the notification area.

Figure 47-3: The Taskbar and Start Menu Properties dialog window.

3. Check or uncheck the options in the Taskbar Appearance area. The options you can select are as follows:

- *Lock the Taskbar*. Prevents resizing or moving the taskbar. If this is unchecked, the taskbar can be resized.

- *Auto-Hide the Taskbar*. Causes the taskbar to disappear when the mouse is not over it. This gives you more of the screen space to use.

- *Keep the Taskbar on Top of Other Windows*. If this is unchecked, windows that you have open may appear on top of the taskbar.

- *Group Similar Taskbar Buttons*. Similar items use the same button. A number appears on the button to let you know how many windows of that type are open. You can then click the button to see a list of the windows of that type. Figure 47-4 presents a taskbar with this option active.

Figure 47-4: The taskbar with similar buttons grouped and one button clicked.

- *Show Quick Launch*. Creates an extra area on the taskbar you can use to place shortcuts to programs you use a lot.

4. Check or uncheck the options in the Notification Area pane. You have two options you can select or unselect:

- *Show the Clock*. This determines whether the time is displayed in the taskbar.

- *Hide Inactive Icons*. If this is selected, icons that have not been used will be hidden. This is useful for keeping the taskbar uncluttered.

5. Click the Apply button to apply the changes.

6. Click the OK button to close the dialog window.

7. Right-click on an empty area of your taskbar. This again pulls up the menu in Figure 47-2.

8. Select Toolbars from the menu. This presents a submenu that lists the different toolbars (or sections) you can have on your taskbar. These include Address, Links, Desktop, and Quick Launch.

9. Select a toolbar you want to have shown or hidden. The toolbars that appear are those with checks next to them. Once you select the option, the menu disappears and your selection takes effect.

10. Repeat Steps 8 and 9 to customize your desktop the way you want it to appear.

tip

If you tend to keep a lot of programs opened, you should select the option to group similar items.

cross-reference

You can learn more about customizing the Quick Launch area in Task 48.

cross-reference

You can drag programs to the Quick Launch area. The program's icon is displayed. See Task 52 to learn how to display a different icon.

tip

You size the taskbar by holding the mouse over the edge and dragging up while holding the mouse button down. This works only if you have not locked the taskbar.

note

If you increase the size of the taskbar, the day of the week and the date are also displayed.

tip

You can use the toolbar to help keep your desktop uncluttered with icons. You can place icons in the shortcut area by dragging them there, and you can access the standard desktop icons by selecting the Desktop toolbar (as shown in Steps 8 and 9).

Task **48**

Customizing the Quick Launch Toolbar

The taskbar contains a number of areas; however, the most useful area to customize is the Quick Launch toolbar area. Within the Quick Launch area, shown in Figure 48-1, you can place icons for programs that you use on a regular basis. Once an icon is on the toolbar, you only have to left-click it once to launch the application.

Menu access   Resizer bar

Quick Launch toolbar

Figure 48-1: The taskbar with an active Quick Launch toolbar.

The following steps walk you through the various customizations available for the Quick Launch bar:

1. **Activate the Quick Launch bar.** If you don't already see the Quick Launch bar on your Taskbar, use Task 47 to activate it.

2. **Resize the Quick Launch bar.** You can change the width of the Quick Launch bar by left-clicking and dragging the resize area that is on the right side of the displayed icons. Your mouse pointer changes to a resize cursor when you are over the bar. The pointer changes to an insert cursor when you are actually resizing the area. Figure 48-2 shows the Quick Launch toolbar being stretched to a larger width.

Figure 48-2: Resizing the Quick Launch toolbar.

3. **Move the location of the Quick Launch toolbar in the taskbar.** You can move the Quick Launch toolbar using the resize bar to the left of its icons. Left-click on this resize bar and drag to the left or right. The Quick Launch toolbar moves as you drag it. You can't move it before the Start button on the left or past the notification area on the right. You may need to resize the toolbar after you move it. Figure 48-3 shows the Quick Launch toolbar moved to the right of the active application icons.

Figure 48-3: The Quick Launch toolbar moved to the right.

note

In older versions of Windows, you would have placed icons on the desktop to make them easy to get to. The Quick Launch area helps to keep your desktop from becoming cluttered with such icons. Additionally, it eliminates the problem of opened windows covering up the icons.

cross-reference

You can learn how to turn on the Quick Launch toolbar in Task 47. Additionally, you can learn how to work with other Toolbar options.

note

If you lock the taskbar, you won't be able to resize or move the Quick Launch toolbar.

tip

If there are programs you rarely use, you probably don't want them on your Quick Launch toolbar. Rather, you can access them from the Start menu. Additionally, if there are programs you use somewhat regularly, you may want to place them on the Quick Launch toolbar's pop-up menu rather than directly on the toolbar.

4. Change the order of the Quick Launch icons. You can change the order by simply left-clicking and dragging the icon to the new location on the toolbar.

5. Remove icons from the Quick Launch toolbar that you are no longer using. To remove an icon, right-click on the icon and then select Delete from the pop-up menu. A prompt similar to the one in Figure 48-4 is displayed asking you to confirm that you want to perform the deletion.

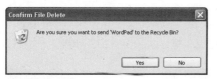

Figure 48-4: Confirm that you want to remove the item.

6. Add additional icons to the Quick Launch toolbar. The easiest way to add an icon is to drag it from another location and drop it onto the toolbar. You can right-click and drag an icon from the Start menu, from the desktop, or from a folder. When you drag the icon over the Quick Launch toolbar, you will see an indicator showing where the icon will be placed. When you drop the item, you are asked to either copy, save, or create a shortcut. Choose to copy or create a shortcut. If in doubt, create a shortcut.

7. Change the display format of the items in the Quick Launch bar. You can change the size of the icons or change the text that is displayed by right-clicking on a blank portion of the Quick Launch bar. You can then select the following items to make the changes. Figure 48-5 shows the impact of changing the Quick Launch bar to use large icons and show text.

   - *View⇨Large Icons*. This causes larger icons to be used.

   - *View⇨Small Icons*. This causes the small icons to be used (the default).

   - *Show Text*. This displays the textual description of an item next to the corresponding icon.

   - *Show Title*. This places the text "Quick Lunch" on the Quick Launch toolbar.

Figure 48-5: The taskbar with the Quick Launch toolbar customized.

note

The items on the Quick Launch toolbar are actually stored in a folder. You can add items to the toolbar by adding them to the Quick Launch folder.

tip

If you have a hard time seeing the small icons on the screen, you can use larger icons on the Quick Launch toolbar. See Step 7 for more information.

Customizing the Start Menu

The Start menu can lead you to all the programs and settings on your computer. Many of the tasks in this book begin with your accessing the Start menu. If you have used previous versions of Windows, you know that the Start menu looks drastically different in Windows XP. If you don't like the new look, however, you can change it. The following steps take you through customizing your Start menu to your own preferences:

1. Right-click on the Start menu, and select Properties from the pop-up menu. This presents the Taskbar and Start Menu Properties dialog window with the Start Menu tab selected, as shown in Figure 49-1.

Figure 49-1: The Taskbar and Start Menu Properties dialog window.

2. Select either Start Menu to use the Windows XP style Start menu or Classic Start Menu to use the older Windows-style Start menu.

3. Click on the Customize button to access additional settings for the Start menu. If you selected Start Menu in Step 2, then the dialog in Figure 49-2 appears. The remaining steps in this task walk you through these options.

4. Select the icon size you want used in your Start menu. You can select either large icons or small icons.

5. Enter the number of program shortcuts you want displayed on the lower-left side of the Start menu. These will be icons leading to programs that you have used the most. Enter the number into the box next to the Number of Programs on Start Menu prompt.

6. Set Internet and email links on your Start menu. On the upper-left side of the Start menu, you can include shortcut icons that link to the Internet and to your email. These are turned on by default.

   If you want to remove them or to change the programs they point to, change the values in the Show on Start Menu section of the Customize Start Menu dialog window. Uncheck the boxes next to Internet and

tip

You can clear the shortcuts on the left side of your Windows XP Start menu by clicking the Clear List button in the Customize Start Menu dialog window. This is the same window you accessed in Step 3.

cross-reference

You can learn more about the email options in the tasks in Part 11.

cross-reference

You can learn more about Internet options in Tasks 138 through 157. You learn about using the Internet with Windows XP in Tasks 133 through 137.

tip

The number of programs to include on the start menu in Step 5 is up to you. Six items generally looks good on the menu; however, you can set the number to anything you want up to 30. The number you select will be the maximum number of items displayed.

E-mail to remove the items from the Start menu. If they are checked, you can select the program to associate the icons to from the drop-down list to the right of the option.

Figure 49-2: The Windows XP Start menu general options.

7. Make changes to the advanced Start menu settings by selecting the Advanced tab (shown in Figure 49-3). Many of the changes on this tab are similar to those in the previous steps.

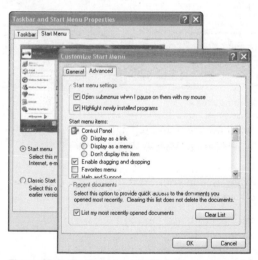

Figure 49-3: The Windows XP Start menu advanced options.

8. Click the OK button once you have made all your changes. This returns you to the Taskbar and Start Menu Properties dialog window. Your changes are not yet implemented.

9. Click the Apply button to implement your changes.

tip

You can include items on the Initial Start menu from the All Programs section of the Start menu. To do this, right-click on the item you want to add to the front, and select Pin to Start Menu from the pop-up menu. To remove the item from the front of the Start menu, right-click on the icon you want to remove and select Unpin from Start Menu from the pop-up menu.

caution

Only an experienced Windows XP user should change the items in the Start Menu Items section of the Advanced tab of the Customize Start Menu dialog window.

tip

You should consider whether you would prefer an item on the Start menu, the desktop, or the taskbar. Your most used items can be placed on the taskbar for the quickest access.

cross-reference

You can place shortcuts to programs on your desktop instead of the Start menu. To learn more about adding shortcuts to your desktop, see Task 50.

Adding Shortcuts to Your Desktop

The desktop in Windows XP is the entire screen that you see. Just like a regular desktop, this is your area to use as you see fit. If there are things you like to have handy, you can place them on your desktop. In Windows XP, you generally don't place the actual item on the desktop, but you place a shortcut to that item. You can place a shortcut to nearly any item on your desktop. The following steps walk you through the standard process:

1. Right-click on an open area of the desktop. A pop-up menu is displayed similar to Figure 50-1.

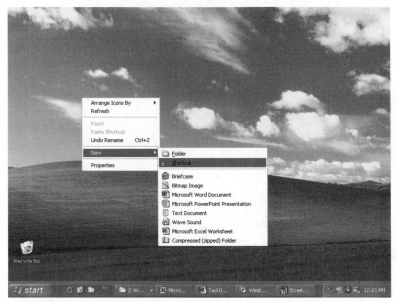

Figure 50-1: The desktop pop-up menu.

2. Select New⇨Shortcut from the pop-up menu. The first page of the Create Shortcut Wizard appears (see Figure 50-2).

Figure 50-2: The first page of the Create Shortcut Wizard.

cross-reference

You may find that it is better to place shortcuts to frequently accessed programs on the taskbar or Start menu rather than on the desktop. When you place items on the desktop, opened program windows will hide the icons. You can learn more about adding items to the Quick Launch toolbar on the taskbar in Task 48. You can learn how to customize your Start menu in Task 49.

cross-reference

The shortcut you create will be placed on the desktop in the location you originally clicked for the pop-up menu. See Task 51 for arranging your desktop to see how to move the icons. Depending on your settings, you may be able to simply drag the icon to a different location on the desktop in order to move it.

3. Enter the location for the item for which you are creating the short-cut. You can either enter the full path to the item on your hard drive or you can select the Browse button and search for the item. For example, to create a shortcut to the Windows calculator, you would enter **\Windows\system32\calc.exe** into the text box.

4. Click the Next button. If you did not select a valid item at a valid location, an error similar to the one in Figure 50-3 appears.

Figure 50-3: The error message for a bad shortcut location.

If you entered a valid location, you are taken to the next page of the wizard, as shown in Figure 50-4.

Figure 50-4: The Select a Title page of the Create Shortcut Wizard.

5. Enter a name for your shortcut. This is the text that will be displayed under the icon on the desktop. By default the name of the item you selected will be displayed.

6. Click the Finish button. The Create Shortcut Wizard ends and the icon is placed on the desktop.

cross-reference

See Task 22 to learn more about browsing for items in Windows XP.

tip

You can click on the Show Desktop icon to minimize all the windows currently opened on the desktop. This allows you to get to an icon on the desktop quicker. This icon is on the Quick Launch toolbar on the taskbar.

caution

Icons placed on the desktop may be hidden when you open programs.

tip

You can create shortcuts on the desktop for items listed on your All Programs menu. To do this, simply right-click and drag the menu item onto an open area of the desktop. Then click Copy Here from the pop-up menu. You can do the same with items in the Quick Launch toolbar on the Task menu.

cross-reference

Don't like the icon used for the shortcut? See Task 52 to learn how to change an icon.

Arranging Your Desktop Items

You can place icons, Web pages, and other items directly onto your desktop so that you can quickly find and use them. By default, these items are placed on your desktop wherever you click. The following steps walk you through arranging the icons and Web pages that you have placed on your desktop:

1. Right-click on an open area of the desktop, and select the Arrange Icons option on the pop-up menu. A submenu appears, as shown in Figure 51-1.

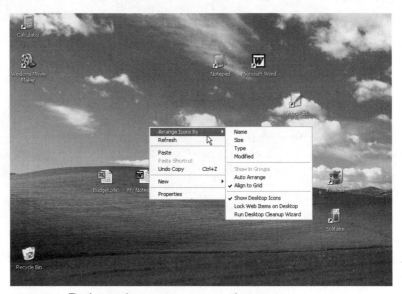

Figure 51-1: The Arrange Icons pop-up menu options.

2. Select Name, Size, Type, or Modified from the menu to automatically arrange the icons on the left side of your desktop in the corresponding order. Figure 51-2 shows the icons on the desktop in Figure 51-1 after Name was selected.

3. Select Auto Arrange from the menu present in Step 1 if you would like to have the icons automatically added to the left side of the desktop. When the auto arranging is active, there will be a check next to it on the pop-up menu. Select Auto Arrange again to turn Auto Arrange off.

4. Select Align to Grid from the menu presented in Step 1 if you want to keep the icons in a somewhat uniform location on the desktop. Icons are aligned within an invisible grid on the desktop when this is active. When this is not active, icons will remain in the exact location where they are placed (unless Auto Arrange is active).

   This option is active when a check mark appears next to this on the menu. To turn it off, select the option on the menu again. This removes the check mark and turns the option off. Figure 51-3 shows

cross-reference

To learn how to add shortcut icons to your desktop, see Task 50. To see how to add one of the standard Windows XP items to you desktop, see Task 53.

cross-reference

You can also place Web pages on your desktop. To learn how to add Web pages, see Task 54.

caution

It is very easy to get into the habit of adding a lot of icons and other items to your desktop. This, however, creates a messy workspace. It's best to only place items on your desktop that you need quick access to or that you need to remember how to get.

caution

If you arrange icons by size, Windows XP will arrange them by the size of the file on the desktop. If a shortcut is on the desktop, the size of the shortcut itself will be used, not the size of the item the shortcut links to.

note

If you move an icon and it ends up moving back to the left side of the desktop, you most likely have the option to automatically arrange the icons turned on.

note

If Auto Arrange is turned on, icons will automatically be aligned within the invisible grid.

a desktop that has Auto Arrange turned off. Icons have been dragged into groups on the desktop to make them easier to find.

Figure 51-2: The icons after being arranged by name.

5. Select Show Desktop Items from the menu presented in Step 1 if you want to hide all the items that are on the desktop. When a check mark is next to Show Desktop Items, all items will be visible on the desktop. If you select this again, the check mark is removed and all desktop items are hidden. Simply select it again to bring the items back.

Figure 51-3: A desktop with Auto Arrange turned off and icons arranged for usability.

tip

If you have turned Auto Arrange off, you can move icons and other content to different locations on your desktop. You can do this by simply left-clicking and dragging the item to its new location. You can move multiple icons at once by left-clicking in an open spot on the desktop and then dragging the mouse cursor on the screen. You will see a rectangle appear as you move the mouse. This selects all the icons within the rectangle. You can then right-click on any of the selected icons and drag the entire group to a new location. Click on an open area of the desktop to unselect the group.

tip

You can select the Run Desktop Cleanup Wizard option from the menu presented in Step 1. This shows you the icons on your desktop that you have not used in a long time, and it will help you to remove them.

Picking a Program's Icon to Display

Programs in Windows XP have icons associated with them. These little graphics can sometimes be fun; however, often they are relatively boring. Within Windows XP, you can change the icon that is used on some programs. More specifically, you can change the icons used on shortcuts. On a shortcut, you can change the icon to any other icon available on your system, or you can even create an icon. The following steps show you how to determine if you can change the icon and if so, how to make the changes.

You can choose an item on the Start menu, the All Programs menu, the Quick Launch bar on the taskbar, or the desktop.

cross-reference

With Windows XP you have everything you need to create your own icons! See Task 64 for the step-by-step details on creating an icon of your very own.

1. Right-click on the item and select Properties from the pop-up menu. If Properties is not an option on the pop-up menu, it is most likely not a valid item for changing the icon. The Properties dialog window for the selected item should be displayed. This dialog window should look similar to Figure 52-1; however, the values displayed will depend on the program that you selected.

Figure 52-1: A Properties dialog window, in this case for the Windows Media Player.

cross-reference

In Task 50 you learn how to add shortcuts to your desktop. You can add new icons to shortcuts created in the manner shown in Task 50.

note

Many programs have icons included with them. Most programs have just one. The number of icons you see in Step 3 depends on what was included with the program. You can see that the Windows Media Player has two different icons included.

2. Look for a Change Icon button. It should be in the same location as the Change Icon button in Figure 52-1. If this button is not available, you cannot change the icon on the selected item. If the button is available, click it. You are presented with the Change Icon dialog. This will be similar to Figure 52-2; however, you will see the icon that was displayed for your item. You may also see additional icons.

3. Select one of the icons presented by clicking on it. If you don't see an icon that you want to use, or if you want to use your own icon instead, continue to Step 4. If you are using one of the presented icons, continue to Step 5.

4. Enter the path and filename for the icon you want. If you don't know where other icons are, then do one of the following:

a. If you know what file to use for an icon, or if you've created your own icon, click the Browse button. This displays a window that lists files in the current folder that *might* contain icons. Navigate in this dialog to that file you want and select it. Press the Open button to return to the Change Icon dialog window.

b. If you don't know the icon you want to use, enter **%SystemRoot%\system32\SHELL32.dll** as the name of the file to look for icons. Press the Enter key. This displays the icons in the `Shell32.dll` file. This file contains a lot of icons that you may want to use. Figure 52-3 shows some of the displayed icons. Select an icon by clicking on it.

Figure 52-2: The Change Icon dialog.

5. Press the OK button to finalize the selection of the icon and to close the Change Icon dialog. You are returned to the Properties dialog window with the new icon shown in the top left.

Figure 52-3: The `Shell32.dll` icons.

6. Click the OK button. Your icon should now be updated.

cross-reference

See Task 22 if you need help using the file window in Step 4a to find a file.

caution

If you want to restore the original icon, you have to remember the file and location where it was originally stored.

caution

When selecting an icon, make sure it fits the program you are associating it to.

Placing Standard Items and Icons on the Desktop

You can customize your desktop by placing an image on it as shown in Task 42. You can also customize it in a number of other ways. In Task 50 you learned how to add icons as shortcuts to your programs. In this task you learn how to add a number of standard icons, as well as other active content onto your desktop.

There are several standard icons you can add to your desktop:

- My Document
- My Computer
- My Network Places
- Internet Explorer

You can add these icons and customize them by following these steps:

1. From the Start menu, select Control Panel.

2. Select Appearance and Theme.

3. Select Change the Desktop Background. The Desktop tab in the Display Properties dialog window appears.

4. Select the Customize Background button. This displays the Desktop Items dialog with the General tab presented, as shown in Figure 53-1.

tip

There is a shortcut to getting to the Desktop tab in the Display Properties dialog window. Instead of Steps 1 through 3, you can right-click on an open area of your desktop. On the menu that appears, select Properties to access the Display Properties dialog window. You can then click on the Desktop tab.

cross-reference

Learn how to create an icon in Task 64. You can use the Browse button in the Change Icon dialog to select your custom icon.

cross-reference

See Task 54 for the steps on placing Web pages on your desktop.

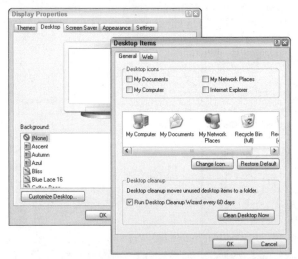

Figure 53-1: The General settings for the desktop.

5. Check the standard desktop icons you want displayed on your desktop. The standard desktop items in the preceding list are shown at the top of the General tab of the Desktop Items dialog window. If you want to remove an icon from the desktop, uncheck the item.

6. Select the icon you would like for each of these standard desktop items.

   a. Click on the corresponding icon in the center of the General tab. For example, you can select My Computer by clicking on it. This highlights the text under the graphical icon.

   b. Click on the Restore Default button to return the icon to the original graphic installed by Windows. If you don't want to use the default icon, skip this step.

   c. Click on the Change Icon button if you want to pick a different graphic for the desktop item. You will be changing the icon of the item selected. A dialog appears that shows the available icons that you can use. You can also use the Browse button to select icons from other locations on your computer's hard drive. Figure 53-2 shows the Change Icon dialog with icons displayed from the `\WINDOWS\System32\shell32.dll` file.

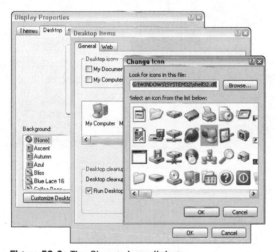

Figure 53-2: The Change Icon dialog.

   d. Click on the icon you want to use.

   e. Click OK to close the Change Icon dialog.

7. Select other desktop items and follow the instructions in Step 6 to change each of their icons.

8. Click OK to exit the Desktop Items dialog window.

9. Click OK to close the Display Properties dialog window and to apply the change you made to the desktop.

tip

You should use this same process to remove the standard icons from your desktop rather than just deleting them. You remove them by removing the check mark next to the standard item in the Desktop Items dialog window.

tip

Icons are stored in files that end with an .ico extension. There can also be icons in other types of files. You'll find standard files in `C:\WINDOWS\explorer.exe` and `C:\WINDOWS\system32\mydocs.dll`. You'll find lots of icons in `C:\WINDOWS\system32\shell32.dll`.

caution

You should pick icons that are related to the item you are assigning them to. Otherwise, you may forget what the icon is tied to.

note

You can set two different icons for the Recycle Bin. You can set a full icon and an empty icon.

cross-reference

Task 52 shows you how to add icons to any programs.

Task 54

Putting Web Pages on Your Desktop

You can add one or more Web pages to your desktop. You can add one big Web page that covers your entire desktop, or you can leave room on the side for your desktop icons. You can also add a number of small windows with different Web pages in them. You can lock these small Web pages into place, or you can allow them to be resized and moved around.

Figure 54-1 shows a desktop with a number of small windows to different Web pages placed on the desktop. These small windows allow easy access to the Web sites.

Figure 54-1: A number of pages displayed on the desktop background.

1. From the Start menu, select Control Panel.

2. Select Appearance and Theme.

3. Select Change the desktop background. The Desktop tab in the Display Properties dialog window appears.

4. Select the Customize Background button. This displays the Desktop Items dialog with the General tab shown.

5. Click on the Web tab. You should see a dialog like the one in Figure 54-2.

6. Select the pages you want displayed on your desktop by checking the boxes next to the names. Remove the check to remove the page from the desktop.

   If the page you want added is not listed, you can add it by clicking the Add button and following the prompts provided in the wizard.

When you add a Web page, it is copied to your machine in case you disconnect from the Internet. If you are no longer using a page in the list, you can click the Delete button to remove it.

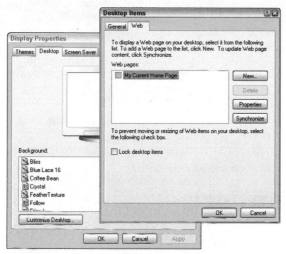

Figure 54-2: The Web settings for the desktop.

7. Check or uncheck the Lock Desktop Item check box. If this is checked, you can't change the size of the Web pages you placed on the desktop. If it is not checked, you can change the size of the Web pages on the desktop. To change the size, place the cursor near the top of the Web page. A title bar is displayed with Full Screen, Most Screen, and Close icons, as shown in Figure 54-3. Click your choice of these.

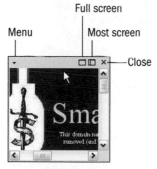

Figure 54-3: The title bar for expanding a Web page window.

8. Click OK to exit the Desktop Items dialog window.

9. Click Apply to place the selected Web pages onto the desktop.

10. Click OK to close the Display Properties dialog window.

caution

The Web pages selected are not added to the desktop until you select either Apply or OK in the Desktop tab of the Display Properties dialog window.

tip

If you are no longer using a Web page on your desktop, you can remove it by using the Delete button on the Web tab of the Desktop Items dialog window (shown in Figure 54-3).

caution

A copy of the Web pages is used on your desktop. If you are connected to the Internet, these will be updated regularly. If you are not connected, these may become outdated and you might click on items or links that don't work. When connected to the Internet, you can click the Synchronize button on the Web tab of the Desktop Items dialog window (shown in Figure 54-3).

cross-reference

You can learn more about Internet connections in Part 9. Surfing the Web to find cool pages is covered in Part 10.

cross-reference

The My Current Home Page window displays the home page you have set in Internet Explorer. See Task 152 to see how to set a home page in Internet Explorer.

Customizing Mouse Options

The mouse is something that you constantly use with Windows XP; however, many people don't realize they can customize it. There are a number of options for the mouse that can be changed. Some of these help you to control the mouse better; others are simply for fun. The following steps will help you customize many of the available mouse options:

1. Select the Control Panel from the Start menu.

2. Click on the Printers and Other Hardware category.

3. Click on the Mouse Control Panel icon in the lower part of the Printer and Other Hardware window. This presents the Mouse Properties dialog window. The Buttons tab appears (see Figure 55-1). If it isn't displayed, click on the Buttons tab.

Figure 55-1: The Buttons tab of the Mouse Properties dialog window.

4. Customize the basic button properties.

   a. Click the box next to Switch Primary and Secondary Buttons if you'd like to change the function of the right and left mouse buttons.

   b. Drag the slider within the Double-Click Speed area to change how much time can pass between clicks to count as a double click.

   c. Select the box next to Turn on ClickLock to turn the ClickLock feature on. Unselect to turn the feature off.

5. Select the Pointer Options tab on the Mouse Properties dialog window. This presents you with options similar to those in Figure 55-2.

note

If you set the speed slider toward Fast, you must click faster to have two clicks count as a double click. If you move it toward Slow, more time can pass between clicks and still count as a double click. You can test the speed by double-clicking on the folder. If the double click registers, the folder will open or close.

cross-reference

Some of the mouse settings can be saved as part of a theme. For example, the pointers you assign will be saved as part of a theme. You learn about creating and saving themes in Task 46.

cross-reference

This task shows you how to customize some of the mouse options. Task 56 shows you how to further customize the mouse pointers. More specifically, you'll learn to change the graphics that are used for your mouse pointer.

note

The Click Lock feature allows you to highlight or drag without having to continuously hold the mouse button down. Rather, you can click and hold for a set amount of time to start the highlighting or to grab an item. You can then click a second time to end the highlight or holding.

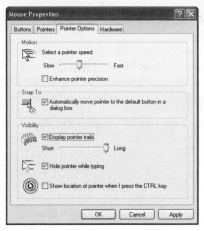

Figure 55-2: The mouse pointer options.

6. Customize your mouse's pointer options:

   a. Set the speed that your mouse pointer moves by adjusting the slider in the Motion section. The closer to Fast that you set the slider, the less you will have to physically move the mouse in order to get the pointer to move. The closer to Slow that you set the slider, the more you will physically have to move the mouse in order to move the pointer, and thus the more precise control you'll be able to exercise.

   b. Check the box next to Display Pointer Trails to turn on mouse trails. This feature causes copies of your pointer to trail behind the primary pointer. The faster you move, the larger the gap in the trails. You can also adjust the gap in the trails by moving the slider between Short and Long. To turn the trails off, uncheck the Display Pointer Trails box.

   c. Check the box next to Hide Pointer While Typing if you'd like to have the pointer disappear when you type. This keeps the pointer out of your way.

   d. Check the box next to the Show Location of Pointer When I Press the CTRL Key if you would like to have help finding the pointer. When this option is checked, when you press and release the Ctrl key, circles hone in on the pointer location. This helps you find the exact location of the pointer.

7. Click the Apply button to save the changes you've selected.

8. Click the OK button to close the dialog window.

tip

If you use the ClickLock feature described in Step 4, you can select the Setting button near it to set the amount of time that you must press and hold the mouse button in order to begin the effect.

tip

If you are left-handed, you may want to switch the functions of the right and left mouse button. You learn where to make this change in Step 4.

note

Some programs, such as Microsoft Word, automatically hide the pointer regardless of the Hide Pointer setting.

note

Your mouse may have special software installed to customize it. If so, your options might be slightly different from those presented in this task.

note

If you have a more advanced mouse, you may have other tabs that can be used to customize features. For example, if your mouse has a wheel, you will see a Wheel tab that allows you to set the number of lines to scroll on the screen.

Task 56

Customizing the Mouse Pointers

Within Windows XP, the default mouse pointer on the screen is a white arrow outlined in black. When the system is busy because a task is taking time, an hourglass is displayed. When you drag an item to an invalid area, the pointer changes to a circle with a slash through it. These are all the standard Windows XP pointers; however, they are not the pointers you have to use! The following steps walk you through customizing your Windows XP pointers:

1. Select the Control Panel from the Start menu.

2. Click on the Printers and Other Hardware category.

3. Click on the Mouse Control Panel icon in the lower part of the Printer and Other Hardware window. This presents the Mouse Properties dialog window.

4. Select the Pointers tab in the Mouse Properties dialog window. You should see a window similar to Figure 56-1.

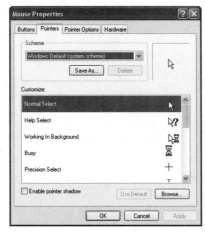

Figure 56-1: The Pointers tab in the Mouse Properties dialog window.

5. Select an item from the Scheme list. The drop-down list within the Scheme area contains different sets of pointers that you can use. When you select an item from this list, the Customize portion of the screen changes to show you the specific pointers in the scheme. You can scroll through the list of pointers in the Customize area. Go through the schemes until you find one that has pointers you like.

   If you like all of the pointers in the scheme you find, you can continue to Step 8. If you want to change one or more of these pointers, continue to the next step.

cross-reference

To learn how to customize the operation and basic features of the mouse, see Task 55.

cross-reference

The mouse pointer settings can be saved as part of a theme. You learn about creating and saving themes in Task 46.

note

Windows XP will generally only have one pointer displayed at a time. This pointer, however, changes shapes depending on what is happening. The shape of the pointer is often a clue for what your system is doing. You should keep this in mind if you change the pointer graphics.

tip

Cursor filenames that end in .ANI are animated. Pointer files that end in .CUR generally are not.

tip

You can double-click on an item in the Customize area to automatically open the Browse dialog window.

6. Change the pointers you don't like. You can change individual pointers within the Customize area. Use the following steps for each pointer you want to change:

   a. Select the pointer you want to change by clicking on it.

   b. Select the Browse button. This presents the Browse dialog window with pointers displayed. The dialog window will look something like Figure 56-2; however, your pointers may be different depending on the extra programs that are installed on your computer. You can use the pointers in this default location, or you can look for pointers in other locations on your computer.

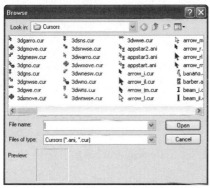

Figure 56-2: The Browse dialog window for selecting pointers.

   c. Select a pointer file by clicking on a pointer name in the Browse dialog, and then click the Open button. The selected pointer is added to the current scheme.

   d. Repeat Step 6 until all the pointers are customized to your liking.

7. Click the Apply button to apply your selections.

8. If you would like to save your pointer selections as your own scheme, select the Save As button in the Scheme area. This displays a pop-up window as shown in Figure 56-3 that you can use to enter a scheme name. Press OK to save the scheme name.

Figure 56-3: The Save Scheme prompt.

9. Press OK on the Mouse Properties dialog window to close it.

Task 57

Setting Keyboard Options

The keyboard and mouse are the two most common devices for interacting with Windows XP, and you can customize a number of settings for both. There are a variety of different keyboards you can use with Windows. Some keyboards include extra buttons and switches for accessing programs, the Internet, or devices on your computer. Most of these features are unique to individual keyboards and not to Windows XP. There are, however, a few settings that you can use to customize regardless of your specific keyboard. These settings include the speed at which your keyboard can start repeating a key press and the frequency at which the key is repeated. Additionally, you can set the rate at which the cursor in your windows blinks. To customize these values, use the following steps:

1. Select the Control Panel from the Start menu.

2. Click on the Printers and Other Hardware category.

3. Click on the Keyboard Control Panel icon in the lower part of the Printer and Other Hardware window. This presents the Keyboard Properties dialog window.

4. Select the Speed tab in the Keyboard Properties dialog window if it is not already displayed. You should see a window similar to Figure 57-1.

Figure 57-1: The Speed tab in the Keyboard Properties dialog window.

5. Set the amount of time to wait before a key being held down begins to repeat. To do this, adjust the slider control for the Repeat Delay. Moving the slider toward Short decreases the delay between the time

cross-reference

In addition to the keyboard, you can customize options for your mouse. See Task 55 for customizing the mouse options.

cross-reference

You change the cursor blink rate in the Keyboard Properties dialog window. You can actually change the cursor in the mouse settings. See Task 56 to learn how to change the cursor that is used for insertions.

the key is pressed and the moment the key value is repeated. Moving the slider toward Long increases the time.

6. Set the speed at which a key's value will repeat as long as the key continues to be held down. This value is set using the slider control for the Repeat rate. Moving this slider control toward Fast causes the key's value to be displayed more often in a shorter period of time. Moving this value toward slow causes the key's value to be displayed less often.

7. Test the settings you've selected. You can test your settings by clicking in the entry box located at the center of the Speed tab. You can then press and hold a key to see how long it takes to start repeating and then how many times it repeats. Figure 57-2 shows two different settings for the keyboard. Within the test area, the letter was pressed and held for two seconds. As you can see, the faster settings allowed a much larger number of repeats to occur than the slower repeat rate settings.

Figure 57-2: Testing the key repeats for approximately two seconds with different settings.

8. Change the cursor blink rate. You can do this by adjusting the slide control within the Cursor Blink Rate area. If you move the cursor closer to None, it blinks less often. If you move it toward Fast, it blinks more often.

9. Click the Apply button to apply the selected changes.

10. Click OK to close the dialog window.

note

The Hardware tab in the Keyboard Properties dialog presents you with information on your keyboard, including the type of keyboard that Windows believes you are using. If you are having trouble with your keyboard, you can go to this tab to see if Windows XP has noticed any problems. You can even do some troubleshooting from this dialog window to try to find the problem.

note

If you have a more advanced keyboard, you may have other options available to customize as well. This may include the ability to customize keyboard buttons to run programs or go to Web pages. You will need to check the documentation that came with the keyboard to learn to customize the keyboard-specific features.

cross-reference

Windows XP has features called StickyKeys and FilterKeys. You learn about these accessibility features in Tasks 206 and 207.

Automatically Starting a Program at Startup

Many programs will run automatically when Windows first starts up and you first log in to your account. You can add additional programs to the startup of Windows. For example, you can have Windows automatically open your media player so it is ready to play music.

To have programs automatically run when Windows XP starts, add them to the Startup folder on the Start⇨All Programs menu. You can do this by using the following steps:

1. Create a shortcut for the program you want to have start up. If the program is listed in the All Programs menu, you can use the existing menu item as the shortcut. Otherwise, see Task 50 for creating a shortcut.

2. Right-click on your shortcut and hold the mouse down. This allows you to drag the shortcut.

3. While continuing to hold the right mouse button down, drag the shortcut over the Start button. The Start menu appears.

4. While continuing to hold the right mouse button down, drag the shortcut over the All Programs item on the Start menu. The All Programs menu appears.

5. While still holding the right mouse button down, drag the shortcut to the Startup item on the All Programs menu. A black line appears above or below the Startup item. Additionally, the submenu for Startup is displayed. If nothing is in the submenu, you will see the word "Empty."

6. While still holding the right mouse button down, drag the shortcut over onto the submenu. If there are no existing items, a black line appears at the top of the submenu above the word Empty as shown in Figure 58-1. If there are items in the submenu, a black line still appears; however, you can move the black line by moving your cursor up and down.

7. Release the mouse button. A pop-up menu appears.

cross-reference

For information on creating a shortcut, see Task 50.

cross-reference

If you want to customize the icon that displays on the Start menu's items, see Task 52.

note

If you no longer want the program to run when Windows XP starts, then delete it from the Startup menu by right-clicking on it and selecting Delete.

note

Many programs place items into the Startup menu so that they will be run automatically. You shouldn't remove items from the Startup menu unless you know why they are being run at start up.

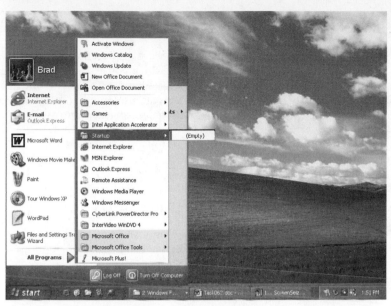

Figure 58-1: The Startup submenu with no items in it.

8. Select Copy. The shortcut is copied to the location where the black line was. Your program will now run the next time — and every time — Windows XP starts. Figure 58-2 shows the Startup menu with the newly added Windows Media Player shortcut.

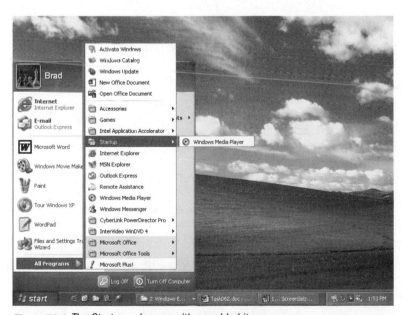

Figure 58-2: The Startup submenu with an added item.

note

Some programs run when Windows XP starts up without placing them into the Startup menu shown in this task. These programs usually make modifications to the Windows XP registry. The registry is an internal area that programs can use. It is an advanced area of Windows XP that should only be accessed if you have an advanced understanding of Windows XP.

Changing Regional Settings

The way dates, times, numbers, and currency are displayed within Windows XP depends on the region of the world in which you are located. For example, in the United States, dates are generally presented in order of month, day, year. In many other regions of the world, dates are presented in day, month, year format. You can set Windows XP to use regional settings. Alternatively, you can make changes to the format of your dates, times, numbers, and currency simply because you want to. The following are steps to help you change some of the primary regional settings within Windows XP:

1. Select the Control Panel from the Start menu.

2. Click on the Date, Time, Language, and Regional Options category.

3. Click on the Regional and Language Options Control Panel icon in the lower part of the window. The Regional and Language Options dialog window appears. The Regional Options tab should be displayed as shown in Figure 59-1. If it isn't, click on its tab.

Figure 59-1: The Regional and Language Options dialog window.

4. Select a specific location from the drop-down list in the Standards and Formats area. The list contains a large number of areas, some of which can be seen in Figure 59-2. Select the region you want. If your region is not listed, select a region that has similar settings. The following steps show you how to customize any of the individual settings.

5. Review the changes made by your region selection. Once you've selected a region, the Samples area of the dialog window changes to show you how the different values will be formatted. Make sure the settings are what you want. Figure 59-3 shows the sample values for the Icelandic region. As you can see, Icelandic settings differ from United States settings in a number of ways. Commas and decimal

cross-reference

If the settings for a region are not exactly what you want, you can customize them. Task 60 presents the steps for customizing numbers and currencies.

cross-reference

Task 5 showed you how to set the computer's clock, including setting the time zone.

note

In Step 3 you selected Regional and Language Options. You could have also selected Change the format of numbers, dates, and times from the tasks. This would have resulted in the same dialog being displayed.

note

On the Regional Options tab, you can also select a region from the list presented in the Location area at the bottom of the dialog window. This setting is used by MSN and other online services to provide you with local news. These products use this setting to determine what is "local." This allows you to get news from a different area than your own, if desired.

points are switched in numbers, the currency is in kronurs, and dates are in dd/mm/yyyy format instead of mm/dd/yyyy.

Figure 59-2: Selecting a region from the list.

6. Add additional language support. Chances are, if you are changing the regional settings, you will most likely want to be able to enter text from that region as well. This will require that you add language support. Language support for entering information can be added using the Languages tab.

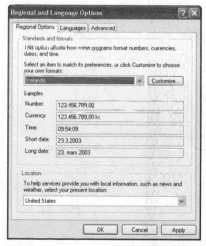

Figure 59-3: The Icelandic regional settings.

7. Click the Apply button to save the changes you've selected.

8. Click the OK button to close the dialog window.

note

You can add support for additional languages as well as for different language keyboards within the Regional and Language Options dialog window. Most of these settings are within the Languages tab. For more on this, see the Windows XP Help and Support Center.

tip

If you want to change the language used in menus and toolbars, you need to obtain the Windows Multilingual User Interface Pack. Contact a Microsoft office for more information.

note

The Regional and Language Options dialog window also contains an Advanced tab. This contains additional settings related primarily to the use of Unicode. You can also select an option on this tab to apply the regional settings to the default user profile on your system.

Changing Number and Currency Formatting

While the way numbers and currency are displayed within Windows XP depends on the region of the world in which you are located and the region you select (see Task 59), you can also customize these to your individual liking. If you don't like commas in your numbers, you can remove them, and if you want to use pounds instead of dollars, then change your Windows XP settings. The following steps show you how to customize how your numbers and currency are displayed:

1. Select the Control Panel from the Start menu.

2. Click on the Date, Time, Language, and Regional Options category.

3. Click on the Regional and Language Options control panel icon in the lower part of the window. The Regional and Language Options dialog window appears. The Regional Options tab should be displayed as shown in Figure 60-1. If it isn't, click on its tab.

Figure 60-1: The Regional and Language Options dialog window.

4. Click the Customize button. The Numbers tab in the Customize Regional Settings dialog window appears, similar to the one shown in Figure 60-2. The values you see depend up on the region that is currently selected.

5. Set the values within the entry boxes to customize how your numbers will be presented. Most of these settings are straightforward. Depending on the value you are changing, you can choose a value from the drop-down list, enter a value, or both. The sample area at the top of the dialog window shows how positive and negative numbers will look based on your current settings.

cross-reference

If you want to change the settings for your numbers and currency based on a specific region of the world, you can use Task 59. It shows how to select regional settings. If you can't find a setting that exactly matches what you want, pick a region that is closest, and then use this task's steps to make the customizations.

cross-reference

Task 5 showed you how to set the computer's clock and the time zone.

note

In Step 3 you selected Regional and Language Options. You could have also selected Change the Format of Numbers, Dates, and Times from the Tasks. This results in the same dialog being displayed.

caution

Your customized settings will be lost if you select a different region after making the customizations.

tip

To clear your customizations, simply select a different region.

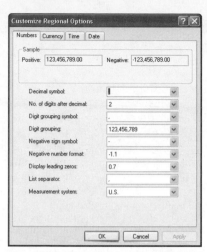

Figure 60-2: The Numbers tab within the Customize Regional Settings dialog window.

6. Click the Currency tab. A dialog window similar to Figure 60-3 appears. Your values may be different depending on your current region.

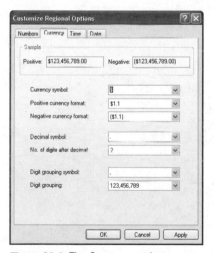

Figure 60-3: The Currency settings.

7. Make changes to the different values on this page. You can use the drop-down lists, enter values, or both. The samples at the top show the results of your changes.

8. Click the Apply button to save the changes you've selected.

9. Click the OK button to close the Customize Regional Settings dialog window.

10. Click OK to close the Regional and Language Options dialog window.

Part 4: Graphics and Digital Photography

Task 61: Copying Pictures from Your Camera to Your Hard Drive

Task 62: Using a Scanner to Capture Photographs

Task 63: Capturing a Picture of Your Screen

Task 64: Creating Your Own Icons in Paint

Task 65: Drawing Pictures in Paint

Task 66: Organizing Your Pictures into Folders and Photo Albums

Task 67: Storing and Retrieving Information about Your Pictures

Task 68: Viewing, Zooming, and Reorienting Your Pictures

Task 69: Resizing a Picture

Task 70: Cropping a Picture

Task 71: Adding Notes and Drawings to a Picture

Task 72: Converting a Picture's File Type

Task 73: Printing a Picture

Task 74: Ordering Prints of Your Pictures Online

Task 75: Putting Your Pictures on the Web

Task 76: Creating a Screen Saver with Your Own Pictures

Task 61

Copying Pictures from Your Camera to Your Hard Drive

Digital cameras come in all shapes and sizes. And different cameras have different ways of connecting to your computer. However, most new cameras work as plug-and-play devices with Windows XP. This means that Windows XP is able to recognize them as cameras as soon as they are plugged in without you needing to install additional software. How do you know if your camera is the plug-and-play type? Just plug it in and see if the wizard comes up (as described in the steps that follow). If not, install the software that came with your camera and follow the directions in your camera's user manual.

1. Plug your camera into your computer. Most cameras come with a cable especially for this purpose — usually a USB cable.

2. Turn on your camera.

3. The Removable Disk dialog appears. Windows XP knows that what you've plugged in is a camera, but in some ways, it treats it as if it were a removable disk drive (like your floppy disk drive).

4. Select the first option. It should have a picture of a camera and text that reads: Copy Pictures to a Folder on My Computer Using Microsoft Scanner and Camera Wizard.

5. Click OK. The opening page of the Scanner and Camera Wizard appears.

6. Click Next. The Choose Pictures to Copy page of the wizard appears (see Figure 61-1). Here you view all the images stored on your camera as thumbnails. Each thumbnail has a check box in the upper right indicating that the picture should be copied to your hard drive. By default, all the pictures are checked.

7. Look through all the images (using the scroll bar on the right to scroll up and down). If there are any you don't want to copy, click the check box to remove the check mark on that picture. Buttons in the lower right allow you to Select All or Clear All check boxes.

8. Click Next. The Picture Name and Destination page appears. Here you can choose where on the hard drive you want to place your pictures.

tip

The first time you plug your camera into your computer, you may see some text pop up in yellow balloons in the lower-right corner of your screen. They might say things like USB Mass Storage or Disk Drive, or give the name of your camera. This is Windows XP installing the appropriate software by itself, behind the scenes, so that it can work with your camera.

tip

Sometimes when people take pictures, they turn the camera sideways to get a better frame around tall skinny things — like a tall building. When you look at pictures like that on the Choose Pictures to Copy page, they appear sideways. You can click on a sideways picture to select it and then click the Rotate Clockwise button or that Rotate Counterclockwise button in the lower left of the window to turn pictures until they are right-side-up.

tip

If you don't have a preference, the default My Pictures folder is a good place to store photos. Just type a name for this set of pictures in the first text box, and the wizard creates a folder with that name under your My Pictures folder and puts all the photos there. If you prefer to choose your own location, click the Browse button. Finally, if you want to clear the pictures off your camera after they are copied (so you'll have room to take more), click the check box.

Task **61**

Rotate Counterclockwise

Rotate Clockwise

Figure 61-1: The Choose Pictures to Copy page.

9. Click Next. The Copying Pictures page appears (see Figure 61-2). The wizard immediately goes to work copying each picture to the hard drive. When it is done, the Other Options page is displayed. Here you have the option to order prints or publish the pictures to a Web site. You'll have the option of doing these things later, too, if you like.

Figure 61-2: The Copying Pictures page.

10. Choose the Nothing. I'm Finished Working with These Pictures option, and click Next. The Completing the Scanner and Camera Wizard dialog appears. Click Finish and you're done! A window appears showing you the folder where you copied your picture files.

Using a Scanner to Capture Photographs

Digital cameras make it easy to download pictures and post them on your Web site or email them to a friend. But what if you have taken pictures with a regular camera that you'd like to get onto your computer's hard drive? That's what scanners are for! You can buy a scanner for around $75 that allows you to scan documents, receipts, or pictures and save the images on your hard drive, just as you would with a digital camera. Once you have your scanner properly installed, follow these steps to scan your pictures to your hard drive.

1. Select My Computer from the Start menu. The My Computer window appears. Look through the items here. You should find your scanner listed.

2. Double-click on your scanner. The opening page of the Camera and Scanner Wizard appears.

3. Click Next. The Choose Scanning Preferences page appears (see Figure 62-1).

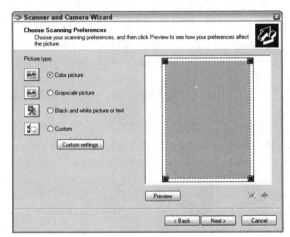

Figure 62-1: The Choose Scanning Preferences page of the Camera and Scanner Wizard.

4. Select an appropriate picture type. If you are scanning a color picture, choose Color picture. If you are scanning a black-and-white picture, choose Grayscale picture.

5. Place the picture you want to scan in your scanner as directed. Click Preview. The scanner does a preliminary scan of the page and shows you the results. If the picture is smaller than a full page, you'll see a dotted line around the picture with boxes at each corner (see Figure 62-2).

caution

Do *not* select Black and White Picture or Text for black-and-white pictures. This is only for pictures that are truly only black and white — like a logo.

tip

You can use the boxes at the corners of the dotted outline to resize the box. This box determines what is actually scanned. If you want to scan in just a part of your picture, you can use these resize boxes to adjust exactly what the dotted line surrounds.

Task **62**

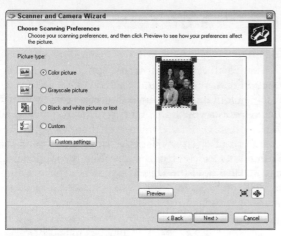

Figure 62-2: After the Preview scan.

6. Click the Next button. The Picture Name and Destination page appears (see Figure 62-3). Here you can choose where on the hard drive you want to place your pictures.

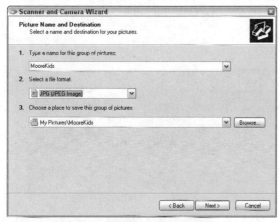

Figure 62-3: The Picture Name and Destination page of the Camera and Scanner Wizard.

7. Click the Next button. The Scanning Picture page appears. Your scanner now does a final scan of the picture. When it is complete, the Other Options page appears. Here you have the option to order prints or publish the pictures to a Web site. You'll have the option of doing these things later, too, if you like.

8. Choose the Nothing. I'm Finished Working with These Pictures option and click Next. The Completing the Scanner and Camera Wizard page appears.

9. Click Finish, and you're done! A window opens showing you the folder where you copied your picture.

note

If you don't have a preference, the default My Pictures folder is a good place. Just type a name for this set of pictures in the first text box, and the wizard creates a folder with that name under your My Pictures folder and puts the photo there. If you prefer to choose your own location, click the Browse button.

cross-reference

To find out how to how to order prints of your pictures after they are on your hard drive, see Task 74. To publish your pictures to a Web site, see Task 75.

Capturing a Picture of Your Screen

Back in the old days when DOS ruled the world, the Print Screen key on your keyboard actually did what you'd expect — it would spit a page out of your printer with all the information that appeared on the screen. This was handy. It meant that if you needed some bit of information you were looking at, to use in another program or in the real world, you didn't have to resort to pen and paper.

Today, it's not as simple. The Print Screen key doesn't print the screen. But it does do something useful — it puts an image of the screen in the Clipboard. This task shows you how to take a snapshot of the screen, save it as a file on your hard drive, and, yes, even print it, if you like. Once you have your screen ready for capture, do the following:

1. Hit the Print Screen key on your keyboard (it may be labeled PrtScn or Print Scr or some other variation). This doesn't appear to do anything, but Windows XP has just snapped a picture of your screen as it looks right now and put that picture in the clipboard.

2. Select Start⇨All Programs⇨Accessories⇨Paint to launch Paint.

3. In Paint, select Edit⇨Paste. A picture of your screen as it appeared when you hit Print Screen appears (see Figure 63-1). You'll only be able to see the upper-left corner, but you can use the scroll bars to see that the rest of it is there.

Figure 63-1: Pasting the screen capture into Paint from the clipboard.

tip

The next time you get a big ugly error message that you want to show to your tech support or help desk person, reach for the Print Screen key instead of a pen and paper.

4. Choose File⇨Save As from the Paint menu. The Save As dialog appears (see Figure 63-2).

Figure 63-2: The Save As... dialog in Paint.

5. Click on the Save as Type drop-down list box. Select the file type you want to use to save the image.

6. Navigate to the location where you want the image stored on your hard drive, give the image a name, and click the Save button. Your image is saved.

7. To print the image on your printer, simply choose File⇨Print from the Paint menu.

tip

If you need a perfect image, as you would if you were saving an image to be printed in a newsletter, magazine, or book, you should choose TIF or BMP. Otherwise, JPG is perfectly readable and creates a much smaller file, making it the better choice if you plan to email the image or put it on a Web site.

cross-reference

For more information on file types and which are best for what purpose, see Task 72.

cross-reference

Depending on your resolution, printing your screen capture may spill over into multiple pages, which you'd have to assemble like a jigsaw puzzle. To avoid this, reduce the size of the image before printing by following the steps in Task 69.

Creating Your Own Icons in Paint

Task 52 demonstrates how you can change a file's icon to one of the default icons or to an icon in an ICO file. But what if you don't see any icons you like among the defaults and you don't have an ICO file that fits the bill either? There's only one thing to do: Create your own! That's what we'll show you how to do in this task.

1. Select Start➪All Programs➪Accessories➪Paint to launch Paint.

2. From the Paint menu, choose Image➪Attributes. The Attributes dialog appears. Be sure the Units (in the middle of the dialog) is set to Pixels. Type **32** for both Width and Height (see Figure 64-1). Click OK.

Figure 64-1: The Attributes dialog.

3. Choose View➪Zoom➪Custom... to display the Custom Zoom dialog. Choose 800% (see Figure 64-2). Click OK.

Figure 64-2: The Custom Zoom dialog.

4. Choose View➪Zoom➪Show Grid. A grid of lines appears (see Figure 64-3).

5. Choose View➪Zoom➪Show Thumbnail. A small Thumbnail window appears with a small white box inside it. Move the window so that it's in a convenient spot beside the grid (see Figure 64-4). The Thumbnail window shows what your icon will look like at its actual size.

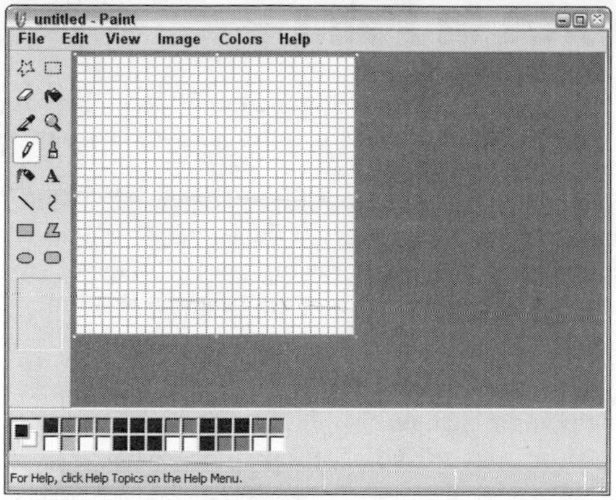

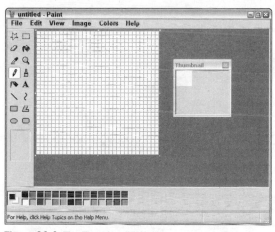

Figure 64-3: The grid is on.

Figure 64-4: The Thumbnail window.

6. Draw your masterpiece! You can use all of Paint's drawing, painting, text, and color tools just as you normally would. Since you are zoomed in and the grid is on, working with individual pixels is relatively easy. And as you make changes on the grid, you'll see them appear in the thumbnail immediately.

7. Choose File⇨Save As... The Save As dialog appears. Find the location on your hard drive where you want the file stored and type a name. Add an **.ico** after the filename you type, like this: **myicon.ico**. This ensures that the file extension is .ico, rather than the usual .bmp.

8. The file is saved. The ICO file will use itself as its icon, so you can use Explorer to go to the spot on your hard drive where you saved the file to see what it looks like.

cross-reference

See Task 65 for a description of the most commonly used features of Paint.

cross-reference

Now that you've created your own icon, go to Task 52 and follow those steps to apply the new icon to your files.

Drawing Pictures in Paint

Paint is a very cool little application, considering it comes free with Windows XP. This task demonstrates some of its most commonly used features.

1. Select Start⇨All Programs⇨Accessories⇨Paint to launch Paint. The Paint window appears. A white box appears in the center of the window. This is the piece of paper you'll be drawing on. If you look closely, you'll see dots at the corners of the white box. These allow you to resize the page.

2. Move your mouse pointer over the dot near the lower-right corner of the white box. The pointer changes to a double arrow. Press and hold the left mouse button, and move the mouse to resize the white box. You can see the size in pixels displayed in the status bar (see Figure 65-1).

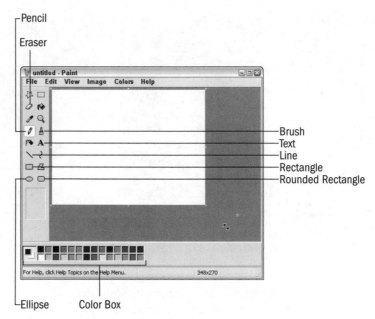

Figure 65-1: Resizing your "paper."

3. Click on the Pencil icon in the toolbar on the left. When you move your mouse pointer around in the white box, it looks like a pencil. When you press the left mouse button, it presses the pencil down onto the paper and you begin to draw. You can draw freehand shapes of all kinds using the pencil.

4. Down at the bottom of the window is a Color Box. On the left you see two boxes that overlap each other. This identifies the foreground and background colors. To the right you see lots of little squares of color. Click on your favorite color, and the foreground box changes to that color. Now when you draw again with your Pencil, you are drawing in the color you selected.

5. Click on the Brush icon in the toolbar on the left. Now your mouse pointer looks like a crosshair. When you press the left mouse button and move the mouse, you find yourself drawing with a thicker line. You can also change your brush's color using the Color Box at the bottom of the Window, just as you did with the Pencil.

6. If you need to clear the page, select the Eraser icon in the toolbar on the left. Now when you draw over lines, they are erased. To clear the entire page, select Image⇨Clear Image.

7. Click the Line button to draw a straight line. Go to where you want to start the line, then press and hold the left mouse button. Now move the pointer where you'd like to end the line, release the button, and the line is drawn. If you immediately press the left mouse button again, you can draw another straight line that begins where the last one ended.

8. The Rectangle, Rounded Rectangle, and Ellipse all work the same way: Press and hold the left mouse button where you want the top-left corner to be, drag the mouse down to where you want the bottom-right corner to be, and release the button.

9. Click the Text button in the toolbar. Now use the same technique you used in the last step to draw a rectangle. A dotted rectangle appears with a flashing cursor in it. You can type any text you like here. You may also notice that a floating Fonts window containing a toolbar appears (see Figure 65-2). This toolbar allows you to change the font, size, and style for the text.

Figure 65-2: The Fonts window toolbar.

tip

To change the background color, use the right mouse button to click in the square of the color you want in the Color Box. This will not change the background of the white box, but it will affect the color that appears when you use the eraser.

tip

With the Brush selected, notice, just below the toolbar, a box with different-sized circles, squares, and lines in it. These are different brush shapes you can choose to draw with. Experiment by clicking on different ones and then drawing in the white box.

tip

Erasing really just means painting with the background color specified in the Color Box. You can erase while using the pencil or brush by pressing and holding the right mouse button instead of the left mouse button.

cross-reference

To find out how to resize a picture in Paint, see Task 69. To crop a picture, see Task 70. To convert a picture to a different file format, see Task 72. To print a picture, see Task 73.

Organizing Your Pictures into Folders and Photo Albums

Windows XP has added a lot of features to the operating system to make it easy for you to work with pictures. Here we show you how to organize your pictures into folders under My Pictures, and we also demonstrate some of the cool features for viewing thumbnails and slideshows with no extra software required!

1. Select Start⇨My Pictures. The My Pictures window appears. This is where folders are created by the Camera and Scanner Wizard to hold images retrieved from your digital camera and scanner. It's a good place to keep and organize all your pictures (see Figure 66-1).

Figure 66-1: Folders show thumbnails of some of the images inside.

2. Double-click on one of the folders here in My Pictures. Your window presents the pictures in a special Photo Album format (see Figure 66-2). Use the scroll bar at the bottom of the window to slide the thumbnails back and forth. Click on any thumbnail, and it is displayed, as big as your window will allow, at the top. Windows XP calls this the Filmstrip view.

3. On the left side of the window are several groups of links labeled Picture Tasks, File and Folder Tasks, and Other Places. These links provide easy access to things you may want to do with your pictures. For example, under Picture Tasks, click the View as a slide show link. Your screen is filled with one of the pictures. Use the left and right arrow keys to move back and forth among the pictures. When you are done, hit the Escape key (Esc) to return to your desktop.

4. Now click the Up button in your window's toolbar to go to the parent folder.

note

You'll notice that the folders icons here appear big and have little thumbnail versions of some of the pictures they contain. This makes it easier to find what you're looking for visually.

cross-reference

See Task 61 to find out how to copy pictures from your digital camera to a folder in My Pictures. Also, see Task 62 to find out how to scan your photographs onto your hard drive.

note

If you don't have any folders of your own here, you can double-click on the Sample Pictures folder that was installed with Windows XP.

note

You can click on your favorite picture in this folder and then, under Picture Tasks, click the Set as Desktop Background link. In a few seconds, you see the picture replace your desktop background.

Figure 66-2: A Photo Album folder.

5. Right-click on the icon for the folder you were just in. A pop-up menu appears. Choose Properties from the menu. The Folder Properties window appears. Click the Customize tab at the top of the window (see Figure 66-3).

Figure 66-3: The Customize tab in the folder Properties window.

6. At the top of the properties window there is a drop-down list box labeled Use This Folder Type as a Template. The current selection is Photo Album — that's why the pictures were presented as thumbnails on a slider below and a big picture at the top. Change this to Pictures. Click OK. Now double-click on the folder again. This time, the pictures appear as a bunch of thumbnails. You can pick the layout you want for each of your folders using the folder's property window.

tip

You can create your own folders inside My Pictures and move pictures around to organize them as you like, just as you would any files. For information on creating folders and moving and copying files, see Tasks 23, 24, and 25.

tip

In the middle of the Folder Properties window, on the Customize tab you'll see a representation of the folder with the small thumbnail images in it. Click the Choose Picture button. Now you see a dialog that shows all the pictures in the folder. Select one and click Open. You return to the Properties window, and the picture you selected now appears on the folder. If you decide you'd prefer the window to look as it did, click the Restore Default button.

tip

Move your mouse over (but don't click) one of your pictures in the folder. Just hover there for a second. You'll see a yellow box pop up with a wealth of information about your picture. To get even more information (and store some of your own!), see Task 67.

Task 67

Storing and Retrieving Information about Your Pictures

In the olden days, before digital pictures, it was common to write information on the back of a photograph — things like when and where the picture was taken or the names and ages of the people in the picture. So how do you keep track of such vital information for your digital pictures? Don't worry, Microsoft has thought of everything!

1. Select Start⇨My Pictures to display the My Pictures window. Now double-click on one of the folders here to see your pictures.

2. Right-click on one of your pictures that is stored in TIF or JPG format (preferably one that was taken with a digital camera, if you have one). From the pop-up menu, choose Properties. Click on the Summary tab at the top of the window (see Figure 67-1).

Figure 67-1: The Summary tab of the picture Properties window.

3. Write any information you want about the picture, who or what is in it, and even the photographer. All the information you enter here will be stored along with the picture. You can use the Properties window to view it any time you like.

4. When you're done, click Apply.

5. Click the Advanced button. The information in this tab changes (see Figure 67-2).

6. Click OK on the picture Properties window. Now allow your mouse to hover over the picture for which you just typed in information. In a couple of seconds, a yellow box appears with the title and comments you entered, along with other information.

caution

You cannot store summary information in a BMP, GIF, PNG, or ICO file. Only JPG and TIF files support this feature. Fortunately, photos are typically stored in either JPG or TIF.

cross-reference

If you have a picture in BMP or some other format that doesn't support summary information, you can convert it to a JPG or TIF file. Task 72 shows you how.

tip

Don't worry; you can always get back to the information you entered by clicking the Simple button!

note

Although the information displayed may be different from what you see in this figure, you should see at least some basic information about the picture, like its height, width, and resolution. If this picture came from a digital camera, you might see lots of additional information about the camera and its settings when the picture was taken, as in the figure. You may also find one other useful bits of information mixed in there: the exact date and time the photo was taken.

tip

This is a handy way to see basic information about your photo without having to pull up the Properties window.

Figure 67-2: The advanced Summary tab.

7. Another way to make some of the summary information easy to see is to use the Details view. Click the Views button in the toolbar of the window. A list of views appears. Choose Details (see Figure 67-3).

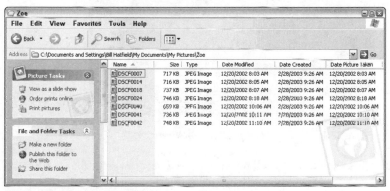

Figure 67-3: Viewing Details.

8. One useful column displayed here is Date Picture Taken. Click on the column header to sort by this column.

9. Other summary information can be displayed here. Right-click on any of the column headers. A pop-up menu appears with a long list of available information you can add as a column in this Detail view. Select Author. The new column appears (you may have to scroll your window to the right to see it). By clicking on this column header, you can now sort by photographer.

Task 68

Viewing, Zooming, and Reorienting Your Pictures

Windows XP includes a picture viewer that responds whenever you double-click a picture file in any common format. It also has a few bells and whistles that we'll demonstrate in this task.

1. Select Start⇨My Pictures to open the My Pictures window. Now double-click on one of the folders here to see your pictures.

2. Double-click on any picture file. The Windows Picture and Fax Viewer appears, displaying your picture (see Figure 68-1).

Figure 68-1: The Windows Picture and Fax Viewer.

3. Click the Next Image button to see the next image in the folder. Click the Previous Image button to go back.

4. Click the Actual Size button. Normally, when the Picture Viewer opens a large picture, it shrinks it down so that it fits comfortably within the window. (This doesn't actually change the size of the image stored in the file, just how it appears in the window.) The Actual Size button puts the picture back to its original size and allows you to use the scroll bars along the right and bottom of the window to move around and see different parts.

5. Click the Best Fit button. The picture is reduced so that it fits comfortably in the window again.

6. Click the Zoom In button. Now click on a specific part of the picture several times. Each time you click on the picture, you zoom in closer to the spot where you click (see Figure 68-2). Click the Zoom Out button repeatedly to zoom out.

cross-reference

To find out how to copy pictures from your digital camera to your hard drive, see Task 61. To find out how to capture photographs using your scanner, see Task 62.

caution

Double-clicking on a file doesn't necessarily open the Windows Picture and Fax Viewer. For example, if you have Corel PhotoPaint installed, it may be selected as the default editor for JPEG files. If so, when you double-click an image, Corel PhotoPaint opens instead. However, you can bypass this without changing the file associations. Right-click on the image and choose Open With⇨Windows Picture and Fax Viewer.

cross-reference

If you edit a TIF file or a fax using the Windows Picture and Fax Viewer, you will see a number of additional buttons that aren't described here. For more information on these additional features, see Task 71.

tip

You can use the plus and minus keys (the ones on the numeric keypad are handy) to zoom in and out from the keyboard.

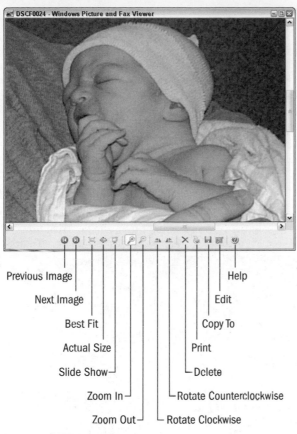

Previous Image

Next Image

Best Fit

Actual Size

Slide Show

Zoom In

Zoom Out

Help

Edit

Copy To

Print

Delete

Rotate Counterclockwise

Rotate Clockwise

Figure 68-2: Zooming in.

7. Sometimes when you take a picture of something tall and narrow, you may turn the camera so that the object fits better in the frame. When you do this, the picture will appear sideways when you view it on your computer. That's what the Rotate Clockwise and Rotate Counterclockwise buttons are for. They allow you to rotate the picture until it's right-side-up.

8. The Slide Show button uses the full screen to display your images one after the other. This is a great way to view your pictures at full resolution. Use the left and right arrow keys on your keyboard to move forward and backward among the pictures.

9. Use the rest of the buttons on this window as needed:

   • The Delete button deletes the picture you are looking at.

   • The Print button launches the Photo Printing Wizard.

   • The Copy To button allows you to copy the file to a new location or give it a new name.

   • The Edit button closes the viewer and launches Paint, automatically opening the picture you were just viewing.

   • The Help button opens the online help for the viewer.

caution

Pushing the Delete button actually erases the file from your hard drive and puts it in the Recycle Bin. You can always retrieve it from the Recycle Bin if you accidentally push this button. See Task 30 to find out how.

cross-reference

To find out how to use the Photo Printing Wizard, see Task 73.

cross-reference

For more information on using Paint to edit pictures, see Tasks 65, 69, and 70.

Resizing a Picture

When you copy a picture from your digital camera or scan a photograph, you may be surprised at how large the resultant image is. If you plan to print the image, that's good — you want a printed image to be as high a resolution as possible so that it looks crisp and clean on paper. But the bigger a picture is, the more room it takes on your hard drive and the longer it will take to download as part of an email message or a Web page. So reducing the size of a picture is something you may do a lot. Fortunately, Paint has a feature for doing just that.

1. Select Start⇨All Programs⇨Accessories⇨Paint to launch Paint.

2. Choose File⇨Open... from the Paint menu. Locate the picture you want to resize, select it, and click Open. The picture appears.

3. Choose Image⇨Attributes... from the Paint menu. The Attributes window appears (see Figure 69-1). Make note of the values in Width and Height here, but do not change them.

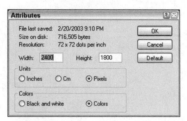

Figure 69-1: The Attributes window.

4. Choose Image⇨Stretch/Skew... from the Paint menu. The Stretch and Skew window appears (see Figure 69-2). This window allows you to resize your image. (You'll be using the top part of the window, not the bottom part. We doubt you'll often have a use for skewing an image.) You can't type in an exact size you want in pixels. Instead, you have to type in a percentage of the current size. This is why we suggested you go check the size using the Attributes window before you came to this window. Any percentage below 100% reduces the size of the image. Any percentage above 100% increases the size of the image.

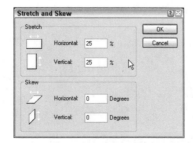

Figure 69-2: The Stretch and Skew window.

al per-
3).

Task **69**

cross-reference

For more information on file
types and which are best for
what purpose, see Task 72.

cation
st not to
ore. If you
e. You
to print it

tip

You might also want to change
the value in the Save as Type
drop-down list. Typically, JPG
files are best for images you
want to send via email or
use on a Web page.

Cropping a Picture

Cropping a picture means simply chopping part of it off. When you take pictures you try to get everything that belongs in the frame in and nothing more. But you aren't always successful. While you can't do much about that picture where you cut Aunt Edna's head off, you can do something about pictures where there's too much stuff in the frame. Sometimes too many things make the picture look busy and distract from the real focus. Other times you are just standing too far away or you weren't zoomed in correctly. Once you get some practice with it, correctly cropping your images can make a big difference in how they look.

1. Select Start➪All Programs➪Accessories➪Paint to launch Paint.

2. Choose File➪Open... from the Paint menu. Locate the picture you want to crop, select it, and click Open. The picture appears. If you need to resize the image, do that first.

3. Maximize the Paint window so that you can see as much of the image as possible. If the image is still larger than you can see all at once, use the scroll bars on the right and bottom of the Paint window to locate the part of the picture you want to *keep*.

4. Click the Select button in the toolbar on the left.

5. Figure out where you want the new top-left corner of the picture to be. Move the mouse pointer there, and then press and hold the left mouse button. Drag the pointer down and to the right until it is located where you want the new bottom-right corner of the picture to be. When you are sure, release the mouse button. A dotted line surrounds what will be the new picture (see Figure 70-1). If you decide that's not right, just click the Select button again and redraw the box.

cross-reference

To find out how to resize an image, go to Task 69.

caution

If the part of the image you want to keep is too large to fit on the screen all at once, even with Paint maximized, then, unfortunately, there's no good way to crop your image in Paint (unless you resize the image to make it smaller). In most image-editing applications, you can zoom out to see even big pictures within the frame of your window. Not so in Paint. There is a zoom feature, but it only lets you zoom in closer, not zoom out.

Figure 70-1: Drawing a dotted line around the portion of the picture you want to *keep*.

6. Choose Edit⇨Copy To... from the Paint menu. The Copy To window appears (see Figure 70-2). Select the location and name of your new, cropped picture. Click Save. The image is saved.

Figure 70-2: The Copy To window.

7. Use Explorer to locate the new, cropped image, and double-click it to see what it looks like (see Figure 70-3). This is often surprising. What looked good in the context of everything around it may look lonely or you may have given too much room on one side and not enough on the other. Not to worry—you still have the original image. Just start over and try again.

Figure 70-3: The newly cropped image.

Adding Notes and Drawings to a Picture

The Windows Picture and Fax Viewer discussed in Task 68 has a few extra features when you edit TIF files or faxes. These are collectively referred to as
annotation features. As the name implies, these features are designed to make it
easy for you to highlight portions of the picture and to make notes. These highlights and notes are then saved as part of the picture so that when others view it,
they see your additions.

tip

If you have a picture that you
want to add annotations to and
it isn't in TIF format, you can
always convert it to TIF format.
See Task 72 to find out how.

tip

There's a check box labeled
Transparent and a button
labeled Color... Clicking the
check box makes the rectangle
transparent, although it still
retains its color and makes
whatever's behind it that color.
This is nice for highlighting a
portion of a picture.

tip

Of course, you can also make
changes to a picture (in *any*
format) using Paint. Many of
the features available here are
available there, as well. See
Task 65 for more information
on using Paint.

1. Select Start⇨My Pictures to open the My Pictures window. Now
   double-click a folder that contains a TIF or fax, then double-click the
   TIF or fax file. The Windows Picture and Fax Viewer appears displaying your picture (see Figure 71-1). You'll notice there are more
   buttons along the bottom than usual.

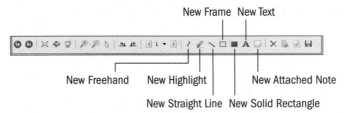

Figure 71-1: The Windows Picture and Fax Viewer window.

2. Click the New Solid Rectangle button. Pick a location on the picture,
   press and hold the left mouse button, and then drag the mouse down
   and to the right. Release the button, and a solid-colored rectangle
   appears. Little boxes called *selection handles* around the rectangle indicate that it is selected.

3. Move your mouse pointer over one of the little boxes. It turns into a
   double arrow. Hold the left mouse button down, and drag the little
   box to change the rectangle's size. Release the button when the size is
   right. Now move your mouse pointer into the rectangle. It turns into
   a four-way arrow. Press the left mouse button and drag. This time
   you move the rectangle around on the picture. You can only move or
   resize a selected rectangle (one that has little boxes around it). To
   select a rectangle, simply click on it.

4. Now select the rectangle and right-click on it. A pop-up menu with two
   options appears: Delete Annotation and Edit Annotation Info. Selecting
   the first option deletes the rectangle. Choose Edit Annotation Info.
   The Annotation Properties window appears.

5. Click the Color... button. The Color dialog appears. Pick your
   favorite color and click OK. Click OK on the Annotation Properties
   window too. Your rectangle is changed to the color you selected.

6. Click the New Attached Note button. Draw a rectangle. It is the
   same color as you chose for the Rectangle in the previous step. Now

click inside the rectangle. The rectangle turns white and a flashing cursor appears. Type some text. When you are done, click elsewhere on the picture. Your text appears against the colored background.

7. Select the Note you just created by clicking on it. Boxes appear around it. Now right-click the Note. The same pop-up appears as you saw on the Rectangle. Click Edit Annotation Info. The Annotation Properties window appears. It looks a little different this time. There are two buttons: Color... and Font.... . Color displays the Color dialog you saw before, changing the background color of the Note.

8. Click the Font button on the Annotation Properties window. The Font dialog appears. Adjust the font face, style, and size as you like. When you are done, click OK. Click OK on the Annotation Properties window too. The font of the text in your note is changed.

9. This same basic process works with all the annotations you can add. Here's a summary of the rest of them:

   • The New Freehand Annotation allows you to draw anything you like as if you were writing on the picture with a pencil.

   • With the New Highlight Annotation, you draw a box and it looks as though you've highlighted it with a yellow highlighting marker.

   • The New Straight Line Annotation draws straight lines.

   • The New Frame Annotation creates a box.

   • The New Text Annotation is just like the New Attached Note, except that it doesn't have a colored background.

10. After annotating your image (see Figure 71-2), save it to a different name and location by using the Copy To button.

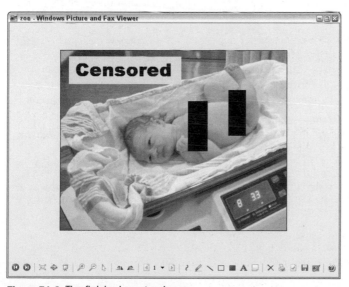

Figure 71-2: The finished masterpiece.

Converting a Picture's File Type

Pictures on your hard drive can be stored using one of several different *file types*. Think of a file type as a strategy for storing the picture information. Some file types try to keep every last detail of the picture intact, but end up creating very large files. Other file types attempt to make the picture file smaller, but compromise some detail in the process. Some file types are best for line drawings and others are best for photographs.

In this task you'll find out how to convert a picture file from one file type to another. In the process you'll discover the strengths and weaknesses of each file type.

1. Select Start➪All Programs➪Accessories➪Paint to launch Paint.

2. Choose File➪Open from the Paint menu. The Open dialog appears. Locate the picture you want to change to a new file type. Select it and click Open. The picture appears.

3. Choose File➪Save As from the Paint menu. The Save As dialog appears (see Figure 72-1). Select the location, and enter a name for the new picture.

cross-reference

For more information on using the Windows Picture and Fax Viewer, see Tasks 68 and 71.

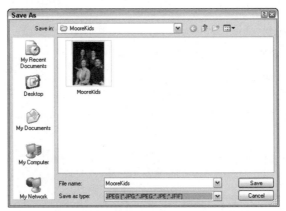

Figure 72-1: The Save As dialog.

4. Click the Files of Type drop-down list box. This shows you all the file types that are supported in Paint. There are dozens of file types in existence, but these five are the most common. Here's a rundown of each file type and its strengths and weaknesses.

   • *Bitmap (.BMP, .DIB).* This is the standard, default Windows picture type. The picture quality is high, but the files it produces are *huge*. Although this format is common, there's almost always a better option. The Files of Type drop-down list box in the Save As dialog includes several items that are all different kinds of bitmap files: Monochrome Bitmap, 16-Color Bitmap, 256-Color Bitmap, and 24-Bit Bitmap. The only difference among these types is the number of colors that are stored. If you create a colorful drawing and save it as a 16-Color Bitmap, the file will be smaller, but your colors will likely be messed up.

- *JPEG (.JPG, .JPEG, .JPE, .JFIF)*. The JPEG (pronounced *jay-peg*) format gets its name from the group that created it: the Joint Photographic Experts Group. Since they are experts, you probably think this has got to be a great format for photographs. You'd be right! This format is the most common format used for pictures on the Web, and it is also the one used by most digital cameras. It stores pictures in surprisingly small files with usually only a small loss in detail. If you're going to email a picture to a friend, this is the format to use.

- *GIF (.GIF)*. GIF is the best choice for line drawings. If you have a cartoon, logo, or diagram, the GIF format will produce a crisp sharp image and take up a minimal amount of space. You can also buy software that lets you create GIF files that have several frames that play in sequence, creating an animation.

- *TIFF (.TIF, .TIFF)*. Another popular format for photographs. TIFF provides a picture with perfect quality, like a BMP, but usually with a much smaller file size (though not as small as a JPEG). It is also an older format, which means that almost every graphics software application out there supports it. If you need a high-quality image for desktop publishing, TIFF is the way to go.

- *PNG (.PNG)*. Although some hail it as the graphics format of the future, right now it isn't nearly as common as the other four.

5. Click the Save button. The file is saved with the name, location, and file type you specified. Now, you'll want to go out and see how big the file is and if the quality of the picture is acceptable.

6. Use Explorer to locate the file on your hard drive.

7. Right-click the file and choose Properties from the pop-up menu. A little less than halfway down the dialog, you should see the Size for the picture. Click OK.

8. Double-click on the picture. The Windows Picture and Fax Viewer opens displaying your picture. Take a good, close look.

---

tip

Actually, in other image-editing programs, you can choose the level of quality you want to use for your JPEG picture when you save it, on a scale of 1 to 10. The higher the quality, the bigger the file. Paint doesn't allow you to change this setting, however.

caution

Converting a JPEG file into a TIFF will not increase its quality. If a file is already in JPEG format, any loss in quality has already happened and you can't get it back.

tip

TIFF is the format used by the Windows XP Fax Service. For more information on that, see Tasks 195 and 196.

tip

Another way of making a file smaller, besides changing its file type, is to reduce the picture's size. For more on that, see Task 69. Cropping also reduces a file's size, and it's discussed in Task 70.

caution

Sometimes if you have another painting or drawing application installed, that application will open instead of the Windows Picture and Fax Viewer. If you have this problem, right-click on the picture and choose Open With⇨Windows Picture and Fax Viewer.

Task 73

Printing a Picture

You might wonder why we'd need to dedicate a task to something a simple as printing a picture. After all, isn't it a matter of just selecting File⇨Print... from the menu in Paint? Well, yes, that's one way to do it. But Windows XP has included another approach that is much more flexible and provides a whole lot more options: the Photo Printing Wizard.

caution

Sometimes if you have another painting or drawing application installed, that application will open instead of the Windows Picture and Fax Viewer. If you have this problem, right-click on the picture and choose Open With⇨Windows Picture and Fax Viewer.

tip

Actually, you don't have to view a picture before you print it. You can just select a picture and click the Print this Picture link under Picture Tasks along the side of the Explorer window. An even easier way is to just right-click on a picture and choose Print from the pop-up menu.

tip

If you want to print all the pictures in this folder, click the Select All button. Clear All, as you might expect, clears all the check boxes so you can start over.

tip

For the best results, use photo-quality paper when you print your pictures. It makes a big difference. Although the paper's a little more expensive, the Photo Printing Wizard helps you make the best use of it by printing several pictures on a page, if possible.

1. Select Start⇨My Pictures to open the My Pictures window. Now double-click on one of the folders here that contains a picture you'd like to print. Double-click on the picture. The Windows Picture and Fax Viewer appears, displaying your picture.

2. Click the Print button. The Photo Printing Wizard appears. Click Next. The Picture Selection page appears (see Figure 73-1). You'll notice the picture you were viewing when you clicked the Print button is automatically checked. You can use this opportunity to click the check box for any other pictures from that folder you'd also like to print at the same time.

Figure 73-1: The Picture Selection page of the Photo Printing Wizard.

3. Click Next. The Printing Options page appears. Here you can choose which printer you'd like to print to (if you have several available). And you can click the Printing Preferences button to change settings for the selected printer. This allows you to select the paper type, black-and-white or color printing, the print quality, and other options.

4. Click Next. Now you see the Layout Selection page (see Figure 73-2). This is where your choices get interesting! Scroll down the list of Available Layouts.

Figure 73-2: The Layout Selection page.

Here are some things you should know about the different options presented here:

- The Full-Page Fax Print is not just for faxes! It is a great option if you want to be sure that you get the biggest print of your picture possible without any cropping. All the rest of the layout options may crop (that is, shave off a little on the side or bottom), as necessary, to fit them onto the page.

- 8 × 10 In. Prints is similar to the Full-Page Fax Print and Full-Page Photo Print option, except that it ensures that picture ends up exactly 8 × 10. Since this is a standard frame size, it is handy. But, unfortunately, it will crop about 6% equally from the short sides of the image (assuming you are working with a standard, full-size, uncropped image from a camera).

- 4 × 6 In. Cutout Prints and 4 × 6 In. Album Prints can be used to get a standard size for use in albums or frames. However, these formats cut about 10% equally from the long sides of the image. That's enough to shave the top of Uncle Ned's head off! To avoid so much cropping, use 3.5 × 5 In. Cutout Prints instead.

- Contact Sheet Prints crams a bunch (up to 45!) of small thumbnail images onto a page, and it puts the filename below the picture. This is a great way to get a look at your entire photo collection at a glance and help you remember which picture is which.

5. Select the layout that best suits your needs. The Print Preview window shows how the page will look with the pictures you selected. Decide how many copies of each picture you want, and enter that value for the Number of Times to Use Each Picture.

6. Click Next. Your pictures are sent to the printer. When they are finished, the final page of the wizard appears. Click Finish.

tip

For the wisest use of your paper, select the number of pictures and the number of copies printed of each carefully. For example, suppose you are using the Wallet Prints layout, which puts nine pictures on one page, but you only want to get prints of three different pictures. By entering a 3 for the Number of Times to Use Each Picture, you can print three copies of each of the three pictures — all on one page!

cross-reference

If you'd prefer to save your ink cartridges, you can order prints online. To find out how, check out Task 74.

Ordering Prints of Your Pictures Online

Color printers are better today than they've ever been. And often you can print your digital pictures yourself and get a very good result, especially if you use photo paper. But photo paper is expensive. And so are the color ink cartridges that you'll need to buy in bulk if you do a lot of picture printing.

Another option that can provide higher-quality prints is to send the electronic pictures to an online service that uses professional printers to make prints and then sends them back to you. In days gone by you'd have had to go to a Web site and upload your pictures yourself. Now, Windows XP makes it as easy as a wizard.

1. Select Start⇨My Pictures to open the My Pictures window. Now double-click on one of the folders here that contains pictures you want to order prints for.

2. Click the Order Prints Online Link under Picture Tasks along the side of the Explorer window. This launches the Online Print Ordering Wizard.

3. Click Next. The Change Your Picture Selection page appears (see Figure 74-1). All the pictures in the folder are displayed. Click the check box associated with the pictures for which you want to order prints.

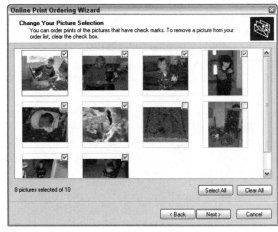

Figure 74-1: Selecting the pictures for which you want to get prints.

4. Click Next. The Select a Printing Company page appears (see Figure 74-2). Choose what company you'd like to use. The companies made available through this wizard are retrieved over the Internet and may change over time. You may see different options than those that appear in the figure.

tip

If you want to order prints for all the pictures in this folder, click the Select All button. Clear All, as you might expect, clears all the check boxes so you can start over.

cross-reference

To print your pictures using your own printer, see Task 73.

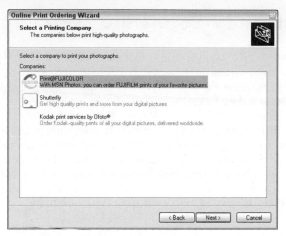

Figure 74-2: Picking a company to make your prints.

5. Click Next. Choose the number of copies and sizes you want for each picture (see Figure 74-3).

Figure 74-3: Choosing the number of copies and sizes for each picture.

6. Click Next. To complete the order, follow the rest of the pages, providing all the required billing information and the shipping information.

Putting Your Pictures on the Web

It's easy today to sign up with a Web hosting company to get your own Web site. Some services, like `Brinkster.com`, have a small account you can set up for free. Many services allow you to set up accounts for as little as $10 or $20 a month. Once you sign up, you have a certain amount of space you can use to store Web pages, pictures, and whatever else you want to show off to the world! If you're interested in setting up even a small personal or family Web site, this is a good way to go.

However, Windows XP also provides an option that is built in to allow you to publish your pictures to the Web. This option is free, but you may be required to set up a Passport account if you don't already have one. You can find out how to do that in Task 183.

1. Select Start➪My Pictures to open the My Pictures window. Now double-click on one of the folders here that contains pictures you want to put on the Web.

2. Click the Publish This Folder to the Web Link under File and Folder Tasks along the side of the Explorer window. This launches the Web Publishing Wizard.

3. Click Next. The Change Your File Selection page appears (see Figure 75-1). All the pictures in the folder are displayed. Click the check box associated with the pictures you want to publish on the Web.

Figure 75-1: Selecting the files you want to publish to the Web.

4. Click Next. The Where Do You Want to Publish These Files? page appears. A list of services is retrieved over the Internet. Select the service you want to use. At the time of this writing, there is only one service available — MSN Groups.

5. Click Next. To use MSN Groups, you must log in with a Microsoft Passport account. So at this point one of several different things may happen. If you already have a Passport and it's associated with your

caution

If you have one or more files selected, you won't see the Publish the Folder to the Web link. Instead you'll see either Publish This File to the Web or Publish the Selected Items to the Web. Regardless, all of these will launch the Web Publishing Wizard.

cross-reference

To email pictures to a friend, see Task 163.

note

MSN Groups is a feature of the MSN Web site that allows you to create your own discussion forums and community sites for virtually any purpose you like. Setting up a group of your own is free. One of the features available to groups is the ability to upload pictures to a group. That's what this wizard utilizes.

note

If you have other options available in the Where Do You Want to Publish These Files? page when you run this wizard, feel free to try them out. But be aware, the wizard may be different for other providers.

Windows XP login, you may not need to sign in at all. If not, you'll see a Passport Sign-in dialog. Or you may see a dialog that asks you to sign up for a new Passport account.

6. After getting through the Passport login, you'll see the Select Where You Want Your Files Stored page (see Figure 75-2). If you are a member of one or more MSN Groups, those groups will appear here. You can also create your own MSN Group. For example, you could create one just to hold your own family pictures. To do so, click Create a New MSN Group to share your files.

Figure 75-2: Creating a new MSN Group to hold your uploaded pictures.

7. Click Next. The Create Your New Group page allows you to enter a name for your group and your email address. Click Next. You can enter a description for your group. Don't publish your group in the directory unless you're interested in strangers finding it and joining. Click Next. You are informed how to access your new group and give the option of putting a link to it in your Favorites. Click Next. You are informed that nonimage files will be stored in a folder called Documents, and image files will be stored in a folder under Documents called Pictures.

8. Click Next. You may see a page that explains that you have a 3MB limit for all files you upload to all MSN Groups and that you may exceed that. It provides a couple of options for getting around that.

9. Click Next. The Do You Want to Adjust Picture Sizes before Publishing? page appears. This page allows you to resize the files as you upload them so that they don't take up as much of your 3MB limit as they normally would. We recommend you click the Yes check box and choose the Small option. Your images will still be plenty big enough to be clearly seen.

10. The pictures are uploaded. After that, you'll see a page that tells you that the upload is complete. Click Next. The final wizard page is shown. Click Finish. Your browser is launched, taking you to your newly created MSN Group.

caution

Before your upload begins, you may be presented with a Passport login window and forced to log in again.

note

For others to see your pictures, they need to come to this Web address and join your group. (They must sign up for a Passport account if they don't have one already.) You can share the address with family and friends, and you can be notified via weekly email as new people join the group.

Creating a Screen Saver with Your Own Pictures

Screen savers are great fun. They were originally created to address a problem: If you walked away from a computer and left it on so that the same image appeared on the screen for too long, the image could become *burned in*. This meant that even when that image wasn't on the screen, you'd see a shadow of it — permanently. Modern monitors aren't nearly so prone to burn-in as they have been in years gone by. And most monitors today shut themselves down to save power anyway if they've been on for more than an hour or so. But screen savers remain, mostly as a fun way of expressing yourself and making your computer environment your own. And what better way to express yourself than by creating a screen saver with your own pictures!

1. Right-click on your desktop (anywhere there's not a window or an icon).

2. From the pop-up menu, choose Properties. This opens the Display Properties dialog.

3. Click the Screen Saver tab at the top (see Figure 76-1). This is where you can choose what screen saver you want to use and adjust its settings. Quite a number of screen savers come with Windows XP.

4. Click the Screen Saver drop-down list box. Choose My Pictures Slideshow from the list.

5. Click the Settings button. The My Pictures Screen Saver Options dialog appears (see Figure 76-2). Here you can decide which pictures are used and how they should be displayed. The most important setting is right in the middle: Use Pictures in This Folder.

6. Click the Browse button. A Browse for Folder dialog appears. Locate a folder that has pictures you want to use for your screen saver.

cross-reference

If you want to find out more about choosing and configuring screen savers, see Task 43.

Figure 76-1: The Screen Saver tab on the Display Properties dialog.

Figure 76-2: The My Pictures Screen Saver Options dialog.

7. Click on the folder, then click OK. You are returned to the My Pictures Screen Saver Options dialog (see Figure 76-2). Now you can set the other options. Following are some of the interesting ones:

   • *Stretch Small Pictures.* The screen saver will automatically shrink big pictures to fit on the screen, but if you want it to stretch small pictures to fill the screen, click this check box.

   • *Show Filenames.* This option displays the filename of each picture.

   • *Use Transition Effects between Pictures.* Adds fades, dissolves, and other cool transitions between your pictures.

   • *Allow Scrolling through Pictures with the Keyboard.* Allows you to use the left and right cursor keys to move forward and backward through the pictures.

8. Once you've set all the options, click OK. You are returned to the Display Properties dialog.

9. Adjust the number of minutes Windows XP should wait before the screen saver kicks in. You can click Preview here to see what the screen saver will look like. When you are done, click OK.

tip

Unfortunately, there's no way to look at the pictures in the Browse for Folder dialog, so you may need to use Explorer to go out to your picture folders yourself, look at the thumbnails, and figure out which folder would be best.

caution

Be aware that stretched pictures often look blocky and ugly — especially if the original picture was small.

tip

If you set up a folder especially for your screen saver, you can name the files there with names that work like captions to your pictures ("Bryce Playing at the Park.jpg"). Then when you turn on the Show File Names option, anyone who's watching your screen saver will see the captions.

Part 5: Working with Digital Music

Task 77: Upgrading Windows Media Player

Task 78: Playing Music CDs

Task 79: Copying Music from a CD to Your Hard Drive

Task 80: Identifying Your Album Name, Artist, and Tracks

Task 81: Finding and Playing Music in Your Media Library

Task 82: Searching for Music to Add to Your Media Library

Task 83: Adding and Viewing Song Lyrics

Task 84: Creating and Listening to a Playlist

Task 85: Downloading Music from the Internet

Task 86: Tuning in to Internet Radio

Task 87: Copying Music to a Portable Music Player

Task 88: Creating Your Own Audio CD

Task 89: Duplicating an Audio CD

Task 90: Making Windows Media Player Beautiful with Skins

Task 77

Upgrading Windows Media Player

Microsoft is continually updating the software that it includes with Windows. So it's likely that the version of Windows Media Player that was installed with Windows XP on your machine is not the latest and greatest. In this task, you'll find out where to go to get the latest version and how to download it and install it. As of this writing, the current version is Windows Media Player 9. That's what we'll use in all the Windows Media Player tasks in this book.

1. Select Start⇨Internet Explorer to open the Internet Explorer window.

2. Type this address into the Address line at the top of the window and hit Enter:

   `http://www.microsoft.com/windows/windowsmedia/`

3. Look for a link that says something like Download Windows Media Player. Click the link. Follow the instructions on the page to download the latest version of Windows Media Player for Windows XP. A File Download dialog appears (see Figure 77-1).

Figure 77-1: The File Download dialog.

4. Click the Save button. The standard Save As dialog appears.

5. Click the Desktop icon along the left side of the dialog and click Save. A progress dialog appears with a bar indicating how far along the download is. When the download is complete, your system should play a sound to let you know. You may need to close the progress window. You should find a new icon on your desktop.

6. Double-click the new icon. After a brief delay, the Setup Wizard for Windows Media Player appears.

7. Click Next. The License Agreement page appears (see Figure 77-2). Read through the agreement, and click the I Accept button. You now see a progress window as Windows Media Player is installed. When the install is complete, the Welcome to Windows Media Player page appears.

8. Click Next. The Select Your Privacy Options page appears (see Figure 77-3). Click to check or uncheck whatever options you like.

9. Click Next. The Customize the Installation Options page appears (see Figure 77-4). Click to uncheck any file types you *don't* want Windows Media Player to play automatically for you. Click Finish.

caution

If you are on a dial-up Internet connection, it may take as long as an hour to download the upgrade.

note

For Windows Media Player 9, the icon's name is MPSetupXP.

cross-reference

To find out how to upgrade Windows Movie Maker, see Task 91.

caution

Read carefully through the privacy options. Microsoft provides these options so that you maintain control of what information is shared with others and what is kept private.

note

Unless you make changes here, Windows Media Player will be the default player that is opened when you double-click to play a file of any of the types listed.

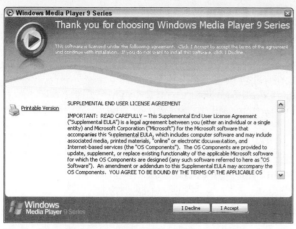

Figure 77-2: The License Agreement page.

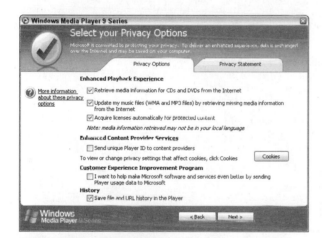

Figure 77-3: The Select Your Privacy Options window.

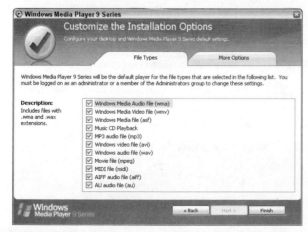

Figure 77-4: The Customize the Installation Options window.

Task **78**

Playing Music CDs

While most software you buy these days is distributed on CD-ROMs, the *other* kind of CD works in your computer too. That's right! Now you can toss out that $100 CD player. The new centerpiece of your stereo system is a $2,000 computer. What a deal! In this task you'll discover all the cool features Windows XP makes available for you to enjoy your favorite music CDs.

1. Insert a music CD in your CD-ROM drive. After a few seconds, you're likely to see the Audio CD window.

2. Click Play Audio CD and click OK.

3. Windows Media Player appears (see Figure 78-1) and immediately starts playing the CD you inserted.

   The name of the album and current song appears in the Video and Visualization pane. The album art appears along the right in the Media Information pane. Windows Media Player uses a free Internet service to identify CDs and download information about them. If it doesn't find your CD, you see Unknown Album.

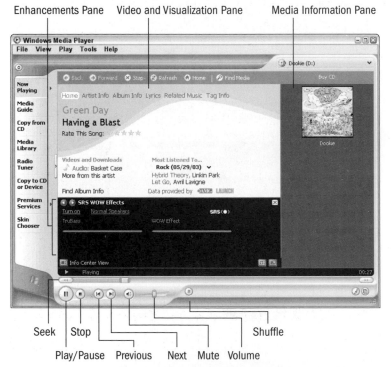

Figure 78-1: Windows Media Player plays your CD.

cross-reference

This task uses Windows Media Player 9. If you don't have this version of Windows Media Player, see Task 77 to find out how to download and install it.

note

If this window doesn't appear and Windows Media Player is launched instead, don't worry about it — that's what you wanted anyway. Just jump to Step 3. If nothing at all happens when you insert your CD, select Start⇨My Computer and double-click on the CD-ROM drive containing your music CD.

tip

If Windows Media Player on your computer doesn't look like the Figure 78-2, then it might be in Skin mode. Hit Ctrl+1 to switch back to Full mode.

tip

If you don't see the Media Information pane, choose View⇨Now Playing Options⇨Show Media Information. If you don't see the Enhancements pane, choose View⇨Enhancements⇨Show Enhancements. If the Video and Visualization pane doesn't look right, choose View⇨Info Center View⇨Always Show.

cross-reference

If Windows Media Player doesn't find your album and track names, see Task 80 to find out how to look them up yourself or enter them manually.

4. Notice the buttons in the lower-left portion of the window. Click the Pause button (or hit Ctrl+P). Click it again to continue playback. Other buttons in the same area allow you to Stop, go to the Previous Track, go to the Next Track, and Mute. Beside these buttons is a Volume slider (you can also use F9 and F10 to decrease or increase the volume). Above the buttons, and stretching across the entire width of the window, is a Seek slider that lets you jump around in the current song.

5. To the right of the Volume slider is the Shuffle button. If shuffle is off, your songs are played in the order they appear on the CD. If it is on, they will play in a random order. If you want to keep playing the CD after all the songs are played, there's no button, but you can select it from the menus: Play⇨Repeat (or hit Ctrl+T).

6. Choose View⇨Now Playing Options⇨Show Playlist. The Playlist pane appears. You can click on a song title to jump to that song and play it.

7. Choose View⇨Enhancements⇨Show Enhancements. This removes the Enhancements pane and gives you more room to view the Video and Visualization pane (see Figure 78-2).

8. Along the top of the Video and Visualization pane, click the Artist Info, Album Info, Lyrics, Related Music, and Tag Info links, in turn. As you do you may find a surprising amount of information is available to peruse about the music you're listening to.

tip

If there are songs you don't like on your CD, click to select them (use the Ctrl key to select more than one), right-click and choose Disable Selected Tracks from the pop-up menu. The disabled tracks will appear gray and won't be played. Windows Media Player will even remember this setting the next time you insert this CD.

tip

Choose View⇨Visualizations⇨ Alchemy⇨Random. The Video and Visualization pane now shows a big light show called a *visualization*. It is an animated, abstract graphical display that responds to the music. It can be quite mesmerizing. You can choose View⇨Visualizations from the menus to select different visualizations.

Playlist Pane

Figure 78-2: Turning the Playlist pane on and the Enhancements pane off.

Copying Music from a CD to Your Hard Drive

cross-reference

This task uses Windows Media Player 9. If you don't have this version of Windows Media Player, see Task 77 to find out how to download and install it.

tip

If nothing happens when you insert the CD, select Start⇨ My Computer and double-click on the CD-ROM drive containing the music CD. Another option is to choose Start⇨ All Programs⇨Windows Media Player.

tip

Be sure you have the correct album name and track titles identified before you copy the music to your hard drive. Otherwise, it'll be difficult for you to find this album again on your hard drive. If any of this information is incorrect (or if you just have values like Unknown Album and Track 1, Track 2, etc.), see Task 80 to find out how to look up the right information or enter it yourself.

I t's nice to be able to pop a CD into your computer and listen to it. But wouldn't it be nicer if you could listen to it *without* popping in the CD? You can — all you have to do is copy the songs on your CD to your hard drive. You can even copy while you're listening. Then, before the CD is done playing, you'll have all the songs transferred. Put that CD away — you won't be needing it anymore!

1. Insert a music CD in your computer. If the Audio CD window appears, choose Play Audio CD and then click OK. Windows Media Player opens.

2. The taskbar is on the left edge of the window with Now Playing at the top. Click the third item down — Copy from CD (see Figure 79-1).

Taskbar

Figure 79-1: The Copy from CD option in Windows Media Player.

3. The check marks beside each track indicate that you want to copy that track to your hard drive. If there are any you *don't* want to copy, clear their check boxes.

4. If you want to listen while you copy, double-click the song you want to begin listening to.

5. Click the Copy Music button at the top of the window. If this is the first time you've tried to copy music to your hard drive, you may see the Copy Options dialog appear. If you do, follow these steps:

a. Read the dialog and select one of the radio buttons indicating whether or not you want to add copy protection to the music you copy.

b. Click the check box at the bottom indicating that you understand that music copied from CDs is protected by law.

c. Click Next. On the second page, you are asked if you would like to change the file type and settings used for storing music on your hard drive. Select an option.

d. Click Finish. If you chose to change your settings, an Option dialog appears, allowing you to make those changes.

6. Each song is copied in turn (see Figure 79-2) until all those you requested are complete.

cross-reference

To find out how to access your music in the Media Library, see Task 81.

note

It is perfectly legal for you to copy music that you own to your hard drive for your own personal use. However, it is *not* legal to copy a CD you don't own to your hard drive. It's also illegal to give files you copied to your hard drive to others who don't own the music already.

Figure 79-2: The music is being copied to the hard drive.

7. In the future, you can access the copied songs through the Media Library.

Task **79**

Task 80

Identifying Your Album Name, Artist, and Tracks

When you insert a CD into your computer, Windows Media Player looks up your CD on a free Internet service called All Media Guide (AMG, www.allmusic.com). (Of course, you have to be connected to the Internet for this to happen.) If your CD is found, Windows Media Player downloads the album name, artist, and track names and displays that information. However, AMG, unfortunately, doesn't have information for every CD ever produced. So you may insert some CDs that it can't find. Here you'll discover how to look up your album manually by name or by artist and how to type in your own information. Of course, typing the information in yourself is a bit tedious (especially for foreign language or classical CDs), but once you do, Windows Media Player always remembers the information and recognizes your CD.

cross-reference

This task uses Windows Media Player 9. If you don't have this version of Windows Media Player, see Task 77 to find out how to download and install it.

1. Click on Copy from CD — the third item down in the taskbar along the left side or your window. A blank list of useless information appears.

2. Click the Find Album Info button in the upper-right portion of the window, above the list. A box opens up in the bottom part of the window, titled Search for Album Information (see Figure 80-1). This part of the window works like a wizard with Previous and Next buttons.

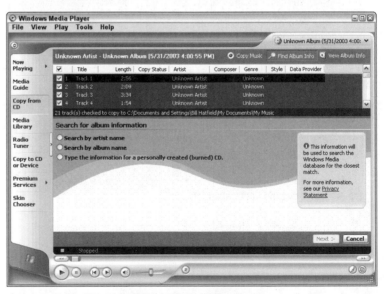

Figure 80-1: The Search for Album Information page.

3. Select one of the three options presented. If you are sure your album won't be found, jump to Step 7. If you choose either of the search options, a text box will appear where you can type what you'd like to search for.

4. Type the name (or part of the name) of your album or its artist. Click Next. A list appears with all the matches and approximate matches. If you see the correct album or artist, click the radio button next to the name. Click Next.

5. If it was the artist you found, a list of the artist's albums is presented. If you see your album, select it and click Next.

6. Once you've identified an album, click Finish to apply that album's information to this CD.

7. If you choose Type the Information and click Next, you are presented with text boxes for entering all the information (see Figure 80-2). Type in all the information, scrolling down as necessary.

Figure 80-2: Entering the information for your CD.

8. When you are finished, click Next. The information is presented to you to look over one last time.

9. If it is correct, click Finish. You are returned to the primary window where all the tracks are listed. From here you can either click Copy Music to copy tracks to your hard drive or you can click Now Playing at the top of the list of links on the left to just listen to your CD.

tip

If at any time during the search process you don't find what you want, click the Search Again button to return to the initial page. Here you can either start another search or choose to type in the information.

tip

Click the Performer and/or Composer links to add a column of text boxes for each song. This allows you to enter different artist names for each song for soundtracks and other multi-artist albums.

cross-reference

For more information on playing a CD, see Task 78. To find out how to copy tracks to your hard drive, see Task 79.

Task 81

Finding and Playing Music in Your Media Library

cross-reference

This task uses Windows Media Player 9. If you don't have this version of Windows Media Player, see Task 77 to find out how to download and install it.

cross-reference

For more information on playing music through Windows Media Player, see Task 78.

cross-reference

To find out more about the Radio option, see Task 86.

note

If this is the first time you've gone to the Media Library, you may see a dialog that asks if you want to search your computer for media. Click No. You can always search later.

Windows Media Player is more than a CD player. It also helps you organize all your electronically stored music with a handy, easy-to-use interface — the Media Library. In this task you'll get a tour of the Media Library and discover how to use it to find just the music you want to hear.

1. If Windows Media Player isn't already running, select Start⇨ All Programs⇨Windows Media Player.

2. The easiest way to begin playing music from your Media Library is by using the drop-down list box that is always in the upper-right corner of the Windows Media Player window. Click it to see a list of all the albums and playlists you have. Select one and it begins playing.

3. For more options, click Media Library on the taskbar on the left edge of the window.

   The window now is divided in two, with a list on the left. In the list are seven items: Now Playing, All Music, All Video, Other Media, My Playlists, Auto Playlists, Radio, and Premium Services (see Figure 81-1).

Figure 81-1: The Media Library in Windows Media Player.

4. Double-click the All Music item in the Tree view on the left to open it (if it isn't already opened). Under All Music, you see three items: Album, Artist, and Genre. These items provide you with easy access to all the music in your media library.

5. Double-click Genre to see the different genres of music in your library. Now click on one of the genres displayed (see Figure 81-2). You'll see a list on the right of all the songs in your library in that genre.

Figure 81-2: Listing all the songs in the Rock genre.

6. Double-click one of the songs on the right. The song begins playing.

7. Double-click Artist to see the different artists in your library. Click one of them. Again, you see all the music by that artist on the right. You can do the same for Album.

8. Click Search at the top of the window. A Search text box appears at the top of the window. Type one or more words to search for, and hit Enter (or click Find Now). Windows Media Player searches the song names, album names, and artists to find matches. The main window now displays all the songs that matched your search (see Figure 81-3).

Figure 81-3: Search results.

tip

To delete a song, right-click on the song and choose Delete from Library in the pop-up menu. A dialog may appear asking if you want to delete the song from the library only or if you also want to delete it from the hard drive. Choose an option and click OK.

cross-reference

There are two kinds of searches you can do in Windows Media Player. The one described in this task allows you to search through your Media Library to find a song you're looking for. Task 82 describes how to search your hard drive for songs to add to the Media Library.

tip

The results of your search actually appear as an item called Search Results, which you can see in the list on the left. If you want to keep the search results, you can store them as a playlist for later reference. Just right-click on Search Results and click Save as New Playlist. Name the playlist whatever you like.

cross-reference

To discover how to create your own playlists and listen to the songs on a playlist, see Task 84.

Searching for Music to Add to Your Media Library

cross-reference

This task uses Windows Media Player 9. If you don't have this version of Windows Media Player, see Task 77 to find out how to download and install it.

caution

There are two kinds of searches you can do in Windows Media Player. The one described in this task searches your hard drive for songs to add to the Media Library. Task 81 describes how to search through your Media Library to find a song you're looking for.

If you've been using your machine for a while, perhaps downloading music from the Internet or sharing music with friends, you may have music files scattered in various places throughout your hard drive. Of course, the point of the Media Library is to give you one place where you can go to access and organize all the music you have on your computer. In this task, you'll find out how you can tell Windows Media Player to search your hard drive (or parts of it) to locate music files and add them to the Media Library.

1. If Windows Media Player isn't already running, select Start⇨ All Programs⇨Windows Media Player.

2. Click Media Library on the taskbar on the left edge of the window (see Figure 82-1).

Figure 82-1: The Media Library in Windows Media Player.

3. Select Tools⇨Search For Media Files (or hit the F3 key). The Add to Media Library by Searching Computer window appears (see Figure 82-2).

Figure 82-2: The Add to Media Library by Searching Computer window.

4. Use the Search option drop-down list box to choose where you'd like to search. Use the Look in Text Box with the Browse Button option to specify a folder where the search should begin. Click to select the New Files Only radio button.

5. Click Search. The progress window shows how far along the search is (see Figure 82-3).

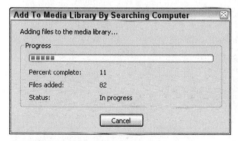

Figure 82-3: The progress window.

6. Click Close on the status window when the search is complete.

7. Click All Audio in the list at the left of the window. Scroll down your list on the right, and look for newly added items. Double-click to listen to them.

caution

If you search your entire hard drive, don't be surprised to find music, video, and sound effects files from games that have been added to your Media Library.

cross-reference

See Task 81 for more information on using the Media Library to organize and locate your songs.

83

Adding and Viewing Song Lyrics

Some people love music for the music and couldn't care less about the lyrics. Others have to be able to understand every line or they can't enjoy the song. For those of you who are more lyrically oriented, Windows Media Player makes it possible for you to keep a song's lyrics with the song. In this task, you find out how to add lyrics to a song and then how to view the lyrics when the song is played.

1. If Windows Media Player isn't already running, select Start⇨ All Programs⇨Windows Media Player.

2. Click Media Library on the taskbar on the left edge of the window (see Figure 83-1).

Figure 83-1: The Media Library in Windows Media Player.

3. In the list on the left, double-click All Music and then on Artist, Album, or Genre to locate the song you want to add lyrics to. When you locate the song, double-click to play it.

cross-reference

This task uses Windows Media Player 9. If you don't have this version of Windows Media Player, see Task 77 to find out how to download and install it.

cross-reference

For more information on navigating the Media Library, see Task 81.

4. Click Now Playing on the taskbar on the left edge of the window.

5. Along the top of the window there are a series of links: Home, Artist Info, Album Info, Lyrics, Related Music, and Tag Info. Click Lyrics. (See Figure 83-2.)

Figure 83-2: The lyrics.

6. Click Add Lyrics. A text box appears where you can type lyrics for the song.

7. Locate the lyrics to the song and type them in. Hit Enter when you want to go to a new line.

8. Click Save Lyrics when you are finished.

tip

Looking for lyrics? Often you can find them included in the booklet that came with the CD. You can also check Web sites like www.purelyrics.com or just go to www.google.com and search for the song title, the artist and the word **lyrics**. Between record company sites, band sites, and fan sites, it's usually pretty easy to find lyrics.

tip

If you found the lyrics on a Web site, you should be able to avoid the typing by simply selecting the lyrics, copying them to the clipboard with Ctrl+C, and then pasting them in the text box with Ctrl+V.

Creating and Listening to a Playlist

cross-reference
This task uses Windows Media Player 9. If you don't have this version of Windows Media Player, see Task 77 to find out how to download and install it.

cross-reference
To find out more about the Media Library, see Task 81.

You can use playlists to create a collection of songs from a variety of different albums. When you create a playlist, you identify exactly what songs should be in it and what order they should play in. For example, you could create a mellow playlist that contains all your favorite relaxing tunes. Or you could create a best-of playlist for your favorite band. In this task you'll find out how to create a playlist, add songs to it, re-order the songs, and then play it whenever you like.

1. If Windows Media Player isn't already running, select Start⇨ All Programs⇨Windows Media Player.

2. Click Media Library on the taskbar on the left edge of the window (see Figure 84-1).

Figure 84-1: The Media Library in Windows Media Player.

3. Click the Playlists button in the upper-left corner of the window. A menu appears. Select New Playlist. The New Playlist window appears (see Figure 84-2).

4. Type the name of the playlist you'd like to create in the Playlist Name text box.

5. Select an option in the View Media Library By drop-down list box. You can view by artist, by album, by genre, or virtually any combination. After you select an option, the appropriate list appears in the list box below.

6. Use the list box on the left to locate songs that you want to add to the playlist. Click on a song to add it to the playlist — the list box on the right shows the playlist songs.

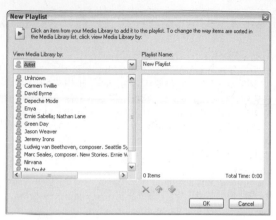

Figure 84-2: The New Playlist window.

7. To delete a song from the playlist, click the song in the list box on the right and then click Delete (the button at the bottom with the big red X).

8. To change the order of the songs in the playlist, click to select a song in the list box on the right and then use the Up and Down buttons (the arrows at the bottom of the window) to change that song's position.

9. When you are finished creating your playlist, click OK. Your playlist appears in the Media Library under My Playlists (see Figure 84-3).

Figure 84-3: The new playlist appears under My Playlists.

10. To play a playlist, simply double-click on its icon.

tip

To change your playlist's name, right-click on the playlist in the list on the left and choose Rename from the pop-up menu. To change the songs in the playlist or their order, right-click and choose Edit.

tip

To delete a playlist, right-click the playlist name and choose Delete from the pop-up menu.

Downloading Music from the Internet

A lot has changed since the wild and wooly days of Napster. Today there is a lot more attention paid to artists' rights and fair compensation for work. But that doesn't mean that you can't get the music you want or that it'll be too expensive to bother with — far from it! In this task you'll discover how you can use Windows Media Player to surf the Web, find, pay for, and download music.

1. If Windows Media Player isn't already running, select Start➪ All Programs➪Windows Media Player.

2. Click Media Guide on the taskbar on the left edge of the window (see Figure 85-1). This part of Windows Media Player essentially works exactly like a Web browser.

Figure 85-1: The Media Guide in Windows Media Player.

3. Click Music in the list of links along the left-hand side of the page. Here you'll see featured music and music videos that you can download. Scroll down a bit and you'll see a group of links along the left where you can select a genre and subgenre that you like and then look at the bands listed (see Figure 85-2).

Figure 85-2: Viewing Rock/Alternative bands that begin with A.

4. When you find an artist that you are interested in, click the artist's name and you will see an Artist Profile. On the right side of the page is a list box labeled Available Media. You can scroll through this list to find songs and entire albums available for purchase and download.

5. Click on a song or album that you'd like to download. A new browser window opens and shows a shopping cart with the song or album in it. (This cart and how it works depends on the provider you are purchasing from.)

6. Follow the steps for checking out, entering billing and shipping information, and downloading. These steps will be different for different providers.

7. When you download the file, save it to your My Music folder (which is inside My Documents).

8. When the download is complete, there's still one step left. You must have Windows Media Player add the new song to your Media Library. Select File⇨Add To Media Library⇨Add File or Playlist. An Open dialog appears. Make your way to your My Music folder, find the file, and double-click it. The song is added to your Media Library.

cross-reference

See Task 83 to find out how to add lyrics to your newly downloaded song.

Tuning in to Internet Radio

Listening to your vast collection of digitized music can be quite satisfying. But after awhile you might miss the friendly voice of a disk jockey. Not to worry! Radio, too, has gone digital — and Windows Media Player is equipped to make it easy to access radio. You can find hundreds of radio stations on the Internet, playing virtually any type of music you enjoy (and some you likely won't enjoy). Many of the stations are actually traditional radio stations from cities throughout the world, while others are Internet-only stations. If you're looking for a friendly voice and cool tunes to accompany you throughout the day, you'll find no lack of options here.

1. If Windows Media Player isn't already running, select Start⇨ All Programs⇨Windows Media Player.

2. Click Radio Tuner on the taskbar on the left edge of the window (see Figure 86-1). This is the opening page for the Radio Tuner. Notice under the Featured Stations is a bar called My Stations. If you've never listened to Internet radio before, this will be empty. You can add stations you like to this list so that you can easily get to them here in the future. It is sort of a Favorites for Internet radio.

Figure 86-1: The Radio Tuner.

3. At this point you can simply select one of the featured stations, click on a favorite genre, or type in keywords to search for. Click your favorite genre. A new page displays a list of the many, many stations that play music of that genre (see Figure 86-2).

Figure 86-2: The stations that play rock.

4. Click on a station. A description of the station opens up, along with a few links. The first link is Add to My Stations. As you might expect, this adds the station you're looking at to the list you'll see when you first come to the Radio Tuner. It also adds the station to your Media Library under Radio Tuner Presets.

Usually you'll also see a Play link here. Some stations will only play through their own Web site, so the link will say Visit Website to Play.

5. Find a station with a Play link, and click it. It will take some time (sometimes 30 seconds or longer) to begin hearing the station.

Often, Windows Media Player opens the station's Web site for you to browse. Minimize the Web browser and click Now Playing in the taskbar. You will see the name of the song and artist.

Some broadband stations may even have video content that is displayed through Windows Media Player. If so, it will play automatically.

6. Try out several different stations and save the best to My Stations so that you can find them again later.

cross-reference

Most stations don't broadcast video, but the visualizations work with radio just as well as they do with recorded music. To find out how to see visualizations, see Task 78.

tip

Looking for a video radio station? Check out The Basement (300K) from Sydney, Australia.

Copying Music to a Portable Music Player

cross-reference

This task uses Windows Media Player 9. If you don't have this version of Windows Media Player, see Task 77 to find out how to download and install it.

caution

Windows Media Player doesn't have the ability to save files in MP3 format unless you purchase an MP3 encoder for it. So make sure your portable music player supports Microsoft's WMA format.

Portable music players (often referred to as MP3 players) are everywhere. Some newer devices actually contain a small hard drive and can hold 10GB, 20GB, or more. In addition, the proliferation of Pocket PC devices provides yet another platform for storing and listening to music. Windows Media Player makes it easy to copy music from your Media Library to whatever device you have so you can enjoy your music anywhere.

1. If Windows Media Player isn't already running, select Start⇨ All Programs⇨Windows Media Player.

2. Click Copy to CD or Device on the taskbar on the left edge of the window (see Figure 87-1). The window is divided into two halves. The left half represents the music you have on your computer right now. The right half represents where you want to copy the music to. There are drop-down list boxes over each half, indicating exactly what is represented by each half of the window.

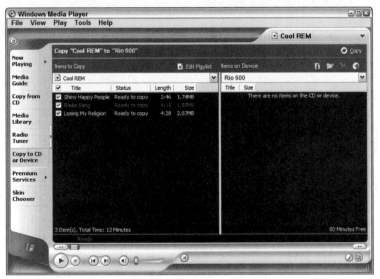

Figure 87-1: Copy to CD or Device in Windows Media Player.

cross-reference

To find out how to create your own playlists and get more details on how to use the Edit Playlist window, see Task 84.

3. Click the drop-down list box at the top of the left half of the window. Select a playlist that contains the songs you want to copy. When you do, the songs from that playlist appear on the left half of the window.

4. Use the check boxes beside each song to indicate whether or not that song should be copied.

5. If you want to reorder the songs or add songs to the playlist, click the Edit Playlist button above the list on the left. The Edit Playlist window appears (see Figure 87-2), and you can use it to add, delete, and re-order the songs in the playlist.

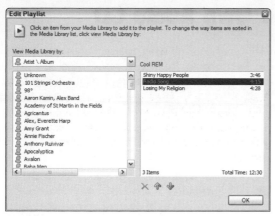

Figure 87-2: The Edit Playlist window.

6. Plug your portable music player into your computer, if it isn't already plugged in.

7. Click the drop-down list box at the top of the right half of the window. Select the name of your portable music player.

8. Click Copy in the upper-right corner of the window. Each song is copied to the device (see Figure 87-3).

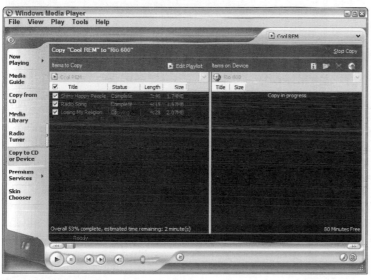

Figure 87-3: Copying songs to the device.

9. Check your device to make sure all the songs are there and that they copied correctly.

---

tip

To find out how to connect your portable music player to your computer, see the manual that came with your portable music player.

caution

If your device doesn't appear in the drop-down list box on the right of the window, you may need to install a driver for your portable music device. The driver probably came on a CD when you purchased the device. You can also check out the Support section of the device manufacturer's Web site.

tip

You can also use Windows Media Player to organize and manage songs on your portable device. Buttons above the right side of the window allow you to delete songs, create new folders, and get additional information about a song.

Task 88

Creating Your Own Audio CD

You created a great playlist for all your relaxing, melancholy songs to help you unwind at the end of the day. Now you're getting ready to go on a trip, and you'd love to be able to listen to your playlist on the plane. Your computer simply won't fit in the carry-on. What do you do? Time to create (or *burn*) your own audio CD that you can listen to in any CD player — including portable ones!

1. If Windows Media Player isn't already running, select Start↩ All Programs↩Windows Media Player.

2. Click Copy to CD or Device on the taskbar on the left edge of the window (see Figure 88-1). The window is divided into two halves. The left half represents the music you have on your computer right now. The right half represents where you want to copy the music to. There are drop-down list boxes over each half indicating exactly what is represented by each half of the window.

cross-reference

This task uses Windows Media Player 9. If you don't have this version of Windows Media Player, see Task 77 to find out how to download and install it.

tip

Be sure to label the CD with a pen or a printed label so that you don't forget its contents.

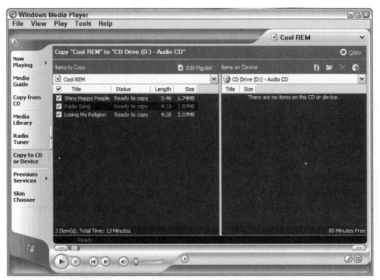

Figure 88-1: Copy to CD or Device in Windows Media Player.

cross-reference

To find out how to create your own playlists and get more details on how to use the Edit Playlist window, see Task 84.

caution

Notice that at the bottom of the left side of the window, something that looks like this: 8 Item(s), Total Time: 37 Minutes. As you check and uncheck songs, keep an eye on this information. You can only transfer about 80 minutes worth of songs to a single audio CD.

3. Click the drop-down list box at the top of the left half of the window. Select a playlist that contains the songs you want to copy. When you do, the songs from that playlist appear on the left half of the window.

4. Use the check boxes beside each song to indicate whether or not that song should be copied.

5. If you want to re-order the songs or add songs to the playlist, click the Edit Playlist button above the list on the left. The Edit Playlist window appears (see Figure 88-2), and you can use it to add, delete, and re-order the songs in the playlist.

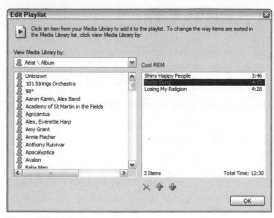

Figure 88-2: The Edit Playlist window.

6. Insert a blank CD into your CD-R or CD-RW drive. (If this causes a window to automatically appear, just close it.)

7. Click the drop-down list box at the top of the right half of the window. Select the CD-R or CD-RW drive where you inserted the blank CD.

8. Click Copy in the upper-right corner of the window. First, each song is converted into the appropriate format for an audio CD. Then each song is copied to the CD (see Figure 88-3). After the last song is copied, the CD will take a few seconds to close and the copy will be complete. The CD is ejected.

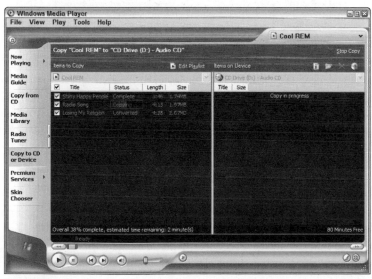

Figure 88-3: Copying the files to the CD.

caution

This process will only work if you have a CD-R or CD-RW drive on your machine, allowing you to create your own CDs.

caution

Although you can play a CD-RW in your computer's CD drive, standard CD players may not recognize it.

cross-reference

To find out how to duplicate a CD, see Task 89.

tip

If you are writing files to a CD-RW (which allows you to make changes after you copy files to the CD), you can use the buttons above the right side of the window to delete songs, create new folders, and get additional information about a song.

Task 89

Duplicating an Audio CD

There's no Duplicate Audio CD option in Windows Media Player. Maybe Microsoft didn't want to take heat for making it too easy to pirate copyrighted music. Regardless of the reasons, it is possible — and not too difficult — to duplicate an audio CD.

Of course, we don't endorse piracy, but suppose you have a CD that you listen to a lot in your car. The heavy use and the unpredictable environment are likely to lead to scratches on the CD and ultimately an unplayable disk. So, before that happens, duplicate it. Then use the duplicated CD and put the original someplace safe. If you end up with scratches and the like, toss the old CD, and make another copy from your original. This is totally legal and a very good idea.

1. Follow the steps in Task 79 to copy all the songs from your source CD to your hard drive.

2. Click Copy to CD or Device on the taskbar on the left edge of the window. The window is divided into two halves. The left half represents the music you have on your computer right now. The right half represents where you want to copy the music to. There are drop-down list boxes over each half, indicating exactly what is represented by each half of the window.

3. Click the drop-down list box at the top of the left half of the window. Select the name of the album you just copied to the hard drive. When you do, the songs from that album appear on the left half of the window (see Figure 89-1).

cross-reference

This task uses Windows Media Player 9. If you don't have this version of Windows Media Player, see Task 77 to find out how to download and install it.

Figure 89-1: Selecting the CD you just copied to the hard drive.

4. Insert a blank CD into your CD-R or CD-RW drive. (If this causes a window to automatically appear, just close it.)

5. Click the drop-down list box at the top of the right half of the window. Select the CD-R or CD-RW drive where you inserted the blank CD.

6. Click Copy in the upper-right corner of the window. First, each song is converted into the appropriate format for an audio CD. Then each song is copied to the CD (see Figure 89-2). After the last song is copied, the CD will take a few seconds to close and the copy will be complete. The CD is ejected.

Figure 89-2: Copying songs to the CD.

caution

This process will only work if you have a CD-R or CD-RW drive on your machine, allowing you to create your own CDs.

cross-reference

To create a CD with your own mix of music on it, see Task 88.

tip

Be sure and label the CD either with a pen or a printed label so that you don't forget its contents.

Task 90

Making Windows Media Player Beautiful with Skins

Nothing is quite so personal to a serious music lover than his or her choice of favorite albums and songs. So why not make playing music a matter of personal expression too? That's the idea behind Windows Media Player skins. Skins can be applied to Windows Media Player to customize how it looks. A number of skins come with Windows XP, and you can download more. They change the color, size, and shape of the Windows Media Player window. Some are designed to make Windows Media Player unobtrusive, providing the most functionality with the least amount of screen real estate, while others are blatantly flamboyant and are more concerned with making a statement. In this task, you'll discover how to select and apply a skin and how to switch back to Full mode (the original appearance).

1. If Windows Media Player isn't already running, select Start⇨ All Programs⇨Windows Media Player.

2. Click Skin Chooser on the taskbar on the left edge of the window (see Figure 90-1). All the skins that came with Windows XP appear here; there are quite a few.

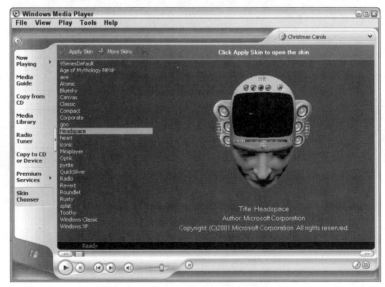

Figure 90-1: The Skin Chooser in Windows Media Player.

3. Click on each skin, in turn. The image at the right changes to show you what the skin looks like.

4. When you find a skin you like, click it and then click Apply Skin in the upper left of the window. Your Windows Media Player is immediately transformed (see Figure 90-2).

cross-reference

This task uses Windows Media Player 9. If you don't have this version of Windows Media Player, see Task 77 to find out how to download and install it.

caution

Skins don't typically make available all the features that are available when you are in Full mode. You can use your mouse to hover over the various buttons to see what they do.

tip

You may want to keep the skinned Windows Media Player on top of your running programs all the time so you have easy access to it. To do that, select Tools⇨Options from the menu, and on the Player tab, click the Display on Top When in Skin Mode check box.

tip

You might have noticed that odd blue square in the lower-right corner of the screen when Windows Media Player is in Skin mode. It is called an *anchor window*. When you click it, you get a pop-up menu with several options. However, this window doesn't really provide any features you can't access elsewhere, so you may want to click on it and choose Hide Anchor Window from its pop-up menu.

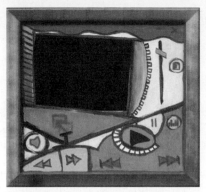

Figure 90-2: The Windows Media Player — transformed!

5. A pop-up menu is available in all skins when you right-click on buttons, links, or labels. This provides access to most of the commonly accessed features.

6. Click Switch to Full Mode in the pop-up menu. The familiar look and feel of Windows Media Player returns.

7. To download a new skin, follow these steps:

   a. Click More Skins in the upper-left portion of the window.

   b. Internet Explorer is launched to a Web page where new skins can be downloaded.

   c. Find a skin you like, and click on the link to download it.

   d. You may see a dialog that asks you to confirm that you want to download the skin. Click Yes.

   e. The Windows Media Download dialog appears (see Figure 90-3). The skin is automatically downloaded to the right location.

Figure 90-3: The Windows Media Download dialog.

   f. When the download is complete, the new skin appears in your list. Click the skin and click Apply Skin.

tip

Here's a keyboard shortcut for going back to Full mode when you are in Skin mode: Ctrl+1. Use Ctrl+2 to go from Full mode back to Skin mode again.

note

You must be connected to the Internet to download new skins.

cross-reference

The few buttons that appear on skins are used for controlling how music is played. For more information on these features, see Task 78.

Part 6: Working with Digital Movies

Task 91:   Upgrading Windows Movie Maker

Task 92:   Playing a Movie on DVD

Task 93:   Playing a Video File

Task 94:   Creating and Deleting Collections in Windows Movie Maker

Task 95:   Importing Clips and Other Items into Your Collections in Windows Movie Maker

Task 96:   Making Movies

Task 97:   Capturing Video from Your Camcorder

Task 98:   Capturing a Photograph from a Video

Task 99:   Capturing Live Video

Task 100: Splitting and Combining Video Clips

Task 101: Trimming a Video Clip

Task 102: Adding Transitions between Your Video Clips

Task 103: Adding Video Effects to Your Clips

Task 104: Adding Titles and Credits to Your Movie

Task 105: Adding Photographs to a Movie

Task 106: Adding Background Music and Sound Effects to a Movie

Task 107: Adding Narration to a Movie

Task 108: Saving a Movie to View on Your Computer

Task 109: Sending a Movie via Email

Task 91

Upgrading Windows Movie Maker

Windows Movie Maker is a great tool for editing your home movies. But the version that was installed on your machine with Windows XP may not have all the latest features. In this task, you'll learn where to go to get the latest version and how to download it and install it. As of this writing, the current version is Windows Movie Maker 2. That's what we'll use in all the Windows Media Player tasks in this book.

1. Select Start➪Internet Explorer to open the Internet Explorer window.

2. Type this address into the Address line at the top of the window and hit Enter:

   `http://www.microsoft.com/windowsxp/moviemaker/`

3. Look for a link that says something like Download Windows Movie Maker. Click the link. Follow the instructions on the page to download the latest version of Windows Movie Maker. A File Download dialog appears (see Figure 91-1).

Figure 91-1: The File Download dialog.

4. Click the Save button. The standard Save As dialog appears. Click the Desktop icon along the left side of the dialog, and click Save. A progress dialog appears with a bar indicating how far along the download is. When the download is complete, your system should play a sound to let you know. You may need to close the progress window. You should find a new icon on your desktop.

5. Double-click the new icon. After a brief delay, you should see Setup Wizard for Windows Movie Maker.

6. Click Next. The License Agreement page appears (see Figure 91-2).

7. Read through the agreement, and click the I Accept the Terms in the License Agreement radio button.

caution

If you are on a dial-up Internet connection, it may take as long as an hour to download the upgrade.

note

For Windows Movie Maker 2, the Desktop icon's name is mm20enu.

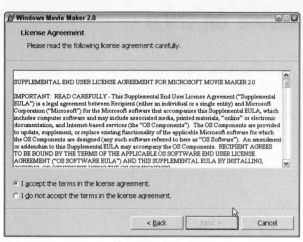

Figure 91-2: The License Agreement page.

8. Click Next. The Ready to Install the Program page appears.

9. Click Install. You now see the Installing Windows Movie Maker page (see Figure 91-3). When the install is complete, the Setup Wizard Complete page appears. Click Finish.

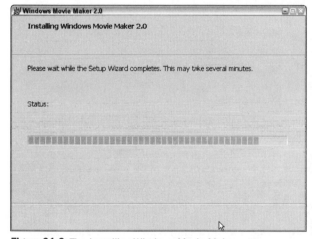

Figure 91-3: The Installing Windows Movie Maker page.

10. To open Windows Movie Maker, select Start⇨All Programs⇨ Windows Movie Maker. The Windows Movie Maker main window appears.

cross-reference

To find out how to upgrade Windows Media Player, see Task 77.

Playing a Movie on DVD

DVDs are everywhere — their quality is much higher than videotape and they last forever. Many computers these days come with a DVD drive. If you have a DVD drive (or you buy one to add to your system), then you can actually watch DVD movies on your PC monitor. Here's how you do it:

1. Insert a DVD in your DVD drive. After a few seconds, you're likely to see a window (see Figure 92-1). (If this window doesn't appear and Windows Media Player is launched instead, don't worry about it — that's what you wanted anyway. Just jump to Step 3.)

Figure 92-1: You've inserted a DVD. What do you want to do about it?

2. Click Play DVD Video using Windows Media Player and click OK.

3. Windows Media Player appears (see Figure 92-2). It immediately starts playing the DVD you inserted.

4. Often DVD movies begin with an opening sequence and then show a menu. From the menu you can usually choose to play the movie, jump to a specific chapter, or view the special features or bonus materials included on the DVD. On this menu you can use your mouse pointer to point at the selection you want and click to select it.

5. Click the Pause button in the lower-left portion of the window. Click it again to continue playback. Other buttons in the same area allow you to stop, jump to the previous chapter, jump to the next chapter, and mute. Beside these buttons is a Volume slider and above them is a Seek slider, which let's you jump around anywhere in the movie.

6. When the video is playing, you'll notice a button below where the video appears labeled Menu. Click this to return to the DVD's opening menu. You can then choose an option there or click the Menu button again to resume playing where you left off.

7. Right-click on the video playing in the middle of the window. A pop-up menu appears. Choose Video Size. You can use this menu to set the size of the video: 50% (half-size), 100% (normal size), or 200% (double size). You can also choose Full Screen from the pop-up menu to blow the video up as big as your monitor will allow.

cross-reference

This task uses Windows Media Player 9. If you don't have this version of Windows Media Player, see Task 77 to find out how to download and install it.

tip

If nothing at all happens when you insert your DVD, select Start⇨My Computer and double-click on the DVD drive containing your DVD. Another option is to choose Start⇨ All Programs⇨Windows Media Player.

tip

Put a check mark in the Always do the selected action? check box at the bottom of the window. Then, in the future when you insert a DVD, you'll go straight into Windows Media Player.

caution

Get an error about a missing *decoder*? A decoder is a little piece of software that Windows Media Player needs to play DVDs. Oddly, Windows XP doesn't come with a decoder. Microsoft counts on computer manufacturers (like Sony, HP, or Dell) to put one in. Usually they do. But if yours doesn't have one, the only way to get one is to buy one from a company that sells them (usually along with their own software for playing DVDs). Check out: www.national.com/ appinfo/dvd or www. intervideo.com.

Figure 92-2: Windows Media Player plays your DVD.

8. Choose View➪Enhancements➪Show Enhancements. A box opens up beneath the video (see Figure 92-3). This box can be used to set a variety of audio and video options. Click the arrows in the upper-left corner of this new box to cycle through all the options.

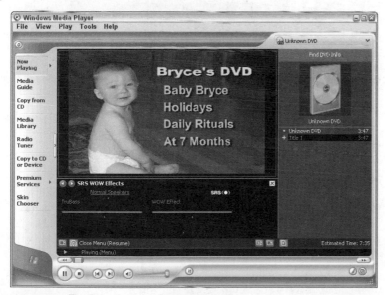

Figure 92-3: The Enhancements box appears.

Task **93**

Playing a Video File

Y ou can download video files from the Internet, or you can capture videos
from your video camera (as in Task 97). But video files are no good unless
you can watch them! In this task you'll find out how to do so.

1. If you are in Windows Explorer, you can simply double-click on a
   video file; Windows Media Player will be launched, and the video
   will begin to play.

2. Alternately, if you are already in Windows Media Player, choose
   File⇨Open. An Open dialog appears. Locate the file, click to select
   it, and click Open to begin playing the file (see Figure 93-1). Notice
   that the name of the video file appears in the lower-left corner of the
   window, just above the Seek slider.

cross-reference

This task uses Windows Media
Player 9. If you don't have this
version of Windows Media
Player, see Task 77 to find out
how to download and install it.

caution

"Windows Media Player is
currently unable to play DVD
video." This error often occurs
because your Windows desktop
resolution and/or color depth
are set too high. (See Task 41
to find out how to change these
settings.) Set your color depth
to Medium (16 bit) and then
try it. If it still fails, try setting
your resolution to 800 × 600
pixels.

tip

If Windows Media Player on
your computer doesn't look like
Figure 93-1, then it might be in
Skin mode. Hit Ctrl+1 to switch
back to Full mode.

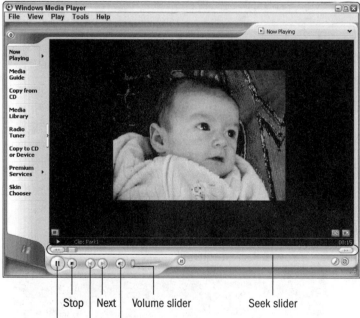

Figure 93-1: Playing the video file.

tip

If you prefer to use the keyboard, you can hit Ctrl+P to
pause/play the DVD, Ctrl+B
for previous chapter, and
Ctrl+F for the next chapter
(presumably standing for Back
and Forward). Use F9 and F10
for volume up and down and
F8 for mute.

caution

The Full Screen option may not
work, depending on your video
card and your video settings.

3. Notice the buttons in the lower-left portion of the window. Click the
   Pause button. Click it again to continue playback. Other buttons in
   the same area allow you to stop, jump to the previous chapter, jump
   to the next chapter, and mute. Beside these buttons is a Volume slider
   and above them is a Seek slider, which let's you jump around anywhere
   in the movie.

4. Right-click on the video playing in the middle of the window. A pop-
   up menu appears. Choose Video Size (see Figure 93-2). You can use
   this menu to set the size of the video: 50% (half-size), 100% (normal

size), or 200% (double size). You can also choose Full Screen from the pop-up menu to blow the video up as big as your monitor will allow.

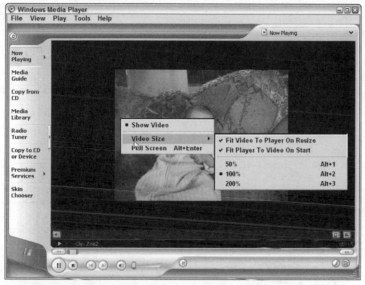

Figure 93-2: The video pop-up menu.

5. Choose View⇨Enhancements⇨Show Enhancements. A box opens up beneath the video (see Figure 93-3). This box can be used to set a variety of audio and video options. Click the arrows in the upper-left corner of this new box to cycle through all the options.

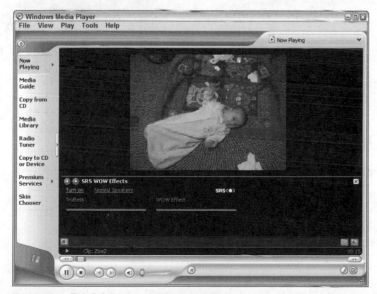

Figure 93-3: The Enhancements box appears.

Task **94**

Creating and Deleting Collections in Windows Movie Maker

cross-reference

This task uses Windows Movie Maker 2. If you don't have this version of Windows Movie Maker, see Task 91 to find out how to download and install it.

cross-reference

To find out how to import items into your collections, see Task 95.

Microsoft's Windows Movie Maker, which comes with Windows XP, is a great tool for capturing, organizing, editing, and producing your videos. In this task, you'll discover how to create and delete collections. A *collection* is simply a folder that holds stuff you might use in a movie — like video clips, still pictures, narration, music, sound effects, and so on. With collections, you can organize your materials any way you want. You can even put folders inside other folders, if you like.

1. Open Windows Movie Maker by selecting Start⇨All Programs⇨ Windows Movie Maker. The Windows Movie Maker main window appears (see Figure 94-1).

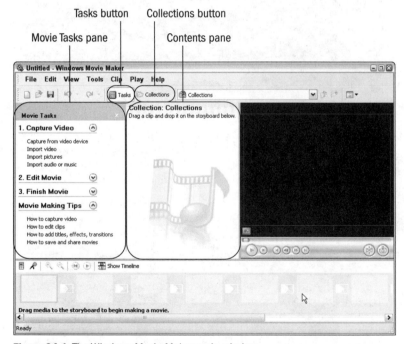

Figure 94-1: The Windows Movie Maker main window.

2. Click the Collections button. The window changes (see Figure 94-2).

tip

To see the Movie Tasks pane again, click the Tasks button.

Collections pane

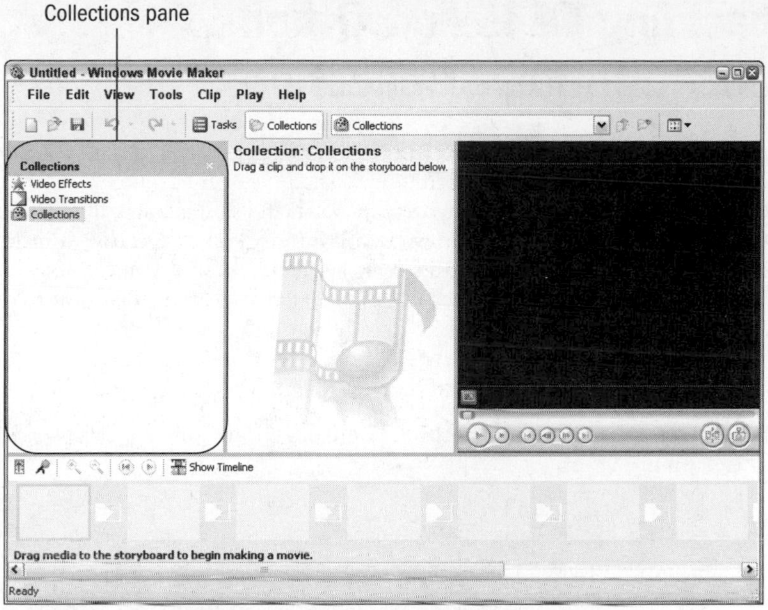

Figure 94-2: The Collections pane replaces the Movie Tasks pane.

The Collections pane displays a list. At the top is Video Effects and Video Transitions. Beneath is a folder called Collections. All your collections will be created within the Collections folder.

3. To create a new collection folder, right-click on the Collections folder and choose New Collection from the pop-up menu. A new folder appears below the Collections folder. Type a name and hit Enter.

4. To create a new collection folder within an existing collection folder, right-click on the existing collection folder and choose New Collection from the pop-up menu. The new folder will appear under the existing folder. Type a name and hit Enter.

5. Click to select a collection folder. When you do, the contents of the folder (if there are any) appear in the Contents pane.

6. To delete a collection and all its contents, right-click on the folder and choose Delete from the pop-up menu.

note

Deleting a collection and its contents simply removes them from Windows Movie Maker. It does not delete the files from your hard drive.

Task 95

Importing Clips and Other Items into Your Collections in Windows Movie Maker

cross-reference

This task uses Windows Movie Maker 2. If you don't have this version of Windows Movie Maker, see Task 91 to find out how to download and install it.

cross-reference

To find out how to capture video from your camcorder, see Task 97.

Collections provide a place for you to store all the things you will use to create your video masterpiece. But how do you import your video clips, music, and other files so they show up in your collections?

1. If Windows Movie Maker isn't already running, select Start⇨ All Programs⇨Windows Movie Maker. The Windows Movie Maker main window appears.

2. Click on the Collections button. The Collections pane appears (see Figure 95-1).

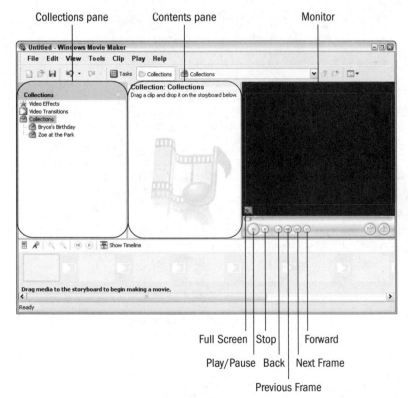

Figure 95-1: The Windows Movie Maker main window with the Collections pane.

3. To import a video clip, sound file, or other item into Windows Media Player:

    a. Click to select the collection folder in the Collections pane where you want to place the new file.

caution

Importing an item does not actually make a copy of the original file. It works more like a shortcut in Windows Explorer. That is, when you work with an item in your collection, it actually refers to the original item on your hard drive. Do not move, delete, or rename an item after you've imported it into a collection. If you do, Windows Media Player will not be able to find it and you'll have to import it again.

b. Choose File⇨Import into Collections from menu. The Import File dialog appears.

c. Locate the file you want to import. Click to select it, and then click Import. If you selected a video file, a new collection is created and the video file is imported and divided into clips for you to easily use. If the file you selected is a music file, sound effect file, or some other file, it is placed in the currently selected collection.

4. To delete a video clip or other item in a collection, click to select the item (hold the Ctrl key while clicking to select multiple items), and then hit the Delete key. The item(s) are removed from the collections folder, but not deleted from your system.

5. To move items from one collection to another:

a. Click on the collection folder that contains the items.

b. In the Contents pane, select an item by clicking on it, or select more than one by holding the Ctrl key down while you click.

c. Press and hold the left mouse button on one of the selected items.

d. Now drag your mouse to the desired collection folder in the Collections pane.

e. Release the button. The items or item is moved.

6. To play a video clip or other item in a collection, click on the collection folder containing the clip. In the Contents pane, click to select the item and then click the Play button on the Monitor.

7. To control how a clip is played:

- Pause stops the video where it is so that when you click Play again it picks up where it left off.

- Stop ends the video and starts over, so that if you then hit Play, the clip begins again at the start.

- Back and Forward cause you to jump to the previous clip or jump to the next clip.

- Previous Frame and Next Frame jump backward and forward one frame at a time.

- Full Screen blows up the video so it fills the screen.

tip

Alternately, you can hit Ctrl+I on the keyboard when you want to import an item into your collections.

tip

You can also use Ctrl+X to cut, Ctrl+C to copy, and Ctrl+V to paste items from one collection to another.

cross-reference

Check out Task 96 to discover how to create a movie using your clips.

Task 96

Making Movies

The first step is getting and organizing raw video, music, sound effects, narration, and so on. To find out how to do that, see Tasks 94 and 95. Once you have everything you need, it's magic time! Whether it's your son's first haircut or your daughter's first step, Windows Movie Maker can help you transform your home movies from ho-hum to wow in just a few simple steps.

1. If Windows Movie Maker isn't already running, open Windows Movie Maker by selecting Start⇨All Programs⇨Windows Movie Maker. The Windows Movie Maker main window appears.

2. Click on the Collections button. The Collections pane appears (see Figure 96-1).

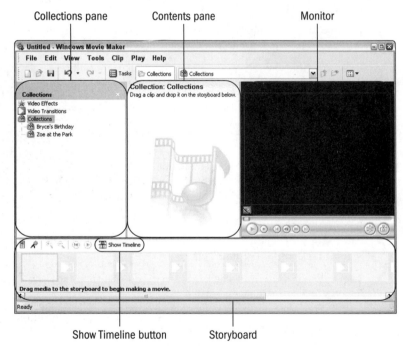

Collections pane   Contents pane   Monitor

Show Timeline button   Storyboard

Figure 96-1: The Windows Movie Maker main window with the Collections pane.

3. Select File⇨New⇨Project (or hit Ctrl+N). The Storyboard is cleared and you are ready to begin creating a new movie.

4. To add video clips to your movie:

   a. Click on the Collections folder in the Collections pane.

   b. In the Contents pane, select one clip by clicking on it or more than one by holding the Ctrl key down while you click.

   c. Press and hold the left mouse button on one of the selected clips.

   d. Drag your mouse to the Storyboard, and release the mouse button. The clip(s) are placed in the Storyboard.

cross-reference

This task uses Windows Movie Maker 2. If you don't have this version of Windows Movie Maker, see Task 91 to find out how to download and install it.

tip

A *project* in Windows Movie Maker refers to the work you do to create a movie. All this work is done in the Storyboard/ Timeline at the bottom of the window. The collections that appear in the top part of the window will stay the same from one project to the next.

tip

You can place a new clip between two existing clips in your movie. When dragging your mouse down to the Storyboard, drag it to the location where you want it placed. When you release the mouse button, it will appear there.

cross-reference

If you want to use just a portion of a clip in your movie, you can trim off stuff at the beginning and/or at the end by using trim points. See Task 101 to find out how.

5. To rearrange clips, just press and hold the left mouse button over the clip you'd like to move, move the mouse to where you'd like the clip to appear in the Storyboard, and then release the button. The clips are rearranged.

6. To remove a clip from your movie, right-click on the clip and choose Delete. This removes the clip from the movie, but it's still in your collection so you can retrieve it and add it back if you need to.

7. To watch a clip from your movie, click on the clip and then click the Play button on the Monitor. This plays the clip and then goes on to play the rest of the movie. To watch the entire movie, click Stop and then push Play on the Monitor.

8. To view the Timeline, click the Show Timeline button. This changes the Storyboard into a Timeline (see Figure 96-2). Instead of each clip appearing in a square box, the clips appear as rectangles of different lengths along a timeline so you can get a more precise view of how long each clip will last. Use the Zoom In and Zoom Out buttons to stretch or shrink the timeline. To go back to the Storyboard view, click the Show Storyboard button.

tip

As you work on creating your movie, you can freely jump back and forth between the Storyboard and the Timeline, using whichever view is most convenient for what you want to do.

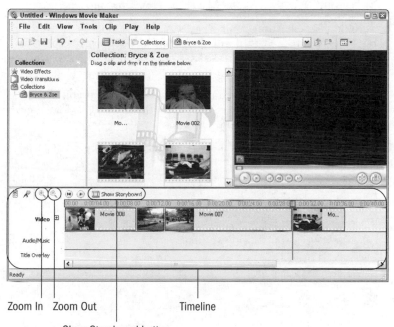

Zoom In   Zoom Out   Timeline

Show Storyboard button

Figure 96-2: The Timeline.

9. As you work on your movie, it's a good idea to save your work frequently. Select File⇨Save Project from the menus. The first time you do this, the Save Project dialog appears and allows you to select a location and name for your project file.

cross-reference

Your movie isn't complete without music, narration, and sound effects. To find out how to add these elements, see Tasks 106 and 107.

cross-reference

Saving your project simply saves the work you are doing in the Storyboard/Timeline; it doesn't produce the final movie. To find out how to produce the final movie, see Task 108.

Task **97**

Capturing Video from Your Camcorder

This task shows you how to use Windows Movie Maker to capture video from a tape in your digital camcorder. Digital camcorders work with your computer very easily because they store information in the same way your computer does — as 1s and 0s. If you do not have a digital camcorder, you'll have to get a video capture device to use with a standard video camcorder. A video capture device may be a card or a box that plugs into your computer. You plug in your standard camcorder, and the video capture device acts as an interpreter, translating standard video into 1s and 0s that the computer can process. Once you have a video capture device installed properly, the process for capturing video from it should be similar to this process.

1. Turn off your camcorder. Plug your camcorder into your computer. This is usually done with a cable that came with your camcorder. The cable might be an i.LINK, FireWire, or USB/USB2 cable. See your camcorder manual for more information on this.

2. If Windows Movie Maker isn't already running, open Windows Movie Maker by selecting Start⇨All Programs⇨Windows Movie Maker. The Windows Movie Maker main window appears.

3. Turn on your camcorder in playback (or VCR) mode. When you do, the Video Capture Wizard will likely appear. If the wizard doesn't appear, choose File⇨Capture Video from the menu (or hit Ctrl+R on the keyboard).

4. Enter a name for the video you are about to capture. If you want to store the video file somewhere other than the My Videos folder, click the Browse button and choose a location.

5. Click Next. The Video Setting page appears (see Figure 97-1). Choose the quality of the video you want to capture.

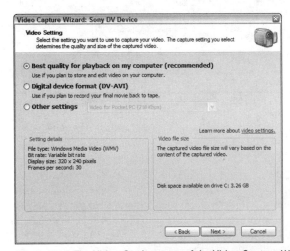

Figure 97-1: The Video Setting page of the Video Capture Wizard.

cross-reference

This task uses Windows Movie Maker 2. If you don't have this version of Windows Movie Maker, see Task 91 to find out how to download and install it.

tip

Camcorders will often go into standby mode if they are not used for a while. If you camera does this, turn it off and then back on in playback (or VCR) mode.

tip

If you'd prefer more (or more descriptive) options, select Other Settings and choose one of the options in the drop-down list. Here, you'll see a long list of detailed options that allow you to pick an option appropriate to what you want to do with the video when you're done (put it on a Web site, send it as email, etc.).

tip

After you select a video setting, the Setting details box in the lower-right corner of the window shows you the technical details about the option you've chosen.

6. Click Next. The Capture Method page appears. Here you can choose to either capture the entire tape or to capture parts of the tape manually. The second option gives you the most flexibility, so choose that one.

7. Click Next. The Capture Video page appears (see Figure 97-2). Use the DV camera controls under the Preview box to rewind the videotape on your camcorder and get it to exactly the point where you want to begin recording. When you play the video, it appears in the Preview box.

Figure 97-2: The Capture Video page of the Video Capture Wizard.

8. Click the Start Capture button. The video begins. When you are done recording, click the Stop Capture button.

9. Click Finish. You return to the Windows Movie Maker main window. A new collection is created with the name you gave to the file, and all the clips from the captured video appear within the collection.

caution

The quality you choose on the Record window is important. Of course, the higher the quality, the better the video is going to look. But you should also know that the higher the quality, the bigger the captured video files will be. For example, if you choose the highest-possible quality (DV-AVI), it could take 11GB to store an hour of video!

caution

These controls won't work if you are recording from a standard, nondigital camcorder. You'll have to use the controls on the camcorder itself to find the location and play the video.

note

As noted on the wizard, you can repeat this process as often as you like to capture different parts of the tape to this same video file.

cross-reference

For more information on working with collections, see Tasks 94 and 95.

note

When Windows Movie Maker captures the video from your camcorder, it notes when you turned your camcorder on and off and breaks up the video into clips that are easier to work with and rearrange as you like.

Capturing a Photograph from a Video

So you're going to a wedding or to a family gathering or to Disney World. Should you take your camera? Or your camcorder? Or both? It's a tough decision. But not anymore! Now you can take your camcorder, videotape everything, and then pull still pictures out of the video when you get home.

1. Turn off your camcorder. Plug your camcorder into your computer. This is usually done with a cable that came with your camcorder. The cable might be an i.LINK, FireWire, or USB/USB2 cable. See your camcorder manual for more information on this.

2. If Windows Movie Maker isn't already running, open Windows Movie Maker by selecting Start⇨All Programs⇨Windows Movie Maker. The Windows Movie Maker main window appears.

3. Click on the Collections button. The Collections pane appears (see Figure 98-1).

cross-reference

This task uses Windows Movie Maker 2. If you don't have this version of Windows Movie Maker, see Task 91 to find out how to download and install it.

caution

While this technique is very handy for pulling out some still pictures to put on the Web or send via email, the quality of the pictures you capture from video aren't nearly as high as the quality you'd get from even an inexpensive digital camera. If you print these pictures at 4"× 6" or larger, you'll probably be disappointed with the results.

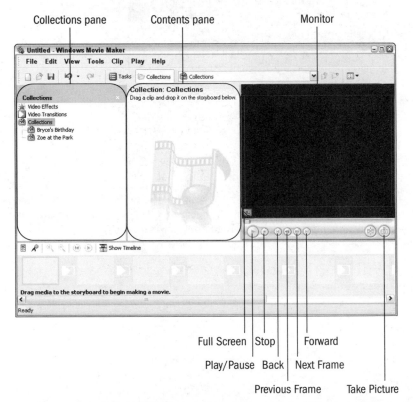

Figure 98-1: The Windows Movie Maker main window with the Collections pane.

4. If you haven't already, capture the video from your camcorder as described in Task 97 or import the video file to a collection as described in Task 95.

5. In the Collections pane, click to select the collection where the video clip is located. In the Contents pane, click to select the video clip.

6. Click Play on the Monitor. When you get near the place where you want to take a snapshot, press the Pause button. Now you can use the Previous Frame and Next Frame controls to move forward or backward in very small increments — and get the exact shot you want.

7. Click the Take Picture button. The Save Picture As dialog appears. Select a location and give your picture a name.

8. Click Save. Your picture is saved as a JPEG file (with a .jpg extension). You can locate it in Windows Explorer and double-click to see how it looks (see Figure 98-2).

Figure 98-2: Viewing the result.

cross-reference
For more information about navigating your hard drive with Windows Explorer, see Task 22.

tip
Pictures you capture from video may seem fuzzy or dark. You can increase the brightness, contrast, and sharpness using a photo-editing application like Microsoft Picture It!

Capturing Live Video

Perhaps you have a security camera connected directly to your PC. Or perhaps it's a video baby monitor. Whatever the reason, there may be times when you need to capture live video to your hard drive immediately, rather than recording the video to tape on your camcorder and then capturing it into your computer as described in Task 97. Fortunately, Windows Movie Maker is up to the task.

1. Connect your camera, camcorder, or other video device to your computer. (When using a camcorder, this is usually done with a cable that came with your camcorder. The cable might be an i.LINK, FireWire, or a USB/USB2 cable. See your camcorder manual for more information on this.)

2. If Windows Movie Maker isn't already running, open Windows Movie Maker by selecting Start⇨All Programs⇨Windows Movie Maker. The Windows Movie Maker main window appears.

3. Click on the Collections button. The Collections pane appears.

4. Turn your camera on, if necessary. Or if you're using a camcorder, turn it on in Record (or Camera) mode. When you do, the Video Capture Wizard will likely appear. If the wizard doesn't appear, choose File⇨Capture Video from the menu (or hit Ctrl+R on the keyboard).

5. Enter a name for the video you are about to capture. If you want to store the video file somewhere other than the My Videos folder, click the Browse button and choose a location.

6. Click Next. The Video Settings page appears (see Figure 99-1). Choose the quality of the video you want to capture.

cross-reference

This task uses Windows Movie Maker 2. If you don't have this version of Windows Movie Maker, see Task 91 to find out how to download and install it.

tip

If you have a video capture board, you can use this same technique to capture video from a videotape playing in a VCR or virtually any other device that produces a video signal.

note

If you'd prefer more (or more descriptive) options, select Other Settings and the click to view the options in the drop-down list. Here, you'll see a long list of detailed options that allow you to pick an option appropriate to what you want to do with the video when you're done (put it on a Web site, send it as email, etc.).

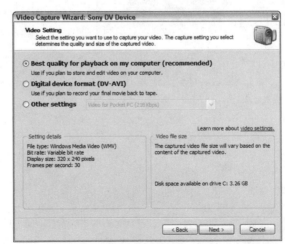

Figure 99-1: The Video Settings page of the Video Capture Wizard.

7. Click Next. The Capture Video page appears (see Figure 99-2). You should see a live image from your camera appear in the Preview window.

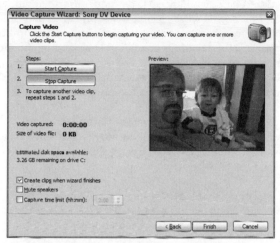

Figure 99-2: The Capture Video page of the Video Capture Wizard.

8. At the bottom of the page, on the left, is a check box labeled Capture Time Limit. You can set this value so that the video is stopped after the specified amount of time has passed. That way, you can walk away after you start the recording without worrying that your hard drive will be filled with video when you get back.

9. Click Start Capture to begin recording. Click Stop Capture to stop recording. Do this as many times as you like.

10. Click Finish. You return to the Windows Movie Maker main window. A new collection is created with the name you gave to the file, and all the clips for the captured video appear within the collection.

cross-reference

For more information on organizing video clips in collections, see Tasks 94 and 95.

Task 100

Splitting and Combining Video Clips

When you capture a video from your camcorder or import a video from a file into your collection, Windows Movie Maker automatically divides the video up into clips. How does it decide what's a clip? It uses the date and time stamp on your videotape to figure out every time you started recording and then stopped recording × and that's a clip. Dividing up your video like this into bite-sized chunks makes them easier to work with when you are making movies. However, you may not always like how the clips are divided up. You may prefer that a long clip be divided into two or three pieces, for example.

You can split or combine clips either in your collections or in the Storyboard/Timeline after they've been added to your movie. Splitting or combining clips in the Storyboard/Timeline has no effect on that same clip in your collections (and vice versa).

1. If Windows Movie Maker isn't already running, open Windows Movie Maker by selecting Start⊃All Programs⊃Windows Movie Maker. The Windows Movie Maker main window appears.

2. Click on the Collections button. The Collections pane appears.

3. If you want to work with a project you saved previously, select File⊃Open Project. Use the Open Project dialog to locate and open your project.

4. To split a clip in one of your collections:

   a. In the Collections pane, click to select the collection holding the clip, and then click to select the clip in the Contents pane.

   b. Use the Seek bar on the Monitor to locate the exact spot where you'd like to split the clip.

   c. Press the Split Clip button on the Monitor. The clip is split into two clips (see Figure 100-1).

5. To combine two clips together in one of your collections:

   a. In the Collections pane, click to select the collection holding the clips.

   b. Click to select the first clip, and then hold the Ctrl key down while you click the second clip.

   c. Right-click on one of the selected clips, and choose Combine from the menu. The clips are combined together into one.

cross-reference

This task uses Windows Movie Maker 2. If you don't have this version of Windows Movie Maker, see Task 91 to find out how to download and install it.

tip

If you want to show only part of a clip in your movie, don't split the clip and delete the parts you don't want. The better approach is to use the clip trimming tools described in Task 101. Trimming makes it easier to correct mistakes later.

tip

You can use Ctrl+L as a shortcut for splitting clips and Ctrl+M as a shortcut for combining clips in your collections and in the Storyboard/Timeline.

Collections pane   Contents pane   Monitor

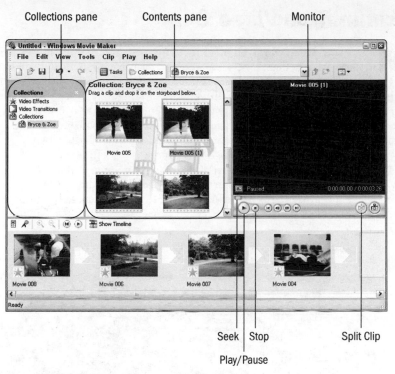

Seek | Stop   Split Clip

Play/Pause

Figure 100-1: The video clip is split in two in a collection.

6. To split a clip in the Storyboard/Timeline:

   a. Click to select the clip in the Storyboard/Timeline.

   b. Use the Seek bar on the Monitor to locate the exact spot where you'd like to split the clip.

   c. Press the Split Clip button on the Monitor. The clip is split into two clips and any clips to the right are moved over to make room for the new clip.

7. To combine two clips together in the Storyboard/Timeline:

   a. Click to select the first clip, and then hold the Ctrl key down while you click on the second clip. If you want to combine more than two, you simply continue to hold the Ctrl key down as you click to select all the clips you want to combine.

   b. Right-click on one of the selected clips, and choose Combine from the menu. The clips are combined together into one.

caution

You cannot combine any two clips. You can only combine clips that you've split previously or that were consecutive when they were recorded on your video camera.

tip

If you want to combine more than two, you simply continue to hold the Ctrl key down as you click to select all the clips you want to combine.

cross-reference

To find out how to work with collections, see Tasks 94 and 95. To discover how to combine clips from your collections to create a new movie, see Task 96.

Task 101

Trimming a Video Clip

cross-reference
This task uses Windows Movie Maker 2. If you don't have this version of Windows Movie Maker, see Task 91 to find out how to download and install it.

Most of your video clips are not going to be packed with wall-to-wall action. In fact it's likely there'll be some good parts surrounded by dull parts at the beginning, at the end, or both. If that's the case, then you need to trim your clip. Trimming simply means that you tell Windows Media Player that, when using a particular clip, it should start at one point and end at another point. You can set these points anywhere in the clip you like. And if you decide later that you accidentally set your end point too early, for example, you can easily move it.

1. If Windows Movie Maker isn't already running, open Windows Movie Maker by selecting Start➪All Programs➪Windows Movie Maker. The Windows Movie Maker main window appears (see Figure 101-1).

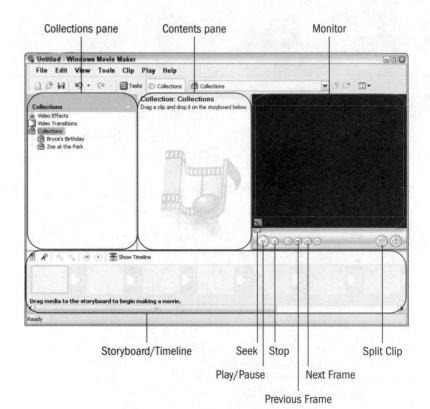

Figure 101-1: The Windows Movie Maker main window.

2. If you want to work with a project you saved previously, select File⇨ Open Project. Use the Open Project dialog to locate and open your project.

3. If the Storyboard is at the bottom of your window, click the Show Timeline button.

4. Click to select a clip in Timeline. Use the Seek bar and other controls on the Monitor to find the exact location where the clip should start (see Figure 101-2).

Figure 101-2: Using the Seek bar to find the spot where the clip should start.

5. Select Clip⇨Set Start Trim Point from the menus.

6. Use the Seek bar and other controls on the Monitor to find the exact location where the clip should end.

7. Select Clip⇨Set End Trim Point from the menus.

8. Click the Play button on the Monitor to view the newly trimmed clip.

9. If you've trimmed too much or too little, select Clip⇨Clear Trim Points and begin again.

cross-reference

To discover how to combine clips from your collections to create a new movie, see Task 96.

tip

As a shortcut, you can use Ctrl+Shift+I (for *In*) to set the start trim point and Ctrl+Shift+O (for *Out*) to set the end trim point. Ctrl+Shift+Delete clears the trim points.

tip

If you don't want to trim anything from the start of the clip, simply place the Set Start Trim Point at the very beginning of the clip. Likewise, you can set the Set End Trim Point at the very end of the clip if you don't want to trim anything from the end.

tip

You can also use the mouse cursor to set beginning and ending trim points within the Timeline. The mouse changes to a red rectangle with a double-headed arrow when positioned at the beginning or end of the box surrounding the clip. Simply drag to set the points. The Monitor shows the location of the clipping.

Adding Transitions between Your Video Clips

cross-reference

This task uses Windows Movie Maker 2. If you don't have this version of Windows Movie Maker, see Task 91 to find out how to download and install it.

When a movie goes from one camera angle to another or from one scene to another, there is always a transition between the clips. Most of the time, the transition is a straight cut, meaning that the transition is instantaneous. This is what happens by default in Windows Movie Maker. Probably the second most common transition is called a *cross-fade*. In a cross-fade, the first clip fades out at the same time the second clip fades in. But there are also wipes and dissolves and dozens of other common transitions. In this task you'll find out how to use the many transitions included with Windows Movie Maker.

tip

If you're looking for a simple cross-fade transition among all the fancy Video Transitions in the Contents pane, it's called Fade.

1. If Windows Movie Maker isn't already running, open Windows Movie Maker by selecting Start➪All Programs➪Windows Movie Maker. The Windows Movie Maker main window appears.

2. Click on the Collections button. The Collections pane appears. In the Collections pane, click the Video Transitions item (see Figure 102-1). All the video transitions Windows Movie Maker includes appear in the Contents pane.

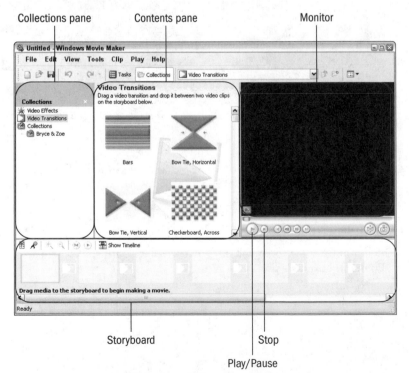

Figure 102-1: The Windows Movie Maker main window with the Collections pane and Video Transitions selected.

3. If you want to work with a project you saved previously, select File⇨ Open Project. Use the Open Project dialog to locate and open your project.

4. If the Timeline is at the bottom of your window, click the Show Storyboard button.

5. To preview what a transition will look like, click on the transition in the Contents pane and then click Play on the Monitor.

6. Select the transition you want.

7. Identify the two clips in your Storyboard you want to create the transition between. Press and hold the left mouse button on the transition, and drag the mouse to the small box between the two clips in the Storyboard. Release the mouse button, and the transition is added (see Figure 102-2).

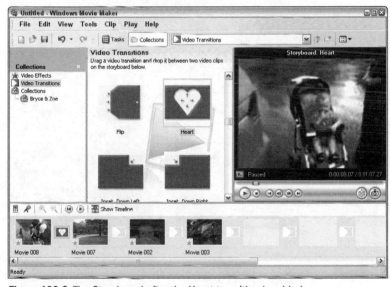

Figure 102-2: The Storyboard after the Heart transition is added.

8. Click to select the first clip in the transition. Press the Play button on the Monitor to view the clip and the transition to the next clip.

tip

When adding transitions between your clips, you may find that the primary action in a scene is being partially obscured as the transition happens. One way to fix this is to readjust your trim points. See Task 101 to find out how to do that.

tip

To delete a transition, simply click on the small box between the two clips and click the Delete button on your keyboard. To replace one transition with another, simply drag a new transition to the small box, and it will replace the old one.

Adding Video Effects to Your Clips

One of the coolest features Windows Movie Maker provides is called Video Effects. Video Effects allows you to add all different kinds of special effects to your clips. For example, you can easily add a fade-in or a fade-out effect to a clip. Or you could change it to black-and-white. Or make it look like an old movie. You can brighten a too-dark video or kick it up to double speed if the action gets slow. Best of all, video effects are easy to add and change.

cross-reference

This task uses Windows Movie Maker 2. If you don't have this version of Windows Movie Maker, see Task 91 to find out how to download and install it.

1. If Windows Movie Maker isn't already running, open Windows Movie Maker by selecting Start⇨All Programs⇨Windows Movie Maker. The Windows Movie Maker main window appears.

2. Click on the Collections button. The Collections pane appears. In the Collections pane, click the Video Effects item (see Figure 103-1). All the video effects available appear in the Contents pane.

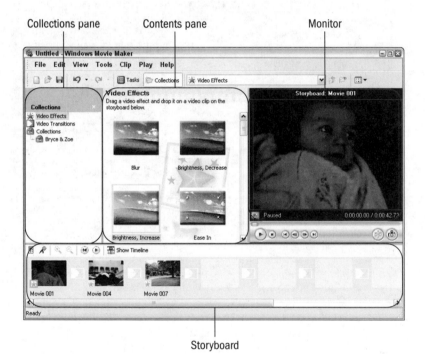

Collections pane   Contents pane   Monitor

Storyboard

Figure 103-1: The Windows Movie Maker main window with the Collections pane and Video Effects selected.

caution

Not all video effects are demonstrated well when you click Play to preview them in the monitor. Since Windows Movie Maker uses still images to demonstrate the effect, you may not see the difference for things that are dependent on motion, like Slow Down or Speed Up.

3. If you want to work with a project you saved previously, select File⇨Open Project. Use the Open Project dialog to locate and open your project.

4. If the Timeline is at the bottom of your window, click the Show Storyboard button.

5. To preview what a video effect will look like, click on the video effect in the Contents pane and then click Play on the Monitor.

6. Identify a clip in your Storyboard that you want to add a video effect to. Locate the video effect in the Contents Panel.

7. Press and hold the left mouse button on the video effect, and drag the mouse to the video clip in the Storyboard. Release the mouse button, and the effect is added (see Figure 103-2). The gray star in the lower-left corner of the clip turns into a blue star to let you know a visual effect has been applied.

Task 103

tip

If a clip has a gray star in its lower-left corner, it has no video effects applied. If it has a single blue star, it has one video effect applied. If it has two blue stars, there are two or more video effects added.

Figure 103-2: The blue star in the lower left of the clip indicates a video effect has been added.

8. Click to select the clip with the video effect. Press the Play button on the Monitor to view the clip and see the video effect in action.

9. You can add additional video effects to the same clip by simply repeating Step 6. To view and change the video effects on a clip, right-click on the clip and choose Video Effects. The Add or Remove Video Effects window appears (see Figure 103-3). Use this window to add or remove effects from the list of available effects.

Figure 103-3: The Add or Remove Video Effects window.

10. Click OK.

Task 104

Adding Titles and Credits to Your Movie

Adding a title at the beginning of your video and credits at the end give it a nice, clean, professional feel. And it gives you the opportunity to put the video in context — When was it shot? Where? How old were the kids? Windows Media Player makes it easy to add simple titles and credits to your movie.

1. If Windows Movie Maker isn't already running, open Windows Movie Maker by selecting Start⇨All Programs⇨Windows Movie Maker. The Windows Movie Maker main window appears.

2. If you want to work with a project you saved previously, select File⇨Open Project. Use the Open Project dialog to locate and open your project.

3. Choose Tools⇨Titles and Credits from the menu. The window changes (see Figure 104-1).

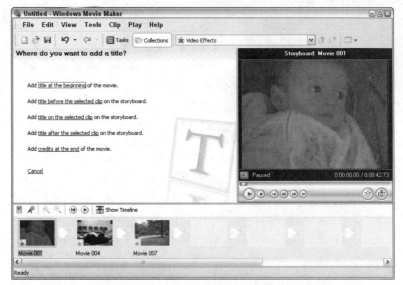

Figure 104-1: The menu for adding titles and credits.

4. Pick the option that best describes what you want to do. Adding a title at the beginning and credits at the end are the options you'll probably use most often. If you want to add some overlay text in the middle of your presentation, you should select the clip in the Storyboard/Timeline before Step 3.

5. When you choose an option, the window changes again (see Figure 104-2). Here you can enter the text that you want to appear in the title. As you do, the text appears in the monitor as it will look in the final presentation.

6. If you'd like to customize your title, use the scroll bar along the side of the pane where you entered your text to scroll down. When you do you'll see more options: Change the Title Animation and Change

tip

Once a title or credit is added, it appears in the Storyboard as if it were another clip. To edit it, simply double-click on the title/credit in the Storyboard. To delete it, right-click on it in the Storyboard and choose Delete from the pop-up menu.

tip

The Add Title on the Selected Clip option allows you to superimpose text over the video clip while the clip is running. This can be a nice effect with the right kind of clip. If you choose this option, you will automatically be switched to the Timeline. You can only work with overlays in the Timeline.

the Text Font and Color. Click the first option. You're presented with a huge number of options (see Figure 104-3).

Figure 104-2: Entering text for a title.

7. Click on the various animation options to see them demonstrated on the monitor. Once you've selected the animation you want, you can scroll down again and choose to go back and edit the title text or change the text font and color. Choose the second option.

Figure 104-3: Title animation options.

8. Select the background color, text color, font, size, transparency, and other options. Click Done, Add Title to Movie.

Task 104

tip

Different boxes are provided where you can type text. Experiment with putting text in different boxes to see how this changes the look of the title.

cross-reference

Another way you can customize your title is by adding a video effect to it. See Task 103 to find out how.

Task 105

Adding Photographs to a Movie

Movies are about *motion* pictures. But often photographs can add an element to your videos you couldn't get any other way. You might want to include a picture of yourself when you were a baby, or a picture of your great-grandmother.

1. If you want to scan in a photograph, do so. If you want to use an existing graphics file on your hard drive, make sure you know where it is.

2. If Windows Movie Maker isn't already running, open Windows Movie Maker by selecting Start⇨All Programs⇨Windows Movie Maker. The Windows Movie Maker main window appears.

3. Click on the Collections button. The Collections pane appears (see Figure 105-1).

Collections pane   Contents pane   Monitor

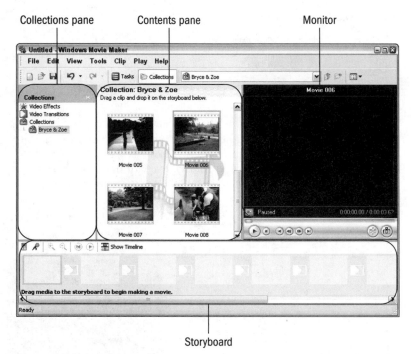

Storyboard

Figure 105-1: The Windows Movie Maker main window with the Collections pane.

4. If you want to work with a project you saved previously, select File⇨ Open Project. Use the Open Project dialog to locate and open your project.

5. Select Tools⇨Options from the menu. The Options dialog appears.

6. Near the top is a number labeled Picture Duration. Set this to the number of seconds you want your imported picture to appear in your movie. The default is 5 seconds. Click OK when you are done.

cross-reference

This task uses Windows Movie Maker 2. If you don't have this version of Windows Movie Maker, see Task 91 to find out how to download and install it.

cross-reference

To discover how to scan photographs using a scanner, see Task 62.

tip

Once you set the Default Imported Photo Duration, all photos imported after that will have the duration you specified. If you change the duration, future imports will have the new duration but previously imported pictures will not. You can delete a picture from your collection and reimport it so that it has the new duration, if you like. For more information on deleting and importing items in your collections, see Task 95.

7. Click to select the collection in the Collections pane where you'd like to put your picture. Choose File➪Import into Collection. The Import File dialog appears (see Figure 105-2).

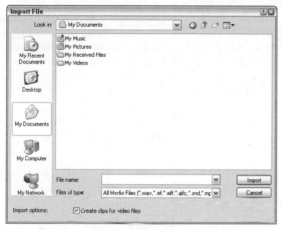

Figure 105-2: The Import File dialog.

8. Locate the picture you want to include. Click to select it, and click the Import button. The picture appears in the selected collection.

9. Press and hold the left mouse button over the picture in your collection. Drag the mouse pointer down to the Storyboard/Timeline at the location in your movie where you'd like for the picture to appear (see Figure 105-3). Release the button. Your picture is placed in your movie.

Figure 105-3: Adding a picture to your movie.

tip

Video effects can be applied to photographs as well as video clips. Ease In and Ease Out are especially good with portraits. To find out more on video effects, see Task 103.

tip

Consider adding a transition between the video clips that comes before and after a photograph. It can add a nice touch. To find out how to do that, see Task 102.

Task 106

Adding Background Music and Sound Effects to a Movie

cross-reference

This task uses Windows Movie Maker 2. If you don't have this version of Windows Movie Maker, see Task 91 to find out how to download and install it.

cross-reference

Task 96 describes the Timeline and how it works.

cross-reference

If you want to use a song from your CD collection, you can copy the song to your hard drive by following the steps in Task 79. Once you've done that, you can import it using the steps in this task.

tip

Looking for great sound effects? You can buy sound effects CDs inexpensively, or you can download free sound effects from sites like www.a1freesoundeffects.com and www.findsounds.com.

It's no wonder that Hollywood pays big bucks for great soundtracks. Nothing can turn a boring movie into an event like music and sound effects. Fortunately, integrating these elements into your movie in Windows Movie Maker is as easy as working with video clips. When you are working with the Timeline, you may have noticed a gray bar below your video labeled Audio/Music. That is where you can place your music and sound effects.

1. Figure out what music and sound elements you want for your movie, and create those elements or locate them if they already exist on your hard drive.

2. If Windows Movie Maker isn't already running, open Windows Movie Maker by selecting Start➪All Programs➪Windows Movie Maker. The Windows Movie Maker main window appears.

3. Click on the Collections button. The Collections pane appears (see Figure 106-1).

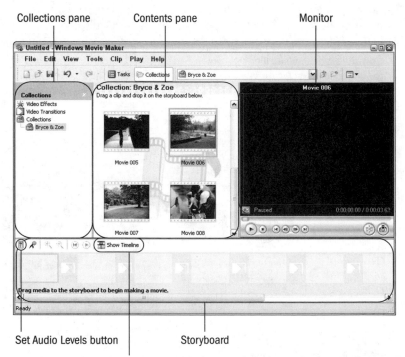

Figure 106-1: The Windows Movie Maker main window with the Collections pane.

4. If you want to work with a project you saved previously, select File➪ Open Project. Use the Open Project dialog to locate and open your project.

5. If the Storyboard is at the bottom of your window, click the Show Timeline button.

6. Click to select the collection in the Collections pane where you'd like to put your music or sound effect. Choose File⇨Import into Collection. The Import File dialog appears.

7. Locate the file you want to include. Click to select it, and click the Import button. The music or sound effect appears in the selected collection.

8. Press and hold the left mouse button over the music or sound effect in your collection. Drag the mouse pointer down to the Storyboard/Timeline and into the gray bar under your video labeled Audio/Music. Place the music or sound effect directly under the video clip where you want the music or sound effect to begin. Release the button. A new bar appears below your video representing the music or sound effect (see Figure 106-2).

Figure 106-2: Adding a little Beethoven.

9. To change when, in the movie, a song or sound effect begins, press and hold the left mouse button on the bar representing the song or sound effect. Then drag the bar left or right to move it where it belongs. Release the button. The sound item is moved.

10. Click to select the video clip where the music or sound effect begins, and then press Play on the Monitor to play the clip and see how you like the music or sound you've added.

Adding Narration to a Movie

What could be more heartwarming than Little Zoe describing what she was doing at the park that day? Or daddy calling the plays at Little Bryce's baseball game? You can add any voice you like alongside your videos by using your computer's microphone. You can even make your own sound effects!

cross-reference

This task uses Windows Movie Maker 2. If you don't have this version of Windows Movie Maker, see Task 91 to find out how to download and install it.

1. If Windows Movie Maker isn't already running, open Windows Movie Maker by selecting Start⇨All Programs⇨Windows Movie Maker. The Windows Movie Maker main window appears (see Figure 107-1).

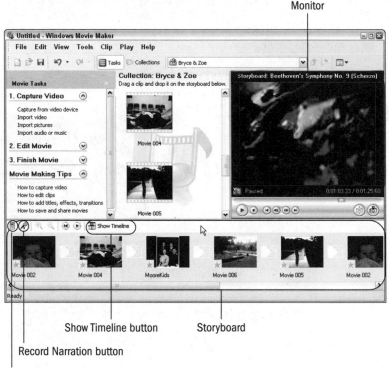

Figure 107-1: The Windows Movie Maker main window.

cross-reference

If you want to use sound effects or music files on your hard drive, see Task 106.

2. If you want to work with a project you saved previously, select File⇨ Open Project. Use the Open Project dialog to locate and open your project.

3. If the Storyboard is at the bottom of your window, click the Show Timeline button.

4. Click the Record Narration button in the Timeline. The window changes to display the Narrate Timeline page (see Figure 107-2).

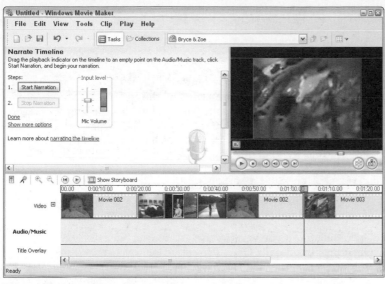

Figure 107-2: The Narrate Timeline page.

5. Click the Show More Options link, and scroll down to the bottom of the page. Click to check the Mute Speakers check box. This turns off the video sound while you are narrating so you don't get feedback. Now click the Show Fewer Options link.

6. Connect a microphone to your computer if you don't have one connected already. It probably plugs into your computer near where your speakers plug in. Now place the microphone a comfortable distance from your mouth and speak in a normal, clear tone of voice. You'll notice a green bar under Input level that goes up and down. If the green bar is mostly bobbing up and down in the lower part of the bar, raise the slider to increase the recording level. If the green bar is mostly in the top part of the bar (and hitting the red often), lower the slider to reduce the recording level.

7. When you are ready, click the Start Narration button. The video plays and you can narrate what you see.

8. When you are done, click the Stop Narration button. The Save Windows Media File dialog appears.

9. Choose the location on your hard drive where you want to save the narration file, and give it a name. Click Save. The file is saved, appears in the current collection, and is automatically placed in your movie.

10. Press Stop and then Play in the Monitor to play your movie. Listen for the narration. Is the volume right? If not, you can click the Set Audio Levels button in the Timeline to change the relative volume of the narration versus the video's audio.

tip

Prepare what you are going to say. You don't need to write it out ahead of time (although this can be helpful!); you need to have a clear idea in mind of what you want to say.

tip

If you mess up, don't worry. Just click Stop, and when the Save Windows Media File dialog appears, just click Cancel. You'll be returned to the main window, ready to start over.

Task **108**

Saving a Movie to View on Your Computer

cross-reference

This task uses Windows Movie Maker 2. If you don't have this version of Windows Movie Maker, see Task 91 to find out how to download and install it.

cross-reference

For more information on creating and saving projects, see Task 96.

There are two different things you can "save" in Windows Movie Maker. When you save a *project*, you are saving all the stuff in the Storyboard/Timeline as it is, so that you can come back and work on it later. However, when you are finished, you probably want to save the *movie* as an actual movie file that others can view using, for example, Windows Media Player. That is what you'll discover how to do in this task.

1. If Windows Movie Maker isn't already running, open Windows Movie Maker by selecting Start⇨All Programs⇨Windows Movie Maker. The Windows Movie Maker main window appears.

2. Open the project you want to save as a movie: Select File⇨ Open Project. Use the Open Project dialog to locate and open your project.

3. Select File⇨Save Movie File from the menus (or hit Ctrl+P on the keyboard). The Save Movie Wizard appears (see Figure 108-1). Click to select My Computer.

Figure 108-1: The Movie Location page of the Save Movie Wizard.

4. Click Next. The Saved Movie File page is displayed (see Figure 108-2). Enter a name for your movie. If you want to put your movie somewhere other than the My Videos folder, click the Browse button and choose a location.

5. Click Next. The Movie Setting page appears (see Figure 108-3). Click to choose the Best Quality for Playback on My Computer, or click Show More Choices... if you'd prefer another option.

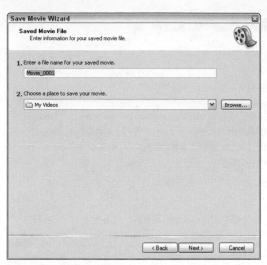

Figure 108-2: The Saved Movie File page of the Save Movie Wizard.

6. Click Next. The Saving Movie page appears, showing the progress as your movie is saved. When it is finished, the Completing the Save Movie Wizard page appears. Click the Play Movie When I Click Finish check box.

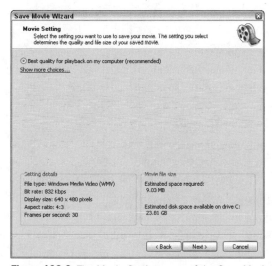

Figure 108-3: The Movie Setting page of the Save Movie Wizard.

7. Click Finish. Windows Media Player is launched and your movie is played.

note

This process of saving your movie may take a while, depending on the length, complexity, and settings you chose.

cross-reference

For more information on viewing movies in Windows Media Player, see Task 93.

Task 109

Sending a Movie via Email

cross-reference

This task uses Windows Movie Maker 2. If you don't have this version of Windows Movie Maker, see Task 91 to find out how to download and install it.

Of course, after you put all that time and effort into creating your cinematic masterpiece, you'll want to share it with everyone you know. Fortunately that's easy with Windows Movie Maker.

1. If Windows Movie Maker isn't already running, open Windows Movie Maker by selecting Start⇨All Programs⇨Windows Movie Maker. The Windows Movie Maker main window appears.

2. Open the project you want to save as a movie: Select File⇨ Open Project. Use the Open Project dialog to locate and open your project.

3. Select File⇨Save Movie File from the menus (or hit Ctrl+P on the keyboard). The Save Movie Wizard appears (see Figure 109-1). Click to select E-mail.

Figure 109-1: The Movie Location page of the Save Movie Wizard.

caution

When you click Next on the Movie Location page, you may see the File Size Is Too Large page. This indicates that your movie is over 1MB and is therefore too big for many email servers. If you know that your email server can handle larger files, increase the number indicated and click Next. If your movie is smaller than the size you specified, the process will continue.

4. Click Next. The Saving Movie page appears. The progress indicator keeps you informed about how long the process should take. When the process is complete, the Ready to Send by E-mail page appears (see Figure 109-2).

5. To preview the movie before you send it, click the first link. To save a copy of the file on your hard drive, click the second link.

Figure 109-2: The Ready to Send by E-mail page of the Save Movie Wizard.

6. Click Next. An email message is created with the movie as an attachment (see Figure 109-3).

7. You are given the opportunity to specify who should receive it, what the subject line should say, and how the message should read. Click the appropriate button to send the email.

Figure 109-3: A new email message, with the movie as an attachment.

tip

The process described in this task makes it easy to send your movie from within Windows Movie Maker. However, if you save your movie as described in Task 108, you can then add the movie file as an attachment to any email message you send. For more information on sending email with attachments, see Task 163.

Part 7: Working with Notepad

Task 110: Creating a New Document Using Notepad

Task 111: Saving a Document from Notepad

Task 112: Changing the Page Setup in Notepad

Task 113: Creating Headers and Footers on a Notepad Document

Task 114: Changing the Font in Notepad

Task 115: Printing a Document in Notepad

Task 116: Finding and Replacing Text in Notepad

Task 117: Creating a Log File with Notepad

Task 118: Creating a Web Page in Notepad

Task 110

Creating a New Document Using Notepad

Notepad is a great program to use when you are interested in creating relatively simple documents or when you want to view a text file. Notepad can also be used to develop computer programs or even Web pages in HTML. Any document that is composed of simple text can be created with Notepad.

Be aware that Notepad will not let you do a lot of fancy formatting, nor will it let you embed items such as figures into your document. Notepad is provided by Windows to allow you to work with simple files only. To create a basic text document in Notepad, follow these steps:

1. Open Notepad. You do this by clicking Start, then selecting on All Programs⇨Accessories⇨Notepad. This opens Notepad, as shown in Figure 110-1.

   You are now in Notepad and can begin to create a document by simply typing.

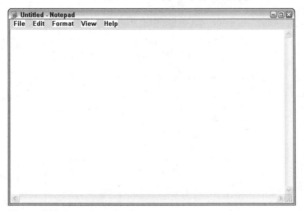

Figure 110-1: Notepad's initial window.

2. If you want to use an existing document, you can open it by following just a couple of steps. First, select Open on the File menu, or press Ctrl+O. (If you have a document opened, or if you have typed anything into the Notepad window, you will be asked if you want to save the changes you had made to the current document.) The Open File dialog appears (see Figure 110-2). By default, this shows you the text files on your system.

3. Use the Open dialog to choose the file you want to open. If you want to open a nonstandard text file (one that doesn't end in .txt), then in the Open dialog, change the value in the Files of Type: drop-down list to All Files instead of Text Documents (*.txt).

4. Click on a file that is displayed in the primary Open window to place the name in the File Name: entry box. You can then click the Open button to open the file. Alternatively, double-clicking on the filename will both select and open the file.

cross-reference

If you need to create documents with special formatting or more than basic text, you should use WordPad instead. Task 119 shows you how to create a document in WordPad.

note

Text files generally end in .txt.

caution

Notepad will open nearly any file whether or not it is a text file. If you open a nontext file and then save it, you may accidentally make a change that can cause the file to no longer be valid. For example, if you open a program file, make a change such as adding a space, and then save it, that program may no longer work.

note

Older versions of Windows had a limit on the size of file that Notepad could open. This limitation has been removed from the version of Notepad in Windows XP. In Windows 2000, if you tried to open a file that is too big for Notepad, you would be automatically switched to WordPad.

note

Notepad is spelled with a lowercase *p*. WordPad is spelled with an uppercase *P*.

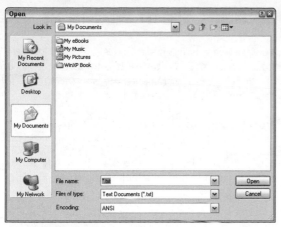

Figure 110-2: The Open dialog for selecting a document.

5. Enter or change the text for your document in the Notepad window. You can enter any text you would like, including basic formatting. You can press the Enter key for blank lines, as well as use tabs, spaces, and any other text keys that are available on your keyboard. Figure 110-3 presents a document that has been entered into Notepad. Note that the formatting was done with tabs and spaces.

6. If you want to use a different font (including a different size, type face, and color), see Task 114 on changing the text style in Notepad. Only one text style can be used in a single Notepad document; however, you can make this one of many styles.

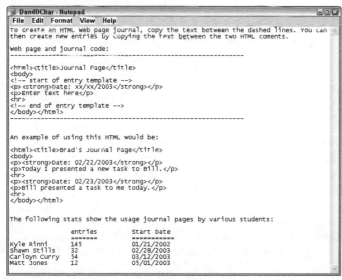

Figure 110-3: A document entered into Notepad.

cross-reference

Notepad is a standard application that comes with Windows XP. If your computer doesn't have Notepad installed, for instructions on installing it, see Task 240, which discusses adding Windows XP components.

cross-reference

If you want to add headers and footers to your text document, see Task 113.

cross-reference

If you want to print your Text document, see Task 115.

note

The tabs in Notepad have a default setting.

cross-reference

See Task 111 for saving and exiting from Notepad.

Saving a Document from Notepad

Notepad can be used to create text documents and files. Task 110 showed you how to open and create a document in Notepad. It is important that you save your documents correctly after you create or make changes to them. The following steps walk you through saving a file in Notepad.

1. Create your file or make changes to an existing file in Notepad.

2. When you are ready to save, select File⇨Save As. The Save As dialog window appears (see Figure 111-1). You use this dialog to name your file, as well as to determine the location to which you will save the file.

Figure 111-1: The Save As dialog window.

3. If you want to save in the default folder, skip to Step 5. The files in the current default folder are displayed in the center of the Save As dialog.

4. If you do not want to save your file in this folder, you can change to a different folder. You can do this a number of ways:

   • *Navigate in the current folder.* To save the file in a subfolder listed in the current folder, double-click on the subfolder name. This replaces the currently displayed files and folders with those in the subfolder. If you want to return to a previous folder, click the Back button near the top of the window. If you want to go to the parent folder of the current folder, click the Up One Level button.

   • *Create a new folder.* You can create a new folder within the current folder by clicking the Create New Folder button.

cross-reference

See Task 110 for information on creating or opening a document in Notepad.

tip

You should save your document frequently to ensure changes are not lost.

note

In Figure 111-1, you can see that there is one text file, called `test`, in the default folder. Also note that on the computer displayed in Figure 111-1, there are four other folders in the default folder. Your system may display different existing files and folders.

caution

You can use the same filename for more than one document as long as each document is in a different folder. If you use the same name for a document that already exists in the current folder, you will overwrite that old file with your new file. It is recommended that you try to give each of your files a unique name.

cross-reference

Task 118 shows how to create and save a basic Web page with Notepad.

note

If you click on a file that is in the current folder, that file's name will be placed in the File Name: entry box. You can then make changes to that name or overwrite that file.

- *Click on a "common location."* On the left side of the Save As dialog are a number of common locations including the desktop and My Documents (which is selected in Figure 111-1). You can click on one of these to change to that location.

- *Select a location from the Save In: drop-down.* At the top of the Save As dialog window is the Save In: drop-down list. Click the down arrow to list the folder structure of your computer (see Figure 111-2). You can then click on items in this list to navigate to a different location on your computer.

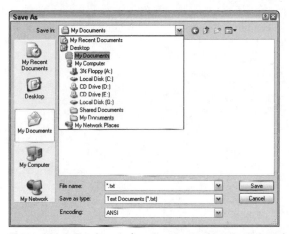

Figure 111-2: The Save In locations in the Save As dialog window.

- *Manually type in a location.* Although not recommended, you can also change locations by typing in the complete location in the File Name: entry box. You should only do this if you are very comfortable with your computer's folder structure.

5. Enter your document or filename into the File Name: entry box near the bottom of the screen. If your files were previously named, that name will be displayed. If this is the first time to save your file, the File Name: box will default to *.txt. You should replace this with the name you would like your file to have. If you are saving a text file, you do not need to include **.txt**. If you are saving a file that should have a different extension, such as an HTML Web page file, you should include the extension.

6. Select the appropriate Save as Type: value. If you are saving your file as a regular text file, leave this with the default value of Text Document (*.txt). If you are a saving other types of standard text files that don't have a .txt extension, change this value to All Files. For example, you can create HTML files for Web pages in notepad. To save an HTML file, select All Files in the Save as Type: list.

7. Click the Save button to save the file or document in the location and filename you chose. You are returned to Notepad and your document.

Task 112

Changing Page Setup in Notepad

Although Notepad limits you to text documents, it does allow you to make a number of changes to the layout. These changes will be applied to your document on any copies you print of your document. Depending on the installed printer, you can specify the size of the margins, the orientation of the paper, which location on the printer you will select paper from, and the type of paper you will use. Note that the changes you make to margin, headings, and layout will not be reflected on the screen in Notepad. They will only be applied when you print.

1. Within Notepad, select File⇨Page Setup.... The Page Setup window appears (see Figure 112-1).

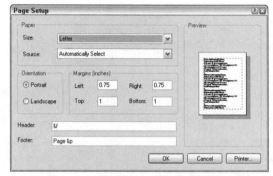

Figure 112-1: The Page Setup dialog window.

2. In the Size: drop-down list, select the size of paper, envelope, or other media that you will be printing to. If you're not planning to print your document, choose the size of paper that best fits the amount of screen space you want to have available.

   Figure 112-2 shows the choices in the Size: drop-down list. Note that the options available may be different depending on what printer you are accessing. Once you've selected your paper, the next step is to set your page margins.

3. Determine the orientation of your paper by selecting either Portrait or Landscape in the Orientation area. Portrait, or a vertical orientation, is the more common layout. You can see the difference between the two in the Preview shown at the top of the window. The Preview shows a mockup of the selections you make.

caution

If you don't have a printer installed, you will receive an error when you try to select Page Setup from the File menu.

note

When using Windows XP, the terms *document* and *file* can be used interchangeably.

cross-reference

Printing to a differently sized or oriented piece of paper is one of the primary reasons for changing the margins and other page settings. Task 115 shows you how to print from Notepad. Note that selecting the Printer button on the Page Setup window may provide additional layout features specific to your printer.

tip

To see the minimum margin sizes for the paper size you have selected, enter zeros (0) into the margin values. The zeros will automatically change to the minimum allowable values.

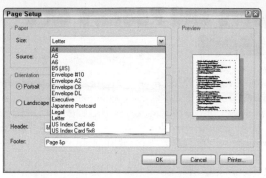

Figure 112-2: Paper size default selections.

4. In the Margins section, set the margins on your page. The margin settings are the amount of space on each edge of the paper. For example, in Figure 112-1, you can see that there is at least .75 inches of space on both the left and right sides of the page. The text starts 1 inch from the top. If the text reaches to within an inch of the bottom of the page, a new page is started.

Figure 112-3 shows different settings from those in Figure 112-1. These settings are for a #10 envelope being printed in landscape mode with minimum margins. Note how the Preview reflects these settings.

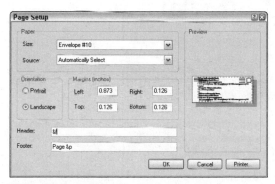

Figure 112-3: Settings for a #10 envelope.

5. Once you have made your changes, select the Print button to set additional settings specific to your printer or select the OK button to save your changes and return to the primary Notepad window.

caution

You can change the margin settings to any value you'd like. Be aware, however, that most printers can't print to the edge of a piece of paper. Because of this, if you enter a value that is too low, the minimum value will instead be placed in the field or you will be given a warning when the document prints.

cross-reference

Task 113 shows you how to add headers and footers that print on each page of your document.

cross-reference

To change the default page setup in Notepad, you must first have a printer or similar device such as a fax machine installed. Task 219 shows you how to install a printer. Task 227 shows you how to access a printer on a network.

Task 113

Creating Headers and Footers on a Notepad Document

In Task 112 you learn how to customize the page setup for your Notepad documents. If you are using Notepad, you are most likely keeping your documents very simple. If you want more complex or structured documents, you should use WordPad. Many people use Notepad to create simple notes, code, or other plain documents.

When printing these plain documents, it is often beneficial to include information at the top and bottom of the printed page. While Notepad doesn't offer many bells and whistles, it does allow you to include a header and a footer that can be customized.

cross-reference

The font of the header and footer will match the font of the Notepad text document. See Task 114 for setting the font face and size.

note

Headers and footers are applied to Notepad, not to your text document. This means that any changes made will be applied to all documents opened with your copy of Notepad until you make new changes.

note

Any text that is entered into the header and footer boxes that is not a special command will be printed as is. For example, you may want to include text such as "***Confidential ***" in your footers or headers.

1. Select File➪Page Setup from the menu. The Page Setup dialog window appears (see Figure 113-1).

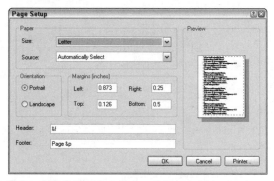

Figure 113-1: The Page Setup dialog window.

At the bottom of the Page Setup window are two entry boxes. One is for the header and the other for the footer. Default values have been placed into both of these entry boxes.

2. Change the value in the Header: entry box to change the header. If you don't want a header on your page, remove the default value that is in the box.

3. Change the value in the Footer: entry box to change the footer. If you don't want a footer on your page, remove the default values that are in the box.

You may have noticed that the values entered into Figure 113-1's Header: and Footer: entry boxes are not normal text. In notepad, &f is code for the filename. Therefore, if you print a notepad document with &f, the actual &f characters are not printed; instead, the filename of the current document prints. Similarly, &p is a special indicator for

Task 113

the page number; **Page &p** prints the word "Page" and the actual page number. So these default settings print the filename at the top of each page and the page number, preceded by the word "Page," on the bottom of each page.

Figure 113-2 shows a number of special character combinations you can use.

Character	Meaning	Description
&d	Date	Inserts the current date from your computer
&f	File name	Inserts the current document's file name. If there isn't a name because you haven't yet saved the document, then this will be the value: **untitled**.
&p	Page Number	Inserts the page number for the current page.
&t	Time	Inserts the current time from your computer
&&	Ampersand	Prints an ampersand (&)
&l	Left	Causes the text that follows to be left justified
&c	Center	Causes the text that follows to be centered
&r	Right	Causes the text that follows to be right justified

Figure 113-2. Special character combinations for Notepad headers and footers.

In addition to the special values in Figure 113-2, you can use any other text that you would like to have printed at the top or bottom of each page. Figure 113-3 shows a few examples of text that can be entered, along with the resulting output (the Notepad document is saved as **MyNotes**).

&lDoc: &f &rPage: &p:

Doc: MyNotes	Page: 1

&l&f &CBrad && Bill &r&d &t

MyNotes	Brad & Bill	Wednesday, February 26, 2003 7:32:11 PM

&f

MyNotes.txt

&c&d

Wednesday, February 26, 2003 7:32:11 PM

Figure 113-3: More character combinations for Notepad headers and footers.

caution

Be careful when using the justification commands (&l, &c, &r). Notepad lets you use these more than once in a single header or footer. The results may not be what you want.

caution

If you use a big font in your document, it will cause big headers and footers. This may cause text to overlap.

Task **114**

Changing the Font in Notepad

While Notepad doesn't allow for fancy formatting, it does provide you with the ability to change the overall font used in the text document. You can only set one font, and that font will apply to the entire document. Additionally, once you change this font, it will be used every time you open a file in Notepad until you change it again. In other words, the font isn't saved with your text document; rather, it is remembered by your copy of Notepad. The following steps walk you through changing the font characteristics of Notepad.

cross-reference

To change the way your document is formatted when printing, see Task 115.

cross-reference

The font is applied to Notepad, not to your document. If you want the font that you use to stay with your text document, you should use WordPad instead of Notepad. Task 124 shows you how to apply fonts to a WordPad document.

note

Styles such as italic, bold, or bold italic are only available if the font includes them. Some fonts only have one or two styles.

tip

More sophisticated word-processing programs such as WordPad and Word let you enter a decimal amount, such as 10.5 for the Font Size.

1. Create a blank document or open an existing document in Notepad, as shown in Task 110.

2. Select Format⇨Font from the menus. The Font dialog appears (see Figure 114-1).

Figure 114-1: The Font dialog opened in Notepad.

3. Select the desired font face from the Font: list. Single-click on the font face name to see a sample displayed.

4. Select the Font Style. The default style is Regular. Depending on the font face you select, you may also be able to choose Italic, Bold, or Bold Italic.

5. Select the Font Size. The larger the number you choose, the bigger the font. You can also enter a number instead of selecting from the size list. As with the other settings on the Font dialog, when you make a selection or a change, the sample is modified to reflect your

current choices. Figure 114-2 shows that a different font face and size have been selected.

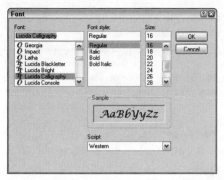

Figure 114-2: Changed font values illustrated in the Sample area.

6. Click the OK button to accept the changes. Click the Cancel button to return to your text document without accepting the changes. Once the changes are accepted, your document is modified to reflect the new font. Figure 114-3 shows the setting from 114-2 applied to Notepad.

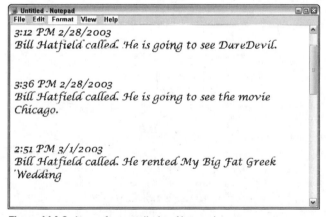

Figure 114-3: A new font applied to Notepad.

Task 115

Printing a Document in Notepad

If you are interested in printing a simple text document, Notepad is a great program to use. If you are interested in printing a document that has formatting or that is more than straight text, consider WordPad instead.

When printing with Notepad, you can set a number of options for the pages you will be printing, as well as set a number of print options. To see how to set the page setup options, see Task 112. To set up the print options and to print the document, use the following steps.

1. Open or create a document in Notepad as shown in Task 110. You can set up margins for printing, as well as select paper sizes, add headers, add footers, and more.

2. Select File⇨Print from the menus, or press Ctrl+P. The Print dialog appears (see Figure 115-1).

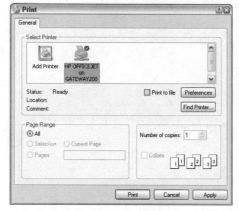

Figure 115-1: The Print dialog window.

3. If the printer you want to use is not selected, click on the desired printer in the Select Printer group at the top of the Print dialog window. If the printer you want to use is not displayed, software for it has not been installed on your computer. In this case, you may want to double-click on the Add Printer icon and follow the wizard.

4. Select settings specific to your printer, if desired.

cross-reference

To change the font, see Task 114.

cross-reference

To set layout options for your document such as margin sizes, paper size, headers, and footers, see Task 113.

note

Several options, such as Selection, Current Page, and Pages:, will be disabled ("grayed out"), because they are not available from Notepad. They are displayed because the Print dialog window is used for many Windows programs for printing.

cross-reference

Refer to Task 219 for more on adding a printer.

Depending on your printer, you may be able to set additional settings. When a printer is selected in the Select Printer area, the Preferences button will be available. Clicking this button provides you with a dialog window of options specific to the printer you selected. Figure 115-2 presents the dialog for the HP OfficeJet displayed in Figure 115-1. The dialog information may be different depending on your printer.

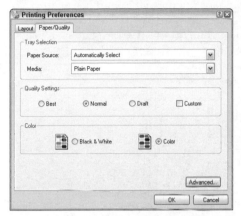

Figure 115-2: The Printing Preferences dialog window.

5. Select the number of copies to print. If you want more than one copy, change the value in the Number of Copies: box. This value can only be changed if your printer supports multiple copies. If your printer cannot support multiple copies, you will get a message such as the one in Figure 115-3 when you try to change the value. The value will be reset to a valid value.

Figure 115-3: An error message.

6. Click the Print button. Your document will print.

Task 115

note

The Find Printer button allows you to search for a printer on your computer or on a network. Your computer still needs to have the correct software installed to use any printers you may find.

caution

If you don't know how to use files specifically formatted for a printer, it is best to avoid using the Print to File feature.

Finding and Replacing Text in Notepad

In small text documents, it is easy to find text within a document; however, what do you do when your document gets very large? For example, in Task 116 you learn to create a log file. A few days of keeping track of phone calls may not be that much text, but what happens after a few weeks, months, or a year? The text document starts to get long, and finding something specific becomes harder to do manually. Notepad provides help for finding and even replacing text.

1. Select Edit⇨Find… from the menu, or press Ctrl+F. The Find dialog appears (see Figure 116-1).

Figure 116-1: The Find dialog.

2. Enter the word or phrase you want to find in the Find What: box.

3. Check the Match Case box if you are searching for a word with the exact casing. Otherwise, your search will not be case-sensitive, and the search function will not differentiate between uppercase and lowercase letters. For example, if Match Case is not checked, searching for Brad finds brad, Brad, and BRAD. If Match case is checked, only Brad will be found.

4. Select Up in the Direction box if you want to search from the current location of the cursor toward the beginning of the document; otherwise, leave the setting at Down (Down is the default), to search from the cursor's current location toward the end of the document.

5. Click the Find Next button. If the text is found, it will be highlighted as shown in Figure 116-2. You can then click the Cancel button to exit the Find dialog or click the Find Next button to search for the next occurrence.

Task **116**

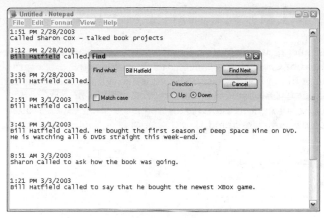

Figure 116-2: Found text using the Find dialog.

6. Select Edit⇨Find Next from the menu, or simply press F3, to find the same text again.

7. If you are also interested in changing text, you can select Edit⇨ Replace or Ctrl+H instead of using the Find option in Step 1. This displays the Replace dialog shown in Figure 116-3.

Figure 116-3: The Replace dialog.

8. Enter the Find What: text and the Replace With: text.

9. Click Find Next or F3 to find the next occurrence of the text.

10. Click the Replace button to replace the highlighted occurrence with the text you entered. Click the Replace All button to change all additional occurrences that appear later in the text document.

note

If text is not found, a warning message is displayed.

Creating a Log File with Notepad

There is one unique, relatively hidden feature that has been built into Notepad: the ability to create a log file that automatically includes the date every time you open the file. Within Notepad, you can add the date and time to the text in a file by selecting File➪Edit➪Date/Time or by pressing F5. This places the date and time at the current location of the cursor in the file. Figure 117-1 shows a new file with the date and time added.

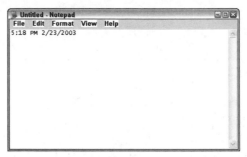

Figure 117-1: The date and time added to a new text file in Notepad.

Creating a log file, however, involves entering a new date every time you open a document. To create a log in a text file, do the following:

1. Create a new text document in notepad. You can also use an existing file if you wish.

2. Open the file and add the text **.LOG** to the first line of the document, as shown in Figure 117-2. Make sure to include the period before the word LOG, that you capitalize LOG, and that you place this in the first line with no leading spaces.

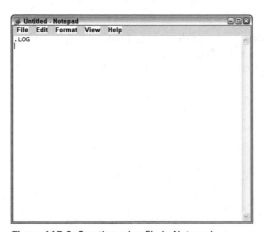

Figure 117-2: Creating a log file in Notepad.

cross-reference

If you don't know how to create or save a text file in Notepad, see Tasks 110 and 111.

caution

The text must be .LOG, with a period and all caps. Additionally, this must be in the first line with no leading spaces. If any of this is different, the date and time will not automatically be added to the file.

3. Save the document. Once saved, anytime you open the document, the date and time are automatically added to the end of the file. Figure 117-3 shows a log file that has been used to track phone calls. A log file like this can be kept on the Windows XP desktop. You can then double-click on the desktop icon to quickly open the file and add new text. You don't have to worry about finding the date and time — it will be automatically added.

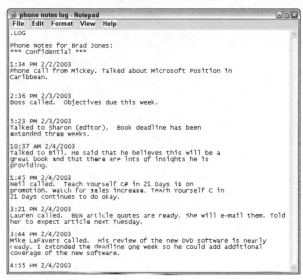

Figure 117-3: A log file in use.

caution

The date and time will be placed at the current location of the cursor. If this is in the middle of a word, the date and time will be placed in the middle of that word. Make sure the cursor is where you want the information to be placed!

tip

If you use a day planner, you can print out your log files and put them in your planner. If your day planner doesn't use a standard size of paper, see Task 112 for setting margins in your Notepad document. You can set the margins to a size that will fit your day planner after doing a little creative cutting.

Creating a Web Page in Notepad

Notepad is the perfect tool for creating text documents, as well as for taking and saving simple notes. What many people don't realize is that Notepad is a great tool for programmers and Web developers as well. You can quickly and easily create Web page documents in Notepad that can be viewed in Internet Explorer. It is beyond the scope of this book to teach Web page development or design; however, in 10 steps or less, you can create and display a simple Web page.

cross-reference

If you don't know how to create or save a text file in Notepad, see Tasks 110 and 111.

tip

You can have both Notepad and Internet Explorer open at the same time. This means that you can make changes in Notepad, save the document without closing, and then refresh the same opened page in Internet Explorer to see the changes. This allows you to quickly see changes you make without closing either program.

1. Create a new text document in Notepad.

2. Add HTML code to your text document. Again, it is beyond the scope of this book to teach you HTML, so for now enter the following text into your document:

```
<HTML>
<Title>My Web Page</Title>
<Body>

<h3>My Web Page</h3>

</Body>
</HTML>
```

After entering this text, your Notepad document should look like the document shown in Figure 118-1.

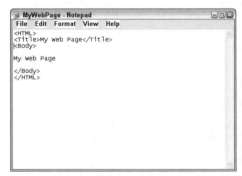

Figure 118-1: A basic HTML file in Notepad.

3. Save the HTML document, giving it a name that ends in **.HTML**, such as **MyWebPage.HTML**. Additionally, in the Save As dialog, change the Save as Type: to All Files. Your file is saved as a Web page

and now has an Internet Explorer icon next to it. Figure 118-2 shows the Notepad Save As dialog ready to save the MyWebPage.HTML file.

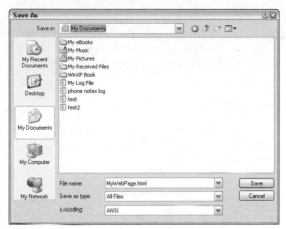

Figure 118-2: The Save As dialog window for saving MyWebPage.html.

4. View your Web page. You can do this by opening Internet Explorer. Within Internet Explorer, select File➪Open from the menus. Within the Open dialog, search for the file you saved in Notepad. When you open the file, it will look similar to Figure 118-3.

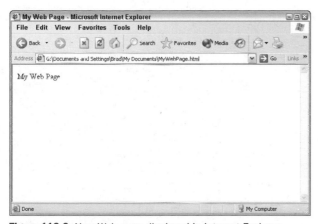

Figure 118-3: Your Web page displayed in Internet Explorer.

cross-reference

To use Internet Explorer to view a Web page, see Task 138.

note

There are lots of HTML commands that allow you to format text, add images, and link to other Web pages.

note

By default, Internet Explorer uses Notepad when people select to view the source code of an HTML page.

tip

Check out *HTML in 10 Simple Steps or Less* to learn all the HTML commands, as well as how to use them.

Part 8: Working with WordPad

Task 119: Creating a New Document in WordPad

Task 120: Saving a Document in WordPad

Task 121: Changing the Page Setup in WordPad

Task 122: Using WordPad's Print Preview

Task 123: Printing from WordPad

Task 124: Changing Font Characteristics in WordPad

Task 125: Formatting Paragraph Margins in WordPad

Task 126: Adding Lists to a WordPad Document

Task 127: Searching and Replacing Text in WordPad

Task 128: Inserting a Picture into a WordPad Document

Task 129: Adding an Object to a WordPad Document

Task 130: Changing Object Properties in a Document

Task 131: Sending a WordPad Document to Someone Else

Task 132: Setting Options in WordPad

Creating a New Document in WordPad

WordPad is a program that comes with Windows XP. With WordPad you can create formatted documents that you can save, print, or share with others. You can use multiple fonts, colors, formatting, and more. You can change the size of your work area in order to print on different paper or envelopes. While WordPad isn't as "full-featured" as word processors such as Microsoft Word, it does offer enough options to do most basic writing tasks.

The place to begin when working with WordPad is to open or create a new document. The following steps walk you through creating or opening a document in WordPad.

1. Open WordPad by clicking Start, then selecting All Programs⇨ Accessories⇨WordPad. This opens WordPad, as shown in Figure 119-1.

Figure 119-1: WordPad's initial window.

2. Open an existing file by doing the following steps. If you are creating a new file, skip to Step 3.

   a. Select File⇨Open, or press Ctrl+O. Alternatively, you can press the Open icon.

   If you have a document opened or if you have typed anything into the WordPad window, you are asked if you want to save any changes you have made. You are shown the Open File dialog, as shown in Figure 119-2. By default, this shows you the Rich Text Format (RTF) files on your system.

   b. Use the Open dialog to choose the file you want to open. If you want to open a document that isn't a Rich Text Format file (doesn't have an .rtf extension), then change the value on the

cross-reference

If you simply want to view a text document, you can use Notepad instead of WordPad. Task 110 shows you how to create a document in Notepad.

note

WordPad can open text files, Rich Text Format files, Microsoft Word documents, and Microsoft Write files.

cross-reference

To learn how to save a WordPad document, see Task 120. To learn how to print a WordPad document, see Task 123.

note

Unlike Notepad, which is also included with Windows XP, WordPad allows you to use more than one font, as well as more than one font size. You can also add images and other objects into your WordPad documents.

caution

If you open a file in WordPad, make sure you know in what format you save it. For example, you can open a Microsoft Word document. If you save the Microsoft Word document, you may lose some of the original formatting. Not all features of Microsoft Word are supported in WordPad.

note

WordPad does not have a spell checker. If you need this feature, you must purchase a full-fledged word processor.

Files of Type: drop-down list to either the document type you would like to open or to All Files.

Figure 119-2: The Open dialog for selecting a document.

   c. Click on a file that is displayed in the primary Open window to place the name in the File Name: entry box. You can then click the Open button to open the file. Alternatively, double-clicking on the filename will select and open the file.

3. Enter or change the text for your document into the WordPad window. You can enter any text you like. You can press the enter key for blank lines, as well as use tabs, spaces, and any other text keys that are available on your keyboard. Additionally, you can change the margins, fonts, text sizes, text colors, and more. Figure 119-3 shows a document that uses many of the available WordPad features.

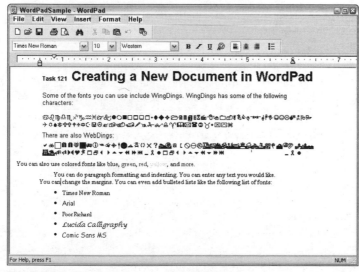

Figure 119-3: A document entered into WordPad.

cross-reference

WordPad is a standard application that comes with Windows XP. If your computer doesn't have WordPad installed, see Task 240, which discusses adding Windows XP components.

note

Once you are in WordPad, you can create a new WordPad document by selecting File⇨ New or by pressing Ctrl+N.

note

While Notepad uses a lowercase *p*, WordPad has an uppercase *P*.

Saving a Document in WordPad

Once you've created or changed a file in WordPad, you will most likely want to save it. By saving the file, you'll be able to open and access it later. Additionally, you'll be able to copy it to disk and share it with others. The following steps walk you through saving a file in WordPad:

1. Create or open a WordPad document as described in Task 119.

2. Make your changes to the document.

3. Select File⇨Save As from the menus when you are ready to save. The Save As dialog window appears (see Figure 120-1). You use this dialog to name your file, as well as to determine where you will save the file.

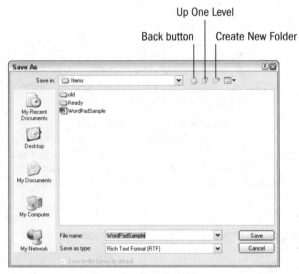

Figure 120-1: The Save As dialog window.

4. Skip to Step 5 if you wish to save in the default folder. Otherwise, you can change to a different folder. There are a number of ways to make changes to where your file will be saved:

   • *Navigate in the current folder.* To save the file in a subfolder listed in the current folder, double-click on the subfolder name. This replaces the currently displayed files and folders with those in the

cross-reference

See Task 118 for information on creating or opening a document in WordPad.

tip

You should save your document frequently to ensure changes are not lost if something goes wrong, such as a power failure or system crash.

note

If you click on a file that is in the current folder, that file's name is placed in the File Name: entry box. You can then make changes to that name or overwrite that file.

caution

You can use the same filename for more than one document as long as each document is in a different folder. If you use the same name for a document that already exists in the current folder, you will overwrite that old file with your new file. Once you overwrite a file in this manner, you cannot get the old file back.

subfolder you selected. If you want to return to a previous folder, click the Back button near the top of the window. If you want to go to the parent folder of the current folder, click the Up One Level button.

- *Create a new folder.* You can create a new folder within the current folder by clicking the Create New Folder button. This displays a folder icon with the highlighted name New Folder. Type a new name for the folder. You can then double-click on it to open it.

- *Click on a "common location."* On the left side of the Save As dialog are a number of common locations, including the desktop and My Documents. You can click on one of these to change to that location.

- *Select a location from the Save In: drop-down list.* At the top of the Save As dialog window is the Save In: drop-down list. Click the down arrow to list the folder structure of your computer. You can then click on items in this list to navigate to a different location on your computer.

- *Manually type in a location.* Although not recommended, you can also change locations by typing in the complete location in the File Name: entry box. You should only do this if you are very comfortable with your computer's folder structure.

5. Enter your document or filename into the File Name: entry box near the bottom of the Save As dialog window. If your files were previously named, that name is displayed. If this is the first time you are saving your file, the File Name: box is blank.

6. Select the appropriate Save as Type: value for the format you wish to use. If you created a basic text file, you can select one of the text document formats. Most likely you added formatting. In this case, you should select the default value of Rich Text Format (RTF). This format retains any formatting you've done. Selecting a Text format (TXT) discards most of the formatting.

7. Click the Save button to save the file or document in the location and with the filename you chose. You are returned to WordPad and your document.

8. Select File⇨Save from the WordPad menu or press Ctrl+S to save the file to the same name and location. If you do this without having previously saved the file, you are presented with the Save As dialog window.

Task 121

Changing the Page Setup in WordPad

WordPad allows you to adjust a number of settings for your document's page layout. These changes are applied to your document when you print. Depending on the installed printer, you can specify the size of the margins, the orientation of the paper you will use for printing, and the type of paper you are using. Note that these changes will not be reflected within the WordPad document window; however, you can view the impact of the changes before printing.

1. Select File⇨Page Setup from the WordPad menus. The Page Setup window appears (see Figure 121-1).

Figure 121-1: The Page Setup dialog window.

2. Select the size of paper, envelope, or other media that you will be printing on. The options available are listed in the Size: drop-down list in the Paper section of the Page Setup window.

   Figure 121-2 presents the choices in the Size: drop-down list. Note that the options available may be different depending on what printer you are accessing. Once you've selected your paper, the next step is to set your page margins.

3. Determine the orientation of your paper by selecting either Portrait or Landscape in the Orientation area. Portrait, or a vertical orientation, is the more common layout. You can see the difference between the two in the Preview shown at the top of the window. The preview shows a mockup of the settings you've selected.

4. In the Margins section, set the margins on your page. The margin settings are the amount of space on each edge of the paper. For example, in Figure 121-1, you can see that there is 1 inch of space on both the left and right sides of the page. The text starts 1.25 inches from the top and bottom. If the text reaches to within this distance (1.25 inches) of the bottom of the page, a new page is started.

Figure 121-2: Paper size default selections.

Change these settings to the desired values Be aware, however, that most printers can't print to the edge of a piece of paper. Because of this, if you enter a value that is too low, the minimum value will instead be placed in the field or you will be given a warning when the document prints. Figure 121-3 shows the settings for a #10 envelope being printed in landscape mode with minimum margins. You can see that the preview illustrates these settings.

Figure 121-3: Settings for a #10 envelope.

5. Select the OK button to save your changes and return to the WordPad document window. The changes you make in the Page Setup dialog window will not impact the display of the document in the primary window. To see the changes, use the print preview feature in Task 122.

Using WordPad's Print Preview

WordPad allows you to modify the setup of a page. This includes changing margins, paper size, paper orientation, and more, as shown in Task 121. Unfortunately, you can't view these changes in the primary document window. You can, however, see the impact of these changes using print preview.

The print preview feature allows you to see what your document will look like when printed. To use this feature, follow these steps with your current document:

1. Make changes to the page setup as shown in Task 120, or if you want to use the default options, skip this step.

2. Select File⇨Print Preview from the WordPad menu. The Print Preview window appears (see Figure 122-1). Although it is somewhat difficult to read because of the smaller presentation of the document, note that this specific document has a page setup with 1-inch margins on letter paper. Also note that the margin is indicated with dashed lines and that the paper size presented matches that of a standard letter-sized sheet of paper.

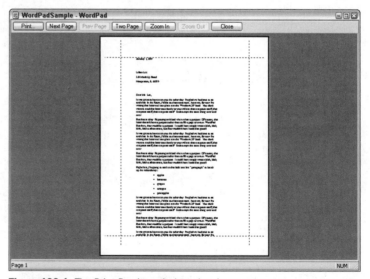

Figure 122-1: The Print Preview window showing a page.

3. Click the Next Page button to see the page following the current one. If you are on the last page, this button is disabled.

4. Click the Previous Page button to see the preceding page. If you are on the first page, this button will be disabled.

5. Click the Two Pages button to see two pages on the screen at once. Figure 122-2 presents the two-page view of the same document used in Figure 122-1. To go back to a one-page view, select the One Page button that replaces the Two Page button.

cross-reference

To change the margins, paper size, and other page features you see in the print preview, see Task 121.

tip

You should always do a quick print preview before printing just to make sure everything looks the way you want.

tip

Print preview makes it easy to ensure that a letter is centered on the page.

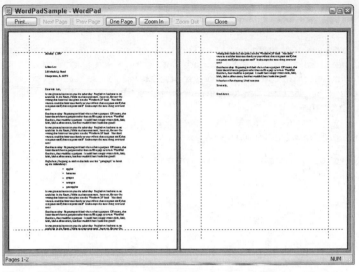

Figure 122-2: The Print Preview window showing two pages.

6. Click the Zoom In button to get a clearer, closer view of the document. You can click this once or twice to get better views. Figure 122-3 shows the same document from the previous figures fully zoomed. You can click the Zoom Out button to go back to a less detailed view.

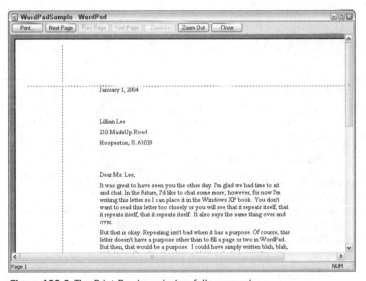

Figure 122-3: The Print Preview window fully zoomed.

7. Click the Print button if you want to go ahead and print the document. The Print dialog window appears, which is covered in Task 123.

8. Click the Close button and return to your WordPad document.

note

You can click the left mouse button on the document in the Print Preview window to zoom. If you click once, it will zoom halfway. Click again and it will zoom the full way. Click a third time and you will return to the default size.

tip

If you are printing envelopes, you can enter multiple addresses and then use print preview to make sure they line up correctly on the envelopes. By adding spaces between the addresses, you can position each address to go onto a separate page.

cross-reference

To understand printing and the Print dialog window, see Task 123.

Printing from WordPad

After creating a document or file in WordPad, there is a good chance you will want to print a copy. With WordPad you can choose to print all or just part of your document. You can choose to print multiple copies. You can choose to print on different printers. You can even print to a file. The following steps walk you through all these options:

1. Open or create a document in WordPad as shown in Task 119.

2. Select File⇨Print from the menu, or press Ctrl+P. The Print dialog appears (see Figure 123-1).

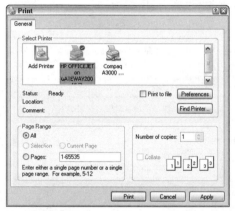

Figure 123-1: The Print dialog window.

3. Click on the printer in the Select Printer group at the top of the Print dialog window. If the printer you want to use is not displayed, the software for it has not been installed on your computer. In this case, you may want to double-click on the Add Printer icon and follow the wizard.

4. Select settings specific to your printer.

   Depending on your printer, you may be able to set additional settings. When a printer is selected in the Select Printer area, the Preferences button will be available. Clicking this button provides you with a dialog window of options specific to the printer you selected. Figure 123-2 presents the dialog for the Compaq 3000 printer shown in Figure 123-1. The display you receive depends on your make of printer.

5. In the Print dialog box, select the number of copies. If you want more than one copy, change the value in the Number of Copies box. This value can only be changed if your printer supports multiple copies. If your printer cannot support multiple copies, a message such as that shown in Figure 123-3 appears when you try to change the value. The value will be reset to a valid value.

cross-reference

To set layout options for your document such as margin sizes and paper size, see Task 121 about Page Setup.

cross-reference

Refer to Task 219 for more on adding a printer.

note

Double-clicking on a printer in the Select Printer area of the Print dialog starts the printing of the document with the current settings.

cross-reference

To see what your document will look like before printing, see Task 122 about print preview. On the Print Preview dialog window, you can select the Print button to be taken to the Print dialog window. You can then go to Step 4 of this task.

note

The Find Printer button allows you to search for a printer on your computer or on a network. Your computer still needs to have the correct software installed to use any printers you may find.

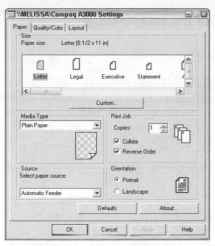

Figure 123-2: The Printing Preferences dialog window for a Compaq 3000 printer.

6. In the Pages text box, select the page range. If your document is more than one page long, you can select to print the entire document, the current page (based on where the cursor is located), or a range of pages. You can also choose to print just a section of the document.

Figure 123-3: An error message.

7. Click the Print button. Your document, or the portion you've selected, will print based on the options you selected.

8. The Print dialog window also includes a box that you can check to have the text document print to a file. If you check the Print to File box, then when you click the Print button, you will be asked for a filename, as shown in Figure 123-4.

Figure 123-4: The Print to File prompt.

Instead of printing to a printer, your text document is formatted and written to a file with the name you enter. This file includes information specific to the formatting you selected in page formatting, as well as for the printer and options that you selected. The information that is written to the file is specifically written for the selected printer. In fact, most of the information in the file will be unreadable.

note

If you select to print more than one copy, you will need to determine if you want to collate the copies. Collating prints all the pages of one document at a time. Check the box next to Collate if you want them collated. If you don't check the box, all copies of the first page will be printed, followed by all copies of the second, and so on.

note

Depending on your printer, you may have additional features that you can use when printing.

caution

If you don't know how to use files specifically formatted for a printer, it is best to avoid using the Print to File feature.

Task 124

Changing Font Characteristics in WordPad

In addition to standard formatting, WordPad lets you change the font style, color, and size. You can customize the font of an entire document or of a single character. By changing the fonts, you can customize a WordPad document to a number of different uses. The following steps walk you through changing characteristics of the fonts.

1. Open or create a document in WordPad as shown in Task 119.

2. Click in your document where you want to enter text.

   Alternatively, you can select the portion of an existing document containing text you want to format. You can select text in a number of ways. The easiest way is to place your mouse cursor at the start of the text you want to select. Click the left mouse button and hold it down while dragging the mouse cursor to the end of the portion of text. When you let up on the mouse button, the area of selected text should be highlighted. Figure 124-1 shows an area of text selected in a WordPad document.

Figure 124-1: Selected text highlighted in a WordPad document.

3. Choose the formatting you want to use. You can either use the format bar (see Figure 124-2) or the Font dialog window. Select Format⇨Font to open the Font dialog window, shown in Figure 124-3. Following are some of the formatting features you can apply:

   • *Changing font.* The font drop-down list in both the format bar and Font window presents a list of the available fonts on your machine. You can select a font to apply to the currently highlighted area.

cross-reference

For additional formatting for paragraphs see Task 125.

tip

You can select all of the text in the entire document by selecting Edit⇨Select All from the WordPad menu or by pressing Ctrl+A.

tip

You can select a single line of text by clicking the left mouse button in the margin area to the left of the line. Double-clicking in the margin to the left selects the paragraph of text on the right. Triple-clicking in the left margin selects the entire document. You can also place the cursor at a location in your page, press and hold the Shift key, then use the arrow keys to select an area. Finally, double-clicking on a word selects that word.

caution

When changing font sizes, you can enter a number not listed. If the font has a TT (indicating a TrueType font) next to it in the Font list, then the font should smoothly scale to the new size. Otherwise the font may not look as smooth if you pick a size other than those listed in the list.

tip

A number of fonts include special images and symbols. For example, Webdings and Wingdings both contain symbols. You can select these fonts and then start typing in your document. You'll see that funny symbols are presented instead of letters.

Font Size   Italic   Font Color

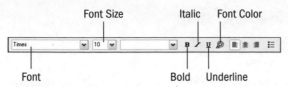

Font   Bold   Underline

Figure 124-2: The format bar.

- *Changing style.* The Font dialog window includes an option to select a font style. This allows you to add bold, italic, or both to the currently selected text. Alternatively, you can click on the bold or italic buttons on the format bar (see Figure 124-2).

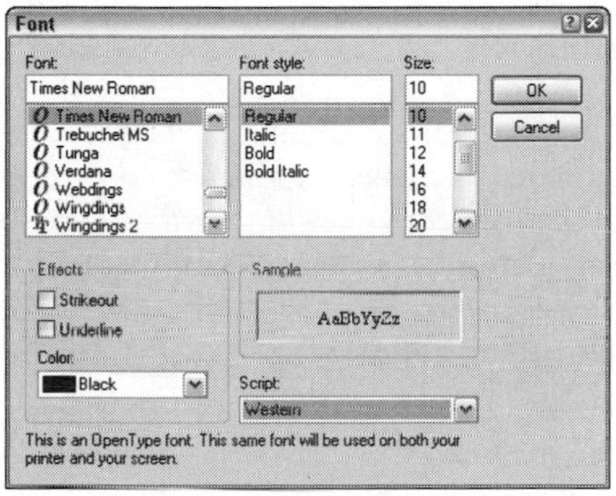

Figure 124-3: The Font dialog window.

- *Changing size.* You can change the size of the text in the current selection by selecting a different Size value. The size value is the available point sizes for the font. A lower number is a smaller font; a larger number is a bigger font. You can select a number from the list or type a new number in the entry box. This works the same in both the Font window and the format bar.

- *Changing color.* To change the color, you can select the color drop-down list in the Color area of the Font dialog window. Alternately, you can select the font color on the format bar by clicking the Color button and then selecting from the presented list.

- *Change other effects.* You can also make two other changes. You can underline the text by checking the Underline option in the Effects box of the Font window or by clicking the Underline button on the format bar. You can strikeout the selected text by checking the strikeout option in the Effects area of the Font dialog. By default, strikeout is not on the format bar.

4. Select the OK button if you are in the Font dialog to apply the formatting. Prior to selecting OK, you can see the impact of your selections in the Sample box.

5. Type additional text into WordPad if you are applying format for new text. If you are formatting a selected area of text, that area will be formatted.

---

note

You can display the format bar by selecting View ➪ Format Bar. A check next to this menu option means that the toolbar is displayed.

---

caution

Although you can change the color of a font, if your printer doesn't support color, your colors will be printed in grayscale or black-and-white.

---

note

Some fonts, especially larger ones, will not display in the WordPad window correctly. To see how they will look when printed, use the print preview feature.

---

note

If you select options from the format bar, they are applied immediately.

Formatting Paragraph Margins in WordPad

A number of features are available in WordPad that you can use to format paragraphs and their margins. You can change the justification of the text in a paragraph from left-justified to centered or right-justified. You can also change the margin settings to be different sizes for different paragraphs. You can even change the amount of indent on the first sentence of a paragraph so that it differs from the rest of the paragraph.

Before making changes to the margins and paragraphs, make sure you have selected the page size that you plan to use. Task 121 shows you the steps for picking paper size. Once your page size is selected, use the following steps to format the paragraphs and margins:

1. Verify that your page view is set to use the ruler width and not the window (or document page) width. If your page is not set to the ruler width, the formatting you apply will not be presented correctly in the WordPad window — only on the printout. To set or verify that the view is set to use the ruler width, do the following:

   a. Select View➪Options... from the WordPad menu. The Options dialog appears, showing the options for the current document type (see Figure 125-1). Each document type supported by WordPad is listed as a tab in the dialog.

Figure 125-1: The Options dialog.

   b. Select the Wrap to Ruler option in order to have the best representation of what your document will look like when printed. This causes your document to use the ruler bar. You can also check the toolbars you would like displayed when you are editing the current document type.

   c. Click the OK button to return to the WordPad document window.

2. Select the paragraph or group of paragraphs that you want to format. Select a single paragraph by double-clicking to the left of it or by triple-clicking within it. Select the entire document by clicking three times in the left margin, by choosing View➪Select All from the WordPad menus, or by pressing Ctrl+A.

cross-reference

To format the text and the text styles, see Task 124.

cross-reference

See Task 121 for setting page margins.

note

WordPad does not offer a justified alignment, which lines up both the left and right sides of the paragraph.

cross-reference

To see the overall look of a document, use the print preview. Task 122 presents the steps for using print preview.

3. Select Format⇨Paragraphs from the WordPad menu. The Paragraph dialog window appears (see Figure 125-2). Alternatively, you can right-click on a paragraph or selected area and then select Paragraph from the pop-up menu that appears.

Figure 125-2: The Paragraph dialog.

4. Set values for the left and right indentation of the selected paragraph(s) by entering numbers into the corresponding entry boxes. Keep in mind that these indentations will be added to any indentations you have set in the page setup.

5. Set a value for any additional indentation you want on the first sentence of the selected paragraph(s). The value entered into the First Line entry box is the amount of additional indentation for the first sentence. Again, this amount is in addition to the left indentation. If you don't want the first sentence to have additional indenting, then leave the value of First Line as 0.

6. Select the alignment of the paragraph from the drop-down Alignment list. Left lines up the left side of the paragraph with the left margin, Right lines up the text in the paragraph with the right margin, and Center centers the lines within the paragraph's margins.

7. Select the OK button to apply the changes.

8. Repeat Steps 2 through 7 for any additional paragraphs that you want to format.

Buttons are available on the format bar to provide a shortcut for formatting the alignment of a paragraph. Clicking these buttons applies the corresponding alignment to the currently selected paragraph(s).

cross-reference

The width you are presented in printing your document is based on the settings you select in Page Setup. For example, if you choose a 4-inch × 6-inch-sized document, then your document width will be no greater than 4 or 6 inches (depending on the orientation you choose). The ruler at the top of the WordPad document actually shows the width of the page minus the values you set as margins in the Page Setup. For more on selecting the page size, see Task 121.

tip

A paragraph is considered any text up to a carriage return. A carriage return is the value from pressing the Enter or Return key. As such, a list of bullets can be treated and formatted as a paragraph. This lets you indent bullets farther into the document if you want.

tip

You can actually start a new line without the larger paragraph break by pressing Shift+Enter. This is called a *soft return* and it forces a manual break that retains formatting for the new line or paragraph.

Task 126

Adding Lists to a WordPad Document

As you build more complex documents in WordPad, one feature that is beneficial is the ability to add lists. WordPad provides you with the option to add bulleted lists to your documents.

1. Open or create a document in WordPad as shown in Task 119.

2. Place the cursor at the location in your document where you want to add a bulleted list.

3. Click the Bullet icon in the toolbar. This will start a bullet list as shown in Figure 126-1. Alternatively, you can select Format⇨ Bullet Style from the menu. Clicking on the Bullet Style menu option places a check mark next to it and starts the bullet list.

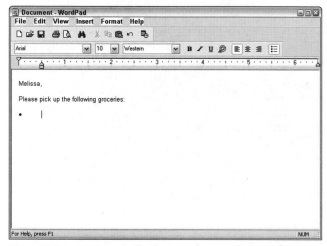

Figure 126-1: Starting a bullet list.

cross-reference

You can format a bulleted list using the Left, Right, and Center buttons as shown in Task 125; however, the bullets will only line up with left justification.

cross-reference

As an advanced feature, you can actually change the distance between the bullet and the text that follows. You do this by adjusting the values in the paragraph indentation settings shown in Task 125. Set the Left value to equal the distance you want from the bullet to the text. Then set the First Line value to the negative of the same value. For example, the default values are .05 inches for the Left indentation and -.05 inches for the First Line value.

cross-reference

Bulleted text can be formatted just like any other text. Thus, you can use bold, italics, underlining, strikeout, and color, as shown in Task 124.

4. Enter text or values for your bulleted item. You can even enter complete paragraphs for each bulleted item.

5. Press Enter to end the current bulleted item and to start a new one.

6. Repeat Steps 4 and 5 until you have entered all the bulleted items that you want in your list.

7. Click on the Bullet icon a second time, or select Format⇨Bullet Style again. This ends the bulleted list. Figure 126-2 illustrates several items that have been entered in a bulleted list.

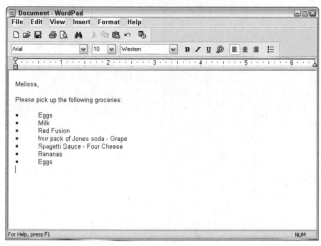

Figure 126-2: An entered bullet list.

8. Continue adding additional text as needed.

9. Convert existing text into a bullered list by highlighting the text and clicking the Bullets button in the format bar. You can remove existing bullets by highlighting the text and clicking the Bullets button.

Searching and Replacing Text in WordPad

WordPad allows you to create large documents. As a document gets larger, it is often hard to find a specific word or phrase that you entered. Additionally, you may find that you want to change a word or phrase. For example, say you entered "Brad" and you want to change all occurrences to "Bradley." You can search for and replace the text in WordPad with the following steps.

1. Open an existing document in WordPad as shown in Task 119. Then place the cursor at the location in your document where you want to start searching.

2. To search for text, select Edit⇨Find, or press Ctrl+F. The Find dialog appears (see Figure 127-1).

Figure 127-1: The Find dialog.

If you want to find and also replace, select Edit⇨Replace instead. The Replace dialog appears (see Figure 127-2).

Figure 127-2: The Replace dialog.

3. Enter into the Find What box the text you would like to find. If you are also replacing, then in addition to the text you enter in the Find What box, also enter the text you want to replace the found text into the Replace With box.

4. Check the Match Whole Word Only box if you don't want to find larger words that contain your search string. For example, if you entered "Brad" into the Find What box, then checking Match Whole Words Only would only find "Brad." It would not find Bradley or Bradford. Leaving it unchecked would find these longer words.

cross-reference

See Task 119 for creating or opening a WordPad document.

tip

You can highlight text before selecting the search dialogs. Doing so places the highlighted text in the Find box of the Search dialog.

note

Searching will start from the current location of the cursor and continue to the end of the document. Once the end of the document is reached, searching will go to the top and continue searching until the original starting location is reached. The result is that the entire document is searched one time.

tip

After searching the first time, you can close the Find dialog by clicking the Close button. You can then select Edit⇨ Find Next... or press F3 to search for the same text another time. This allows you to search for text without having the Find dialog window in the way.

5. Check Match Case if you want to only find words with the same casing. For example, if you check this option and enter Brad for the Find What value, then brad and BRAD would not be found. Clearing this check box would find all three.

6. Click the Find Next button. WordPad finds the first occurrence of the text entered in the Find What box. This occurrence is highlighted as shown in Figure 127-3.

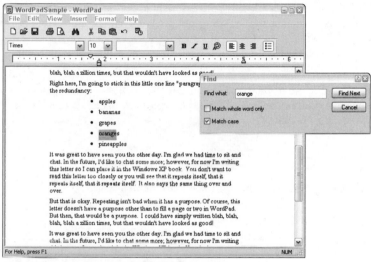

Figure 127-3: Found text in a WordPad document.

7. If you are only finding text and not replacing, click the Find Next button again to find the next occurrence. When you have gone through the complete document, a warning message is displayed (see Figure 127-4).

Figure 127-4: This message is displayed when WordPad can't find the text anymore.

8. If you are finding and replacing text, you will have a Replace button that you can click. Clicking the Replace button also looks for the next occurrence of the text. Continue clicking the Replace button or the Find Next button until you've made all the changes you want.

9. Click the Cancel button to close the Find or Replace dialog.

Task 127

note

If WordPad can't find the text you entered, you will get the same message as the one displayed in Figure 127-4.

tip

Click the Replace All button in the Replace dialog to change all occurrences of the Find What text to the Replace With text. Be sure you want to change all occurrences before using this feature.

cross-reference

Once you find text, you can change its font or other characteristics. Task 124 shows you how to change the look of text.

Inserting a Picture into a WordPad Document

Wordpad gives you the ability to insert a picture or image into a WordPad document. By being able to add pictures, you can create much more impressive documents. For example, creating a document that says "free kittens" is great, but adding a picture of the kittens would increase the odds of finding homes. If you are writing a letter, you can include digital pictures. You can find lots of different scenarios when adding pictures to a WordPad document makes sense. The following steps show you how to add such a picture:

1. Open or create a document in WordPad as shown in Task 119.

2. Select an image to paste into WordPad. You will need to copy an image from another application or from a Web page. Following are two ways to do this.

   From a Web page:

   a. Find the image you want on a Web page.

   b. Right-click on the image. A pop-up menu as shown in Figure 128-1 appears.

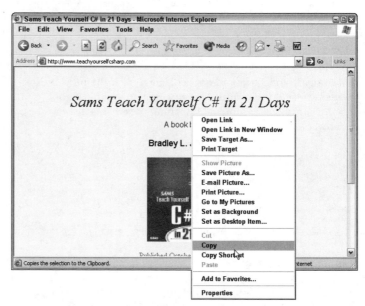

Figure 128-1: Right-clicking a Web page image (in this case the book cover).

   c. Select Copy.

   From Microsoft Paint:

   a. Open the picture in the Windows XP program, Microsoft Paint.

cross-reference

A picture is just one type of object that can be inserted into WordPad. For inserting or linking to other objects, or for linking to an external picture, see Task 129.

caution

You need to be using an RTF file type to add pictures. Text files cannot contain images, so the picture will be dropped along with any other advanced formatting.

cross-reference

See Task 65 for more on using Microsoft Paint.

   b. Select Edit⇨Select All from the Paint menus or press Ctrl+A to select the entire picture.

   c. Select Edit⇨Copy from the Paint menus or press Ctrl+C to copy the image.

3. Place the cursor at the location in your document where you want to add the image.

4. Select Edit⇨Paste from the WordPad menu or press Ctrl+V to paste the copied image into WordPad document. Figure 128-2 shows the result of pasting the image copied from Figure 128-1 at the beginning of a new line.

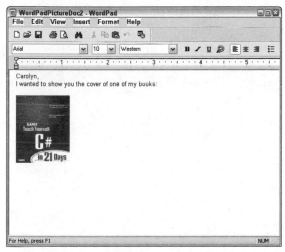

Figure 128-2: WordPad with a pasted image.

5. Save your WordPad document.

6. Repeat Steps 2 through 5 to add additional images to your WordPad document.

tip

A picture does not have to be at the beginning of a line. You can use spaces or text to move an image to the right. You can also justify to the left, right, or center. See Task 125 to learn how to do justification.

cross-reference

You can also create images directly in WordPad by inserting a bitmap object. This is covered in Task 129.

note

You cannot wrap text around an image in WordPad. You can have a single line of text on the same line, but not multiple lines.

note

Clicking on the image will place eight little boxes (handles) around the image. You can use your mouse to select and drag these boxes. This will cause the image to be skewed. Using a corner box, you can actually increase or decrease the size of the image.

Adding an Object to a WordPad Document

WordPad enables you to link or embed objects into a document. There are a variety of different objects that you can use, including bitmap images, media clips, Microsoft Excel charts, Microsoft Excel worksheets, Microsoft Word pictures, MIDI sequences, packages, Microsoft Paint pictures, video clips, wave sounds, and other WordPad documents.

You can either link each object or embed it. Linking an object does not put the actual object in your document. Rather, it links to an object stored in some other place. Embedding places the object within your document. The difference is that if you copy or send your document to someone else, embedded objects are included automatically. Linked objects are not.

1. Place the cursor at the location in your WordPad document where you want to add the object. This can be anywhere, even in the middle of a sentence.

2. Select Insert⇨Object. The Insert Object dialog appears (see Figure 129-1).

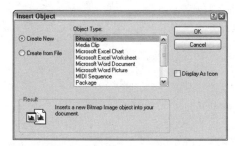

Figure 129-1: The Insert Object dialog.

3. Select the type of object you want to use from the Object Type: list.

4. Select either Create New or Create from File. If you select Create New, a program corresponding to the object type you selected is used to create a new object. If you select Create from File, the Insert Object dialog changes to that in Figure 129-2. Use the Browse button to find an existing file to use.

5. Check or clear the Link check box. The Link option is only available if you selected the Create from File option. If you want to embed the object into your document, make sure this button is cleared. If you want to link to an object that is outside of your document, click the Link check box.

6. Click the OK button to accept your values. If you selected Create from File, your object is placed in the document, and you are done.

   If you selected Create New, an editor or other corresponding program appears that creates the type of object you created. For

cross-reference

In Task 128 you learn how to add a picture or image to a WordPad document. The procedures in this task also work with pictures.

cross-reference

When using this task, if you find that adding a picture causes the name of the picture to be placed in your document rather than the actual picture, use the steps in Task 129 to add the picture.

cross-reference

You can learn how to send a WordPad document via email in Task 131.

caution

If you are using an external object, then changes to a linked object will change the original. Changes to an embedded object will not impact the original.

example, if you selected Wave Sound, then a Sound Recorder, as shown in Figure 129-3, appears.

Figure 129-2: The Insert Object dialog with the file prompt.

7. Create your file or document based on the object type you selected.

Figure 129-3: The Sound Recorder.

8. Click the OK button or close the program when you have completed creating your new object. You are returned to your document. Depending on the type of object you selected, either an icon or the object is presented. For example, with the Wave Sound, an icon of a speaker appears in your document. With a chart object, the chart appears. Figure 129-4 shows a document with several objects added.

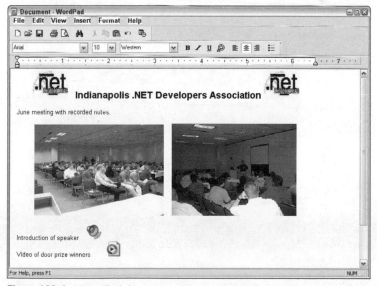

Figure 129-4: A WordPad document with sound and picture objects embedded.

note

The bottom of the Insert Object dialog includes a box that provides a description of the currently selected object type. This description tells you what the result will be of selecting the OK button.

cross-reference

To understand how to use the different editors or programs that create objects, check out the other tasks throughout this book. For example, you can learn about the creating sounds in task 197. Task 79 discusses recording songs. In Task 96 you discover how to make movies. All of these objects, as well as many others, can be linked into a WordPad document.

tip

If desired, you can display all inserted objects as icons. You can force an icon to be displayed instead of the actual objects by checking the Display as Icon option on the Insert Object dialog.

Changing Object Properties in a Document

WordPad lets you link or embed objects into a document, as shown in Task 129. Once these objects are in your documents, you may find that you want to change them. You can change the object, as well as some of its display features.

1. Click on the object you want to use within your WordPad document. Small boxes called *handles* appear in each corner and on the edges of the object.

2. Select Edit⇨Object Properties from the WordPad menu or press Alt+Enter. A property dialog window for the object appears (see Figure 130-1).

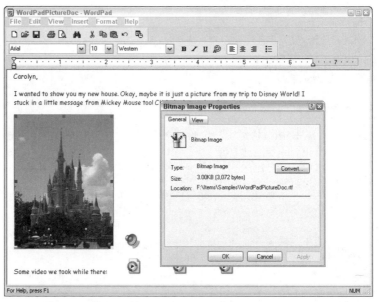

Figure 130-1: An object property dialog for a picture.

3. Select the View tab. The dialog shown in Figure 130-2 appears. This dialog gives you options for changing the size or the icon of what is being displayed.

4. Select whether you want to change your object to or from an icon. You don't have to change this setting. If you originally put an icon on the page, you can select the Display as Editable Information option to place the item in the document.

5. If you want to change the icon, use the following steps:

    a. Click the Change Icon button. The Change Icon dialog appears (see Figure 130-3).

cross-reference
In Task 129 you learn how to add an object to a WordPad document.

caution
Opening an image by double-clicking on it may cause a blank image to be inserted. This is true if you used the steps shown in Task 128 to insert the image. You can press Esc to get back to the document without saving the blank document.

tip
You can often find icons to use by browsing the program for the inserted object. For example, the program file sndrec32.exe contains icons for the sound recorder.

note
If you have not selected an object, the Edit⇨ Object Properties menu option will be disabled. You must have an object selected by clicking on it in order to use this option.

Figure 130-2: The view values of an object.

b. Select the icon you want to use on your document. You can choose icons from another file by selecting From File and entering a filename or browsing.

Figure 130-3: The Change Icon dialog.

c. Change the text in the Label box. This text will be displayed under your icon. You can change the text to something more descriptive.

d. Click the OK button to return to the object's properties dialog.

6. Click the Apply button to apply any changes to your document.

7. Click the OK button to return to your document.

note

You should note that many types of objects — such as sounds and videos — have what appears to be an icon placed in your document; however, these are editable connections to the document. As such, when you view the properties dialog, the Display as Editable Information option will be selected.

cross-reference

Learn how to create your own custom icons in Task 64.

note

If the object you select can be changed to a different format, then the Convert button in the object's property dialog will be usable. If the format cannot be changed, then the button will be disabled. A picture is an example of an object that can be converted to a different format.

tip

Double-clicking on an object opens it so you can edit it.

Sending a WordPad Document to Someone Else

Once you've created a document in WordPad, you may want to share it with someone else. You can save the document as shown in Task 120 and pass it to someone else by copying it to a disk. You can also share it with someone else by sending it via email. To send a document via email, you must have an email account and your computer must be connected to the Internet.

1. Create or open a document in WordPad as shown in Task 119. Make any changes you want. When you are ready to send the document, continue to the next step.

2. Select File⇨Send from the WordPad menus. If you have never sent an email on your computer, the Internet Setup Wizard appears. Follow the steps in the wizard. You'll only need to do this once. After the wizard, or if you are already set up for the Internet, you are presented with a New email message (see Figure 131-1). Your document will be listed as an attachment in this message.

cross-reference

For information on saving a WordPad document, review Task 120.

cross-reference

For more information on setting up your email, see Task 158.

cross-reference

For more information on sending email, see Task 161.

cross-reference

For more information on the options available for sending messages, see the tasks in Part 11.

caution

Make sure that the email address you enter is valid.

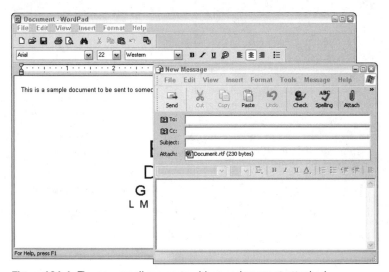

Figure 131-1: The new email message with your document attached.

3. Expand this message dialog if desired. You can increase the size of this dialog to display all of the options and buttons. Figure 131-2 shows the expanded view of the dialog.

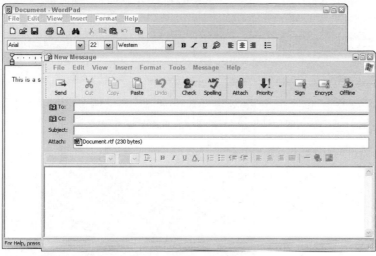

Figure 131-2: The expanded New Message dialog.

4. Fill in the additional information. At a minimum, you need to enter the email address of the person you are sending the document to. You can also fill in a subject line and a message.

5. Click the Send button or select File⇨Send Message from the New Message dialog's menu. A status bar similar to Figure 131-3 appears, showing the status.

Figure 131-3: The status of the message being sent.

Once the message with your document has been sent, the dialog in Figure 131-1 is automatically closed and you are returned to WordPad.

tip

You can enter more than one email address in the To box of the New Message dialog if you want to send the document to more than one person. Separate each address with a semicolon. You can put additional addresses in the CC box as well.

tip

You can send yourself a copy of your document as a backup.

tip

You can press Crtl+S while in the New Message dialog to send a message.

note

Windows XP uses Outlook Express as the default mail program. If you have installed a different email program on your computer, you may use it to send the document instead. In this case, the steps in this task may not work exactly as stated.

Setting Options in WordPad

WordPad allows you to set a few options such as measurement types, word wrapping, and toolbars to display. By default, the ruler and measurements used in WordPad for margins are measured in inches. You can change this to a different unit of measurement, such as points, centimeters, or picas. The following steps show you how to change the measurement setting, as well as how to set values for the way words are wrapped on the screen and the toolbars that are displayed.

cross-reference

The way paragraphs are displayed on the screen is based on the options you set in this task. Task 125 shows you how to work with paragraphs in WordPad.

tip

You can use different settings for each type of document you use in WordPad. For example, your settings for text documents do not have to match those for RTF files.

note

RTF stands for Rich Text Format. This is the standard format for WordPad files. RTF files store the fonts, colors, and other changes you make in your documents.

cross-reference

See Task 121 for changing additional WordPad settings that impact the way your document will look when you print.

note

WordPad lets you set options for Word and Write. You may not have these programs on your machine; however, WordPad lets you open documents that were created with them. Word is available at a separate cost as a standalone program or as a part of Microsoft Office. Write is a program found in older versions of Microsoft Windows. It is similar to WordPad.

1. Select View⇨Options from the WordPad menu. The Options dialog appears (see Figure 132-1).

Figure 132-1: The WordPad Options dialog.

2. Click on the Options tab in the Options dialog. The Measurement Units options are, as shown in Figure 132-2.

Figure 132-2: The WordPad Measurement Units options.

3. Click on the measurement unit that you want to use. Clicking on the name selects that unit.

4. Click on the Automatic Word selection box if you want to be able to select full words when using the mouse cursor. If you want to be able to start or end in the middle of a word when using the mouse to select, then uncheck this box.

5. Set values for specific document types. In the remaining tabs in the Options dialog, you can select options that apply to specific document types or to embedded objects. You can set the Word Wrap value, and you can determine which toolbars are displayed. The options you select in each tab will apply to any documents you use of the corresponding type. For example, following are the steps for setting the Text Document options:

a. Select the Text tab in the Options dialog. See Figure 132-3.

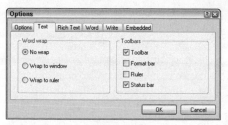

Figure 132-3: The Text tab in the Options dialog.

b. Select the Word Wrap option. No Wrap means that the text will continue to the right on the screen (and off the screen) until you press the Enter key or until the end of a paragraph is reached. Wrap to Window wraps the text based on the actual WordPad window. Wrap to Ruler uses the margin setting.

c. Select the toolbars you want displayed. Selected toolbars will have checks next to them. Figure 132-4 shows the four toolbars that are available in WordPad.

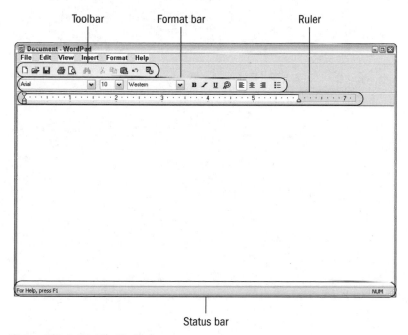

Figure 132-4: The WordPad rulers.

d. Select the other document type tabs and set the options as shown in Steps b and c.

6. Click the OK button to return to your WordPad document.

Part 9: Getting Connected to the Internet

Task 133: Creating an MSN Account to Access the Internet Using a Modem

Task 134: Connecting to the Internet with a Modem Using Another ISP

Task 135: Connecting to the Internet with a Broadband Cable or DSL Line

Task 136: Connecting to the Internet with a LAN and a Router

Task 137: Connecting to a Virtual Private Network

Task 133

Creating an MSN Account to Access the Internet Using a Modem

If you don't have access to the Internet through an Internet service provider (ISP), the easiest way to get online in Windows XP is probably through the Microsoft Network (MSN). In this task, you'll walk through the process of creating an MSN account and getting on the Internet through that account using your modem. Before you begin, you should have a modem in your machine that is configured correctly and that is connected to your telephone line.

1. Access the MSN Explorer Wizard through the New Connection Wizard:

   a. Choose Start⇨All Programs⇨Accessories⇨Communications⇨ New Connection Wizard. The New Connection Wizard appears.

   b. Click Next. The Network Connection Type page is displayed. Select Connect to the Internet. Click Next. The Getting Ready page appears. Select Choose from a list of Internet service providers (ISPs).

   c. Click Next. Choose Get Online with MSN. Click Finish.

   d. The Use MSN Explorer? window asks, "Would you like to get on the Internet and write e-mail through the Start menu using MSN Explorer?" Click No. The Welcome to MSN Explorer Wizard appears.

2. Click Continue. You may see a page asking what region you live in. If you do, choose the appropriate option and click Continue. The Do You Want MSN Internet Access? page is displayed (see Figure 133-1). Choose "Yes, I would like to sign up for MSN Internet Access and get a new MSN e-mail address."

3. Click Continue. The Check Your Dialing Options page is displayed. Click the check box beside any options that apply to your situation.

4. Click Continue. The Dialing... page appears, and then the Connecting... page. After Windows XP is connected, you may see a Do You Want MSN Internet Access? page just as you did in Step 2. If you do, choose the same option and click Continue.

5. Now you will see a series of pages that ask you for your name, birthday, occupation, address, and phone number. Enter the information required on each page and click Continue.

6. The next several pages ask you to choose a plan (there may be only one option, depending on where you live), confirm the access numbers (it selects the nearest ones automatically), and confirm that you read the license agreement. Select the appropriate information on each page and click Continue.

note

If you need to dial a number to get out (such as 9) or a certain set of numbers to disable call waiting (such as *70), enter those values on the Check Your Dialing Options page.

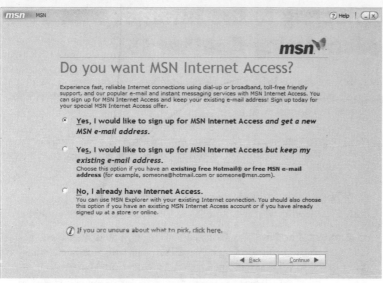

Figure 133-1: The Do You Want MSN Internet Access? page.

7. The Credit Card Information page that pops up allows you to enter your credit card information. Do so.

8. Click Continue. The next two pages ask you to enter the password you want to use to access MSN and choose an email name. Enter the information required on each page and click Continue.

9. The Customer Experience Improvement Program page is displayed. Select I Don't Want to Right Now. Click Continue. The final window is displayed. Click the Sign In! button.

10. The Welcome to MSN Explorer page is displayed. Click the icon beside your name. MSN Explorer dials a local number and connects you to the service (see Figure 133-2).

Figure 133-2: The Connect dialog.

note

When you type in the Password and Confirm Password text box, you won't see the actual letters you're typing. You'll just see dots. This is to help keep your password private.

tip

Be careful to type the user ID and password exactly as given to you by your ISP, including appropriate uppercase and lowercase characters. If this isn't right, it won't work.

note

Don't worry — the number Windows XP calls is toll-free. You'll probably hear your modem dial the number, the ring, and the high-pitched screech as the computers communicate. If Windows XP can't get through, it may wait a few seconds and then retry with another toll-free number.

caution

If the email name you choose is already in use by someone else, you'll be presented with a list of alternatives. You can either choose one of them or type in a different one.

cross-reference

Now that you are connected to the Internet, check out Part 10 to find out how to use Internet Explorer to surf the Web. Also see Task 158 to find out how to set up your email. The rest of the tasks in Part 11 show you how to use Outlook Express to send and receive email.

Task 134

Connecting to the Internet with a Modem Using Another ISP

I f you already have an ISP, or you've decided you want to sign up with a service other than MSN, this task shows you how to configure Windows XP to use your modem to connect with to it.

Before you begin, you should already be signed up with your ISP. When you do, the provider will give you important information that you'll use to configure your computer in this task.

tip

Some ISPs give you a CD to install on your computer. If you have such a CD, go ahead and install it and follow those directions instead of doing this task. The CD will likely configure your system automatically.

1. Choose Start⇨All Programs⇨Accessories⇨Communications⇨ New Connection Wizard. The New Connection Wizard appears.

2. Click Next. The Network Connection Type page is displayed. Select Connect to the Internet. Click Next. The Getting Ready page appears (see Figure 134-1). Select Set Up My Connection Manually.

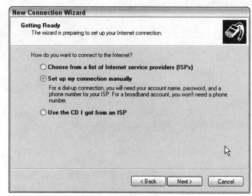

Figure 134-1: The Getting Ready page of the New Connection Wizard.

3. Click Next. Now you see the Internet Connection page.

4. Select Connect Using a Dial-up Modem. Click Next. The Connection Name page appears. Type the name of your ISP (like **Earthlink**, **NetZero**, or **AT&T Worldnet**) in the text box.

5. Click Next. The Phone Number to Dial page appears. Type in the phone number your ISP provided. Your modem will call this number to get a connection to the Internet.

6. Click Next. The Internet Account Information page appears (see Figure 134-2). Type in the user ID and password for your Internet account, provided by your ISP. Type your password a second time in

note

When you type in the Password and Confirm Password text box, you won't see the actual letters you're typing. You'll just see dots. This is to help keep your password private.

tip

Be careful to type the user ID and password exactly as given to you by your ISP, including appropriate uppercase and lowercase characters. If this isn't right, it won't work.

the Confirm Password text box, so that the wizard can be sure you didn't mistype. Leave the three check boxes at the bottom part of the page checked.

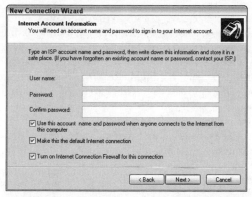

Figure 134-2: The Internet Account Information page of the New Connection Wizard.

7. Click Next. The Completing the New Connection Wizard page appears. Click the Add a Shortcut to This Connection on My Desktop check box.

8. Click Finish. The wizard ends and you are returned to the Windows XP desktop. A new icon appears on the desktop with your ISP's name.

9. Double-click the new icon. The Connect dialog appears (see Figure 134-3). Click Dial. You are connected to the Internet. Now when you open Internet Explorer, you'll access the Web.

Figure 134-3: The Connect dialog.

cross-reference

Now that you are connected to the Internet, check out Part 10 to find out how to use Internet Explorer to surf the Web. Also see Task 158 to find out how to set up your email. The rest of the tasks in Part 11 show you how to use Outlook Express to send and receive email.

Task 135

Connecting to the Internet with a Broadband Cable or DSL Line

If a modem is too slow for you, there are two common options you should consider: DSL and cable. DSL is a service you get through a local phone company that makes it possible for your computer to communicate in a different, faster way over your telephone lines. Cable service is available through your local TV cable company and uses the (coaxial) cable TV line instead of your telephone line. Call your local phone and cable companies to check to see if either of these options is available in your area.

This task assumes that your service is installed and that all appropriate hardware has been set up with your computer.

1. If you have broadband cable service:

    a. Obtain a cable modem. You can often rent or purchase these from your broadband cable service provider.

    b. Connect your cable TV cable to your cable modem.

    c. Connect the cable modem to your computer. This is typically done with a network cable and requires that you have a network (Ethernet) card in your computer. (Some cable modems have a USB connection instead, which makes the network card unnecessary.)

2. If you have broadband DSL service:

    a. Purchase a DSL bridge. You can often obtain these from your broadband DSL service provider.

    b. Connect your telephone line to the bridge.

    c. Connect the bridge to your computer. This is typically done with a network cable and requires that you have a network (Ethernet) card in your computer.

3. Choose Start⇨All Programs⇨Accessories⇨Communications⇨ New Connection Wizard. The New Connection Wizard appears.

4. Click Next. The Network Connection Type page is displayed (see Figure 135-1). Select Connect to the Internet.

5. Click Next. The Getting Ready page appears (see Figure 135-2). Select Set Up My Connection Manually.

6. Click Next. Now you see the Internet Connection page (see Figure 135-3). Select Connect Using a Broadband Connection That Is Always On.

tip

Some cable/DSL service providers give you a CD to install on your computer. If you have such a CD, go ahead and install it, and follow those directions instead of doing this task. The CD will likely configure your system automatically.

tip

Even though DSL uses the same telephone line as you use for your phones and fax, it doesn't tie up your line when you're on the Internet like a dial-up connection does. With DSL you are connected to the Internet all the time and you can still use the phone any time as you normally would. Likewise, use of broadband cable has no impact on your reception of TV cable channels.

note

See your cable modem or DSL bridge manual for details on connecting and configuring the modem/bridge to work on your computer. Your cable/DSL provider should also provide support to help you get everything going correctly.

cross-reference

Now that you are connected to the Internet, check out Part 10 to find out how to use Internet Explorer to surf the Web. Also see Task 158 to find out how to set up your email. The rest of the tasks in Part 11 show you how to use Outlook Express to send and receive email.

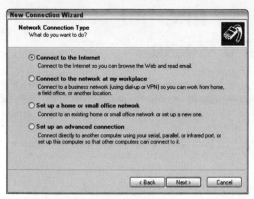

Figure 135-1: The Network Connection Type page of the New Connection Wizard.

7. Click Next. The wizard is complete. Click Finish.

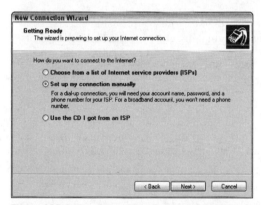

Figure 135-2: The Getting Ready page of the New Connection Wizard.

8. Open Internet Explorer by selecting Start⇨Internet Explorer. The browser opens, and you can surf the Web.

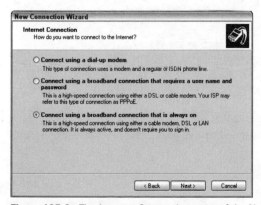

Figure 135-3: The Internet Connection page of the New Connection Wizard.

Task 136

Connecting to the Internet with a LAN and a Router

If you have a LAN set up in your home or small business, you can share a broadband Internet connection. Instead of connecting the cable modem or DSL bridge to a single machine, you connect it to a router and then connect the router to the network. This makes the Internet available for everyone to share. This task assumes that you have your LAN set up and configured correctly before you begin.

1. Purchase a router designed to allow you to share your broadband connection over the Internet.

2. If you have broadband cable service, connect your cable TV cable to your cable modem. If you have broadband DSL, connect your telephone line to the bridge.

3. Connect the cable modem/bridge to your router using a network cable. Be careful to plug the cable into the port marked "WAN" or "Internet."

4. Connect your router to your network hub using a network cable.

5. For each of the computers on the network, repeat Steps 6 through 10.

6. Choose Start➪All Programs➪Accessories➪Communications➪ New Connection Wizard. The New Connection Wizard appears.

7. Click Next. The Network Connection Type page is displayed (see Figure 136-1). Select Connect to the Internet.

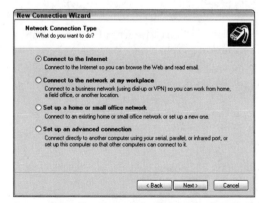

Figure 136-1: The Network Connection Type page of the New Connection Wizard.

cross-reference

For more information on setting up and configuring a LAN, see Part 18.

note

See your router manual for details on connecting and configuring the router to work on your LAN with your broadband connection.

note

You can use your cable modem at the same time you watch cable TV. Although they both use the same cable, they do not interfere with each other. The same is true for a DSL connection. You can make and receive phone calls normally while you use your DSL connection.

tip

Most routers have a network hub built in so that you can connect several computers directly to it. If you're setting up your network and you only have a few computers to connect, you may not need to purchase a separate hub.

8. Click Next. The Getting Ready page appears (see Figure 136-2).
    Select Set Up My Connection Manually.

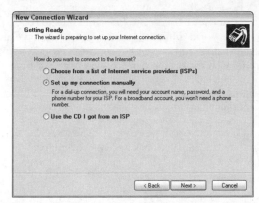

Figure 136-2: The Getting Ready page of the New Connection Wizard.

9. Click Next. Now you see the Internet Connection page (see Figure
    136-3). Select Connect Using a Broadband Connection That Is
    Always On. Click Next. The wizard is complete. Click Finish.

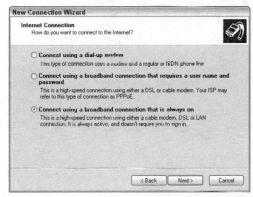

Figure 136-3: The Internet Connection page of the New Connection Wizard.

10. Open Internet Explorer by selecting Start⇨Internet Explorer. The
    browser opens, and you can surf the Web.

Connecting to a Virtual Private Network

A Virtual Private Network (VPN) provides a way for you to access your company's network over the Internet from home (or while on the road), just as if you were sitting at your desk at work. This task assumes that you have an Internet connection installed and configured on your computer and that your company has a VPN server configured to receive connections over the Internet.

cross-reference

To find out how to set up a dial-up Internet connection, see Task 134. To find out how to set up a broadband Internet connection, see Task 135.

1. Choose Start⇨All Programs⇨Accessories⇨Communications⇨ New Connection Wizard. The New Connection Wizard appears.

2. Click Next. The Network Connection Type page is displayed (see Figure 137-1). Select Connect to the Network at My Workplace.

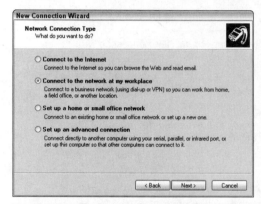

Figure 137-1: The Network Connection Type page of the New Connection Wizard.

3. Click Next. The Network Connection page appears (see Figure 137-2). Select Virtual Private Network Connection.

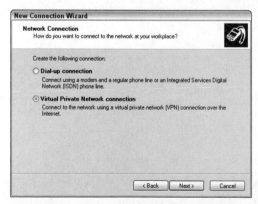

Figure 137-2: The Network Connection page of the New Connection Wizard.

4. Click Next. Now you see the Company Name page. Enter your company's name.

5. Click Next. The Public Network page appears (see Figure 137-3).

   • If your standard Internet connection is through a dial-up modem, select Automatically Dial This Initial Connection, and choose the name of your Internet service from the drop-down list.

   • If your standard Internet connection is through a broadband (cable or DSL) service, select Do Not Dial the Initial Connection.

Figure 137-3: The Public Network page of the New Connection Wizard.

6. Click Next. The VPN Server Selection page appears (see Figure 137-4). Enter the DNS name or IP address of the VPN server you wish to access.

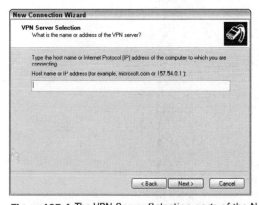

Figure 137-4: The VPN Server Selection page of the New Connection Wizard.

7. Click Next. The wizard is complete. Click the Add a Shortcut to This Connection to My Desktop check box, and then click Finish.

8. You return to the Windows XP desktop. Double-click the new icon there to connect to your VPN. Click Connect, and your network resources (drives, printers, and so on) should be available just as they are when you're at work.

tip

A DNS name looks something like a Web address. An IP address looks like a series of numbers separated by periods, like this: 198.162.0.11. You can get the VPN server's DNS name or IP address from your company's network administrator or whoever set up the VPN server there.

note

If you don't already have a connection to the Internet open, Windows XP offers to make one. You'll be asked for your username and password to log in to your company's server.

caution

If your VPN connection doesn't work, check with your company to see if they set up the VPN server to use encryption. They should be able to give you instructions on how to configure your machine to work appropriately with that encryption.

Part 10: Surfing the Web with Microsoft Internet Explorer

Task 138: Using Internet Explorer for the First Time

Task 139: Going to a Site's Address with Microsoft Internet Explorer

Task 140: Searching the Web

Task 141: Saving a Web Page

Task 142: Emailing Web Pages

Task 143: Printing Web Pages

Task 144: Downloading Files from the Web

Task 145: Copying and Saving Images from the Web

Task 146: Keeping a Favorites List of Sites

Task 147: Organizing Your Favorites List of Sites

Task 148: Customizing the Links Bar

Task 149: Checking Your History in Internet Explorer

Task 150: Clearing and Customizing History Features

Task 151: Deleting Temporary Internet Files

Task 152: Setting Your Home Page

Task 153: Customizing Internet Explorer's Support Programs

Task 154: Customizing Internet Explorer's Tools and More

Task 155: Choosing Privacy Settings

Task 156: Choosing Security Settings

Task 157: Restricting Objectionable Materials

Task 138

Using Internet Explorer for the First Time

The very first time you use Microsoft's Internet Explorer, you may be prompted to walk through a couple of steps to set it up. Sometimes these steps are performed before you get the computer. The following steps walk you through running Internet Explorer the first time.

1. Start Microsoft Internet Explorer by selecting All Programs⇨Internet Explorer from the Start menu. If Internet Explorer has not been set up, you are presented with a page similar to Figure 138-1. As you can see, you are being asked to set MSN as your home page. You can always change your home page to something else later. If Internet Explorer is already set up, you are taken directly to a Web page, in which case you can skip the rest of this task.

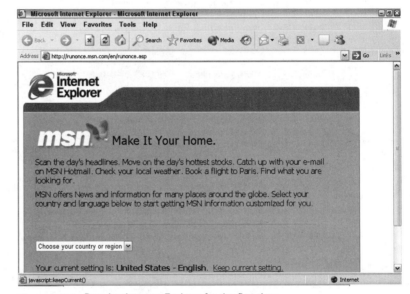

Figure 138-1: Running Internet Explorer for the first time.

2. Your default country and language are displayed at the bottom of the page. If these are not correct, or if you want to set a different country and/or language as your default when browsing the Web, then select

cross-reference

In Task 139 you learn how to go to a specific Web page using Internet Explorer.

note

You may have a shortcut on your desktop for Internet Explorer. If so, you can double-click it instead of using the menu option shown in Step 1.

note

If Internet Explorer has already been used on your user account, you may not be prompted as shown in this task.

cross-reference

You should set up different user accounts for each person that is working on your computer on a regular basis. This allows each person to have his or her own home page and other settings when using Internet Explorer. Task 209 shows how accounts can be created.

cross-reference

In Task 152 you learn how to change your home page to a different Web page.

note

When new user accounts are created, the user is prompted with the steps in this task the first time he or she uses Internet Explorer.

new options from the drop-down list. If you are satisfied with the country and language that are listed, click the Keep Current Settings link.

A pop-up dialog message is displayed (see Figure 138-2). This pop-up asks if you want to make your home page — the page that is displayed when Internet Explorer starts — www.MSN.com.

Figure 138-2: The prompt for setting your home page to MSN.com.

3. Click Yes if you want to make MSN.com your home page. You are taken to MSN, as shown in Figure 138-3. The details of what you see will be different because this page is updated daily.

Figure 138-3: The MSN Web page.

Click No if you don't want to make MSN.com your home page.

note

MSN.com is a Web site run by Microsoft that provides news, weather, shopping, and much more. It also provides you with the ability to create a customized version that includes your local weather, news, and more.

note

Even if you select No in regard to making MSN your home page, MSN may still end up being your default home page.

Going to a Site's Address with Microsoft Internet Explorer

Using the Web, you can catch up on the local news, do your banking, shop, make phone calls, chat with others, play games, and much more. More people hand out their Web addresses rather than their home or business address. Most businesses would rather you go to their Web site when you need help than call them.

Windows XP comes with the software you need to go to a Web page. Included with Windows XP is Microsoft Internet Explorer — a program that can be used to browse the information on the Web. The following steps walk you through viewing Web pages using Microsoft Internet Explorer.

1. Select All Programs⇨Internet Explorer from the Start menu. Internet Explorer opens and automatically goes to your home page. Your home page is the page that you have set as the default page for Internet Explorer. Figure 139-1 shows Internet Explorer opened to my home page — the MSN Web page.

cross-reference

Before you can go to a Web page, you need to have Internet access set up on your computer. Tasks 133 through 137 show you how to establish an Internet connection.

note

A Web address may also be called a *URL* (for Uniform Resource Locator) or a *domain name*.

note

The Internet and the Web are not actually interchangeable terms, even though most people believe them to be. The Web is just a part of the Internet. The Internet includes the World Wide Web, email, newsgroups, and more.

cross-reference

Your home page is the default page for Internet Explorer. Task 152 shows you how to set your own home page.

note

"The Web" is short for the World Wide Web, or WWW.

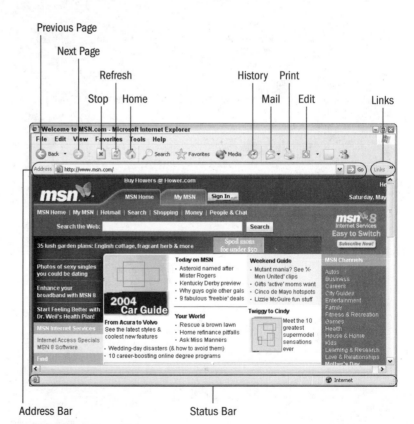

Figure 139-1: Internet Explorer.

2. In the address bar, enter the Web address that you want to go to. If you want to look at my personal page, you can go to www.Jones123.com. Figure 139-2 shows you the results of entering www.Jones123.com into the Address box and then clicking Go (or pressing the Enter key). As you can see in Figure 139-2, the Jones123.com site is accessed. Figure 139-2 also shows you where the Address box and other important items in Internet Explorer are located.

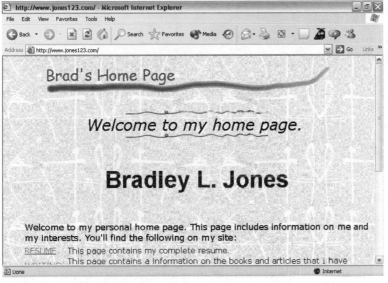

Figure 139-2: The results of entering www.Jones123.com into the address bar and pressing Go.

3. To return to the home page, you have several options:

   a. Click the Home page icon as shown in Figure 139-2.

   b. Click the Back icon. This takes you to the previous page — the home page, in this case.

   c. Enter the address of the home page into the address bar, and click Go or press the Enter key.

4. Repeat Step 2 to go to a different page.

note

A Web site is a group of related Web pages. A Web page is simply a single page that you can view in your browser's primary window. For example, Amazon.com is a Web site that is composed of thousands of Web pages.

tip

A Web address is generally composed of three sections separated by periods. The first section is generally www. The middle is the general name for the site. The third is generally a three-character suffix such as com, org, edu, or gov, although this can also be a suffix of two or more letters. Sometimes, this is a two-letter country identifier, such as uk for the United Kingdom.

note

The extensions .com, .org, .edu, and .gov have meanings. They generally — but not always — indicate the type of site you are going to. For example, .org is usually used by organizations rather than by companies. .gov is used for government sites. .edu is used by educational institutes. .com is often used for commerce sites.

note

You may see "http://" displayed in the name. This is an indicator to your browser that the Web is being used. You generally don't have to enter the http://.

Searching the Web

T he Web is very, very big. Finding what you are looking for is not always easy. There are a number of ways to narrow down what you are looking for, such as by using search engines. Additionally, Internet Explorer gives you a couple of options for searching for Web sites, addresses, music, places, and other information.

The following task walks you through some of the search options you can use from within Internet Explorer:

cross-reference
You can save a page containing search results. See Task 141 to learn more about saving a Web page.

1. From within Internet Explorer, click the Search button or select View⇨ Explorer Bar⇨Search. The Search Companion (see Figure 140-1).

Figure 140-1: The Search Companion in Internet Explorer.

2. Enter a sentence or question into the indicated box for what you want to find.

3. Click the Search button. The Search Companion looks for all the Web pages that contain the key words that you entered into the box. The results are displayed as shown in Figure 140-2. In this case, the question, "What books are written by Bradley Jones?" was entered.

note
The options you see in the Search Companion after the initial search page depend on the search criteria you enter. Some assumptions are made based on terms you enter. For example, if the word `book` is in the question you enter, you will be given options to look for reviews or to find books on different bookstore sites.

4. Navigate through the search results to see if what you want has been found. If not, continue with the remaining steps. You can navigate by simply scrolling and choosing links, or you can use the Highlight Words on the Result Page feature by doing the following:

    a. In the Search Companion, click Highlight Words on the Results Page. This displays the key words that were used in the search. More specifically, it tells you how many times each was found on the current page displayed in the right pane. As you can see in Figure 140-3, the first 15 results of a search are displayed.

tip
You can also press Ctrl+E to open the Search Companion.

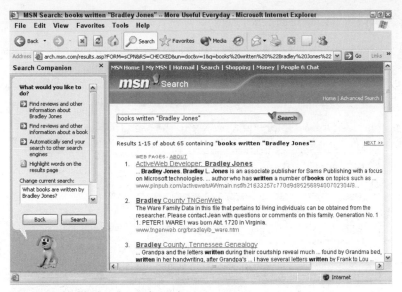

Figure 140-2: Displayed search results.

b. Click one of the items in the list to highlight the first instance of that word. The cursor will go to that word in the right frame.

c. Click the Highlight Next button to go to the next instance of the selected word.

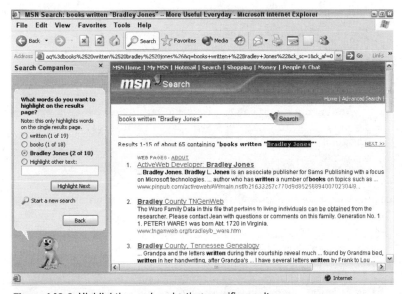

Figure 140-3: Highlighting and navigating specific results.

5. Select an option in the Search Companion to further refine your search or to find related items. As you can see in Figure 140-2, you are given additional options based on the question you entered.

note

You can also search for a word or phrase on the current Web page by selecting Edit⇨Find (on This Page) from the Internet Explorer menus.

note

A *link* is a connection to another Web page. When you click on a link, your Internet Explorer loads the new Web page. Links on a Web page are generally identified by underlined text.

tip

You can also search without using the Search Companion. You can type the words **go**, **find**, or a question mark (**?**) into the address bar, followed by the information you want to find.

tip

You can also use search engines or searching sites to find information on the Web. For example, you can go to a site like www.Google.com. Google is a site that allows you to search other sites on the Web.

Saving a Web Page

At times you will want to keep a copy of a Web page. This may be a confirmation page for an order you place online, search results that you've found, or simply be a piece of information. Using Internet Explorer, you have the option to save a page to your local machine.

cross-reference

You can also save a link to a site that you like rather than saving the actual site. To learn the best way for saving links to sites you like, see Task 146. Note that saving links means you will only view the page when you connect to the Web site, whereas saving the page means you can view it anytime. However, a saved page may not be the most current version.

note

The base file for a saved Web page will be an HTML file. Also saved may be a number of image files in a subfolder. Deleting the base file also deletes the supporting files and the subfolder.

cross-reference

You can delete a saved Web page in the same way you delete other files. You can also copy and move the page or items saved with the page. See Tasks 23, 24, and 25 for more on manipulating files.

cross-reference

See Task 22 for more on navigating what is on your hard drive. After you save a Web page, it is stored where you save it. You can navigate to the page files at the location you save it.

1. Open Internet Explorer and browse to the page you want to save.

2. Select File⇨Save As from the Internet Explorer menus as shown in Figure 141-1.

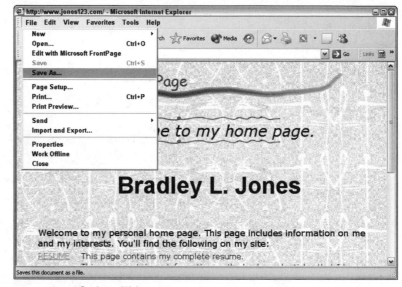

Figure 141-1: Saving a Web page.

3. Click Yes to continue if you received the warning message shown in Figure 141-2. A saved copy of a Web page may not operate like the original.

Figure 141-2: A warning message.

4. Use the Save Web Page dialog as shown in Figure 141-3 to navigate to the location where you want to save the page.

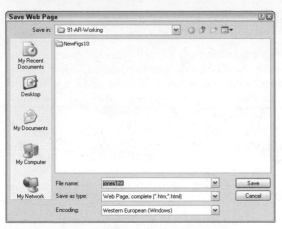

Figure 141-3: Save Web Page dialog window.

5. Enter a new name or use the default name to save the Web page.

6. Click the Save button. The current Web page is saved. Additionally, any figures on the current page are saved in a folder along with the page. This allows the saved page to be displayed on your local machine without you needing to be connected to the Internet. Open the saved page, and note that it looks similar to the original. Figure 141-4 shows the saved copy of the www.Jones123.com Web page. As you can see, this looks just like Figure 141-1.

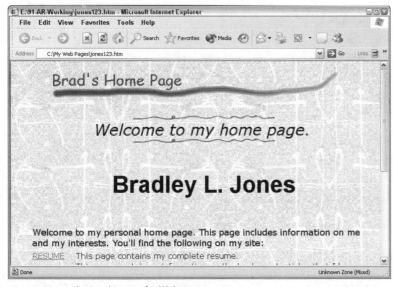

Figure 141-4: A saved copy of a Web page.

caution

Many pages are dynamically generated or contain code that won't be saved along with the page. This means that some of the functionality of a page may not be available when a page is saved. Additionally, if this code generates the look of the page, the saved copy of the page may look different from the original.

note

You may also want to save a page so that you can look at the HTML code that was used to display it. Many people save pages they find on the Web and then use them as a starting point to create their own pages.

Task 142 Emailing Web Pages

When you find a Web page with something on it that you want to remember, a number of options are available to you. You can save a copy of the page to your computer, you can print a copy of the page, you can add a link to the page from your computer, or you could simply email a copy of the page to yourself. You can also email a copy of a Web page to friends or family.

This task presents you with the steps involved with emailing Web pages. You can email a link to a Web page or you can email the Web page itself. One reason for mailing the page rather than simply a link is that the content on the web page may change. For example, news-oriented pages like MSN.com are constantly changing. A mortgage site may allow you to enter values to calculate loan and payment amounts. Emailing a copy of the results would allow you to have a copy that you can forward or compare to later. Regardless of your reasons, the following steps walk you through emailing a Web page.

cross-reference

You can also save a link to a site that you like rather than emailing it. To learn the best way for saving links to sites you like, see Task 146.

caution

Many pages are dynamically generated or contain code that won't be saved along with the page. This means that some of the functionality of a page may not be available in the copy that is emailed.

1. Open Internet Explorer and browse to the page you want to email.

2. Select File⇨Send from the menu. The Send dialog appears (see Figure 142-1).

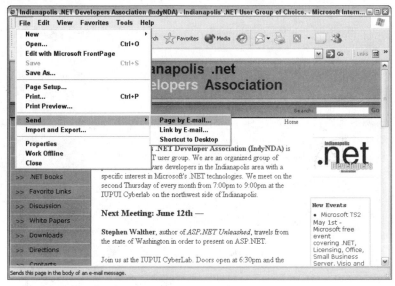

Figure 142-1: The Send menu options.

cross-reference

See Task 158 to learn about setting up email.

3. To send a link via email, select Link by E-mail. If you do not have an email program configured on your machine, you will receive an error message. If you receive this error, you need to set up an email program before continuing with this task.

   If you do have email already configured for your machine, an email message is created, as shown in Figure 142-2.

4. To send the page via email, and not just a link to a page, select Page by E-mail from the File⇨Send menu. Again, if you do not have an email program configured on your machine, you will receive an error message. If you do have email already configured for your machine, an email message is created, as shown in Figure 142-3.

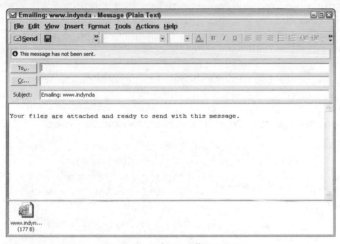

Figure 142-2: An email message for sending a link.

5. Fill in the address of the person or people who will receive the link or page.

6. Add any additional information to the subject or body of the message.

7. Click the Send button. The message is sent using the default email program.

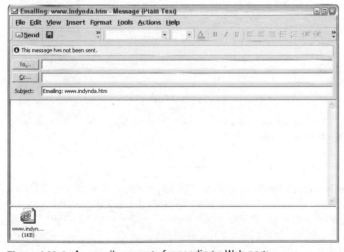

Figure 142-3: An email message for sending a Web page.

note

Notice that the messages created for sending links and pages look very similar. The big difference is in the attachment. A link that is a small file is being sent in Figure 142-2. The person receiving this will use the attachment to go to the page on the Web. In Figure 142-3, a copy of the page is being sent. The person receiving this page doesn't need to connect to the Web to see the page — he or she can merely view the copy he or she receives.

cross-reference

See Task 152 to learn how to set the default email program for Internet Explorer to use.

note

The subject line of the email will generally be the URL (the address) of the Web page. Some URLs — like the ones from a site like Amazon.com — are complex. Such complex email may get truncated when added to the subject line.

Task 143 Printing Web Pages

There are a number of ways you can share or keep a copy of a Web page. One of the more common ways is to simply print a copy, and at times, printing a copy makes more sense than saving or emailing a copy. For example, if you book airline tickets using the Web, you can get e-tickets. One requirement of e-tickets is that you have a printed copy of your itinerary and receipt. You can obtain this by printing a page from the travel company that you used. You would print this receipt just like you would print any other Web page.

The following steps walk you through the process and options for printing Web pages.

1. Using Internet Explorer, go to the Web page you want to print.

2. Select File⇨Print Preview from the Internet Explorer menus. A preview of what will be printed on each page appears (see Figure 143-1). As shown in the figure, a line of text is printed at the top of each page identifying the site. The URL and date are printed at the bottom of each page.

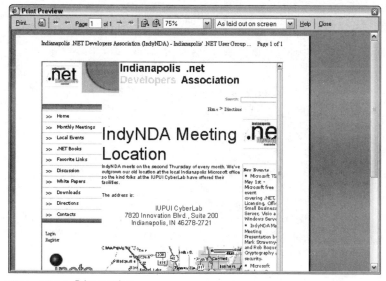

Figure 143-1: Print preview.

3. Click the Close button to close the Print Preview dialog window.

4. Select File⇨Print (or press Ctrl+P) to display the Print dialog window (see Figure 143-2). The actual printers displayed depend on what you have set up on your computer.

cross-reference

See Task 219 for more information on adding and setting up a printer on your computer.

note

Depending on your printer, you may have additional features that you can use when printing, such as quality level, the choice between printing in color or black-and-white, and the number of copies you'd like to print.

tip

You can go directly from the Print Preview dialog window to the Print dialog by clicking the Print button.

Figure 143-2: The Print dialog window.

5. Click on the printer in the Select Printer group at the top of the Print dialog window. If the printer you want to use is not displayed, software for it has not been installed on your computer. In this case, you may want to double-click on the Add Printer icon and follow the wizard.

6. Select settings specific to your printer.

7. Click the Options tab. A dialog similar to the one in Figure 143-3 appears. This dialog allows you to print pages linked to the current page or to print a table of links from the current page. If the page you are printing uses frames, this dialog allows you to determine which portions of the page will actually print.

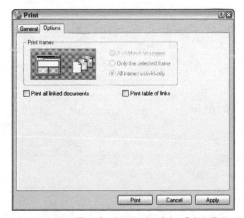

Figure 143-3: The Options tab of the Print dialog window.

8. Click the Apply button to save your selections.

9. Click the Print button. Your document, or the portion you've selected, prints based on the options you selected.

tip

Double-clicking on a printer in the Select Printer area of the Print dialog starts the printing of the document with the current settings.

note

The Find Printer button allows you to search for a printer on your computer or on a network. Your computer still needs to have the correct software installed to use any printers you may find.

note

When a printer is selected in the Select Printer area, the Preferences button is available. Clicking this button provides you with a dialog window of options specific to the printer you selected. What is displayed depends on your printer.

Downloading Files from the Web

Songs, pictures, and games are just a few of the things you can get from the Web. There are sites on the Web that share a number of different types of items. Often these sites include procedures that allow you to get a copy of these items and store it on your own machine. Other times, the procedures are not as clear. This task shows you the steps to copy files from Web pages. Depending on the setup of the Web site, some of these features may be automatic or some may be disabled.

1. Using Internet Explorer, go to the page that has the item you want to download.

2. Click on the item or link to see if the item automatically starts to download. If it does, the dialog in Figure 144-1 appears. Skip ahead to Step 5.

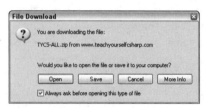

Figure 144-1: Download dialog.

3. If the item did not automatically start to download, right-click on the item or the link. A pop-up menu similar to the one in Figure 144-2 appears.

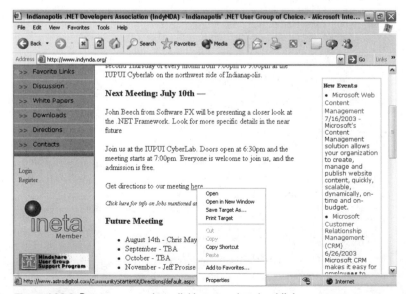

Figure 144-2: Pop-up menu when clicking on a download link.

note

Downloading refers to copying an item from the Web to your local computer. *Uploading* refers to copying an item from your machine to the Web. In more general terms, downloading is receiving a file, and uploading is sending a file.

note

You can also click the Open button in the dialog shown in Figure 144-1. This opens the program that is linked. If this is a compressed program, Windows XP will attempt to open the compressed file. If it is executable program, then it will be run.

tip

You can do other things on your computer while a file is downloading. If you surf the Web, it will slow down the download; however, the download should still proceed.

cross-reference

See Task 141 for saving a copy of an entire Web page.

4. Select Save Target As from the pop-up menu. The dialog shown in Figure 144-1 appears.

5. Select the Save button to save a copy of the file. The Save As dialog box appears (see Figure 144-3).

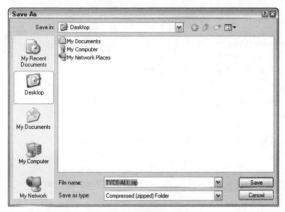

Figure 144-3: The Save As dialog window.

6. Navigate to the location where you want to save the file.

7. Click the Save button on the Save As dialog window. This starts the download processes of the file. A dialog similar to Figure 144-4 appears, showing the status of the download as it progresses. When the download is complete, the file is copied to the location you specified.

Figure 144-4: Download progress dialog.

8. Click Open to open the copy you downloaded, click Open Folder to open the folder where you saved the file, or click Close to simply close the download dialog.

Task 145

Copying and Saving Images from the Web

Most Web pages have images and pictures on them. You can easily copy nearly any picture or other graphical item from a Web page.

This task shows you the steps to copy a picture — which is just an image — from a Web page. Depending on the setup of the Web site and the browser you are using, some of these features may have been disabled.

1. Using Internet Explorer, go to the page that has the graphic you want to copy and save.

2. Right-click on the graphic. A pop-up menu similar to the one in Figure 145-1 appears.

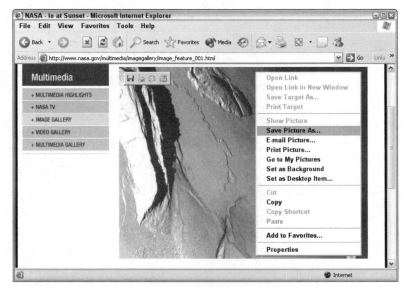

Figure 145-1: Pop-up menu when right-clicking on a Web graphic.

3. Select Save Picture As from the pop-up menu. A Save Picture dialog window appears, similar to the one in Figure 145-2. By default, this will open to your My Pictures folder.

4. Navigate to the location where you want to save the graphic.

5. Click the Save button. The download processes of the picture starts, and a dialog is displayed, showing the status of the download as it progresses. When the download is complete, the picture is copied to the location you specified.

note

Downloading refers to copying an item from the Web to your local machine. *Uploading* refers to copying an item from your machine to the Web. In more general terms, downloading is receiving a file, and uploading is sending a file.

caution

Copyright and trademark laws apply to the Internet and Web. Just because you *can* copy or get an item doesn't mean it is legal to copy the item. For example, most images are covered by copyrights. Additionally, making copies of copyrighted songs is also illegal.

note

Some animated graphics on the Web may not actually be picture files. They could be programs or Flash animations. If this is the case, when you right-click on them, you will see a menu different from those shown in Figure 145-1. You may not be able to copy these files.

cross-reference

See Task 141 for saving a copy of an entire Web page.

Figure 145-2: The Save Picture dialog window.

6. Navigate to the location where you stored the picture to verify that it was saved correctly.

You can also save an image from the Web as your background. In Step 3, select Set as Background from the pop-up menu. This sets your Windows XP desktop background to the selected image. You can see in Figure 145-3 that the background has been set to the image selected in Figure 145-1.

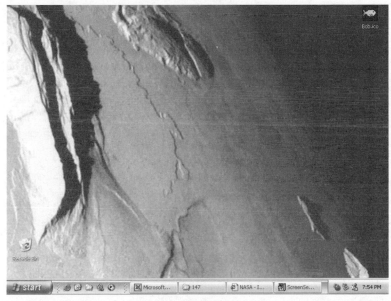

Figure 145-3: Saving a picture as your background image.

note

The amount of time required to download a file depends on the size of the file, the speed of the Internet connection you have, and the speed of the connection the site you are downloading from has.

cross-reference

See Task 22 for more on navigating your computer's folders.

note

There are a number of great sites with pictures and photos. The picture used in this task is of the mountains on Jupiter's moon IO. This is from the NASA site (www.nasa.gov), which contains a number of pictures that are not copyrighted.

cross-reference

See Task 140 to learn more about searching the Web. You can find picture and other graphics files. It just takes a little searching!

Task 146

Keeping a Favorites List of Sites

The more you use the Web, the more sites you will find that you really like. Rather than keeping track of the names on sticky notes that you put on your computer monitor, you can keep a list of favorites directly in Microsoft Internet Explorer. This list of favorites can be organized into folders or left as one big long list. Even better, the list of favorite links is then available from the menus or from a button within Internet Explorer.

Accessing your list of favorites is as simple as selecting the site link after clicking on the Favorites button or after selecting the Favorites menu option. The following steps show you how to add new links to your favorites.

1. From within Internet Explorer, navigate to the Web page you would like to add as a new Favorite.

2. Select Favorites⇨Add to Favorites. The Add Favorite dialog box appears with the title of the current Web page displayed. Figure 146-1 shows this dialog for the Web page www.HTMLGoodies.com.

Figure 146-1: The Add Favorite dialog window.

3. Change the name that you'd like have displayed in the list of Favorites. If you like the default name, you can keep it.

4. If you want to place the link in the primary Favorites menu, skip to Step 7; otherwise, select the Create In button if you want to place the link into a folder. The Add Favorite dialog window will expand, as shown in Figure 146-2. The current folders within your Favorites list are shown.

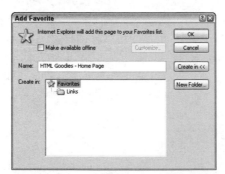

Figure 146-2: The expanded Add Favorite dialog window.

5. Click the New Folder button if you want to store the link in a new subfolder. A dialog window is displayed that allows you to enter the new folder name (see Figure 146-3).

Figure 146-3: The Create New Folder prompt.

6. If creating a new folder, enter the name of the new folder and press the OK button. The new folder is added to the expanded Add Favorites dialog window. Figure 146-4 shows a new folder called Helpful Web page sites.

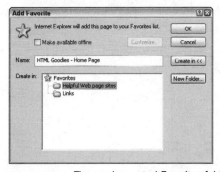

Figure 146-4: The newly created Favorites folder.

7. Click to select the folder where the link being added will be placed. If you added a new folder, you can select it.

8. Click the OK button. The link is added. You can now access the link from the Favorites menu or by clicking the Favorites button. The Helpful Web page sites folder has been added, along with the link to the current site (www.HTMLGoodies.com). If you select this new item, you are returned to the site.

cross-reference

The folder called Links that is within the Favorites folder is special. It contains the links that can be displayed in the Links bar. You can learn more about the Links bar in Task 148.

tip

Don't add every Web site you like to your Favorites list. Only add the sites you believe you will visit again or that you want to remember.

Organizing Your Favorites List of Sites

The more you use the Web, the more sites you find that you really like. As you find sites you like, you will likely add them to your Favorites list, as shown in Task 146. After a while, however, you may find that you have links that are no longer your favorites. Additionally, you may find that some links no longer go to valid Web sites. Also, you may find that you have a number of similar sites that would be better organized in a folder. By organizing your Favorites list in Internet Explorer, you can do all of these changes.

The following steps show you how to organize the links in your Favorites.

1. From within Internet Explorer, select Favorites⇨Organize Favorites Links from the menus. The Organize Favorites dialog window appears.

2. Click on a folder item. The links within that selected folder appear. In Figure 147-1, you can see that the Organize Favorites dialog window with the Helpful Web page links folder selected. Note that this folder contains one link to HTML Goodies.

Figure 147-1: Expanding a folder.

3. Click an item to select it. Select an item you want to organize from the list of folders and links on the right side of the Organize Favorites dialog window. When you select an item, notice that information about the item is displayed in the box on the lower left-hand side of the dialog window.

4. Click the Rename button to rename the selected link. A box appears around the name, as well as highlighting, telling you the name can now be edited (see Figure 147-2). Enter a new name.

4. Click the Delete button to remove the selected item. A prompt appears, where you can confirm that you want to delete the item.

5. Click on the Create Folder button to create a new folder to store the item. A folder item is added to the list on the right, as shown in Figure 147-3. You can now enter a new name for the folder.

cross-reference

Task 146 shows you how to add a link to your Favorites.

note

Clicking the Favorites button causes the Favorites items to be listed in the left side of Internet Explorer. Clicking the button a second time hides the Favorites links from the window. You can click the Organize link in this displayed list to access the Organize Favorites dialog window discussed in this task.

cross-reference

The folder called Links that is within the Favorites folder is special. It contains the links that can be displayed in the Links bar. You can learn more about the Links bar in Task 148.

cross-reference

Deleting an item places it into the Recycle Bin. You can learn more about the recycle bin in Tasks 30 and 31.

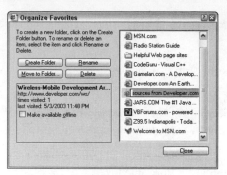

Figure 147-2: Renaming a link.

6. Click Move to Folder to move the selected item to a folder. The Browse for Folder dialog appears (see Figure 147-4). Select the folder to move the item into by clicking on its name and pressing the OK button.

7. Move an item within a folder by dragging it up or down the list.

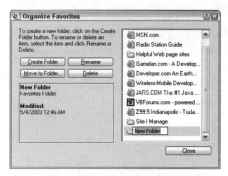

Figure 147-3: Creating a new folder.

8. Click the Close button to close the Organize Favorites dialog window.

Figure 147-4: The dialog window for selecting a folder to move an item into.

note

The actual folders displayed in Figure 147-3 depend on the folders in your Favorites list.

Task 148

Customizing the Links Bar

Internet Explorer has a number of different toolbars you can use. One of the toolbars is called Links. The Links bar can be used for shortcuts to other Web sites or locations on your computer.

note

Most of your links should go into your Favorites list and not onto the Links bar. You should reserve the Links bar for only your most frequently used links and shortcuts.

1. Start Internet Explorer by selecting All Programs⇨Internet Explorer from the Start menu. When you run Internet Explorer, you should see a Links bar as one of the toolbars near the top of the window. If the Links bar is not shown, you can display it by selecting View⇨ Toolbars⇨Links from the Internet Explorer menus.

2. Click on the double right arrows (>>) next to the Links title. The list of links appears, as shown in Figure 148-1.

Figure 148-1: The opened Links bar in Windows Explorer.

cross-reference

You must be connected to the Internet to access online Web pages. Tasks 133 to 136 show you how to connect to the Internet.

3. Add a new item to the Links bar by doing the following:

   a. If you are adding a Web page, open the link by entering it into the address bar and clicking the Go button or pressing the Enter key. Once opened, click on and drag the page icon next to the address in the Address bar to the Links list. The address is added to the Links bar.

   b. If you are adding a link to a program, click on and drag the icon or program from the Start menu, taskbar, desktop, or other location, and then unclick to drop it onto the Links bar. A shortcut is added to the Links bar.

4. Remove an item from the Links bar by doing the following:

   a. Right-click on the item to be removed.

   b. Select Delete from the pop-up menu that will be displayed.

cross-reference

Task 154 shows you how to turn on or off the various toolbars in Internet Explorer. This task also shows you how to move the toolbars and resize them within Internet Explorer.

5. To rearrange the items on the Links bar, simply drag them to the new location where you want them.

6. Change the icon on a Links bar item by doing the following:

   a. Right-click on the item.

   b. Select Properties. The properties dialog window for the item appears, as shown in Figure 148-2.

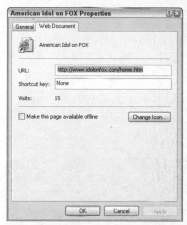

Figure 148-2: A Links bar item's Properties dialog window.

   c. Click Change Icon. A dialog window similar to Figure 148-3 appears.

Figure 148-3: The Change Icon dialog window.

   d. Select an icon.

   e. Click OK. You are returned to the Properties dialog window.

   f. Click OK to save the icon.

tip

You can right-click on an item in the Links list and then select Sort by Name.

note

You go to a link in the Links bar by clicking on its name.

note

The items in your Links list can also be accessed from a folder in your Favorites list called Links.

cross-reference

You learn how to customize the Favorites list in Task 147.

Checking Your History in Internet Explorer

Internet Explorer enables you to go to the previous pages you've seen while in a current Internet Explorer session. Once you move back, you can then go forward as well as long as you don't go to a new page.

While the forward and back navigation features are useful, the history feature Internet Explorer provides is more so. History makes it much easier for you to find sites you — or others that may have been using your machine — have been to. The following steps walk you through looking at the history on your computer:

1. From Internet Explorer, select View⇨Explorer Bar⇨History from the menus. The History pane in the Internet Explorer window appears, similar to Figure 149-1.

Figure 149-1: The History links.

2. Click the time frame you want to see. For example, to see the sites that have been traversed today, click on Today. To see the items from last week, click on Last Week. Figure 149-2 shows the Today list expanded on my computer.

3. Click on a site to expand it. A list of the key pages from the selected site appears. If you click on one of the links, the corresponding page is displayed in the Internet Explorer window.

tip

You can see where someone else has gone on the Internet by looking at the history on his or her computer.

cross-reference

You can set the number of days that history is tracked. Task 150 shows you how to set this option.

tip

The Search button allows you to search your history and more.

note

You can delete individual items from your history by right-clicking and selecting Delete from the pop-up menu.

cross-reference

You can clear the history from your computer. Task 150 covers this. There are other temporary files you can check and clear as well. Clearing these additional files is covered in Task 151.

Figure 149-2: Expanding a History link.

4. Change the order in which items are displayed by doing the following:

   a. Select View at the top of the History window. A drop-down menu appears, with four options; By Date, By Site, By Most Visited, By Order Visited Today.

   b. Click on the item that indicates the sort order you want applied. Selecting an option other than By Date causes all the dates to be sorted together. For example, Figure 149-3 shows the selection of By Most Visited using the history from my computer.

note

The history will include files that you've worked with, as well as the Web sites and pages that you've visited. This includes tracking history information about the files you have accessed on your computer, such as WordPad and picture files.

Figure 149-3: The History links sorted by Most Visited.

Clearing and Customizing History Features

Internet Explorer gives you the ability to go to the previous pages you've seen while in an Internet Explorer session — it keeps a history of where you've been. This tracking is done automatically and lasts for a specified number of days. By default, Internet Explorer keeps track of the last 20 days.

Task 149 shows you how to view and sort your history information. This task shows you how to clear your history.

To get the basic view of your history, select View⇨Explorer Bar⇨History. The History pane in the Internet Explorer window is displayed, as shown in Figure 150-1. You can click on a date to expand the historical information.

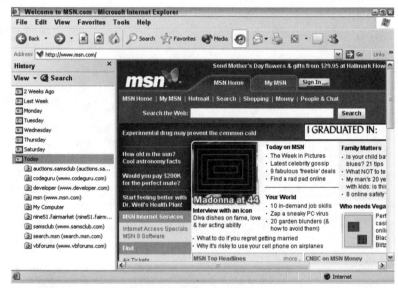

Figure 150-1: Displayed history information sorted by date.

The following steps show you how to change the number of days tracked, as well as how to clear the current history information:

1. From Internet Explorer, select Tools⇨Internet Options. The Internet Options dialog for Internet Explorer appears. The General tab should be selected, as shown in Figure 150-2.

2. Use the up and down spinner buttons or type a new number of days to track into the Days to Keep Pages in History Box in the History section of the dialog.

3. Click Apply to apply this change.

4. Click OK to close the Internet Options dialog.

cross-reference

Task 149 shows you how to review and sort your history information.

tip

Clearing your history files can help hide where you've been. You should, however, also clear the temporary Internet files and cookies. Task 151 shows you how to clear these other files.

note

You can delete individual items from your history by right-clicking and selecting Delete from the pop-up menu.

note

Increasing the number of days tracked will not regain the history from prior days. It will only apply to future tracking.

note

The history will include files that you've worked with, as well as the Web sites and pages that you've visited. This includes tracking history information about the files you have accessed on your computer, such as WordPad and picture files.

Figure 150-2: The Internet Explorer Options dialog.

5. Click the Refresh button or select View⇨Refresh from the menus in your browser. The tracking will be changed to reflect your new selection. In Figure 150-3, four weeks of history are shown.

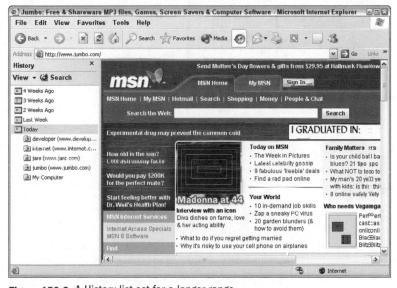

Figure 150-3: A History list set for a longer range.

6. Return to the Internet Options dialog if you want to clear the history. You did this in Step 1 by selecting Tools⇨Internet Options from the Internet Explorer menus.

7. Click the Clear History button on the General tab. You are prompted with a dialog to confirm that you want to clear the history. Once cleared, it is gone.

8. Click Yes to clear the history. You are returned to the Internet Options dialog window. Click OK.

caution
Once you clear your history, you cannot retrieve it.

note
When viewing the sites you have seen by date, the farther back you look, the larger the groupings of the sites.

tip
You can adjust how far back the history tracks. You can both increase and decrease this information.

note
Shortcuts are stored to create the history list. The longer you are tracking, the more short-cuts that may be stored.

Task 151

Deleting Temporary Internet Files

When you are browsing the Web, a number of files are copied to your computer. These files help to make future visits to the same Web page faster or more personalized. Additionally, Internet Explorer keeps track of the actual sites that you've visited. These temporary files and historical information can take up space on your computer. You can, however, control the amount of space they take. Additionally, you can clear these files.

To learn how to clear the historical information that indicates what sites you have visited, see Task 150, which discusses clearing and adjusting the history tracking. This task shows you how to clear the temporary graphics and Web page files that are copied to your computer, as well as the temporary files that may be written to your machine to keep track of personalized information about you for a specific site.

To learn how to clear the historical information that indicates what sites you have visited, see Task 150, which discusses clearing and adjusting the history tracking.

note

Many Web sites create a tiny file on your machine that keeps track of personal information. This information is then grabbed when you come back to the site. This allows the site to dynamically customize the settings for you. These small personal files are called *cookies*. Cookies are also used to help Internet Explorer remember your password and login IDs when you return to a site as well.

1. From Internet Explorer, select Tools⇨Internet Options. The Internet Options dialog for Internet Explorer appears. The General tab should be selected, as shown in Figure 151-1.

Figure 151-1: The Internet Explorer Options dialog.

cross-reference

To hide where you've been, you need to clear cookies, temporary Internet files, and history. Task 150 shows you how to clear history. This task helps with the other two types of files. Even clearing all three of these may not totally hide where you've been; however, it will make it much harder for people to figure it out.

2. Click the Delete Cookies button to clear cookies. A prompt appears to confirm that you are sure you want to delete your cookies (see Figure 151-2). Once deleted, the cookies are gone.

Figure 151-2: Confirming you want to clear your cookies.

3. Click OK to clear the cookies. You'll be returned to the Internet Options dialog window.

4. Click Delete Files to remove temporary Internet files. A confirmation prompt appears to verify that you really want to clear the files (see Figure 151-3).

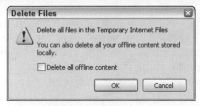

Figure 151-3: Confirming you want to clear your temporary files.

5. Check Delete All Offline Content in the prompt if you want to clear all of the offline files. This includes pages that you've asked to be able to view offline. If you only want to delete the temporary files, don't check this box.

6. Click OK to confirm the delete. The files are removed from your system and are no longer retrievable.

7. Click Settings if you want to adjust the amount of space used to store temporary files. The Settings dialog window appears (see Figure 151-4).

Figure 151-4: The temporary file settings dialog window.

8. Adjust the slider or enter a new value into disk space prompts within the Temporary Internet Files Folder section. This sets aside the amount of space you indicate.

9. Click OK to save your change.

10. Click OK to close the Internet Options dialog window.

note

You can set the amount of temporary space to use to 1MB if you want to avoid storing any significant amount of temporary files. This will, however, prevent you from being able to take advantage of speed increases by using these temporary files when you return to a Web site.

tip

Windows sets aside a default amount of space to use for temporary files. If you don't have a lot of disk space, set this to a lower value.

note

The upper limit that you can set for the amount of space to use for temporary Internet files can vary depending on the size of your hard drive.

Setting Your Home Page

When you start Internet Explorer, it opens the Web page that you set as your home page. Your home page can be any Web page, or it can even be set to be blank. While a home page is usually set by default the very first time you use Internet Explorer, you can change your home page at any time.

It is important to note that some Web sites will try to hijack your home page. This occurs when the site tricks you into clicking on a button or other item that executes a program. This delinquent program then makes the change to your home page. Other sites will pop up a prompt asking if you would like to set the site to your home page. Regardless, if you want to change your home page, the following steps should help:

1. Select Tools⇨Internet Options from the Internet Explorer menus. The Internet Options dialog window appears (see Figure 152-1). The General tab should be showing.

Figure 152-1: The Internet Options dialog window.

2. Click Use Blank if you want to use a blank home page, as shown in Figure 152-2.

3. Click on Use Current if you want to use the Web page that is currently displayed in your browser as your default home page. This is the easiest way to set up your home page.

4. Click Use Default if your home page was changed because you installed another browser or program that changed the home page.

cross-reference

There are a number of great sites that can be set as a home page. www.msn.com allows you to create a custom page that you can use for your home page. You can also use other news, hobby, or other special interest sites for your home page. To find a site, you can search the Web. Task 140 shows you how to search for Web pages that may be of interest to you.

tip

You can go to your home page at any time by clicking on the Home page icon (picture of a house).

caution

If you install a different Web browser on your computer, it may cause your home page to be changed. You can, however, reset back to your default Internet Explorer home page.

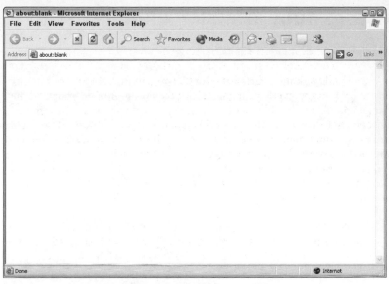

Figure 152-2: Internet Explorer opened with a blank home page.

5. As an alternative to pressing one of the buttons, you can enter the address of the specific Web page you want to use for your home page. Enter this address into the Address entry box.

6. Click Apply. The change based on the selection you made in Steps 2 through 5 is applied. You now have access to the new Web page.

7. Click OK to close the Internet Options dialog window.

8. Click Home in the toolbar or select View➪Go to➪Home Page to verify that the home page was changed.

caution

The Internet Options dialog will not validate the Web address should you type one. You will need to make sure it is correct.

caution

Some sites will try to take over your Web site. Many adult-oriented sites will try to reset your home page to their sites. If a Web site pops up a dialog, you are best to close the dialog with the close button (the × button in the top right corner) if you are not famil-iar with the site.

tip

Pressing Alt+Home takes you to your home page.

Task 153

Customizing Internet Explorer's Support Programs

When you are using Internet Explorer, you will find that there are lots of things you can do that interact with other programs on your computer. For example, you may go to a Web site that lets you send an email. Internet Explorer will check your settings to determine the email program to use. If you're a bit technical, you may want to look at the code behind a Web page. Again, you can determine what program on your local machine is used to open the code file. In all, you can set programs for the following:

- Email
- Newsgroups
- Internet calls
- Calendar
- Contacts
- HTML editor

The following steps show you how to change the default setting for these programs.

cross-reference

See Task 142 to learn how to email a Web page to someone else. The email program that is used in that task is determined by your settings in this task.

tip

If an option was initially blank, then no program was associated. Once you select a program to associate, you will no longer be able to reset the option back to a blank. There should be no reason to reset it in this manner.

note

The Reset Web Settings button only resets changes that a different browser may have made. It does not reset changes you make in the Programs tab of the Internet Options dialog window.

1. From within Internet Explorer, open the options page by selecting Tools⇨Internet Options from the menus. The Internet Options dialog window appears (see Figure 153-1).

Figure 153-1: The Internet Options dialog for Internet Explorer.

2. Select the Programs tab. The program options for Internet Explorer are displayed in a dialog similar to Figure 153-2.

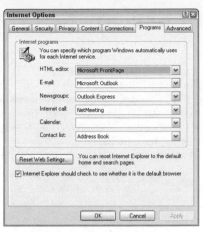

Figure 153-2: The Programs options.

3. Select the programs you would like to use for each of the listed items in the Program Items area. Select these from the drop-down list. The items listed depend on the actual programs installed on your machine. For example, for email, my machine has the options shown in Figure 153-3. Your machine may not have Microsoft Outlook.

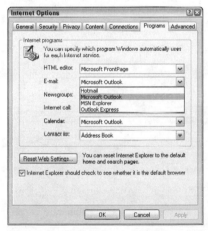

Figure 153-3: The options for Email on my machine.

4. Click Apply after you have selected the default options. These options are now Internet Explorer's defaults.

5. Check the box next to Internet Explorer Should Check to See Whether It Is the Default Browser if there is a chance another browser may be installed on your computer. By checking this box, you make sure that Internet Explorer is not dropped as the primary browser (the browser starts if you click on a Web link).

note

You can use the Cancel button to leave a dialog. As long as you have not clicked the Apply button, any changes will be thrown out.

cross-reference

You will see a number of other tabs and options in the Internet Options dialog window. Many of these options are detailed in Tasks 138 through 157.

Task 154

Customizing Internet Explorer's Tools and More

There are a number of toolbars and other items that can be used within Internet Explorer. Task 148 shows you how to customize and use the Links bar for easily accessing a number of Web sites. In this task, you learn how to turn on and off these toolbars, as well as a number of additional ones. You also learn how to rearrange or change the buttons that are displayed on the Standard Buttons bar. Figure 154-1 shows some of the different buttons, along with the three critical toolbars: the Standard Buttons bar, Address bar, and Links bar. You can also see the status bar at the bottom. Each of these four items can be turned on or off.

cross-reference

Customizing Links is covered in Task 148.

tip

By turning off all the toolbars, you give more room on your screen to the actual Web page.

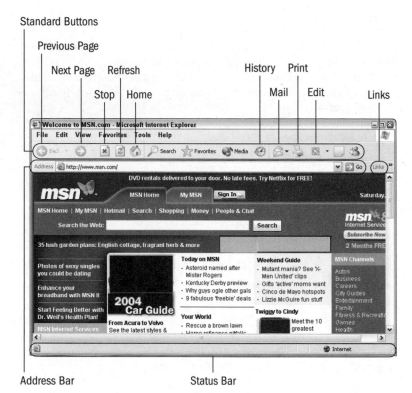

Figure 154-1: The standard toolbars and other items.

cross-reference

Customizing Favorites is covered in Tasks 146 and 147.

note

A check mark on the menus next to Status Bar, Standard Buttons, Favorites, or Links means that the option is currently on.

1. Turn on or off the status bar by selecting View➪Status Bar. Each time you select this menu option, the option toggles on or off.

2. Turn on or off the Address bar, Standard Buttons bar, or Links by selecting them from the View➪Toolbars menu. Each time you select each of these from the menu, the option will toggle on or off.

3. To move or resize the toolbars, you may follow these additional steps:

   a. Unlock the toolbars if they are locked. Locking them prevents them from accidentally being moved or resized. To unlock the toolbars, select View⇨Toolbars⇨Lock the Toolbars (the check mark means they are already locked). If there is not a check mark next to Lock the Toolbars, skip this step.

   b. Using the mouse, drag and drop the toolbars to the locations you would like them placed. You can also change the widths of the different toolbars by dragging the small vertical bars that appear on the left side of the toolbar when you place your mouse pointer there.

   c. Lock the toolbars so they don't get moved or resized. Do this by selecting View⇨Toolbars⇨Lock the Toolbars again.

4. You can customize the Buttons bar by selecting View⇨Toolbars⇨Customize from the Internet Explorer menus. A dialog window appears, as shown in Figure 154-2. You can then use this dialog to add, remove, or move items.

Figure 154-2: The Customized Toolbar dialog window.

5. Select Close to close the Customize Toolbar dialog window.

note

Add an item to the button bar by first selecting it in the left pane of the Customize Toolbar window. Follow this by clicking the Add button. This will move the item to the right side, which lists the items on the toolbar.

note

Remove an item from the button bar by first selecting it in the right pane of the Customize Toolbar window. Follow this by clicking on the Remove button. This will remove the item from the right side and thus off the toolbar.

note

Move items on the toolbar by selecting them in the right pane and then using the Move Up and Move Down buttons. You can also drag them up or down to a new location.

tip

You can reset the Standard Buttons toolbar back to the original buttons and original order by selecting Reset in the Customize Toolbar dialog (see Figure 154-2).

tip

You can add separators to your Standard Buttons toolbar. These are displayed as vertical lines.

Choosing Privacy Settings

Microsoft Internet Explorer lets you change your privacy settings. These changes can impact how much or how little information can be obtained before you are warned. You should understand that in general, a site will not be able to get information about you unless you provide it.

More important to privacy is the information that is maintained about you when you go to a site. Many sites will get information from you that they will retain for the next time you return. This information, however, is generally stored on your computer in a small file called a *cookie*. The cookie file that is written can only be accessed by that Web site — other Web sites cannot read cookies they did not create.

You can choose to ban these cookie files, to ask for warnings before they are written, or to allow any sites to write them whenever they want. You can also do a number of customized settings. The following steps walk you through the process of changing your privacy settings in Internet Explorer:

1. Select Tools➪Internet Options from the Internet Explorer menus. The Internet Options dialog window appears.

2. Select the Privacy tab. The standard privacy options appear (see Figure 155-1).

Figure 155-1: The Privacy options.

cross-reference

Task 151 shows you how to remove the temporary files that can be written to your computer when you visit a Web site. To clear all the cookies off your machine, click the Delete Cookies button on the General tab of the Internet Options dialog window.

tip

Click the Default button to set the default privacy settings. This will generally be the Medium setting.

3. Move the slider in the Settings section. Moving the slider up increases the amount of privacy you will have. Lowering the slider decreases the settings. In Figure 155-1, you can see that the standard setting of Medium is selected. A description of this setting is provided in the dialog window. As you move the slider, each setting is described.

4. Set exceptions. You can have Internet Explorer make exceptions for specific Web sites. The following steps walk through setting these exceptions. If you are not making exceptions, you can go to Step 10.

5. Click the Edit button in the Web Sites section of the Privacy tab in the Internet Options dialog window. The Per Site Privacy Actions dialog window appears (see Figure 155-2).

Figure 155-2: The Per Site Privacy Actions dialog window.

6. Type the address of the site into the Address of Web Site entry box.

7. Click the Block button to block all cookies from the entered site. The site will be added to the Managed Web sites list.

8. Press the Allow button to allow all cookies from the entered site. The site will be added to the Managed Web sites list.

9. Click OK to close the dialog window and return to the Internet Options.

10. Click OK to close the Internet Options dialog window.

note

If you completely block cookies, some Web sites may not work as you expect. There are many Web sites that expect cookies to be enabled.

note

The terms first party and third party are used in the descriptions of privacy. A *first party* is a site that you are currently visiting. A *third party* is something that occurs — such as writing a cookie — when another site other than the one you are currently visiting writes a cookie.

note

You can remove items from the Managed Web Sites list by selecting them and then clicking the Remove button.

tip

If you don't want a Web site to know your name, address, phone number, credit card, or other information, then don't enter it onto Web pages. The best way to keep most of your privacy is to avoid submitting personal information.

cross-reference

Task 156 presents a few of the security features of Internet Explorer. If you do have to give out private information, you will want to make sure you provide it in a secure manner and only to a trusted Web site.

Choosing Security Settings

Some site are secure, others are not. When providing information to a Web site, you should consider the confidential nature of what you are providing. When you enter information into a Web site, it is being sent from your machine, across the Internet through other machines, and finally to the destination machine. If the information is confidential, you will want to make sure that it is protected from people grabbing it along its way.

Internet Explorer provides settings for security that you can change. The following steps walk through configuring your security settings:

1. Select Tools⇨Internet Options from the Internet Explorer menus.

2. Select the Security tab from the Internet Options dialog window. Figure 156-1 shows the Security tab.

Figure 156-1: Security options for Web sites.

3. Set the options for Web sites you trust (Trusted Sites), don't trust (Restricted Sites), or Don't Know (Internet). You can create custom settings for each of these areas, or you can set them to a default setting. To use one of the default settings, do the following:

   a. Click on the zone at the top of the Security tab to select it. (Figure 156-1 shows the Internet zone selected.)

   b. Click the Default level button. As shown in Figure 156-2, this changes the display in the security level for this zone area to allow you to use a slider control to select one of four levels of security. Your four choices are High, Medium, Medium-low, and Low.

   If you try to select a level lower than the recommended level, you will be given a warning message.

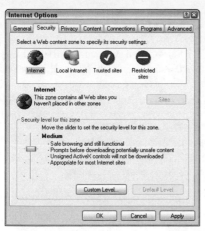

Figure 156-2: Adjusting the default security level setting.

4. Add sites to the trusted or restricted zone lists. You can increase or decrease the security for a site by placing it in either of these lists. As you saw in Step 3, the settings for these areas can be different from the settings for standard Internet access. If you don't want to add sites to these zones, skip to Step 5.

   a. Select the zone you want to define for a site, either Trusted Sites or Restricted Sites.

   b. Click the Sites button. The Trusted Sites dialog window appears (see Figure 156-3).

Figure 156-3: The Trusted Sites dialog window, which is similar to the Restricted Sites dialog window.

   c. Enter the address of a site that you wanted added to this zone's list. Enter the address into the Add this Web Site to the Zone entry box.

   d. Click Add. The site address is added to the Web sites list.

   e. Click OK.

5. Click OK to close the Internet Options dialog box.

cross-reference
Task 154 shows how to turn on the status bar if it is not displayed at the bottom of your Internet Explorer window.

note
While people generally think of credit cards when talking about security, it is just as important to make sure other information such as your email address, your birth date, your tax ID or social security number, and your home address are all kept secure as well.

Restricting Objectionable Materials

The Web is open to everyone in the world. As such, you can find anything in the world on the Web. This includes material that is illegal or illicit. Nudity, profanity, violence, and more are all on the Web for people to find.

Internet Explorer cannot stop everything that you or others using your computer may come across; however, it can filter a lot of it. Internet Explorer provides the Content Advisor to prevent your browser from being used to go to certain sites. Using the Content Advisor, you can control the access that your computer has to the certain types of content. The following steps walk you through turning on the Content Advisor:

1. Select Tools➪Internet Options from the Internet Explorer menus.

2. Select the Content tab from the Internet Options dialog window. Figure 157-1 shows the Content tab.

Figure 157-1: Content options.

3. Click the Enable button in the Content Advisor section to turn on the Content Advisor. A Password dialog is displayed, as shown in Figure 157-2. Here you can create an Administrator password.

Figure 157-2: Setting the Administrator password.

cross-reference
In addition to watching content, you can also secure your computer from downloading unwanted files. See Task 156 for more on security and Task 155 for more on privacy.

caution
If you put the content settings too low, you may find you can't get to very many sites. For example, setting Language to Inoffensive Slang; No Profanity may result in a large number of sites being blocked.

caution
Once Content Advisor has been turned on, any future changes will require that the password be entered.

note
It is critical to remember the Content Advisor password.

tip
You can change the Content Advisor password via the General tab in the Content Advisor dialog. The Content Advisor dialog is accessed with the Settings button on the Content tab of the Internet Options dialog window.

4. Fill out the password and a hint to help you remember the password. This password will be used to make changes to the Content Advisor and to override any Web pages that are blocked.

5. Click OK to save the password and hint. You can now fill out the settings for the content. Figure 157-3 shows the Content Advisor's primary settings page with the Ratings tab displayed. You will determine the ratings for Language, Nudity, Sex, and Violence using this dialog window.

Figure 157-3: Content settings.

6. Click the category that you want to set.

7. Adjust the slider to determine the allowed viewable level for the given category. The description on the page will help you to see what the setting level means.

8. Repeat Steps 6 and 7 for each of the four category areas. Click OK.

   When you go to a Web site, if it does not have a rating, you will be required to enter the Content Advisor password into a dialog similar to Figure 157-4 in order to access the page.

Figure 157-4: Content Advisor warning page.

note

You should consult the online help for more information on settings that can be configured in the Content Advisor. This includes applying a rating service to your browser that can help identify Web sites that are both trusted and untrusted.

note

Unless you configure a rating system into your browser (see online help), you may not be able to get to a lot of Web pages. You can, however, unblock a Web page or Web site by clicking an option on the dialog that pops up (see Figure 157-4). You can also unblock a Web page in the Content Advisor's Settings dialog under the Approved tab.

note

Keep in mind that a password hint for the Content Advisor password will be displayed every time the prompt for the password is displayed.

note

You should review all of the options in the Content Advisor's Settings tabs. You'll find that there are a number of additional options that you can set.

Part 11: Interacting with Email

Task 158:   Setting Up Your Email

Task 159:   Retrieving and Viewing Email Messages

Task 160:   Opening and Saving Received Attachments

Task 161:   Creating and Sending Email

Task 162:   Forwarding or Replying to a Message

Task 163:   Sending a Picture or File as an Attachment

Task 164:   Using Stationery

Task 165:   Creating Your Own Stationery

Task 166:   Creating and Using a Signature

Task 167:   Organizing Your Inbox

Task 168:   Filing Your Email into Folders

Task 169:   Finding a Message

Task 170:   Using Your Address Book

Task 171:   Creating Your Own Virtual Business Card

Task 172:   Sending Virtual Business Cards

Task 173:   Adding Virtual Business Cards to Your Address Book

Task 174:   Using Message Rules to Kill Spam and Do Other Cool Stuff

Setting Up Your Email

Email has changed the way we communicate more profoundly than any invention since the telephone. It provides a quick, easy way to stay in touch with those who are across town or across the world. It's easier than sending a letter and less obtrusive than a telephone call.

But before you can take part in this communications revolution, you have to get set up. Windows XP comes with a very handy application called Outlook Express for sending and retrieving email, and in this task you'll find out how to make it work for you.

1. Open Outlook Express by choosing Start⇨All Programs⇨ Outlook Express.

2. The Internet Connection Wizard appears (see Figure 158-1).

Figure 158-1: The Internet Connection Wizard.

3. Type your first and last name. Click Next. The Internet E-mail Address page appears.

4. Type your email address. Click Next. The E-mail Server Names page appears (see Figure 158-2).

5. Select the type of email server you are accessing, and fill in the additional information required:

   • If you use a Hotmail or MSN account, choose HTTP. When you do, another drop-down list box appears: My HTTP Mail Service Provider Is. Select Hotmail.

   • If you can access your email via the Web, you may also want to choose HTTP and then select Other for My HTTP Mail Service Provider Is. Type in the URL of your email server for Incoming mail.

tip

If the Internet Connection Wizard doesn't appear and all you see is the Outlook Express main window, select Tools⇨Accounts... from the menu to display the Internet Accounts dialog. Click the Mail tab and then click the Add button and choose Mail... from the pop-up menu. Now you'll see the Internet Connection Wizard.

note

If you don't have the information required in this wizard, contact your ISP, and they will provide you with this information.

- If your email account is one that was given to you when you signed up for Internet access, you should probably choose POP3. Then type in the address for your Incoming Mail and Outgoing Mail servers.

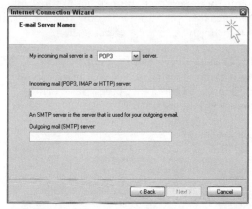

Figure 158-2: The Internet Connection Wizard, E-mail Server Names page.

6. Click Next. The Internet Mail Logon page appears (see Figure 158-3).

Figure 158-3: The Internet Mail Logon page of the Internet Connection Wizard.

7. Enter the account name and password for your email account.

8. Click Next. You are done! Click Finish. You may see a dialog that asks if you want to "download folders for the mail server you added." If you do, click Yes.

tip

Click to check the Remember Password check box on the Internet Mail Logon page if you want Outlook Express to log on automatically. If you don't, you'll have to type your password each time.

cross-reference

Once you're set up, you'll want to try out your account before retrieving your email. See Task 159 to find out how.

Task 159

Retrieving and Viewing Email Messages

It's become part of the morning routine — newspaper, coffee, email. There's something irresistible about retrieving your email and seeing who's been thinking about you recently. While there's nothing difficult about retrieving and viewing your messages, this task takes the opportunity to show you a few features Outlook Express provides to make the whole process even easier.

1. Open Outlook Express by choosing Start⇨All Programs⇨Outlook Express. You see the Outlook Express main window (see Figure 159-1). This opening page provides links to Outlook Express' three primary functions: email, newsgroups, and contacts.

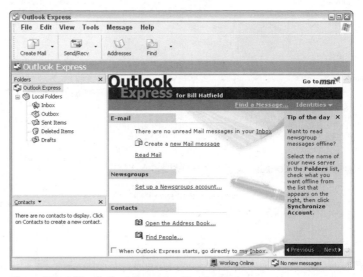

Figure 159-1: The Outlook Express main window.

2. Click the Read Mail link. Now you are looking at your Inbox (see Figure 159-2).

3. Click the Send/Recv button in the toolbar. A progress window appears, flashing messages so quickly you may not be able to read them all. Essentially, it's just telling you that Outlook Express is connecting to your email server, sending your login information, and retrieving your email messages.

tip

Notice the check box at the bottom of the opening page: When Outlook Express starts, go directly to My Inbox. It's pretty self-explanatory, but we thought we'd point it out because it's a nice option — and it's easy to overlook.

cross-reference

For more on working with contacts in Outlook Express, see Task 170. For more on newsgroups (which are basically Internet discussion forums), check out Tasks 175 through 182.

tip

Outlook Express, by default, sends and receives automatically every half hour. You can change this setting (or turn it off) by selecting Tools⇨Options from the Outlook Express menu and then changing the Check for New Messages Every option. If you turn it off, Outlook Express only sends and receives when you push the Send/Recv button.

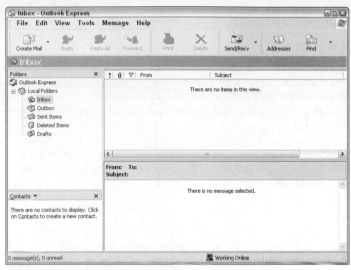

Figure 159-2: Your (empty) Inbox.

4. When the progress window disappears, you find out whether or not you've received any new email. If you have, it appears in the List pane at the top of the window (see Figure 159-3). You can click on each message in turn to see its contents in the Preview pane below.

Folder list   List pane

Preview pane

Figure 159-3: The Inbox — with new mail!

Opening and Saving Received Attachments

Got a message in your Inbox with a little paperclip beside it? That means it's more than just a message! The sender has also included a file of some type with your message. In this task you'll find out how to open the file and save it to your hard drive.

1. Open Outlook Express by choosing Start➪All Programs➪Outlook Express. On the Outlook Express opening page, click the Read Mail link to see your Inbox.

2. Retrieve your messages by clicking the Send/Recv button.

3. Select a message that has an attachment. If the attachment is a picture, you can simply scroll down in the message to see the picture (see Figure 160-1).

cross-reference

To find out how to retrieve your messages, see Task 159.

cross-reference

To find out how to send an attachment to someone else, see Task 163.

Folder list   List pane

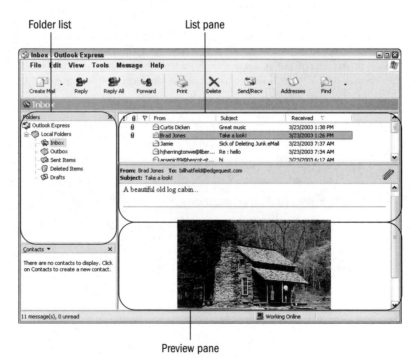

Preview pane

Figure 160-1: Viewing a picture attachment in the message itself.

4. To open the attachment (that is, to view a picture, open a document, or run a program that was sent to you):

   a. Click on the Paperclip icon in the gray bar at the top of the Preview pane. A pop-up menu appears (see Figure 160-2).

   b. Select the attachment from the menu that you want to open. For example, if you select a picture, the Picture Viewer will be

caution

Be *very* careful with any attachment you receive — especially if it is an application (an executable, or EXE, file). This is one way viruses are spread! But the virus can't infect your computer unless you open the executable file by selecting it from the attachment pop-up menu. If you aren't sure, don't do it! First check with the sender to find out what it is and if they meant to send it to you.

launched, displaying the picture. If you select a WordPad document, WordPad will open, displaying the document. If you select a music file, Windows Media Player will open, playing the song. If you select an application (an executable file, with the extension .exe), the application will open.

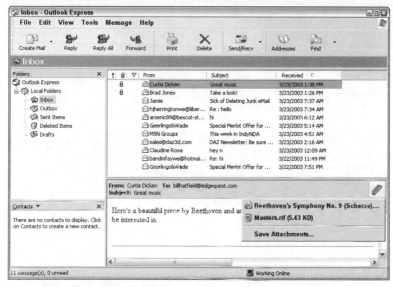

Figure 160-2: The attachment pop-up menu.

5. To save the attachment to your hard drive:

   a. Click on the Paperclip icon in the gray bar at the top of the Preview pane. The pop-up menu appears.

   b. Select Save Attachments... from the pop-up menu. The Save Attachments dialog appears (see Figure 160-3).

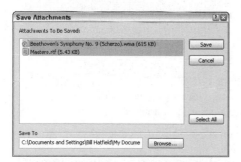

Figure 160-3: The Save Attachments dialog.

   c. Click the Browse button to select a folder where the attachments should be saved. You cannot choose a different folder for each one — they are all saved in the same folder.

   d. Click the Save button. The attached files are saved in the location you specified.

Creating and Sending Email

If you want people to send you letters, you've got to write letters. The same is true for email. On the other hand, in these days of junk mail and spam, that's really not as true as it once was! Nevertheless, if you want email you *care* about, it helps to send out some love to others.

1. Open Outlook Express by choosing Start⇨All Programs⇨Outlook Express. On the Outlook Express opening page, click the Read Mail link to see your Inbox (see Figure 161-1).

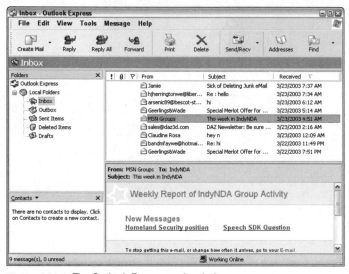

Figure 161-1: The Outlook Express main window.

2. Click the Create Mail button on the toolbar (or hit Ctrl+M on the keyboard). The New Message window appears (see Figure 161-2).

3. In the To text box, type in the email address of the person you want to send this message to. If you want to send the message to more than one person, separate the email addresses with a comma or semicolon.

4. In the CC text box (it stands for *carbon copy*), type in the email address of anyone you want to send a copy of this email. Again, separate multiple email addresses with a comma or semicolon.

5. Select View⇨All Headers from the New Message window menu. The BCC line (it stands for *blind carbon copy*) appears, and you can type additional email addresses here.

6. Type descriptive text in the Subject text box. This same text will appear in the title bar of the New Mail window.

Task **161**

Italic

Paragraph Style   Underline

Font   Size   Bold   Font Color

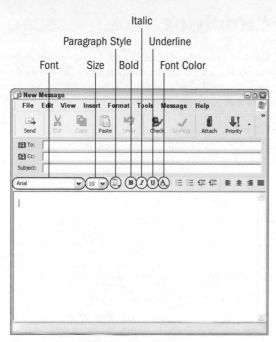

Figure 161-2: The New Message window.

7. Now type your message in the bottom half of the window.

8. Format your text with the formatting toolbar above the message area of the window. First select the text you want to format, and then use one of the controls in the toolbar:

   - Use the Font and Size drop-down list boxes to change the style and size of your text.

   - Use the Paragraph Style button to change the current paragraph to a heading, add numbers, add bullets, and perform lots of other options.

   - Use the Bold, Italic, and Underline buttons to apply these styles to your text.

   - Use the Font Color drop-down list to brighten up your email with a splash of color.

9. Set the priority level of your message appropriately. By default, a message is considered normal priority. Click the Priority button in the New Message window toolbar to identify this message as High Priority so that your reader will know to look at it right away. Click the Priority button again to set the priority of this message to Low Priority. Click it a third time to set it back to normal.

10. Click the Send button on the New Message window to send your message.

caution

If the person receiving your email isn't using Outlook Express or Outlook as his or her email application, the formatting may or may not come through. The person will be able to read your text, but he or she may not see the styles you added.

cross-reference

To find out how to send an attachment or a picture with your message, see Task 163.

caution

When you click Send, your message is not sent right away. Instead, it goes into the Outbox and waits until the next time you hit the Send/Recv button. Outlook Express, by default, sends and receives automatically every half hour.

Task **162**

Forwarding or Replying to a Message

Getting new email is fun. Responding to a big pile of email is not so much fun. But it must be done, so Outlook Express tries to help you out. In this task you'll discover two important features: forwarding a message you received on to others and replying back to someone (or several someones) who sent you a message.

1. Open Outlook Express by choosing Start⇨All Programs⇨Outlook Express. On the Outlook Express opening page, click the Read Mail link to see your Inbox (see Figure 162-1).

Folder list   List pane

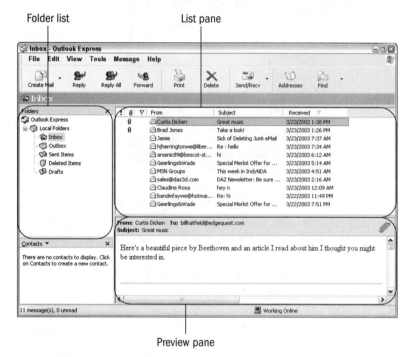

Preview pane

Figure 162-1: The Outlook Express main window.

2. Click to select the message in the List pane you want to work with. The contents of the message appear in the Preview pane.

3. To forward the selected message to others:

   a. Click the Forward button on the toolbar (or press Ctrl F on the keyboard). A message window appears (see Figure 162-2).

   b. In the To and CC text boxes, type the email addresses of the people you want to forward the message to. If you want to put more than one email address in each text box, separate them with a comma or semicolon.

tip

If you forward a message that has an attachment, the attachment is forwarded too. If you reply to a message with an attachment, the attachment is *not* included in the reply. For more on sending attachments, see Task 163. For more on receiving attachments, see Task 160.

cross-reference

To find out how to retrieve and view your messages, see Task 159.

tip

It's great to forward funny or inspiring emails you receive to your friends. However, some people get carried away and barrage their friends with several such forwards a day. Be considerate and always be sure you are sending stuff that you're sure your recipient will want to receive.

Figure 162-2: A forward message window.

  c. In the message area of the window, type any message you like —
     perhaps explaining how you received this message or why you
     thought it might be interesting to those you're forwarding it to.

  d. Click Send.

4. To reply to the sender of the selected message:

  a. Decide whether you want to send your reply to the sender only
     or (if the original message was sent to several people) if you want
     to reply to the sender and everyone else on the To and CC lines.
     To reply to the sender only, click the Reply button (or press
     Ctrl+R on the keyboard). To reply to everyone, click the Reply
     All button. A message window appears. Notice that the To and
     CC lines are already filled in appropriately.

  b. In the message area of the window, type your reply. Notice that
     the email that the sender sent to you appears below your message
     so that he or she can go back and trace the course of the conver-
     sation, if desired.

  c. Click Send.

Sending a Picture or File as an Attachment

Sending email messages is much like writing a letter. But what if you'd rather do something more like send a package? That's what email attachments are for. They allow you to send, along with your message, a picture, a song, or almost any other kind of file that might be on your hard drive.

1. Open Outlook Express by choosing Start➪All Programs➪Outlook Express. On the Outlook Express opening page, click the Read Mail link to see your Inbox (see Figure 163-1).

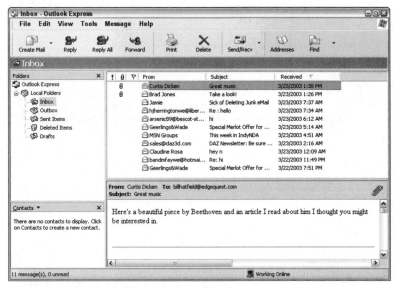

Figure 163-1: The Outlook Express main window.

2. Click the Create Mail button on the toolbar. The New Message window appears. Enter the information requested.

3. Click the Attach button in the New Message window's toolbar. The Insert Attachment dialog appears (see Figure 163-2).

4. Browse to the folder where the attachment is located, and click to select it. If you want to attach several files in the same folder, you can hold down the Ctrl key while you click on additional files.

5. Click the Attach button. A tiny icon and the name of the file(s) appear in the Attach line of the message header (see Figure 162-3).

cross-reference

For details on how to create an email message, see Task 161.

caution

If you are sending a file to someone who has a dial-up Internet connection, be very careful about the size of the file you send him or her. A big file might end up taking hours to download. However, if you *need* to send a big file, it's usually a good idea to call or send an email ahead of time to warn the person that it's coming.

note

When you are sending a picture to someone as an attachment, the picture does not appear below the message as it does when you receive a picture. However, if your recipient is using Outlook Express, he or she will see the picture below the message upon receipt.

Figure 163-2: The Insert Attachment dialog.

6. If you wish to add additional attachments in the same email, repeat Steps 4 and 5 as often as you like.

7. If you decide you don't want to send a file that you've already added to the attachments, just click on that file's name and hit the Delete key. The attachment will disappear (but the file is still on your hard drive).

8. Click Send.

cross-reference

To find out how to save an attachment to your hard drive that was sent to you by someone else, see Task 160.

Figure 163-3: The New Message window with attached files.

Task 164

Using Stationery

When you write letters, you can let the people you are writing to know they are really special by using fancy stationery. Why can't you do that with an email message? You can! Sort of... While you can't imitate the textured feel of expensive paper, you can make your emails look a lot snazzier.

1. Open Outlook Express by choosing Start⇨All Programs⇨Outlook Express. On the Outlook Express opening page, click the Read Mail link to see your Inbox.

2. Look closely at the toolbar near the Create Mail button. You'll notice a little down arrow beside it. Click on this down-arrow. A menu appears that gives you options for creating a new mail message in different ways (see Figure 164-1). The numbered items listed first are different kinds of stationery you can choose.

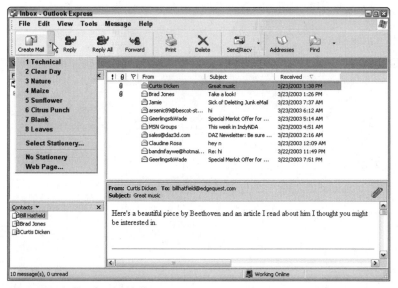

Figure 164-1: The Create Mail menu.

3. Choose Select Stationery... By choosing this option, instead of selecting one of the stationery by name, you cause the Select Stationery window to appear (see Figure 164-2). This window allows you to click on the different stationery available and get a thumbnail view of what it looks like. Click on each of the stationery in turn and see what it looks like in the Preview box.

4. Select your favorite stationery from the group. Click OK. A New Message window appears with the stationery in the message part of the window.

Figure 164-2: The Select Stationery window.

5. Enter the information requested in the New Message window, and click Send.

6. If you decide you like a particular stationery and want to use it all the time, you can set it as your default:

   a. Select Tools⇨Options from the menus on Outlook Express's main window. The Options dialog appears.

   b. Click the Compose tab.

   c. In the Stationery section, click to check the Mail check box. When you do, the Select... button is enabled.

   d. Click the Select... button. The Select Stationery window appears.

   e. Select the stationery you want to use as your default. Click OK. The Options dialog shows your default stationery (see Figure 164-3). Click OK.

Figure 164-3: The Compose tab on the Options dialog.

   f. Once you do this, you can simply click the Create Mail button, and your stationery will appear in the New Mail window automatically.

cross-reference

For more information on creating and sending email messages, see Task 161.

caution

If your recipient is not using Outlook Express or Outlook to get his or her email, the stationery may not look right upon receipt. (However, the recipient will still be able to read your message without trouble.)

tip

If you would like to find more stationery, there are plenty of Web sites where you can download it for free. Start with www.stationery.org and www.thundercloud.net, or just search for **Outlook Express stationery** using your favorite search engine.

Task **165**

Creating Your Own Stationery

Outlook Express includes some nice-looking stationery to choose from. And you can download more from the Web. But if you really want to make a personal statement, you can create something uniquely your own.

1. Open Outlook Express by choosing Start⇨All Programs⇨Outlook Express. On the Outlook Express opening page, click the Read Mail link to see your Inbox.

2. Click on the little down arrow beside the Create Mail button. Choose Select Stationery... The Select Stationery window appears. Click the Create New... button. The Stationery Setup Wizard appears.

3. Click Next. The Background page is displayed (see Figure 165-1). Here you can select a picture or a background color for your page. There are quite a number of pictures available in the drop-down list box. When you select one, it appears in the Preview box on the right. If you'd rather use a different graphic, you can click the Browse button to locate one on your hard drive.

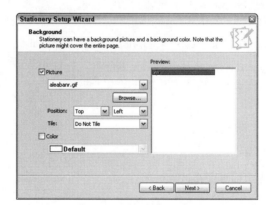

Figure 165-1: The Background page of the Stationery Setup Wizard.

4. Select a position where the graphic should appear on the page. Then decide how the graphic should be tiled.

5. Click Next. The Font page is displayed (see Figure 165-2). Select the font, size, and color you want for the text in your email messages.

6. Click Next. The Margins page appears (see Figure 165-3). Here you can decide where your text should appear on the page, leaving space at the top and/or along the right. If you have a graphic at the top or down the left side, you'll want to set your margins so that the text isn't on top of the graphic (unless you want it to be).

---

cross-reference

Before you create your own, you'll want to explore the stationery that Outlook Express provides, if you haven't already. See Task 164.

note

If your graphic isn't tiled so that it covers the whole page, or you decide not to use a graphic, you can choose a background color for your page.

note

Tiling means simply repeating the graphic over and over again, either horizontally, vertically, or all over the page. Some graphics are designed to be tiled and look nice that way. Some aren't. Experiment with the different graphics and different tile options to see how they work.

caution

When selecting a font color, keep in mind the background color you chose. Keep it readable!

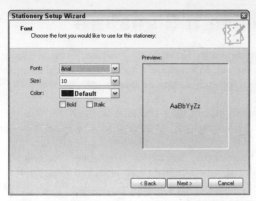

Figure 165-2: The Font page of the Stationery Setup Wizard.

7. Click Next. Give your new stationery a name, and click Finish.

8. Your new stationery appears in the Select Stationery window so that you can put it to use right away. Select it and click OK. A New Message window appears with your new stationery.

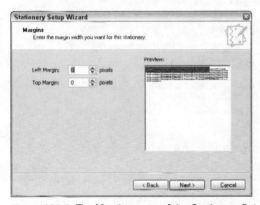

Figure 165-3: The Margins page of the Stationery Setup Wizard.

Task

166

Creating and Using a Signature

In days gone by, a person was known by his or her signature. Today we have to work a little harder to make our mark. Outlook Express allows you to create your own signature lines that might include your name, your title, the company you work for, or even a joke or funny quote. Once you create it, you can easily drop it into any email message or you can have Outlook Express do it for you, automatically.

cross-reference

If you're looking for more ways to add a personal touch to your email, check out the stationery. See Tasks 164 and 165.

1. Open Outlook Express by choosing Start⇨All Programs⇨Outlook Express. On the Outlook Express opening page, click the Read Mail link to see your Inbox (see Figure 166-1).

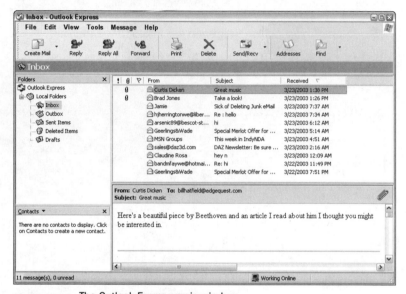

Figure 166-1: The Outlook Express main window.

2. Select Tools⇨Options from the menu. The Options dialog is displayed. Click the Signatures tab (see Figure 166-2).

3. Create an official, business signature:

   a. Click New. An entry called Signature #1 appears in the Signatures list box.

   b. Under Edit signature, in the Text box, type your name, hit Enter, and then type your company name.

   c. Click the Rename button. Type in **Business Signature**. Hit Enter.

Figure 166-2: The Signatures tab on the Options dialog.

4. Now create a fun, personal signature:

   a. Click New. An entry called Signature #1 appears again.

   b. Under Edit Signature, in the Text box, type your name, hit Enter, and then type a favorite quote or joke.

   c. Click the Rename button. Type in **Personal Signature**. Hit Enter.

5. Click OK on the Options dialog.

6. Click the Create Mail button on the toolbar. Enter an email address for the To line, and type a Subject and some text in the message.

7. Move your cursor to the bottom of your message, and on the New Message window menus, choose Insert⇨Signature⇨Personal Signature. The text from your signature appears in the message.

8. Click Send to send the message.

9. To make Outlook Express automatically add your signature to every email (without having to select it from the Insert menu):

   a. Select Tools⇨Options from the Outlook Express main window menu. The Options dialog is displayed. Click the Signatures tab.

   b. Click to check the check box labeled Add Signatures to All Outgoing Messages. Click to select the signature you want as your default in the Signatures list box. Click the Set as Default button.

   c. Click OK on the Options dialog.

Organizing Your Inbox

When you work with your email you spend most of your time at your Inbox. So it's worth spending a little time becoming familiar with how it works and what you can do with it. In this task we show you some tricks for viewing and organizing your email to make your life a little simpler.

cross-reference
To find out how to save email attachments you receive to your hard drive, see Task 160.

1. Open Outlook Express by choosing Start⇨All Programs⇨Outlook Express. On the Outlook Express opening page, click the Read Mail link to see your Inbox (see Figure 167-1).

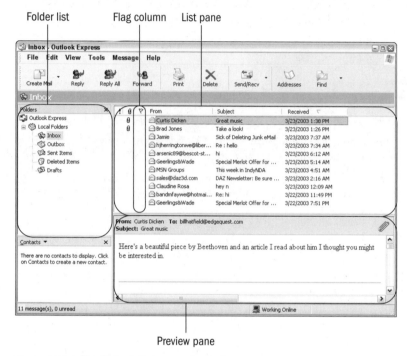

Folder list   Flag column   List pane

Preview pane

Figure 167-1: The Outlook Express main window.

2. To adjust the relative pane sizes in your Outlook Express window:

   a. Move your mouse pointer to the line that separates the List pane from the Preview pane. Your pointer turns into a double arrow.

   b. Press and hold the left mouse button and move your mouse. You can move this separator bar up and down, making the List pane bigger and the Preview pane smaller or vice versa.

   c. Release the mouse button to drop the line where you want it.

   d. Use the same technique with the vertical line that separates the Folder list from the List pane. You can move it back and forth to change the relative size of each.

tip
Another way to sort is by selecting View⇨Sort By from the menu.

3. To print an email message on your printer:

   a. Select the message you want to print in the List pane.

   b. Click the Print button in the toolbar (or hit Ctrl+P on the keyboard). The Print dialog appears.

   c. Enter the number of copies you want to print (if it's more than one).

   d. Click the Print button. The message is printed on your default printer.

4. To delete one or more email messages:

   a. Select a message that you want to delete in the List pane. (Hold the Ctrl key down to select multiple messages.)

   b. Hit the Delete key on your keyboard, or click the Delete button on the toolbar.

5. If you would like to flag a message to deal with later, In the List pane, click in the flag column next to one of your messages. When you do, a flag appears in the column beside that message (see Figure 167-2).

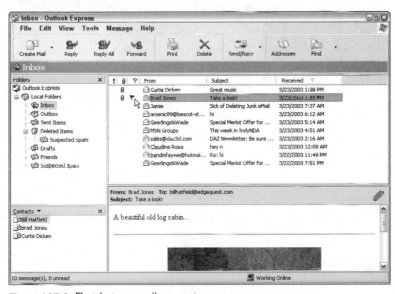

Figure 167-2: Flagging an email message.

6. To sort the email in the List pane:

   a. Click the column header at the top of the List pane. The email items are sorted based on that column.

   b. Click the same column again. The email items are sorted in reverse order. (Notice the little triangle in the column heading pointing up or down.)

tip

When you delete a message it isn't actually deleted right away. Instead, it is put in the Deleted Items folder. To retrieve a message you accidentally deleted, click to select the Deleted Items folder and move the message back to the Inbox. To find out how to move messages from one folder to another, see Task 168.

tip

To empty the Deleted Items folder, right-click it and choose Empty 'Deleted Items' Folder.

tip

You can also click in the Flag column beside a flagged message to remove the flag. This indicator is for you to use however you want — it has no effect on anything else.

note

You'll usually sort your email chronologically by clicking on the Received column header. However, you can sort your Inbox on any column. For example, you can click the ! column header to bring all the high-priority emails to the top of the list. Or can click the Flag column header to bring all the messages you've flagged to the top.

Filing Your Email into Folders

Just as Windows Explorer uses folders to organize the files on your hard drive, so Outlook Express provides folders to help you organize your email. Several special folders are created for you when you first begin using Outlook Express: Inbox, Outbox, Sent Items, Deleted Items, and Drafts. In this task you'll discover how to create your own folders and how to move email between folders to help you stay organized.

1. Open Outlook Express by choosing Start⇨All Programs⇨Outlook Express. On the Outlook Express opening page, click the Read Mail link to see your Inbox (see Figure 168-1).

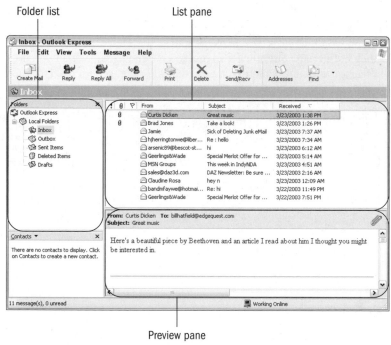

Figure 168-1: The Outlook Express main window.

2. To create a new folder:

   a. Right-click on Local Folders in the Folder list. From the pop-up menu choose New Folder. The Create Folder dialog appears.

   b. Type the name of the folder you want to create in the Folder Name text box.

   c. Click OK. The new folder appears in the Folder list.

3. To move an email message from one folder to another folder:

   a. Click on the folder that contains the message in the Folder list.

   b. Press and hold the left mouse button on the email message in the List pane.

tip

You can create folders inside of other folders. Instead of right-clicking on Local Folders, right-click on the folder you want to create another folder within.

tip

You can use the Ctrl key to select two or more messages and move them all at once.

c. Move the mouse to the destination folder in the Folder list. The destination folder is highlighted (see Figure 168-2).

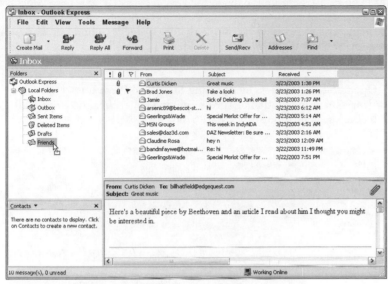

Figure 168-2: Dragging a message from one folder to another.

d. Release the mouse button. The email message is moved.

You can use this technique to move emails you've already dealt with into a folder you created. You can also use this technique to retrieve email that you accidentally deleted, moving it from the Deleted Items folder back to the Inbox.

4. To rename a folder:

a. Right-click on the folder.

b. Select Rename from the pop-up menu. The Rename Folder dialog appears.

c. Type the new name and click OK. You can see the renamed folder in the Folder list.

5. To delete a folder:

a. Right-click on the folder

b. Select Delete from the pop-up menu. A dialog appears asking if you are sure you want to delete the folder. Click Yes.

c. The folder and its messages are moved to the Deleted Items folder.

cross-reference

To find out how to delete an individual email message, see Task 167.

tip

To empty the Deleted Items folder, right-click the Deleted Items folder and choose Empty Deleted Items Folder.

Finding a Message

Once you've used Outlook Express for a while, created your own folders, and organized your email in a way that's comfortable for you, you might find that you're beginning to get so many emails that it's difficult to find just what you're looking for by browsing through your folders. That's why Outlook Express includes a Find feature.

1. Open Outlook Express by choosing Start⇨All Programs⇨Outlook Express. On the Outlook Express opening page, click the Read Mail link to see your Inbox (see Figure 169-1).

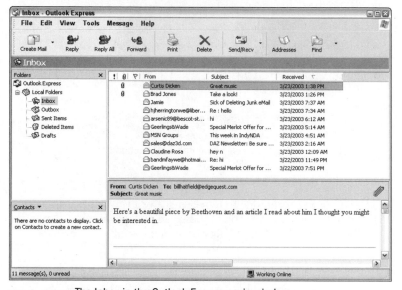

Figure 169-1: The Inbox in the Outlook Express main window.

2. Click the Find button on the toolbar. The Find Message window appears (see Figure 169-2).

Figure 169-2: The Find Message window.

3. Click the Browse button. Select the folder where you want to search for the message.

4. Use the From, To, Subject, and Message text boxes to type in what you know about the message you are searching for. For example, if you know the message included the word **transubstantiation**, type that word into Message. If you know the subject included the word **Calvinism**, type that.

5. If you have some idea when the message was received, you can use the Received Before and Received After drop-down list boxes to identify a range.

6. Use the Message Has Attachment(s) and Message Is Flagged check boxes to further narrow the search, if you remember these details.

7. Click the Find Now button. The window opens up at the bottom to reveal a list of messages that meet your criteria (see Figure 169-3). You can double-click on a message to view its details. You can even drag the messages from the Find Message window to one of the folders in the Folder list on the main window.

tip

If you have no idea what folder your message is in, select Local Folders and click OK. Then make sure the Include Subfolders check box is checked. This ensures all folders are searched.

tip

As with any search, the more specific the information you provide, the more likely it is that the search will be able to zero in on exactly the message you're looking for.

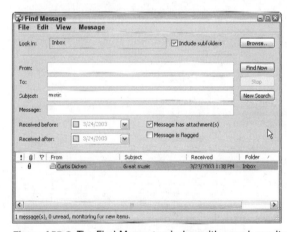

Figure 169-3: The Find Message window with search results.

8. If your search brought back too many results, or the wrong results, you can modify your search criteria and click Find Now again. Or you can click New Search to clear everything out and start over again.

cross-reference

Another way to look for a message is by sorting the columns in the List pane in different ways. To find out how to do that, see Task 167.

Task 170

Using Your Address Book

Now your little black book has a home on your computer. The Outlook Express address book helps you keep track of all the contact information for business associates, friends, and enemies. It also remembers all those complicated email addresses so you don't have to type them out every time you want to send someone a message.

1. Open Outlook Express by choosing Start➪All Programs➪Outlook Express. On the Outlook Express opening page, click the Read Mail link to see your Inbox (see Figure 170-1).

Folder list   List pane

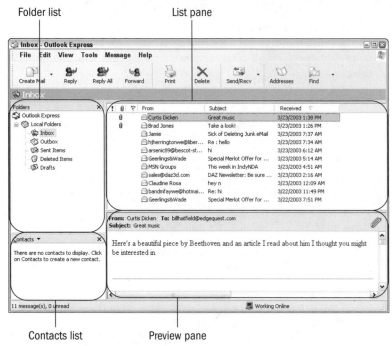

Contacts list   Preview pane

Figure 170-1: The Inbox on the Outlook Express main window.

2. To add a new contact to your address book:

   a. Select File➪New➪Contact... The contact Properties window appears.

   b. Fill in all the information you have about the contact. The first five tabs are the ones you're most likely to use: Name, Home, Business, Personal, and Other. Click OK. The contact's name appears in the Contacts list.

3. To create a new contact for a person who has sent you an email message:

   a. Right-click the email message in the List pane and choose Add to Address Book from the pop-up menu. A new contact is created and added to the Contacts list.

tip

If you already have a pretty complete address book in some other application you use on your computer, there's a chance that you can import that address book into Outlook Express. Just select File➪ Import➪Other Address Book.

b. Right-click the new contact in the Contacts list. Select Properties from the pop-up menu. The contact Properties window appears. Fill in any additional details you know about the contact and click OK.

4. To delete a contact, right-click the contact's name in the Contacts list. Select Delete from the pop-up menu. A dialog confirms that you want to delete the contact. Click Yes.

5. To address a new email message to contacts in your address book:

   a. Click Create Mail button on the toolbar. The New Message window appears.

   b. Click on the To:, CC:, or BCC: label (not the text box, but the label identifying the text box). The Select Recipients dialog appears (see Figure 170-2).

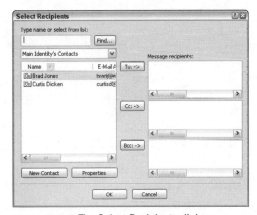

Figure 170-2: The Select Recipients dialog.

   c. Click to select a contact's name and then click the To, CC, or BCC button. The contact's email address is added.

   d. Repeat this process for as many of your contacts as you like.

   e. Click OK when you are done. You are returned to the New Message window with the To, CC, and BCC lines filled in appropriately.

tip

Here's a shortcut to sending an email to one of your contacts: Just double-click on the contact name in the Contacts list. A New Message window appears already addressed to the contact.

cross-reference

For more information on sending email, see Task 161.

Task **171**

Creating Your Own Virtual Business Card

These days, even business cards have gone virtual. Now you can share all your contact information with friends and business associates easily with Outlook Express vCards. When you send out a vCard with your email, it makes it easy for others to add all your contact information to their address book. And this way you can be sure they get all the information right. In this task, you'll find out how to create your own vCard.

tip

You can use this same technique to make vCards for others in your Contacts list if you want to share their information with others.

1. Open Outlook Express by choosing Start⇨All Programs⇨Outlook Express. On the Outlook Express opening page, click the Read Mail link to view your Inbox (see Figure 171-1).

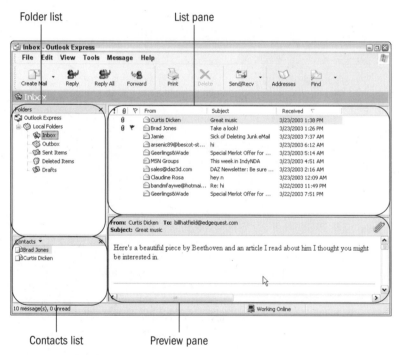

Figure 171-1:The Outlook Express main window.

2. Click the Address button on the toolbar. The Address Book window appears (see Figure 171-2).

3. Click the New button on the Address Book window toolbar. A menu appears.

tip

You could actually create two or three vCards for yourself. For example, one could have your complete information for close friends, while another has only the information you want to share with business associates.

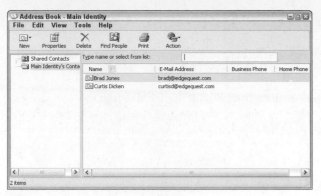

Figure 171-2: The Address Book window.

4. Choose New Contact... from the menu. The contact Properties window appears (see Figure 171-3).

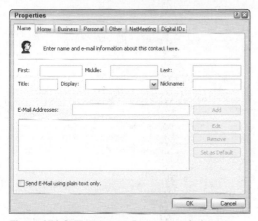

Figure 171-3: The contact Properties window.

5. Fill in all the information you want to share about yourself. The first five tabs are the ones you're most likely to use: Name, Home, Business, Personal, and Other. Click OK on the Properties window. Your name appears in the Contacts list on the Address Book window.

6. Click to select your name, and choose File⇨Export⇨Business Card (vCard).... The Export window appears.

7. Select a location and a name for your business card. Click Save. Close the Address Book window to return to the main window.

cross-reference

To find out how to send and receive your new business card, see Tasks 172 and 173.

Sending Virtual Business Cards

rading business cards will never be the same again. Email your business card
out to others, and they'll never spell your name wrong again.

cross-reference

You can't send your business
card out to others until you've
created it. If you haven't done
that yet, see Task 171.

1. Open Outlook Express by choosing Start➪All Programs➪Outlook
   Express. On the Outlook Express opening page, click the Read Mail
   link to see your Inbox (see Figure 172-1).

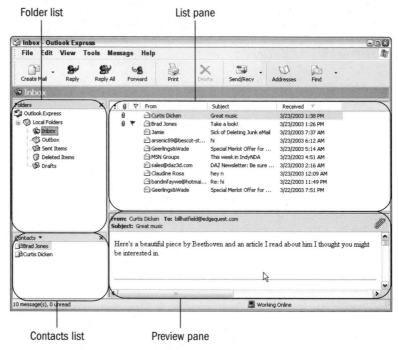

Figure 172-1: The Inbox in the Outlook Express main window.

cross-reference

For more information on adding
attachments to your email messages, see Task 163.

2. Click the Create Mail button on the toolbar. The New Message
   window appears. Enter the information requested.

3. Click the Attach button in the New Message window's toolbar. The
   Insert Attachment dialog appears (see Figure 172-2).

Figure 172-2: The Insert Attachment dialog.

4. Locate the vCard file you want to attach to your email message, and click to select it.

5. Click the Attach button. The vCard appears in the Attach line of the message header (see Figure 172-3). Click Send to send the message.

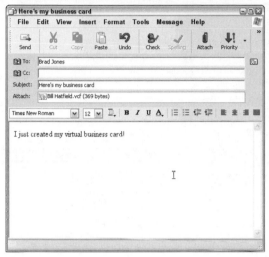

Figure 172-3: The New Message window with an attached vCard.

6. To ask Outlook Express to include your virtual business card with every email:

   a. Select Tools⇨Options... from the menus. Click to view the Compose tab (see Figure 171-4).

   b. In the Business Cards section at the bottom of the dialog, click the check box beside Mail. Use the drop-down list box to choose your virtual business card.

   c. Click OK. Now whenever you send an email, your vCard is automatically attached.

Figure 172-4: The Compose tab on the Options dialog.

caution

Your recipient may not be able to make use of your Virtual Business Card if they do not use Outlook or Outlook Express as their email application.

cross-reference

To find out how to add a Virtual Business Card you receive to your Address Book, see Task 173.

Task 173

Adding Virtual Business Cards to Your Address Book

When someone emails you their Virtual Business Card, you can easily turn it into an entry in your Contacts list.

cross-reference

To find out how to create your own Virtual Business Card, see Task 171. To find out how to send your card to others, see Task 172.

1. Open Outlook Express by choosing Start⇨All Programs⇨Outlook Express. On the Outlook Express opening page, click the Read Mail link to see your Inbox (see Figure 173-1).

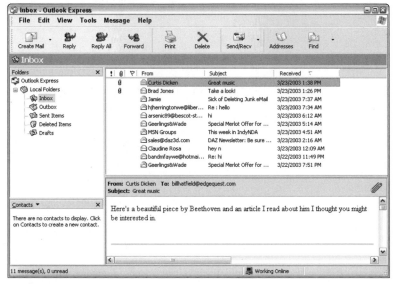

Figure 173-1: The Inbox on the Outlook Express main window.

2. Click to select the email message in your List pane that has an attached vCard.

3. Click on the Paperclip icon in the gray bar at the top of the Preview pane. A pop-up menu appears.

4. Select the vCard attachment from the menu.

5. You may see an Open Attachment Warning window. If you do, select Open it and click OK.

6. A properties window appears (see Figure 173-2).

cross-reference

To find out how to open and save other kinds of attachments, see Task 160.

Figure 173-2: The vCard properties window.

7. Click the Add to Address Book button at the top of the window. The window transforms into a contact entry, and you can make any changes you like to the information.

8. Click OK. The contact is added to your Contacts list.

tip

If you already have an entry for a contact in your Contacts list and you try to add a vCard, you'll get a message that says, "Your Address Book already contains a contact named Brad Jones. Do you want to update the existing contact with the new contact?" Click Yes. This adds the vCard information to the contact information you already have.

Using Message Rules to Kill Spam and Do Other Cool Stuff

Once you get your folders set up and a system for organizing your email (as described in Tasks 167 and 168), you may begin to wish you could have a robot around that would just do some of the automatic stuff like, "OK, this message is from Brad, so it goes in the Friends folder" and "This one is from my boss, so it goes in the Work folder," and so forth. It turns out that Outlook Express *does* include a robot! It's called Message Rules, and we'll show you how it works in this task while walking you through an example that will help kill some of your spam (the email equivalent of junk mail).

1. Open Outlook Express by choosing Start⇨All Programs⇨Outlook Express. On the Outlook Express opening page, click the Read Mail link to see your Inbox.

2. Select Tools⇨Message Rules⇨Mail from the menus. The New Mail Rule dialog appears (see Figure 174-1). The list of check boxes at the top of this window allows you to specify what kind of condition you want to check for. The second list of check boxes allows you to specify what kind of action you want to take.

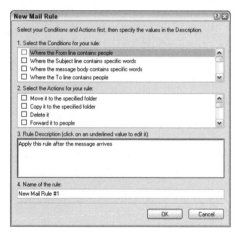

Figure 174-1: The New Mail Rule dialog.

3. Click the Where the Subject Line Contains Specific Words check box in the first list box.

4. Click the Move It to the Specified Folder check box in the second list box.

   Now in the Rule Description (below the two list boxes) you see two links. One for Where the Subject Line Contains Specific Words and the other for Move It to the Specified Folder. These links allow you to fill in the details.

5. To identify what words will trigger this rule:

   a. Click the Where the Subject Line Contains Specific Words link. The Type Specific Words dialog appears (see Figure 174-2).

Figure 174-2: The Type Specific Words dialog.

   b. In the Type Specific Words text box at the top of the dialog, type **Viagra** Click Add. The word is added to the list box below.

   c. Go ahead and add as many words as you like. The trick is to try to find words that often appear in the subject line of spam messages that you get, but are not likely to appear in subject line of your normal emails.

   d. When you are done, click OK. You are returned to the New Mail Rule dialog.

6. To identify what folder offending messages should be moved to:

   a. Click the Move It to the Specified Folder link. The Move dialog appears.

   b. Click on Local Folders to select it, and then click the New Folder button. Type the name of the new folder you want to create: **Suspected Spam**. Click OK.

   c. Click the Suspected Spam folder in the folder list to be sure it's selected and then click OK.

   The New Mail Rule dialog's Rule Description should be complete now. Read over it to be sure. You can click on the links, as necessary, to make changes.

7. Type a name for your rule: **Spam Killer**. Click OK. The Message Rules dialog appears. From now on whenever you want to create a new rule, you can do it here, by clicking the New button. Click OK.

   Now whenever a new message is received in your Inbox, the rule you just created will check to see if the message matches its condition. If it does, the message will be moved into the Suspected Spam folder.

cross-reference

For more information on creating and using folders, see Task 168.

tip

Of course, you can do a whole lot more with Message Rules than simply catch spam. Use it to organize your messages based on sender or content. Or you can automatically reply or forward messages based on certain criteria. Play around with it — the possibilities are endless!

caution

There's always the chance that your rule will accidentally snag a message that you do want to read (the friend who wants your opinion about Viagra, for example). So check the Suspected Spam folder every few days or so to make sure that nothing important has slipped through. And as you get new spam, you'll get ideas for additional words you can add to your rule to make it stronger.

Part 12: Discussing with Newsgroups

Task 175: Connecting to a Newsgroup Server

Task 176: Searching for and Subscribing to Newsgroups

Task 177: Reading Newsgroup Messages

Task 178: Posting a New Message to a Newsgroup

Task 179: Replying to a Newsgroup Message

Task 180: Downloading Newsgroup Message Attachments

Task 181: Downloading Multipart Newsgroup Message Attachments

Task 182: Searching for Messages in a Newsgroup

Task **175**

Connecting to a Newsgroup Server

The term *newsgroups* is deceiving; it sounds like a place where you go to read news. But the emphasis in the word is on *groups*, not on *news*. Newsgroups would be better named discussion forums. They are simply a place where people can post messages on a topic and read messages that others have posted. As such, they become ongoing discussions. While some Web pages offer similar capabilities, newsgroups are the original Internet discussion forum, and newsgroup servers receive hundreds of thousands of posts every day in thousands of very active forums.

In this task you'll find out how you can use Outlook Express to connect to a newsgroup server so that you can begin to see what's out there.

note

When Outlook Express starts, you may go directly to the Inbox (and never see the opening page). If that happens, click on the top item in the Folders list labeled Outlook Express. The opening page will appear.

cross-reference

When Outlook Express starts, if you immediately see the Internet Connection Wizard, refer to Task 158 to find out how to fill it in appropriately.

1. Open Outlook Express by choosing Start⇨All Programs⇨ Outlook Express. You see the Outlook Express opening page (see Figure 175-1).

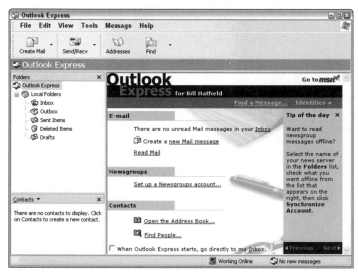

Figure 175-1: The Outlook Express opening page.

note

Although this wizard has the same name as the wizard discussed in Task 158, it collects different information. The wizard in Task 158 collects information about your email server. This wizard collects information about your newsgroup server.

note

Your Internet service provider (ISP) should have provided the newsgroup server name to you when you signed up for service with them.

2. Click the Set Up a Newsgroups Account link under Newsgroups in the middle of the page. The Internet Connection Wizard appears.

3. Enter your name (it might already be filled in for you). Click Next. Enter your email address (again, it might already be filled in).

4. Click Next. The Internet News Server Name page appears (see Figure 175-2). Enter the name of your newsgroup server. (If you are required to log in to your newsgroup server, click the check box and then click Next. You'll be given the opportunity to enter an account name and password.)

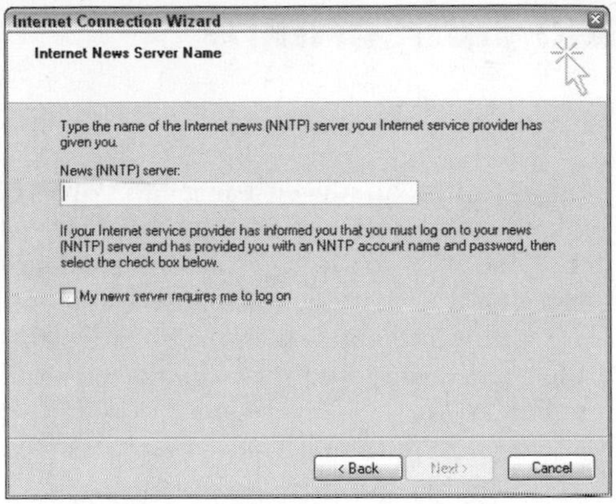

Figure 175-2: The Internet News Server Name page of the Internet Connection Wizard.

5. Click Next. The wizard is complete. Click Finish. A dialog is immediately displayed asking if you'd like to "download newsgroups from the news account you added?"

6. Click Yes. The names of all the newsgroups on your server are downloaded (see Figure 175-3).

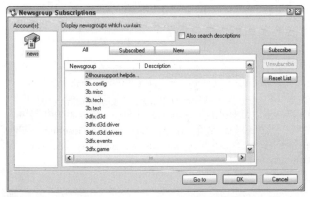

Figure 175-3: Downloading the newsgroup names.

7. The Newsgroup Subscriptions dialog presents the list of available newsgroups to you (see Figure 175-4). If you find one that looks interesting, click to select it and then click the Go To button.

Figure 175-4: The Newsgroup Subscriptions dialog.

note

Newsgroups are a part of the Internet, and since the Internet is worldwide, you'll see postings from people all over the world.

cross-reference

To find out how to search for newsgroups that match your interests, see Task 176.

Task 176
Searching for and Subscribing to Newsgroups

There are tens of thousands of newsgroups. So it isn't realistic to think you'll just scroll through the list, looking at them all, to find something interesting. That's why Outlook Express offers a handy search feature that makes looking for cool newsgroups a breeze. And once you find newsgroups that you like, you can subscribe to them so that they'll be readily available whenever you want to check them out. In addition, if you decide a newsgroup isn't for you, you can also unsubscribe to remove it from the Folder list.

1. Open Outlook Express by choosing Start➪All Programs➪ Outlook Express. You see the Outlook Express opening page.

2. Click the Subscribe to Newsgroups link under Newsgroups. The Newsgroup Subscriptions window appears (see Figure 176-1).

3. In the text box at the top labeled Display Newsgroups Which Contain:, type a word that indicates what you're looking for, like **game**. When you finish typing, the list below changes so that only newsgroup names that have "game" somewhere in them appear.

4. Press the space bar and type another word that narrows the search further, like **chess**. The list changes again to list only newsgroups with names that contain both words typed. You can enter as many words as you like.

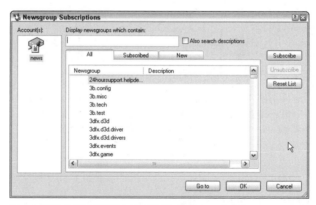

Figure 176-1: The Newsgroup Subscriptions window.

5. When you find one or more newsgroups you'd like to subscribe to, click the newsgroup name to select it (hold the Ctrl key down while you click to select more than one). Then click the Subscribe button. An icon appears beside the newsgroups to indicate you've subscribed to them (see Figure 176-2).

note

When Outlook Express starts, you may go directly to the Inbox (and never see the opening page). If that happens, click on the top item in the Folders list labeled Outlook Express. The opening page will appear.

cross-reference

If you don't see a Subscribe to Newsgroups link on the opening page under Newsgroups, it may be because you haven't set up a newsgroup server. See Task 175 to find out how to do that. Alternately, it might be because you've already subscribed to at least one newsgroup. To find out how to read messages in a newsgroup, see Task 177.

tip

You should type **game** rather than **games**, because **game** will find all titles that have **game** or **games** in it. Similarly, if you are looking for **puppy** or **puppies**, it's probably best just to search for **pupp**, so that you will find all mentions of either **puppy** or **puppies**.

caution

Be aware that when you type a second keyword, you are effectively only searching *within* the list found by the first keyword. If you want to search for newsgroups with *either* **eBay** or **auction** in the title, you need to do them as separate searches. Typing both will only find newsgroups with *both* words in the title.

Figure 176-2: An icon appears beside newsgroups you've subscribed to.

6. Clear out the text box at the top, type different words to do another search, and follow the same process to subscribe to as many newsgroups as you like.

7. Click OK. You are returned to the Outlook Express main window. Notice in the Folders pane on the left, the newsgroup server appears with the newsgroups you subscribed to under it. Click on one of the newsgroups to open it (see Figure 176-3).

Folder pane

Newsgroup server

Subscribed newsgroups

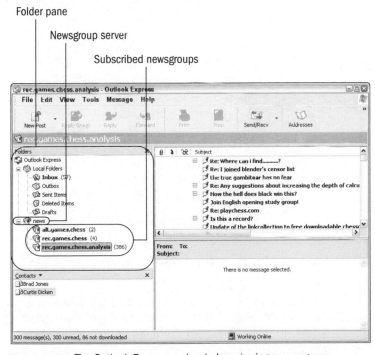

Figure 176-3: The Outlook Express main window, viewing a newsgroup.

Reading Newsgroup Messages

Newsgroups are like an ongoing, disconnected conversation. The cool thing is that not everyone has to be present to make the conversation work. You can just check in whenever you like and see who has posted new messages to the group.

1. Open Outlook Express by choosing Start⇨All Programs⇨Outlook Express (see Figure 177-1).

cross-reference

You may run across messages that have a paperclip beside them. This indicates that the message has an attachment — a file that was sent along with the message. For more information on downloading and opening newsgroup message attachments, see Tasks 180 and 181.

Folder pane

Newsgroup server

Subscribed newsgroups

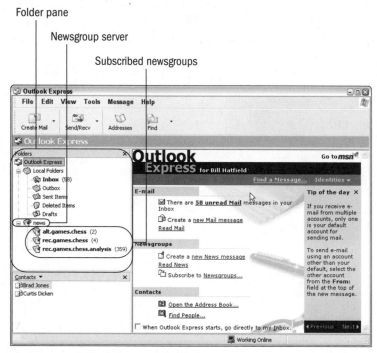

Figure 177-1: Outlook Express main window.

cross-reference

If you don't see the newsgroup server in your Folder list, it may be because you haven't set up a newsgroup server yet. See Task 175 to find out how to do that. If you see a newsgroup server, but no newsgroups below, it's probably because you haven't subscribed to any. To find out how to do that, see Task 176.

tip

If you want to search for additional newsgroups to subscribe to, choose Tools⇨Newsgroups from the menus. This opens the Newsgroup Subscriptions window, which is described in Task 176.

2. Click on one of the newsgroups you've subscribed to in the Folders pane, under the newsgroup server. The window changes so that the messages in that group are displayed in the List pane (at the top on the right side of the window).

3. Click on a message in the List pane. The contents of the message appear below, in the Preview pane (see Figure 177-2).

4. Notice the little plus sign beside some of the messages. Click on one of them (see Figure 177-3). New messages appear below the first message. These are *replies* that people have posted to that message. Some people even reply to the replies, creating a tree structure.

Folder pane   List pane

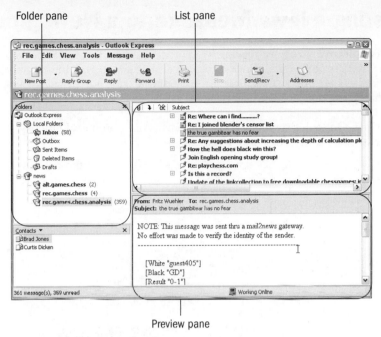

Preview pane

Figure 177-2: Reading a message.

tip

Although the tree structure created by replies to a message
and replies to the replies can
seem complicated at first, it is
designed to organize discussions. If you are interested in
the replies to a message, you
can open them up and look at
them. If not, it's easy to just go
on to the next message.

You can read messages in order or skip around. You can read the
replies to a message or skip them. Or you can just look for the subject
lines that interest you.

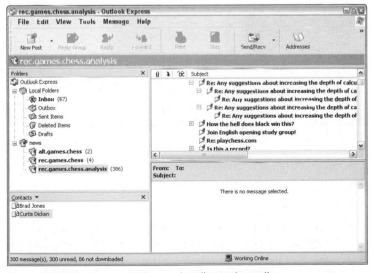

Figure 177-3: A message, replies, and replies to the replies.

Task 178

Posting a New Message to a Newsgroup

You can learn a lot by just reading what others have posted, but a conversation isn't really a conversation unless you can take an active part. In this task you'll find out how to post a message in a newsgroup that others will see and (hopefully!) respond to.

1. Open Outlook Express by choosing Start⇨All Programs⇨Outlook Express. You see the Outlook Express opening page.

2. Click on one of the newsgroups you've subscribed to in the Folders pane, under the newsgroup server. The window changes again so that the messages in that group are displayed in the List pane (at the top on the right side of the window). Click on a message in the List pane. The contents of the message appear below, in the Preview pane (see Figure 178-1).

Folder pane   List pane

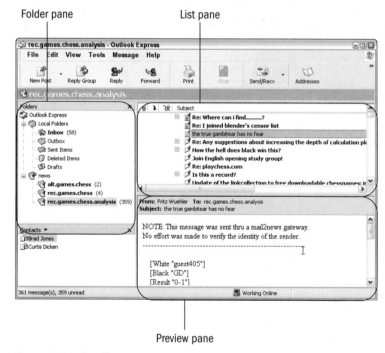

Preview pane

Figure 178-1: Reading a message.

3. Click New Post on the toolbar. The New Message window appears (see Figure 178-2). Note that the Newsgroups text box is already filled in with the newsgroup you were in when you clicked the New Post button.

4. Fill in the Subject text box with a descriptive title for your message.

5. Type your message in the bottom part of the window.

---

caution

Never post a message in a newsgroup that isn't related to the topic of the newsgroup — it is considered rude.

cross-reference

If you don't see the newsgroup server in your Folder list, it may be because you haven't set up a newsgroup server yet. See Task 175 to find out how to do that. If you see a newsgroup server, but no newsgroups below, it's probably because you haven't subscribed to any. To find out how to do that, see Task 176.

tip

You can post to several newsgroups at once. In the New Message window, click on the Newsgroups label itself (not the text box beside it). The Pick Newsgroups window appears and allows you to select other newsgroups to post your message to at the same time.

tip

If you want to send your message as an email as well as a newsgroup post, you can type email addresses into the CC line of the New Message window. You can also click on the CC label itself to display your address book so that you can select people from there.

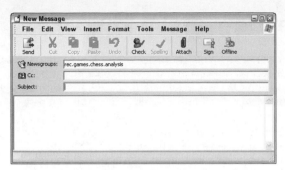

Figure 178-2: The New Message window.

6. If you want to attach a file to your message:

   a. Click Attach to open the Insert Attachment window.

   b. Locate the file you want to attach and click to select it. (You can use the Ctrl key when you click to select more than one.)

   c. Click OK. A new line appears in the top part of the window labeled Attach. Your file appears there (see Figure 178-3).

Figure 178-3: The New Message window with an attachment.

   d. Repeat the process to attach additional files.

7. When your message is complete, click Send in the toolbar of the New Message window. The message may not appear immediately in the newsgroup where it was posted. It may take a few minutes.

tip

Some newsgroup servers have a limit on the maximum size your message can be (including attachments). Often it's 1MB. If you have an attachment that's bigger than this limit, you can tell Outlook Express to post your attachment as a multipart attachment, dividing a large file into several postings, each with a small piece of the complete file. To do so, select Tools⇨ Accounts, then click the News tab. Click to select your newsgroup server, and click Properties. Click the Advanced tab, and then click the check box labeled Break Apart Messages Larger Than. Set the maximum size for each part (to 1000KB, for example).

note

Some newsgroups are monitored — that is, they are overseen by a person who's in charge of the group. The monitor ensures that all messages posted to the group are on-topic and relevant to the conversation. If you post to a moderated newsgroup, it may take longer than usual for your message to appear, since it must be reviewed by the monitor first.

Replying to a Newsgroup Message

You usually post a message to a newsgroup to ask a question or add your own thoughts to the conversation. However, in this task you'll discover how to reply to a message that someone else has posted. This is a great way to answer a question someone else has asked or to go off on a tangent that isn't a part of the main conversation.

1. Open Outlook Express by choosing Start⇨All Programs⇨Outlook Express. You see the Outlook Express opening page.

2. Click one of the newsgroups you've subscribed to in the Folders pane under the newsgroup server. The window changes again so that the messages in that group are displayed in the List pane (at the top on the right side of the window). Click on a message in the List pane. The contents of the message appear below, in the Preview pane (see Figure 179-1).

cross-reference

If you don't see the newsgroup server in your Folder list, it may be because you haven't set up a newsgroup server yet. See Task 175 to find out how to do that. If you see a newsgroup server, but no newsgroups below, it's probably because you haven't subscribed to any. To find out how to do that, see Task 176.

Folder pane   List pane

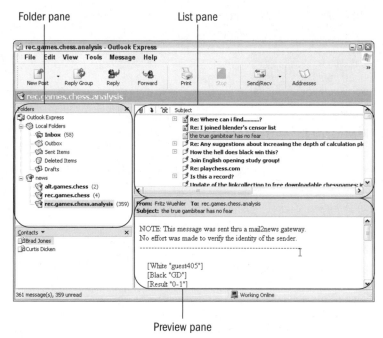

Preview pane

Figure 179-1: Reading a message.

3. Read through the newsgroup messages.

4. When you come across a message you want to respond to, click to select the message and then click the Reply Group button on the toolbar. The message window appears (see Figure 179-2). Note that the Newsgroups text box is already filled in with the newsgroup you were in and that the original email's contents appear in the bottom part of the window. This allows you to use parts of the original message in your posting.

tip

Sometimes the person posting a message may request that you respond to him or her privately or in addition to posting to the newsgroup. That's because he or she may not monitor the newsgroup that often, checking for new messages. To reply to a message posting privately, click the Reply button instead of the Reply Group button. This sends an email to the person who posted the message instead of posting your message to the newsgroup.

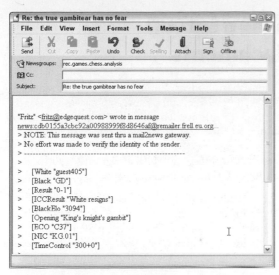

Figure 179-2: The message window.

5. The Subject text box is already filled in with the original subject and an Re: in front if it. You can change that if you want to give your posting a more specific subject.

6. Type your message in the bottom part of the window.

7. If you want to attach a file to your message,

   a. Click Attach to open the Insert Attachment window.

   b. Locate the file you want to attach and click to select it. (You can use the Ctrl key when you click to select more than one.)

   c. Click OK. A new line appears in the top part of the window labeled Attach. Your file appears there.

   d. Repeat the process to attach additional files.

8. When your message is complete, click Send in the toolbar of the message window. The message may not appear immediately in the newsgroup where it was posted. It may take a few minutes to be posted. When it is posted, it will appear under the message you responded to, so you might have to click the plus sign beside the original message to see yours.

tip

If you want to send your message as an email as well as a newsgroup post, you can type email addresses into the CC line of the New Message window. You can also click on the CC label itself to display your address book so that you can select people from there.

Task 180

Downloading Newsgroup Message Attachments

Most newsgroups are about sharing ideas. Some newsgroups are more about sharing files and pictures. These files and pictures appear as message attachments in Outlook Express. In this task you'll find out how to access an attachment, view it (if it's a picture) and save the file to your hard drive.

cross-reference

To find out how to post a message with an attachment, see Task 178.

cross-reference

If you don't see the newsgroup server in your Folders pane, it may be because you haven't set up a newsgroup server yet. See Task 175 to find out how to do that. If you see a newsgroup server, but no newsgroups below, it's probably because you haven't subscribed to any. To find out how to do that, see Task 176.

tip

If the attachment is a picture, you can often simply scroll down in the message to see the picture.

1. Open Outlook Express by choosing Start⇨All Programs⇨Outlook Express. You see the Outlook Express opening page.

2. Click on one of the newsgroups you've subscribed to in the Folders pane, under the newsgroup server. The window changes again so that the messages in that group are displayed in the List pane (at the top on the right side of the window). Click on a message in the List pane. The contents of the message appear below, in the Preview pane.

3. As you click on different messages, sometimes a paperclip appears beside the message. This indicates that the message has an attachment (see Figure 180-1).

Folder pane   List pane

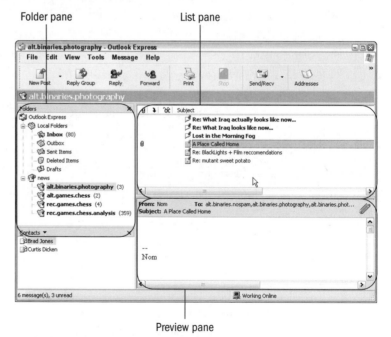

Preview pane

Figure 180-1: A message with an attachment.

4. To open the attachment (that is, to view a picture, open a document, or run a program that was sent to you):

   a. Click on the Paperclip icon in the gray bar at the top of the Preview pane. A pop-up menu appears (see Figure 180-2).

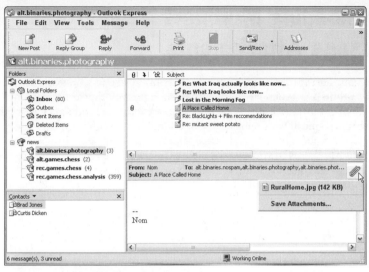

Figure 180-2: The attachment pop-up menu.

b. Select the attachment that you want to open from the menu. For example, if you select a picture, the default application to view that picture is launched, displaying the picture. Likewise for other types of files.

5. To save the attachment to your hard drive:

a. Click on the Paperclip icon in the gray bar at the top of the Preview pane. The pop-up menu appears.

b. Select Save Attachments from the pop-up menu. The Save Attachments dialog appears (see Figure 180-3).

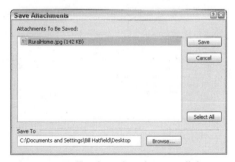

Figure 180-3: The Save Attachments dialog.

c. Click Browse to select a folder where the attachments should be saved. You cannot choose a different folder for each one — they are all saved in the same folder.

d. Click Save. The attached files are saved in the location you specified.

caution

Be *very* careful with any attachment you download — especially if it is an application (an executable, or EXE, file). This is one way viruses are spread! But the virus can't infect your computer unless you open the executable file by selecting it from the attachment pop-up menu. If you aren't sure, don't do it!

cross-reference

You may run across messages that have numbers in their subject line like this: [1/4]. This may indicate that the message has a multipart attachment. To find out how to retrieve a multipart attachment, see Task 181.

Downloading Multipart Newsgroup Message Attachments

Newsgroup servers sometimes limit the maximum size of a message (including attachments). So when large attachments are posted, they are sometimes divided up into several messages, each with an attachment holding a part of the complete file. Typically, the subject line of a multipart attachment message includes two numbers inside brackets, separated by a slash, like this: [1/4] or [2/7]. The second number is the number of pieces the complete attachment is divided into, while the first number indicates which piece *this* message contains. So [1/4] indicates that the message is the first part of a four-part message attachment.

Unfortunately, Outlook Express has no way of identifying what messages go together or in what order. So you have to show it how to put the pieces back together.

1. Open Outlook Express by choosing Start⇨All Programs⇨Outlook Express. You see the Outlook Express opening page.

2. Click on one of the newsgroups you've subscribed to in the Folders pane, under the newsgroup server. The window changes again so that the messages in that group are displayed in the List pane (at the top on the right side of the window). Click on a message in the List pane. The contents of the message appear below, in the Preview pane.

3. When you see a group of messages that belong to a multipart attachment (see Figure 181-1), click to select the first one and then hold the Ctrl key down as you select each of the rest of them.

caution

Sometimes when you see numbers inside brackets (like [2/5]) it is *not* a multipart attachment. Sometimes when the same person posts five different pictures, for example, he or she will put numbers like this in the subject line just to indicate that this is the second of five pictures being posted.

cross-reference

To open or save a normal attachment (one that isn't multipart), see Task 180.

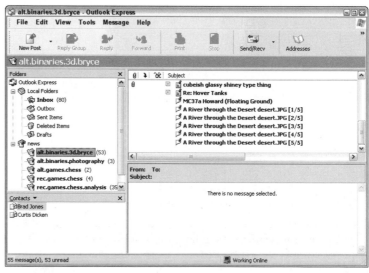

Figure 181-1: A multipart attachment.

4. When you have all the messages selected, right-click on one of the selected messages. Select Combine and Decode... from the menu (see Figure 181-2).

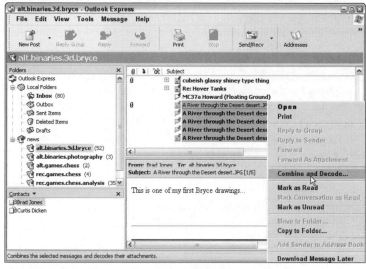

Figure 181-2: Combine and decode the multipart attachment.

5. The Order for Decoding window appears (see Figure 181-3). The messages should be listed in order from first to last. If they are not, click on one of the messages that is in the wrong place and use the Move Up and Move Down buttons to put it in the right place. Repeat this as often as necessary to get them all where they belong.

Figure 181-3: The Order for Decoding window.

6. When the files are in the correct order, click OK. The attachments are downloaded from the newsgroup server and combined together. Depending on the number and size of the attachments, this could be a very quick or a somewhat slow process.

7. When the process is complete, a message window appears with the complete file shown as an attachment. Right-click the attachment in the message window and choose Save As from the menu.

8. The Save Attachment As dialog appears. Pick a location for the file and click Save.

tip

If the attachment is a picture, you can often just scroll down in the message window to see the picture. Or you can double-click the picture to see it in the Windows XP picture viewer.

Task 182

Searching for Messages in a Newsgroup

cross-reference

For more information on reading newsgroup messages, see Task 177.

Some newsgroups get a lot of postings, and it would be very difficult to read every one. Fortunately, Outlook Express provides a feature that allows you to search through all the messages in a newsgroup to find messages on the specific topic you're interested in.

1. Open Outlook Express by choosing Start➪All Programs➪Outlook Express. You see the Outlook Express opening page.

2. Click on one of the newsgroups you've subscribed to in the Folders pane, under the newsgroup server. The window changes again so that the messages in that group are displayed in the List pane (at the top on the right side of the window). Click on a message in the List pane. The contents of the message appear below, in the Preview pane (see Figure 182-1).

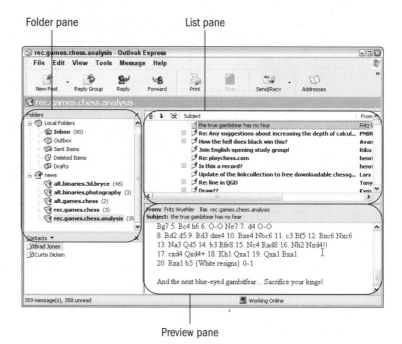

Figure 182-1: Reading a message.

tip

When entering words to search for, type **pawn** instead of **pawns**, because pawn will find all messages that have pawn *or* pawns in it.

3. Choose Edit➪Find➪Message from the menu. The Find Message window appears (see Figure 182-2). You can type in words to search for in the various parts of the message.

Figure 182-2: The Find Message window.

4. Use the From, To, Subject, and Message text boxes to type in what you know about the message you are searching for. For example, if you know the message included the word **bishop**, type that word into Message. If you know the Subject included the word **gambit**, type that.

5. If you have some idea when the message was posted to the newsgroup, you can use the Received Before and Received After drop-down list boxes to identify a range.

6. Use the Message has Attachment(s) and Message is Flagged check boxes to further narrow the search, if you remember these details.

7. Click Find Now. The window opens up at the bottom to reveal a list of messages that meet your criteria (see Figure 182-3). You can double-click on a message to view its details. You can even drag the messages from the Find Message window to one of the folders in the Folders pane on the main window.

tip

If your search brought back too many results, or the wrong results, you can modify your search criteria and click Find Now again. Or you can click New Search to clear everything out and start over again.

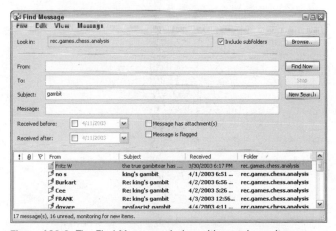

Figure 182-3: The Find Message window with search results.

Part 13: Exploring Windows Messenger

Task 183: Creating a Passport Account

Task 184: Adding and Deleting Contacts

Task 185: Carrying On a Conversation

Task 186: Changing Your Look in Windows Messenger

Task 187: Sending a File or a Picture

Task 188: Receiving a File or a Picture

Task 189: Configuring Your Audio and Video in Windows Messenger

Task 190: Adding Voice and Video to Your Conversation

Creating a Passport Account

When you've spent some time on the Web, it doesn't take long before you acquire a collection of usernames and passwords that you have to remember to access all the different Web sites you've joined. Wouldn't it be nice if you could have just one username and password, and when you surf the Web, sites would instantly recognize you without your having to log in separately to each one? That's the vision Microsoft has in Passport. The only catch is that not all Web sites use it yet. But you can be sure all Microsoft sites do! So if you want to get a Web email account on Hotmail (owned by Microsoft), you have to get a Passport account. The same is true if you want to use Microsoft's Windows Messenger software. Fortunately, getting Passport is pretty easy. And, best of all — it's free!

1. Open Windows Messenger by selecting Start⇨All Programs⇨ Windows Messenger. A simple window appears.

2. Click on the Click Here to Sign In link in the middle of the window. The .NET Passport Wizard appears. Click Next. The Do You Have an E-mail Address? page appears (see Figure 183-1). Click Yes.

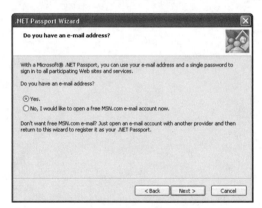

Figure 183-1: The .NET Passport Wizard with the Do You Have an E-mail Address? page displayed.

3. Click Next. The What Is Your E-mail Address? page appears. Enter your email address.

4. Click Next. The Create your password page appears (see Figure 183-2). Pick a password and type it in twice (so the wizard can be sure you didn't mistype). Be sure the Save My .NET Passport Information in My Windows User Account check box is checked.

5. Click Next. The Choose and Answer a Secret Question page appears. If you ever forget your password, you can reset it by answering the secret question correctly.

6. Click Next. The Where Do You Live Page appears. Select your country, then enter your state and zip code (if appropriate). Click Next. The Review the .NET Passport Terms of Use page appears. Review the text and click I Accept the Agreement.

tip

If you don't have an email address or you don't want to associate your email address with your Windows Messenger account, you can choose No on the Do You Have an E-mail Address? page, and the wizard will create a new MSN email account for you.

note

When you type in the password and confirm it, you won't see the actual letters you're typing. You'll just see dots. This is just to help keep your password private.

tip

The Save My .NET Passport Information in My Windows User Account check box saves the Passport email address and password so that all you have to do is log in to Windows, and it knows your .NET Passport information. It can use this information to log you in to Passport automatically. This is a convenient feature, but if there's any chance that someone else could use your PC, it's probably a good idea to put a password on your Windows XP user account. (See Task 214 to find out how.) Otherwise, anyone who gets on your PC has access to all your Passport Web sites.

Figure 183-2: The Create Your Password page of the .NET Passport Wizard.

7. Click Next. The Share Your Information with Participating Sites? page appears. Be sure both check boxes are not checked.

8. Click Next. The wizard is complete. Click Finish. You are signed in using your new Passport account, and the Windows Messenger window is a lot more lively now (see Figure 183-3).

Figure 183-3: The Windows Messenger window, after logging in.

9. Retrieve your email. You should find two messages from Microsoft .NET Passport, one with the subject Welcome to Microsoft .NET Passport! and the other with the subject Please Verify Your Microsoft .NET Passport E-mail Address. Open the latter email. You see a link.

10. Open the page indicated by the link. A page appears that says Please Verify Your E-mail Address. Click Continue. You see a login dialog. Enter the password you selected in Step 4. Click to check the Sign Me in Automatically check box. You'll now see a page that says Verification Successful.

caution

You can check the check boxes on the Share Your Information with Participating Sites? page if you like, but it's really just begging for them to send you junk email!

cross-reference

To find out how to set up Outlook Express to access your email account, see Task 158. To find out how to retrieve your email, once Outlook Express is set up, see Task 159.

note

It may seem odd that you have to go to all this trouble of receiving an email, going to a site, and clicking a button just to activate your account, but it's necessary so that Microsoft can confirm that the email address is real and that it belongs to you.

184 # Adding and Deleting Contacts

Windows Messenger acts like a "buddy list" for your computer. If your friends or business associates use Windows Messenger, you can add them as a contact. Once you do, you'll be able to see when they are at their computer and start up a conversation with them!

cross-reference

If this is the first time you've opened Windows Messenger and you haven't set up a Passport account, see Task 183 to do so. You can't use Windows Messenger until you have a Passport account.

1. If Windows Messenger isn't already open, open it by selecting Start↷ All Programs↷Windows Messenger. The Windows Messenger window appears (see Figure 184-1).

Figure 184-1: The Windows Messenger window.

tip

If you don't see the I Want To... list at the bottom of the window, select Tools↷Show Actions Pane.

2. Click the Add Contact link at the top of the I Want To... list at the bottom of the window. The Add a Contact Wizard appears (see Figure 184-2).

Figure 184-2: The Add a Contact Wizard.

3. If you know the email address of the person you are searching for, select By E-mail Address or Sign-in Name. If you don't, choose Search for a Contact. Click Next.

4. If you choose to add a contact by email address or sign-in name:

   a. Enter your contact's email address.

   b. Click Next. The wizard searches for the email address you entered.

   c. If the email address is found, the contact is added to your list. Click Finish. You are done. Repeat the process to add another contact.

   d. If the email address is not found, you are informed. Click Back and enter a different email address, or click Cancel and start over again.

5. If you choose to Search for a contact:

   a. Enter your contact's first name and last name (see Figure 184-3). Enter the country if you like. If the country you select is United States, you can also enter a city and state.

Figure 184-3: Enter the contact's name and location.

   b. Click Next.

   c. If one or several entries are found, they are displayed and you can select from the correct one. Click Next. The contact is added.

6. When you add a person to your contacts list, he or she sees a message pop up on his or her machine (either immediately or next time that person logs in) that asks if it's OK for you to add that individual to your list. If the person chooses to allow it, you will see his or her icon in the Online section when his or her computer is on and running Windows Messenger. When the person is not online, he or she appears in your Not Online list.

7. To delete a contact, simply right-click the contact's name in the Windows Messenger window and select Delete Contact. A window asks if you're sure. Click Yes. The contact disappears from your list.

---

caution

Unfortunately, you can only connect with others who use Windows Messenger (also called MSN Messenger in previous versions of Windows). Currently there's no way to talk to people who use other instant messaging programs like AOL Instant Messenger (AIM) or ICQ.

tip

Keep in mind that the email addresses you type in here must be the email addresses they have used with Windows Messenger. If they created an MSN email account just for Windows Messenger, for instance, you won't find them by searching for their normal email address.

note

The search will only find your contact if you type the first and last name exactly as he or she entered it.

caution

If no one was found with the criteria you entered, you are informed. Click Back and try being less specific. If too many entries were found, you'll also be informed. Click Back and try to be more specific.

note

Just because you can't find the person you're looking for using the search doesn't mean he or she isn't using Windows Messenger. It may just mean the person chose not to put his or her name in the directory. The best solution is just to call the person and find out what his or her email address is!

Carrying On a Conversation

Using Windows Messenger is a little like being in the same room with all your contacts. You can see when they come and go, and whenever you like, you can start up a conversation with them.

1. If Windows Messenger isn't already open, open it by selecting Start⇨ All Programs⇨Windows Messenger. The Windows Messenger window appears (see Figure 185-1).

Figure 185-1: The Windows Messenger window.

2. Double-click on the contact you want to have a conversation with. The Conversation window appears (see Figure 185-2).

Figure 185-2: The Conversation window.

tip

If you want to start a new line while typing, don't hit Enter! That will send your message. Instead, hit Shift+Enter.

tip

Watch the status bar at the bottom of the Conversation window. It lets you know when your contact is in the process of typing a message to you. This way, you can tell if the contact is typing a long message or simply ignoring you!

tip

You can also add emoticons to your message by typing their corresponding keys. For example, if you type a colon and a right parenthesis, it will look like a little yellow smiley face when you send your message. For a complete list of all the emoticons and their corresponding keys, see the Windows Messenger online help, which you can access by choosing Help⇨Help Topics from the Windows Messenger window.

3. Click to place your cursor in the bottom part of the window. Type some text. Hit Enter or click the Send button to send your message to the contact. Your message appears in the top part of the window.

4. Wait for a response. Any response your contact sends appears below your message. As you go back and forth typing messages, the top part of the Conversation window scrolls as necessary, keeping a running document of the conversation.

5. If you want to add a little pizzazz to your messages, use emoticons. Emoticons are little icons that you can drop into your text anywhere you like. Just click the Emoticons icon in the Conversation window (see Figure 185-3). Then select one of the emoticons. It is placed right in the message you are creating.

Figure 185-3: The emoticons.

6. If you want to invite a third or fourth person to the conversation, simply click the Invite Someone to This Conversation link in the I Want To... list along the right side of the Conversation window. The Add Someone to This Conversation window appears. Double-click on the contact you want to add, and they are added to the conversation.

7. When you are done talking, choose File⇨Close on the Conversation window to end the conversation.

cross-reference

To find out how to send a file or picture to your contact via messenger, see Task 187.

note

If you don't see the I Want To... list along the right side of the Conversation window, just choose Actions⇨Invite Someone to This Conversation.

note

You can have a total of five people (including you) in a conversation.

caution

When you save a conversation as a text file, keep in mind that none of the font styles or colors are saved. Neither are the emoticons.

tip

You can save an entire conversation as a text file, if you like. Simply choose File⇨Save As... in the Conversation window. The Save As dialog appears. Pick a location and a filename for the text file. You can open it later, if you like, using Notepad.

Task 186

Changing Your Look in Windows Messenger

Your self-image is important — even in Windows Messenger. In this task you'll discover several ways to present yourself in messenger in a more informational and stylish way. You'll find out how to change the name others see when you log in, how to tell others not to bug you because you're busy, how to change the font and color of your text in a discussion, and how to block someone you don't want to communicate with from seeing you at all.

1. If Windows Messenger isn't already open, open it by selecting Start⇨All Programs⇨Windows Messenger. The Windows Messenger window appears.

2. To change the name other people see on their list for you:

   a. Choose Tools⇨Options from the Windows Messenger window menus.

   b. At the top of the Personal tab (see Figure 186-1), there's a textbox labeled Type Your Name as You Want Other Users to See It. Change the name to whatever you like.

   c. Click OK.

3. To change your status:

   a. Click on your name at the top of the Windows Messenger window. A drop-down menu appears.

tip

The name used for you, by default, is your email address. It's best to choose something more descriptive, but be sure it's also unique. Using your first name is fine if your name is Cedric, but probably not if your name is Bill. You can use your last name or a nickname.

note

Use the status to indicate to your contacts what you're up to. Of course, it's bad manners to disturb someone who has their status set to Busy. Your status will automatically be set to Away if you don't do anything for 10 minutes. (To change this duration, choose Tools⇨ Options... menu option from the Windows Messenger window and click on the Preferences tab on the Options dialog.)

Figure 186-1: The Personal tab of the Options dialog.

b. From the menu (see Figure 186-2), choose what you want to set your status to. The status appears beside your name and changes the look of your icon on your Contacts list.

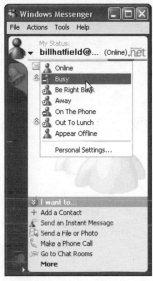

Figure 186-2: The status menu.

4. To change the font and color of your text in a conversation:

   a. Double-click on the contact you want to have a conversation with. The Conversation window appears.

   b. Click the Font button in the Conversation window. The Change My Message Font window appears.

   c. Choose a font, style, and size. The Color drop-down list is in the lower left of the window. The Sample shows you what the result will look like.

   d. Click OK. When you type a message, it will appear as you specified.

5. To block a specific contact so that he or she can't see you or send a message to you:

   a. Right-click on the contact in the Windows Messenger window.

   b. Choose Block from the pop-up menu. A crossed-out icon appears beside the name of the person blocked. You'll still be able to see his or her online status, but he or she can't see yours.

cross-reference

To find out more about having a discussion in Windows Messenger, see Task 185.

note

To unblock a blocked contact so that he or she can see you again and send you messages, right-click on the blocked contact in the Windows Messenger window and choose Unblock from the pop-up menu. The icon is returned to normal.

Sending a File or a Picture

Perhaps you want to send a document you've been working on to a coworker to review. Or maybe you want to show off those pictures of your new baby. Windows Messenger allows you to send pictures and other files to your contacts quickly and easily without having to open up an email program.

1. If Windows Messenger isn't already open, open it by selecting Start⇨ All Programs⇨Windows Messenger. The Windows Messenger window appears.

2. Double-click on the contact you want to send a file to. The Conversation window appears (see Figure 187-1).

Figure 187-1: The Conversation window.

3. Click the Send File or Photo link in the I Want To list along the right side of the Conversation window. The Send a File window appears (see Figure 187-2). Locate and click to select the file you want to send.

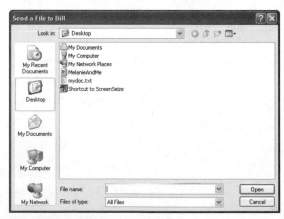

Figure 187-2: The Send a File window.

note

If you don't see the I Want To... list along the right side of the Conversation window, just select File⇨Send a File or Photo from the menu.

note

If you are in a conversation with more than one person (see Task 185 to find out how to do this), a window appears asking who, of those in the conversation, should receive the file.

tip

Here's a quicker, easier way to send a file: Locate the file in Windows Explorer. Press and hold the left mouse button on the file. Drag the file over to the Windows Messenger window and over the contact you want to send it to. Release the button. A Conversation window opens and the file is immediately sent.

4. Click the Open button. Windows Messenger sends a message to the contact asking him or her whether he or she wants to accept or reject the file. You see a "Waiting..." message (see Figure 187-3).

Figure 187-3: The Send a File window.

5. When the receiver accepts the transfer, a connection is made and the file is transferred (see Figure 187-4). In the status bar at the bottom of the window, you can track the transfer's progress.

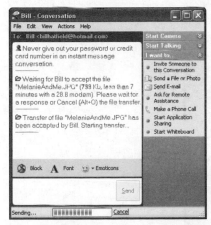

Figure 187-4: The transfer is in progress.

6. You can continue to carry on a conversation by typing messages back and forth while the transfer is taking place. Once the transfer is complete, you are informed with a message.

tip

Notice that the "Waiting..." message informs you how big the file is and how long it will take to transfer using a modem. This gives you a chance to cancel and avoid a transfer that is longer than you anticipated.

tip

You can click the Cancel link in the status bar at the bottom of the Conversation window (or by hitting Alt+Q) anytime during the course of the transfer to stop it.

caution

You may not be able to send files from your office to people outside your company. Sometimes corporate firewalls block that. If this is a problem, you can just email your recipient and send the file as an attachment. For more information on how to do that, see Task 163.

cross-reference

To find out how to receive a file or picture sent by someone else, see Task 188.

Task 188

Receiving a File or a Picture

When one of your contacts sends a file or picture to you, you can receive it and save it on your hard drive. This task shows you how.

1. If Windows Messenger isn't already open, open it by selecting Start⇨All Programs⇨Windows Messenger. The Windows Messenger window appears.

2. When one of your contacts attempts to send you a file and you are not already having a conversation with him or her, you see a small window appear in the lower-right corner of your screen (just above your clock) (see Figure 188-1).

Figure 188-1: Someone is trying to send you a file.

3. Click on the text inside the window. This causes a Conversation window to appear (see Figure 188-2). There's a message in the window that lets you know who's trying to send the file, what the file's name is and how big the file is.

Figure 188-2: The Conversation window — Want to receive the file?

4. Click the Accept link. You may see a message dialog appear (see Figure 188-3) warning you that some files contain viruses and so on.

Figure 188-3: The warning dialog.

5. Click OK. A connection is made and the file is transferred (see Figure 188-4). In the status bar at the bottom of the Conversation window, you'll see a progress bar and messages that keep you up-to-date on what's going on.

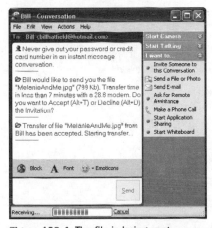

Figure 188-4: The file is being sent.

6. You can continue to carry on a conversation by typing messages back and forth while the transfer is taking place. Once the transfer is complete, you are informed with a message. You'll be informed exactly where the file was saved.

7. To quickly access the sent file, choose File➪Open Received Files. A window opens showing the contents of the folder where your received files are stored.

cross-reference

To find out how to send a file or picture to someone else, see Task 187.

Task 189

Configuring Your Audio and Video in Windows Messenger

Windows Messenger makes it possible to have audio and video calls. But in order to take advantage of these features, you need to first set up your microphone and speakers and then use the Audio and Video Tuning Wizard to verify that it's all working correctly.

1. If Windows Messenger isn't already open, open it by selecting Start⇨All Programs⇨Windows Messenger. The Windows Messenger window appears.

2. Choose Tools⇨Audio Tuning Wizard from the menus. The Audio and Video Tuning Wizard appears. Do as it says and be sure you close down any other applications that play or record video or sound. Also be sure your camera, microphone, and speakers are all plugged in and turned on.

3. If you have a webcam connected to your computer:

   a. Click Next. Choose the camera from the drop-down list box. If you only have one, the default is likely correct.

   b. Click Next. The image your video camera sees right now appears in the wizard's window (see Figure 189-1). Be sure the camera is aimed correctly and that everything looks good.

Figure 189-1: The Audio and Video Tuning Wizard — Your video.

4. Click Next. Read and follow the instructions for configuring your microphone (see Figure 189-2).

5. Click Next. Select the microphone and speakers you wish to use.

6. Click Next. The Audio and Video Tuning Wizard appears, allowing you to test your speakers (see Figure 189-3). Click the Click to Test Speakers button. A sound is then played continuously. Adjust the volume of your speakers using the slider. Click Stop when you are done.

note

The default values for these settings are probably correct. If you are using headphones, click the I Am Using Headphones check box.

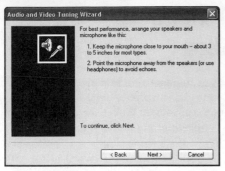

Figure 189-2: The Audio and Video Tuning Wizard — Read the instructions.

7. Click Next. Now you are asked to read text into a microphone (see Figure 189-4). As you do, you'll notice the green bar rises and falls with the sound of your voice. You can use the slider to adjust the microphone's sensitivity.

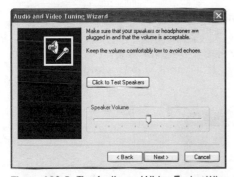

Figure 189-3: The Audio and Video Tuning Wizard — Testing your speakers.

8. Click Next. The wizard is complete. Click Finish.

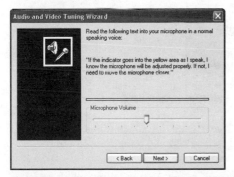

Figure 189-4: The Audio and Video Tuning Wizard — Testing your microphone.

tip

Adjust the microphone sensitivity so that the green bar is registering strongly, but not so high that it is hitting the top and staying there.

cross-reference

Once you have completed this configuration, you are ready to try out Windows Messenger's voice and video conversations. See Task 190.

Adding Voice and Video to Your Conversation

Windows Messenger can make your fingers tired. Fortunately, it provides a feature that practically turns your PC into a telephone — or even a video-phone! To make use of the telephone features, you'll need an audio card on your PC where you can plug in speakers (or headphones) and a microphone. To use the video features, you'll need a webcam. With these simple accessories, you can talk to your friends just as if they were sitting next to you. And it's free — even if they live in Elbonia!

1. If Windows Messenger isn't already open, open it by selecting Start⇨ All Programs⇨Windows Messenger. The Windows Messenger window appears.

2. Double-click on the contact you want to have a conversation with. The Conversation window appears.

3. To start a voice conversation:

   a. In the sidebar along the right side of the Conversation window, click on Start Talking (or choose Actions⇨Start Talking from the menu). The Speakers and Microphone volume controls display (see Figure 190-1).

Figure 190-1: The Conversation window for a voice call.

   b. Wait for your contact to accept your call. Once it is accepted, you'll see a message that says "[*Contact's Name*] has accepted your request to have a voice conversation."

   c. Now simply speak into your microphone. You'll hear your contact's response through your speakers or headphones. You can also type messages as you would normally.

cross-reference

If this is the first time you've tried to use the audio/video features of Windows Messenger, you may see the Audio and Video Tuning Wizard appear. It is described in Task 189.

tip

In Windows Messenger, there's a difference between a *voice conversation* and a *phone call*. What you're reading about in this task is a voice conversation. You can also make phone calls from Windows Messenger, which means that you can communicate through your computer with anyone who has a phone. You just type their phone number, and when they pick up, you talk to them through your microphone and speakers. Unfortunately, in order to make phone calls, you have to purchase an additional service that costs a monthly or yearly fee.

tip

You can use any combination of text, audio, and video in a call. For example, if you don't have a microphone hooked up to your computer, you can still do a video call without the audio and use text to commu-nicate. Or, if you have a video camera and your contact doesn't, you can still do a video call — the contact will see you, but you won't see the contact.

caution

Voice and video may not always work. If you try a voice/video from your office to someone outside your company, for example, the corporate firewall may stop it.

4. To add video to your conversation:

a. In the sidebar along the right side of the Conversation window, click on Start Camera (or choose Actions⇨Start Camera from the menu). A screen appears in order to show the video (see Figure 190-2).

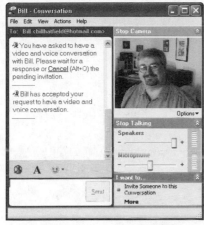

Figure 190-2: The Conversation window for a video and voice call.

b. Wait for your contact to accept your call. Once it is accepted, you'll see a message that says "[*Contact's Name*] has accepted your request to have a video and voice conversation."

If both of you have cameras that are hooked up and working properly, you should see each other in your Conversation window.

c. To see the video you're sending out, click on the Options button below the video. A menu appears. Choose Show My Video as Picture-in-Picture (see Figure 190-3).

Figure 190-3: It even has picture-in-picture!

---

caution

Voice conversations usually work fine over a dial-up connection, but video is a different story. Over dial-up your "video" is more likely to look like a series of grainy still pictures.

---

tip

If you're going to do something you don't want your contact to see, you can also choose Stop Sending Video from the Options menu. This freezes the current picture on the contact's Conversation window and doesn't send your video until you select the option again.

Part 14: Exploring the Other Accessories

Task 191: Using the Basic Calculator

Task 192: Using the Scientific Calculator

Task 193: Performing Statistical Calculations

Task 194: Converting Numbers

Task 195: Configuring Your Computer to Send Faxes

Task 196: Sending a Fax

Task 197: Recording Sounds: The Sound Recorder

Task 198: Mixing and Modifying Sounds

Using the Basic Calculator

A computer can be used for a number of functions. One of the most common utilities available on Windows is also one that you can find the most reasons to use: the calculator. Whether you are balancing your checkbook or simply trying to figure the tip to pay the pizza delivery person, the basic calculator can help you. Using the calculator is as simple as the following steps:

1. From the Start menu, select All Programs⇨Accessories⇨Calculator. The Calculator program appears (see Figure 191-1).

2. Determine the type of operation you want to perform. For addition, subtraction, multiplication, or division, do the following:

   a. Enter the first number that will be used in the calculation. You can enter this number by either pressing the number keys at the top of your keyboard, by using the keypad on your keyboard with the number lock key turned on, or by clicking on the numbered buttons in the calculator. Figure 191-1 shows the calculator with the number 54321 entered.

Figure 191-1: The calculator with a number entered.

   b. Select the symbol for the type of operation you want to perform:
      - Select + for addition
      - Select – for subtraction
      - Select / for division
      - Select * for multiplication

   c. Enter the second number for the calculation.

   d. Click the equal sign or press the Enter key. The result of the operation is displayed. You can then use this value as the first value in a new calculation.

3. To determine a square root:

   a. Enter the number to be used for calculating the square root.

   b. Click the Sqrt button. The square root is displayed.

note

If the scientific calculator is shown, you can select View⇨Standard from the menu to display the standard calculator.

cross-reference

If you want to do complex calculations, including calculations that use trigonometry, see Tasks 192 and 193.

cross-reference

If you want to do calculations in a different number system, see Task 194.

4. To figure percentages (such as calculating how much to pay the pizza boy for a tip):

   a. Enter the first number. For example, you can enter a number such as 12.50 (roughly the cost of a pizza delivered).

   b. Press an operator key. To figure the amount to pay for a tip, press plus because you are adding to this value.

   c. Press the number representing the percentage you want to pay. If you are paying 15%, then enter **15**.

   d. Press the percentage button. The result is displayed as shown in Figure 191-2. This is the percentage amount. In the case of calculating a tip, this is just the tip portion.

Figure 191-2: The calculated percentage.

5. Press the Equal button. This finalizes the operation, performing the calculation you entered. It takes the original number and applies the percentage number that was shown in Step 4. (In the example, it adds the original number of 12.50 to the tip amount of 1.875.) As you can see, Figure 191-3 displays the result of 14.375 (the amount to pay the pizza delivery person, although you'll want to round this up).

Figure 191-3: The final value of the calculation.

tip

If you enter a digit that you didn't mean to enter, clicking the Backspace key will move back and erase it.

note

You can find the reciprocal of a number using the 1/x button. For example, the reciprocal of 3 is 1/3 or 0.33333333333333 333333333333333333333.

note

The CE button clears the value currently displayed. The C button clears the current calculation.

cross-reference

If you want to do calculations that involve the value of pi (such as determining the radius of a circle), you should switch to the scientific calculator. It has a button that will enter the value of pi for you. Task 192 shows you how to use the scientific calculator.

note

Larger numbers can be harder to read. To make them easier to read, you can turn on grouping. This puts spaces into binary, octal, and hexadecimal numbers. A separator will be put into decimal numbers based on your region. Generally this will be a comma.

cross-reference

See Task 60 to learn how to set the separator that will be used for your decimal numbers.

Using the Scientific Calculator

Windows XP includes an advanced version of the calculator that has a number of functions you'd find on a scientific calculator. This includes the ability to do trigonometry functions such as calculating the sine, cosine, and tangents for a number, as well as doing exponentials, logarithms, factorials, and more.

note

When you originally open the calculator, it will be in the view that you last used. For example, if the last time you used the calculator, it was in scientific view, then when you open it again, it will still be in scientific view.

cross-reference

Task 191 shows how to use the basic calculator to do basic mathematical tasks.

tip

You can press the S key instead of clicking the Sin button. You can press the C button instead of clicking the Cos button. Likewise, you can press the T button instead of clicking the Tan button.

cross-reference

Task 193 shows how to perform statistical calculations that require more than two numbers.

cross-reference

Task 194 shows how to use different number systems with the scientific calculator.

note

Larger numbers can be harder to read. To make them easier to read, you can turn on grouping. This puts spaces into binary, octal, and hexadecimal numbers. A separator will be put into decimal numbers based on your region. Generally this will be a comma.

1. Display the calculator by selecting Start⇨All Programs⇨ Accessories⇨Calculator. The basic calculator appears (see Figure 192-1).

Figure 192-1: The standard calculator.

2. Select View⇨Scientific from the calculator's menu. The scientific calculator appears (see Figure 192-2). As you can see by comparing Figure 192-2 and 192-1, the scientific calculator offers a much larger number of operations.

Figure 192-2: The scientific calculator.

3. Determine the type of operation you would like to do.

4. To calculate an exponent:

   a. If you want to square a value, enter the value and press the x^2 button.

b. If you want to cube a value, enter the value and press the x^3 button.

c. To calculate the value of a number raised to the power of any other number, enter the base number, then click the x^y button followed by the number for the value of the power. For example, to calculate 3 raised to the 10th power, enter **3**, click x^y, then enter **10**. Press the Equal button to display the value.

5. To calculate a standard trigonometry function:

a. Enter the decimal number to be used.

b. Perform the specified trigonometry function by clicking on the associated controls as specified in Table 192-1.

cross-reference

See Task 60 to learn how to set the separator that will be used for your decimal numbers.

Table 192-1: Trigonometry Routines

Routine	How to Perform
Sine	Click the Sin button
Arc sine	Click the check box next to Inv, then click the Sin button
Hyperbolic sine	Click the check box next to Hyp, then click the Sin button
Arc hyperbolic sine	Click the check boxes next to both Inv and Hyp, then click the Sin button
Cosine	Click the Cos button
Arc cosine	Click the check box next to Inv, then click the Cos button
Hyperbolic cosine	Click the check box next to Hyp, then click the Cos button
Arc hyperbolic cosine	Click the check boxes next to both Inv and Hyp, the click the Cos button
Tangent	Click the Tan button
Arc tangent	Click the check box next to Inv, then click the Tan button
Hyperbolic tangent	Click the check box next to Hyp, then click the Tan button
Arc hyperbolic tangent	Click the check boxes next to both Inv and Hyp, the click the Tan button

6. To calculate the remainder value of a division operation (modulus):

a. Enter the first value for the operation.

b. Click the Mod button.

c. Enter the second value of the division operation. This value is divided into the first value.

d. Click the Equal button or press Enter. The solution is displayed. For example, 5 mod 2 equals 1.

Performing Statistical Calculations

The Windows XP calculator can be used to do statistical calculations. In simple terms, this means you can use the calculation to figure things such as the average of a group of numbers. If you need to do advanced math, you can get values such as averages, sums, and standard deviations. To perform statistical calculations, you usually enter a group of numbers and then perform the operation. The following steps walk you through this process for calculating the average of a group of numbers:

cross-reference

Statistics are done with the scientific calculator. See more about this calculator in Task 192.

note

You can remove a value from the Statistics box. To do this, select the value by clicking on it, then press the CD button. This removes the current data item. You can clear all of the values from the Statistics box by clicking the CAD button. This clears all the data.

cross-reference

The standard number system is decimal. You can also use different numbers systems when doing statistical calculations. See Task 194 to learn more.

note

If other windows hide the Statistics box, you can pull it to the front by clicking the Sta button in the calculator again. You can also click on its button in the taskbar.

1. Open the calculator by selecting All Programs➪Accessories➪ Calculator. The calculator program is displayed.

2. Select the Scientific view if it is not already displayed. Select this view by selecting View➪Scientific from the calculator's menu. You should see the scientific calculator as shown in Figure 193-1.

Figure 193-1: The scientific calculator used for statistical calculations.

3. Press the Sta button. The Statistics box appears (see Figure 193-2). The Statistics box is used to hold the values you will use in your calculation.

Figure 193-2: The Statistics box is used for holding entered values.

4. Return to the calculator leaving the Statistics box open. Return to the calculator by either selecting the RET button in the Statistics box or by simply clicking on the calculator window.

5. Enter the values for your calculation by entering a number into the calculator. Once you've entered the number, press the Dat button in

the lower-left corner of the calculator. This adds the number to the Statistics box. In Figure 193-3, you can see the result of entering the number 111 and pressing Dat.

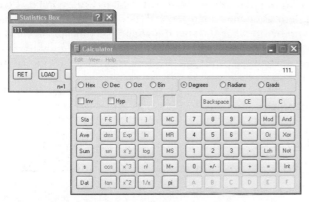

Figure 193-3: The Statistics box with the first value entered.

6. Continue entering numbers as shown in Steps 4 and 5 until all numbers are entered.

7. Press the Ave button to obtain the average of the numbers you have entered. The average of the numbers is displayed in the calculator's entry window.

8. Press the Sum button to obtain the sum of the numbers you have entered. The sum of the numbers is displayed in the calculator's entry window.

9. Press the S button to obtain the standard deviation for the numbers you have entered. The standard deviation is displayed in the calculator's entry window, as shown in Figure 193-4.

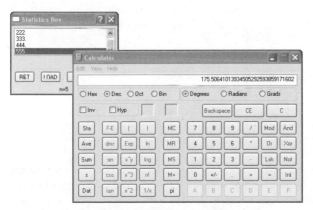

Figure 193-4: The standard deviation being displayed.

tip

You can enter numbers into the calculator by typing them or clicking on the corresponding buttons. You can use the number pad on your keyboard as long as the Num Lock is turned on.

tip

As numbers are entered, you will see the value at the bottom of the Statistics box increase. The value after n= is the number of items that have been entered.

caution

If you close the Statistics box, the data is cleared.

note

Clicking the Load button in the Statistics box copies the currently selected value from the Statistics box to the calculator's entry box.

See more on the scientific calculator in Task 192.

Task 194

Converting Numbers

In general, we use a decimal number system. There are times, however, when you may want to convert a number to a different system. For example, if you wanted to convert a number so you could represent it with just 1s and 0s, you would convert this number to binary. While this sounds technical, it is very simple with the calculator provided in Windows XP. To convert numbers from decimal to hexadecimal, binary, or octal, use the following steps:

cross-reference

See more on the scientific calculator in Task 192.

tip

Select File⇨Copy or press Ctrl+C to copy a value from the calculator. Once copied, you can paste this value into any Windows application.

cross-reference

You can use octal, hexadecimal, or binary numbers for doing calculations. To see how to do statistical calculations, see Task 193.

tip

You can also change number systems using the options on the View menu or by pressing F5 for hexadecimal, F6 for decimal, F7 for octal, or F8 for binary.

note

Larger numbers can be harder to read. To make them easier to read, you can turn on grouping. This puts spaces into binary, octal, and hexadecimal numbers. A separator will be put into decimal numbers based on your region. Generally this will be a comma.

1. Open the calculator by selecting Start⇨All Programs⇨ Accessories⇨Calculator.

2. Use the Scientific view by selecting View⇨Scientific from the calculator's menu. A screen similar to Figure 194-1 appears.

3. Select the number format you want to use. By default, decimal (Dec) will be selected.

4. Enter the number you want to convert. Figure 194-1 shows the number 12345 entered into the calculator.

Figure 194-1: A decimal number in the calculator.

5. Select Bin to convert to binary. The result of clicking Bin is shown in Figure 194-2. As you can see, 12345 equals 11000000111001 in binary.

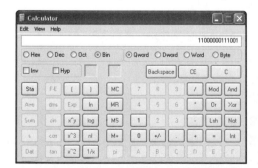

Figure 194-2: A binary number in the calculator.

To make the binary number easier to read, you can turn on digit grouping. Do this by selecting View⇨Digit Grouping from the menus. Figure 194-3 shows the binary number again, this time with digit grouping.

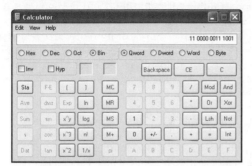

Figure 194-3: A binary number in the calculator with digit grouping.

6. Select Hex to convert to hexadecimal. The result of clicking Hex is shown in Figure 194-3. As you can see, 12345 equals 3039 in hexadecimal.

Figure 194-4: A hexadecimal number in the calculator.

7. Select Oct to convert to octal. The result of clicking Oct is shown in Figure 194-5. As you can see, 12345 equals 30071 in octal.

Figure 194-5: An octal number in the calculator.

note

Binary is a base 2 number system. Base 2 means there are two digits to represent numbers — 0 and 1. Octal is a base 8 system. This means there are eight digits to represent numbers 0, 1, 2, 3, 4, 5, 6, and 7. Hexadecimal is a base 16 system. This means 16 digits are used. These are 0 through 9, followed by A, B, C, D, E, and F. A is equivalent to a decimal number 10. You can see that the scientific calculator has the letters A through F as buttons. When you select Hexadecimal, these are available to use to enter numbers.

cross-reference

See Task 60 to learn how to set the separator that will be used for your decimal numbers.

note

When you change number systems, some items on the calculator may change or have their protection changed. For example, changing to binary protects the numbers 2 through 9 because they are not valid for binary numbers.

Task 195

Configuring Your Computer to Send Faxes

Windows XP comes with a program that lets you send and receive faxes if you have a modem installed or attached to your computer. Before you can send faxes, you must set up and configure the Microsoft Fax software — it is not installed by default when Windows XP is installed. Once you have installed and configured this software, you can send and receive faxes, as well as keep track of your fax activity. The following steps show you how to set up and configure the Microsoft Fax software:

1. Open the Control Panel by selecting it from the Start menu.

2. Within the Control Panel, select Add or Remove Programs. The Add or Remove Programs dialog window appears (see Figure 195-1).

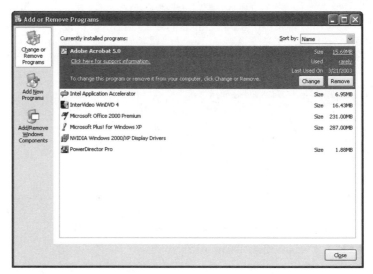

Figure 195-1: The Add or Remove Programs dialog window.

3. Select Add/Remove Windows Components on the left side of the screen. This starts the Windows Component Wizard, shown in Figure 195-2.

4. Select Fax Services by checking the block next to it.

5. Click the Next button. This starts the installation of the Fax Services. A progress bar appears, indicating the status of the installation.

   Unless you have a copy of the Windows installation files on your hard drive, you are prompted to insert your Windows XP CD, as shown in Figure 195-3.

6. Insert your Windows XP CD and click OK. The installation continues. When the installation is complete, a completion message appears.

cross-reference

To use the Microsoft Fax software, you need a fax machine or a fax modem that is built to work with a computer system. See Tasks 217 through 223 for information on installing hardware.

note

Most built- in modems for newer computers include the ability to send and receive faxes.

note

The Microsoft Fax software is not set up by default when Windows XP is installed. Because of this, you may need to install it yourself.

note

You can perform this task even if you don't have a fax installed. You will, however, receive warnings when you try to configure the software.

cross-reference

This task shows you how to set up and configure the fax software. Task 196 shows you how to send a fax.

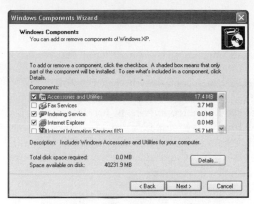

Figure 195-2: The Windows Component Wizard.

7. Click the Finish button. You now have fax services added to the All Programs menu.

8. Select Start⇨All Programs⇨Accessories⇨Communications⇨Send a Fax.... The first time you select this, you should be prompted with the Fax Configuration Wizard. When you run this wizard, the dialog in Figure 195-4 appears.

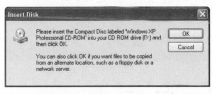

Figure 195-3: The prompt to insert your Windows XP CD.

9. Enter your information into this dialog and press Next. This executes the rest of the wizard. A final screen appears, confirming the wizard is complete.

10. Press Finish. The fax software is now installed and configured with your information.

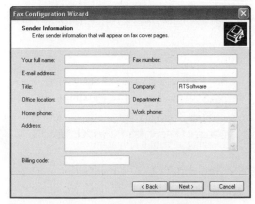

Figure 195-4: The Fax Configuration Wizard.

note

Some programs, such as Microsoft Word, allow you to select a menu option that will send a document by fax.

note

Once installed, you can get to the fax programs by selecting Start⇨ All Programs⇨Accessories⇨ Communications⇨Fax.

note

Windows XP sets up the fax as a printer, which you can print to from any Windows application. Just choose it from the list " of available printers in that software.

Task 196

Sending a Fax

Windows XP comes with a program that lets you send and receive faxes if you have a fax machine or fax modem installed or attached to your computer. You can use the following steps to send a fax using the Fax Console.

1. Run the Fax Console program by selecting Start⇨All Programs⇨ Accessories⇨Communications⇨Fax⇨Fax Console. The Fax Console is shown in Figure 196-1.

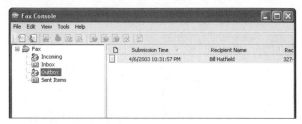

Figure 196-1: The Fax Console.

2. From the File menu of the Fax Console, select Send a Fax. The Send Fax Wizard dialog window appears.

3. Click Next to begin the wizard. If this is the first time you have used the wizard, you are presented with the Location Information dialog.

4. Enter the information into the Location Information dialog and click Next. You are prompted with the Phone and Modem options.

5. Select the area code for the location rules that you are calling from by clicking on it, then click OK. A dialog window for entering the recipient information appears (see Figure 196-2).

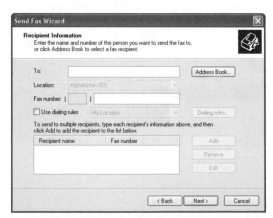

Figure 196-2: Dialog window for entering recipient information.

cross-reference

To use the Microsoft Fax software, you need a fax machine or a fax modem that is built to work with a computer system. Additionally, you need the fax software in Windows XP installed before you can use it. Task 195 shows you how to install and configure the Microsoft Fax software.

note

Some programs, such as Microsoft Word, allow you to select a menu option that will send the current document by fax. This program usually opens the Fax Wizard shown in this task.

note

You can see the faxes you have scheduled to send by selecting Outbox in the Fax Console Window (see Figure 196-1).

note

The area code information is only displayed the first time you run this program.

note

You can set up multiple locations for sending faxes. These locations can include different area codes or access numbers. This is very useful if you have multiple fax machines connected to your computer or if you are using a fax modem in a notebook computer from different locations.

6. Enter the recipient information and press Next. This takes you to the Cover Page dialog window (see Figure 196-3).

Figure 196-3: The dialog window for preparing a cover page.

7. Enter the information for the cover sheet. Select a template for the fax, and then enter a subject line and any notes you want on the coversheet. Once you have entered this information, press Next to continue. The Schedule dialog window appears.

8. Select the time and priority you want assigned to this fax. The time is when the fax will be sent. Click Next when you are done with this information. The completion dialog window appears (see Figure 196-4).

Figure 196-4: The final dialog window for sending the fax.

9. Verify the information presented in the Completing the Send Fax Wizard dialog window is correct. If so, press Finish. The fax is added to the Outbox and will be sent at the time you scheduled.

tip

You can use different templates to format your faxes. You can select the different templates in the cover page dialog when you are running the Fax Wizard.

note

You can see faxes you have sent by selecting Sent Items in the Fax Console.

note

There are a number of advanced features within the Microsoft Fax software. This includes the ability to create your own cover page templates. See the Windows XP help for more on these features.

Task 197

Recording Sounds: The Sound Recorder

Windows XP comes with a program that allows you to record sounds. This includes the ability to record yourself — or others — talking as well as to record from a CD-ROM. Using the sound recorder, you can create and manipulate sound files that can then be played back later. These recordings can also be used with other programs or they can be set as sounds that you can use within Windows XP. To record with the Sound Recorder, do the following:

1. Select Start⇨All Programs⇨Accessories⇨Entertainment⇨Sound Recorder. The Sound Recorder appears (see Figure 197-1). As you can see, this is a relatively simple program; however, it offers a lot of features.

Current offset in recording

Current position in recording

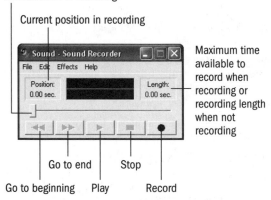

Maximum time available to record when recording or recording length when not recording

Go to end   Stop

Go to beginning   Play   Record

Figure 197-1: The Sound Recorder.

2. Clear the Sound Recorder so you can create a new sound file. Do this by selecting File⇨New from the menus. If anything has been recorded already, you are prompted with the message in Figure 197-2. Click No if you receive this message and have not already recorded something. This clears the Sound Recorder.

Figure 197-2: Confirmation message for the Sound Recorder.

3. Make sure your microphone is plugged into the computer and turned on.

4. Click Recording to begin recording. The amount of time recorded is displayed in the recorder. Note also that the slider bar moves as you are recording.

5. Click Stop when you are done recording or when you want to stop or pause. This stops the recorder, but leaves the position at the end. You can add additional sound to this recording by pressing the Record button again. You can do this as often as you like.

6. Press Play to play back the sound and verify it is what you want. You can stop the playback by pressing the Stop button at any time.

7. From the Sound Recorder menu, Select File⇨Save to display the Save dialog window, shown in Figure 197-3.

Figure 197-3: Saving the recorded sound file.

8. Select the format to save the file. You can skip this step to save as the default format; however, by default, sound files are saved as relatively large WAV files. You can adjust the format size by clicking Change in the Save As dialog window. The Sound Selection dialog appears (see Figure 197-4). Click OK to save your selection.

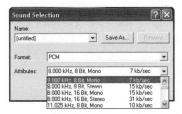

Figure 197-4: The Sound Selection dialog.

9. Enter the filename to save your recording.

10. Press OK to save your recording.

---

note

The higher the MHz value and the more bits used to record, the higher the quality of the recording; however, it will also increase the amount of hard disk space needed to store the recording.

note

There is a lot that can be adjusted based on your selection in the Sound Selection dialog. The key thing to know is that the size on the right side of the Attribute list is roughly the amount of disk space needed for each second of recording time. If you want to save disk space, select a lower value option with a lower Kb value.

caution

You cannot record sounds if your computer does not have a microphone attached. Some keyboards and monitors have built-in microphones. Additionally, you can add a separate microphone to most computers.

cross-reference

In Task 198 you learn to mix and manipulate the sounds you record. This includes adding echo, cutting out pieces of a sound file, and adding sound files together.

cross-reference

If you want to record a song from a CD-ROM, you are better off using the Microsoft Media player, as shown in Task 78. You can use the Media Player to convert the recording from the CD to a WAV file that can then be opened in the Sound Recorder.

Mixing and Modifying Sounds

Microsoft Sound Recorder allows you to make a number of changes to an existing WAV sound file. You can open and work with any existing WAV file, or you can create new WAV files to use. The following steps walk you through a number of different changes you can make to your sound files:

1. Create a new file or open an existing file in the Sound Recorder. The file is presented in the Sound Recorder as shown in Figure 198-1.

Figure 198-1: A sound loaded in the Sound Recorder.

2. To change the file to play backward, select Effects⇨Reverse from the menu. Selecting this a second time puts the file back to normal.

3. To make a file play faster, select Effects⇨Increase Speed (by 100%). This shortens the length of the recording by "scrunching" it. You can also stretch a recording by selecting Effects⇨Decrease Speed from the menus.

4. To combine two sound files into one, do the following:

   a. Select and open the first file.

   b. Place the slider at the location within the first file where you want the second file inserted. If you want to append the file to the end, place the slider at the end. You can also place the slider in the middle.

   c. Select Edit⇨Insert File from the menus. The Insert File dialog window appears.

   d. Select the file to be inserted and click Open. The file is inserted into the original file.

5. To overlay two files so that they mix together, do the following:

   a. Select and open the first file.

   b. Place the slider at the location within the first file where you want the beginning of the second file to be mixed into the first. If you want to append the file to the end, place the slider at the end. You can also place the slider in the middle.

cross-reference

You learn how to record and save sound files in Task 197.

caution

When you make changes to a sound file, the quality may be slightly degraded. For example, if you increase the speed and then decrease the speed, the resulting file may not exactly match the original.

note

Open the Microsoft Sound recorder from the menus by selecting All Programs⇨ Accessories⇨Entertainment⇨ Sound Recorder. Open a file in the Sound Recorder by selecting File⇨Open from the menu.

note

Some sound files are compressed. A compressed sound file cannot be modified. When a sound file is compressed, the green line will not be presented when the file is opened.

   c. Select Edit⇨Mix with Files. The file dialog window for file selection appears.

   d. Select the file to be mixed and click Open. The file is mixed with the original file.

6. To clip out sections of the current file, do the following:

   a. To delete the beginning of a sound file, move the slider to the new starting point, then select Edit⇨Delete before Current Position. The slider location becomes the new starting location.

   b. To delete the end out of a sound file, move the slider to the new ending point for the sound file, then select Edit⇨Delete After Current Position. The end of the file is removed.

7. To add an echo effect to the file, select Effects⇨Add Echo.

8. Save your file when you've completed your changes by selecting File⇨Save As. The Save As dialog window appears (see Figure 198-2). Enter a filename and press Save.

Figure 198-2: The Save As dialog window.

caution

If you don't want to overwrite the original sound file, make sure you use the Save As menu option instead of Save, which will overwrite the original file.

note

Using Add Echo is similar to mixing the same file with itself using just a small offset.

Part 15: Accessibility Features

Task 199:   Changing the Windows Font Size

Task 200:   Using the Magnifier

Task 201:   Using the Narrator

Task 202:   Using the On-Screen Keyboard

Task 203:   Selecting the On-Screen Keyboard Layout

Task 204:   Setting Usability Feature Options

Task 205:   Setting Usability Feature Options with the Accessibility Wizard

Task 206:   Using and Setting StickyKeys

Task 207:   Using and Setting FilterKeys

Changing the Windows Font Size

There are a number of ways to make Windows XP easier to use. One of the most obvious changes is the size of the font. If the fonts you are using are small, it can be hard to clearly read what is being displayed. By increasing the size of the fonts, you can make it much easier to read what is being presented. Beyond changing the fonts, you can change the DPI, or dots per inch, that are used by the computer. This will increase the displayed text on the screen, as well as increase the size of some of the icons and other graphics. To change the DPI and thus the font size of everything, do the following steps:

1. From the Start menu, select Control Panel.

2. Select Appearance and Theme.

3. Click the Display icon. The Display Properties dialog window appears.

4. Select the Settings tab to show the display options for the resolution and colors, as shown in Figure 199-1.

5. Select the Advanced button on the Settings tab. The advanced dialog appears. This dialog will be different depending on the graphics card that is in your machine. Figure 199-1 shows the dialog for a machine with a NVIDIA GeForce4 MX 440 graphics card. Regardless of your graphics card, you should see a general tab with similar settings to those shown in this dialog.

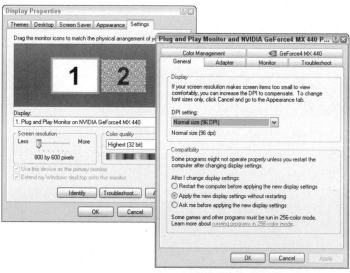

Figure 199-1: The Advanced features of the display property settings.

6. Change the value of the DPI setting. For example, to double the font size, double the DPI number. Figure 199-1 shows the current, normal DPI setting to be 96. Changing this by 200% to 192 would double the size of everything on the screen (which would be huge, as you can see in Figure 199-2).

tip

You can decrease the font size to get more items on your screen. This will, however, generally make displayed information harder to read.

cross-reference

You can increase the size of the fonts displayed on your screen by decreasing the resolution used. This will, however, cause less information to be displayed on the screen as well. To learn more about changing the resolution to one of the standard resolutions, see Task 41.

note

By lowering the DPI (dots per inch) setting, your machine will display fewer dots per inch of screen. This means that fonts and such will actually get bigger. Increase the DPI setting value by a factor equal to the size you'd like fonts to grow.

note

If you select to do a custom setting for the DPI value, an additional dialog will be displayed showing a ruler for the font and DPI setting. You can enter a percentage of your own or select one of the values from the drop-down list. Once selected, the ruler will be rescaled.

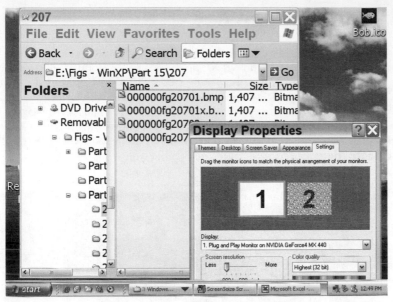

Figure 199-2: A screen shot at 800 × 600 resolution with the DPI doubled to 192.

To change the DPI setting's value, do the following:

a. Click on the DPI setting's drop-down list.

b. Select one of the custom values. Such as Large (120 DPI), or

c. Select Custom Setting to set your own custom value into the DPI.

7. Select a value from the Compatibility list. These options are descriptive; however, it is recommended that you restart your computer regardless of what setting you choose.

8. Select OK to close the advanced options. You may see some of the screen change immediately to the new DPI.

9. Select OK to close the Display Properties dialog window.

10. Restart your computer to make sure the new settings are applied to everything.

cross-reference

In Task 44 you learned how to change the font size to Normal, Large Fonts, or Extra Large Fonts by making a change in the Appearance table of the display properties. Changing the font as shown in Task 44 will only impact the text in window headers, icon labels, and menus.

note

You can also get to the Display Properties dialog window by right-clicking on an open area of the desktop and then selecting Properties from the pop-up menu.

note

Although the DPI was changed, you will notice that the background did not change size. Your screen's resolution remains consistent with the setting in the Display Properties dialog window.

caution

You may notice that not all text was changed. If this is the case, make sure you have rebooted your machine. Some settings will not be updated until Windows XP has been rebooted.

caution

It is possible to increase the DPI to a point where dialog boxes become bigger than the screen. This means you may not be able to see the buttons that you need to press in order to close the dialog window.

Using the Magnifier

If you have a hard time seeing small objects, or you simply want to zoom in on a portion of your screen, Windows XP provides an accessibility tool called the Magnifier. The Magnifier uses a separate window to display a zoomed-in portion of the screen. The location zoomed can be based on the current location of the mouse pointer, the location where you are typing text, or the location of the cursor from the keyboard. For example, Figure 200-1 shows the Magnifier when the cursor is run over the Start button. The following steps show you how to turn on and use the Magnifier.

Figure 200-1: The Magnifier in use.

1. Start the Magnifier by selecting from the Start menu All Programs⇨ Accessories⇨Accessibility⇨Magnifier. The Magnifier is displayed, along with an initial dialog window displaying informative text and a link to the Microsoft Web site (see Figure 200-2).

2. Close the Microsoft Magnifier message dialog window. Click the box next to Do Not Show This message Again if you don't need to see the message box again. Click the OK button to close the message window. This leaves you with the Magnifier Settings dialog window.

3. Place the Magnifier window on the screen where you want it. As you can see in Figures 200-1 and 200-2, the Magnifier window is located at the top of the screen by default. You can click on the window and drag it to another location. You can also leave it as a standard window. If you drag it near one of the edges of the screen, it will connect to that edge.

note

The Magnifier is limited and is not intended to be a comprehensive solution for people with vision impairments. Rather, it is only a tool to help.

cross-reference

See Task 199 to learn how to increase the overall size of the icons, text, and other display features.

caution

Closing the Magnifier Settings dialog window closes the Magnifier. You need to minimize the Magnifier Settings dialog window instead.

tip

After determining your settings for the magnifier, you should select the Start Minimized option. The Magnifier Settings dialog window will be minimized when you run the Magnifier in the future.

Figure 200-2: The Magnifier, along with its Settings dialog window.

4. Determine the level of magnification you want to have displayed in the magnification area. You can select this from the Magnification Level drop-down list in the Magnifier Settings dialog. Selecting a value of 2 doubles the normal size. A value of 9 will be much larger.

5. Determine the tracking you want to occur. You can select Follow Mouse Cursor, Follow Keyboard Focus, and Follow Text Editing.

6. Select your presentation settings:

   a. Select Invert Colors to flip the colors in the magnification area. By inverting the colors, you may make it easier to read the magnification area.

   b. Select Start Minimized to have the Magnifier Settings box minimized when you run the Magnifier program.

   c. Select Show Magnifier to have the Magnifier window displayed. If you uncheck this presentation option, the Magnifier window will not be displayed.

7. Minimize the Magnifier Settings dialog window. If you select the Exit button, the Magnifier window will be closed.

tip

You can also run the Magnifier by pressing Ctrl+Esc to display the Start menu, followed by pressing R to display the Run dialog window, entering **Magnify** into the Open entry box, and clicking OK or pressing the Enter key.

note

Selecting Follow Mouse Cursor causes the Magnifier to follow the mouse cursor. Selecting Follow Keyboard Focus causes the Magnifier to follow the current location of the cursor when you press the Tab key or use an arrow key. Selecting Follow Text Editing will cause the Magnifier to zoom in on the area where you are typing.

tip

You can dock (attach) the Magnifier window to any of the four edges of the screen. Once docked, you can increase the width or height by clicking and dragging the edge.

tip

You can right-click on the Magnifier window to get a pop-up menu with three options. These options allow you to hide the Magnifier window (Hide), open the Magnifier Settings dialog window (Options), or close the Magnifier window (Exit).

cross-reference

You can also set Magnifier settings when using the Utility Manager. Task 204 covers the Utility Manager.

Using the Narrator

Windows XP will talk to you! Within Windows XP, the Narrator program has been provided to enable Windows XP to speak to you. More specifically, it is a text-to-speech program that was designed to help blind or vision-impaired people use Windows XP.

The Narrator will read words, as well as tell you what is currently displayed on your screen. This includes the contents of the current window and menu options you may have. To start and use the narrator, do the following steps:

1. From the Start menu, select All Programs⇨Accessories⇨ Accessibility⇨Narrator. The Narrator program appears, as shown in Figure 201-1. You should note that the first time you use the Narrator, the informational dialog window is displayed along with the Narrator settings dialog window.

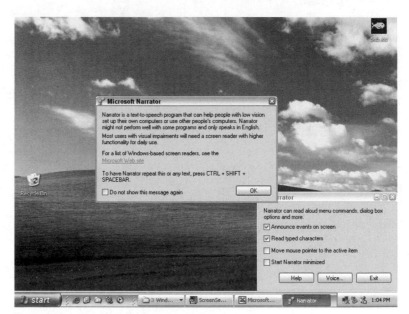

Figure 201-1: The Narrator program.

2. Close the Microsoft Narrator dialog window. Click the box next to Do Not Show This Message Again if you don't need to see the message box again. Click OK to close the message window. This leaves you with the Narrator settings dialog window.

3. Set the standard Narrator options. As you can see in Figure 201-1, there are four standard options that can be set for the Narrator:

   • Select Announce Events on Screen to have Narrator read events that occur.

   • Select Read Typed Characters if you want to have the Narrator program read characters that you type.

- Select Move Mouse Pointer to the Active Item if you want to have the Narrator program move the cursor to the current active item.

- Select Start Narrator Minimized if you want to have the Narrator settings dialog window minimized when you start it. Once you've made your selections for the settings, you will probably want to select this option.

4. Change voice settings. If you like the basic voice of the Narrator, you can skip this step; however, if you'd like to change it, then do the following:

   a. Select the Voice button at the bottom of the Narrator settings dialog. The Voice Settings dialog window appears (see Figure 201-2).

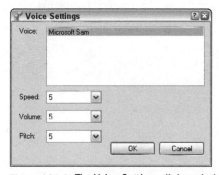

Figure 201-2: The Voice Settings dialog window.

   b. Select the voice you want to use with Narrator. If you only have one voice — such as the example in Figure 209-2 — then you will not be able to change this value.

   c. Select a value for Speed. This determines how fast the voice will read. Lower numbers are slower. Higher numbers are faster.

   d. Select a value for Volume. Selecting a higher number increases the volume.

   e. Select the Pitch. You can change the pitch by selecting a value from 1 to 9 from the drop-down list.

   f. Click OK to close the Voice Settings dialog window.

5. Minimize the Narrator dialog to save screen space.

cross-reference

The Utility Manager covered in Task 204 also uses the Narrator.

note

The Narrator is only supported in the English version of Windows XP.

tip

You can also run the Narrator by pressing Ctrl+Esc to display the Start menu, followed by pressing R to display the Run dialog window. Enter **Narrator** into the Open entry box, followed by clicking OK or pressing the Enter key.

caution

Closing or pressing the Exit button on the Narrator will close the Narrator program. To keep the program running, you need to minimize it instead of closing it.

Using the On-Screen Keyboard

Window XP comes with a built-in keyboard — that is, a keyboard that can be displayed on the screen. While this keyboard was provided to allow accessibility to people who may not be able to use a regular physical keyboard, anyone can access it.

The built-in keyboard can be operated in three different modes. It can also be customized in a number of different ways, including changing the number of keys, as well as fonts and other settings. In this task, you will learn the steps necessary for using the on-screen keyboard, as well as for customizing features such as font, typing mode, and more.

1. Start the On-Screen Keyboard by selecting from the Start menu All Programs➪Accessories➪Accessibility➪On-Screen Keyboard. The On-Screen Keyboard is displayed, along with a message dialog box (see Figure 202-1).

Figure 202-1: The On-Screen Keyboard.

2. Close the On-Screen Keyboard message dialog window. Click the box next to Do Not Show This Message Again if you don't need to see the message box again. Click OK to close the message window. This leaves you with the On-Screen Keyboard displayed.

3. Customize the way keys are selected on the On-Screen Keyboard by selecting Settings➪Typing Mode from the On-Screen Keyboard's menus. The Typing Mode dialog window appears (see Figure 202-2).

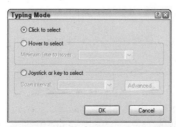

Figure 202-2: The Typing Mode settings dialog window.

cross-reference

Task 203 shows you how to select the layout for the On-Screen keyboard.

tip

If you'd like to hear a clicking sound when a key is selected on the On-Screen Keyboard, select Settings➪Use Click Sound. A check next to this menu option means that clicking is active. Selecting the menu option again turns off the clicking.

note

The benefit of the Hover to Select typing mode is that no buttons need to be clicked and no keys need to be pressed.

note

The benefit of the Joystick or Key to Select typing mode is that a single button or key can be used to select values on the keyboard.

You can pick one of the three typing modes displayed in the Typing Mode settings dialog window:

a. Select Click to Select if you want to click on the keys on the On-Screen Keyboard with your mouse.

b. Select Hover to Select if you want to use the mouse pointer to select keys from the On-Screen Keyboard by hovering over them. You can set the amount of time that the pointer hovers over the key before it is selected.

c. Select Joystick or Key to Select if you want to use a single button or key to select values from the On-Screen Keyboard. Pressing the assigned button or key causes highlighting to occur on the On-Screen Keyboard. The highlighting cycles through rows on the keyboard as shown in Figure 202-3.

Figure 202-3: Using the Joystick or Key to Select option, which highlights rows then individual keys.

When the row you want is highlighted below, you can press the button or key again. This will cause the highlighting to cycle through either a set of keys or the individual keys in that row. When the character you want is highlighted, you can press the button or key again to select it.

Set the amount of time that the highlighting should remain on a selection before moving to the next. Select the Advanced button to choose whether a button or keyboard key is used, as well as which key will be used. Figure 202-4 shows the Scanning Options dialog window.

Figure 202-4: The Scanning Options for the Joystick or Key to Select typing mode.

4. Open or switch to the application that you want to use with the keyboard. Place the cursor at the location where you want to type.

5. Use the On-Screen Keyboard based on the typing mode you selected in Step 3. You should see corresponding keys or characters displayed in the active application.

Task **203**

Selecting the On-Screen Keyboard Layout

cross-reference

Task 202 shows you how to use the On-Screen Keyboard, as well as how to set some of the options.

tip

If you'd like to hear a clicking sound when a key is selected on the On-Screen Keyboard, select Settings⇨Use Click Sound. A check next to this menu option means that clicking is active. Selecting the menu option again turns off the clicking.

note

If the Block Layout is selected, you will only be able to use the 101 Keys Keyboard. The 102 and 106 Keys Keyboards will be unavailable.

note

The 102 Keys Keyboard has an extra forward slash on the lower-left side next to the Shift key.

Window XP's On-Screen Keyboard can be customized with a number of different layouts. These layouts impact the positioning of the keys, as well as the number of keys displayed. The following steps walk you through the different keyboard layouts that you can choose from:

1. Start the On-Screen Keyboard by selecting from the Start menu All Programs⇨Accessories⇨Accessibility⇨On-Screen Keyboard. The On-Screen Keyboard appears, along with a message dialog box (see Figure 203-1).

Figure 203-1: The On-Screen Keyboard.

2. Close the On-Screen Keyboard message dialog window if it is displayed by clicking OK.

3. Select the Keyboard menu on the On-Screen Keyboard. Figure 203-2 shows the keyboard menu options you can choose.

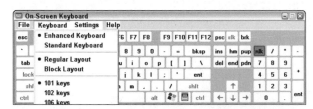

Figure 203-2: The Keyboard menu on the On-Screen Keyboard.

4. Select either Standard Keyboard or Enhanced Keyboard. The Enhanced Keyboard includes the additional arrow keys and number pad as shown in Figure 203-1. The Standard Keyboard is smaller and is shown in Figure 203-3.

Figure 203-3: A Standard Keyboard layout.

5. Select to use either the Regular Layout or the Block Layout from the Keyboard menu. The Regular Layout matches a standard keyboard and is the same as the layouts in Figures 203-1 and 203-3. The Block Layout groups characters into blocks of characters with the most frequently used characters grouped together. Figure 203-4 displays the Enhanced Keyboard with the Block Layout selected.

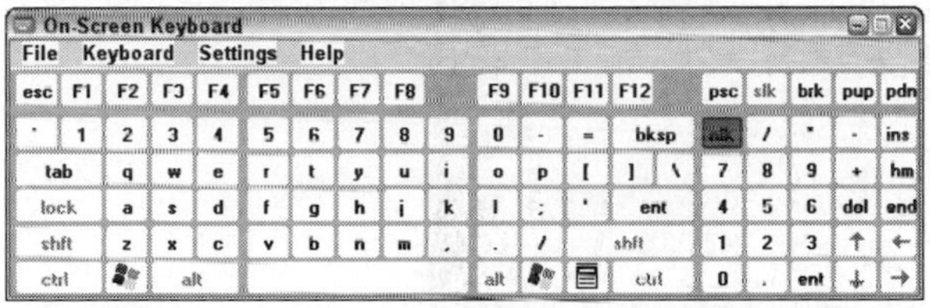

Figure 203-4: The Enhanced Keyboard using the Block Layout.

6. Select the number of keys that your keyboard should have. There are three options:

- *101 Keys*. This is the standard keyboard layout used in the United States (see Figure 203.3).

- *102 Keys*. This is a more standard layout that is used around the world (see Figure 203-5).

Figure 203-5: The 102 Keys Keyboard layout.

- *106 Keys*. This layout contains several additional Japanese keys.

caution

The On-Screen Keyboard is not usable within all applications. For example, some games take over the entire screen, causing the On-Screen Keyboard to be hidden.

Setting Usability Feature Options

Usability features allow you to customize Windows XP to make its use easier if you have trouble with your vision or if you are unable to effectively use a standard keyboard. The Utility Manager is a program that allows you to set the standard status of the three accessibility programs: the On-Screen Keyboard, the Narrator, and the Magnifier. Using the Utility Manager, you can set these programs to run automatically when you log in to your computer or when you start the Utility Manager. To use the Utility Manager and to set the accessibility programs to run automatically, use the following steps:

1. Press the Window logo key+U. This starts the Utility Manager. You can press this key combination from the Windows XP Welcome Screen or after you are logged in to your Windows XP account. The first time you press this key combination, you may see dialog windows similar to those in Figure 204-1. You may also see the Narrator, On-Screen Keyboard, and Magnifier launch depending on what your settings are.

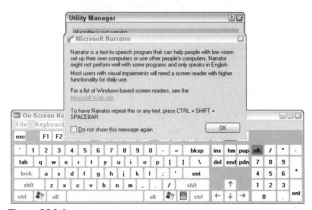

Figure 204-1: Launching the Utility Manager.

cross-reference

You can run a wizard that will walk you through setting values for the accessibility of your computer. Task 205 walks you through this wizard.

Do not start the Utility Manager by selecting from the Start menu Accessories➪Accessibility➪Utility Manager. This will result in a message being displayed as shown in Figure 204-2. As you can see from the message, you shouldn't use the menu to run this program.

Figure 204-2: Launching the Utility Manager from the Start menu.

2. Clear any message windows. If your Utility Manager has any of the accessibility programs set to run automatically, message dialogs for those applications may be displayed. Figure 204-1 showed the message dialog for the Narrator program. Close these message dialogs by selecting the OK buttons. After they are closed, you should see the Utilities Manager window. This should look similar to Figure 204-3. You may also see option windows for some of the utility programs.

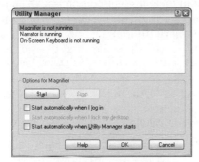

Figure 204-3: The Utility Manager.

3. Select the accessibility program you want to start, stop, or change running options on. In Figure 204-3, the Magnifier was selected. You can select a different program by clicking on the item in the box.

4. Select the Start button in the Options area to start the selected program.

5. Select the Stop button to immediately stop the running program.

6. Check the Start Automatically When I Log In option if you want the currently selected program to start when you log in.

7. Check the Start Automatically When I Lock My Desktop option if you want the currently selected program to start when you lock your computer.

8. Check the Start Automatically When Utility Manager Starts option to start the currently selected program when you start the Utility Manager program.

9. Repeat Steps 3 through 8 for the other accessibility programs.

10. Click OK to save your settings. The accessibility programs are now activated based on the options you set.

cross-reference

Task 201 walks you through setting the options for the Narrator.

cross-reference

Task 200 walks you through setting the options for the Magnifier.

cross-reference

Tasks 202 and 203 walk you through setting the options for the On-Screen Keyboard.

caution

If your computer is on a network and the network has security in place, you may not be able to run the Utility Manager from the Windows Welcome screen.

Setting Usability Feature Options with the Accessibility Wizard

T he Accessibility Wizard is one of the most complex wizards you can use in Windows XP. The overall dialog windows that are presented depend on the selections you make. If you want to have Windows XP customize itself to become more accessible, this wizard will help. Based on your selections, it can change the font sizes, whether accessibility programs run automatically, the types of cursors that are used, the color scheme, and much more. You should walk through each dialog of the wizard and review its options closely. The following steps get you going with the Accessibility Wizard:

1. From the Start menu, select All Programs⇨Accessories⇨ Accessibility⇨Accessibility Wizard. This starts the Accessibility Wizard with a welcome message.

2. Click the Next button to begin the process of customizing your accessibility options. This displays the text size options shown in Figure 205-1.

Figure 205-1: Options for setting text size.

3. Set the text size. Select one of the three sizes of text by clicking on it. A rectangular box appears around the currently selected item. Click the Next button to continue. This takes you to the next step in the wizard, as shown in Figure 205-2. This window shows you the display settings that were selected based on the text size you chose.

4. Confirm that the options selected are what you want, and then click the Next button. The options shown in Figure 205-3 appear. These options configure the settings for vision, hearing, and mobility.

5. Check the statements that are true, and then press the Next button. The remaining screens that you will see are based on your selections in Figure 205-3. If you don't select any options in the dialog presented in Figure 205-3, you will be given an error message.

note

This wizard can change everything from display settings to accessibility settings to sound settings. This is all done based on the questions and other prompts presented in the wizard.

tip

If you change your mind about the changes you are making, you can click the Cancel button at any time. Doing so gives you the option to keep some of the changes made to that point or to throw the changes out entirely.

cross-reference

You can learn more about changing the Windows XP font size in Task 199. You can learn more about using the Magnifier in Task 200.

note

In Step 3 you can select an option to turn off the personalized menus. Personalized menus are menus that hide items you have not used in a while.

cross-reference

You can learn more about other accessibility features by reviewing Tasks 199 through 207.

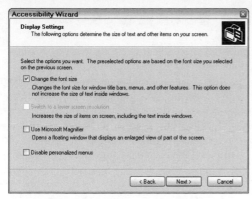

Figure 205-2: Options for setting text size.

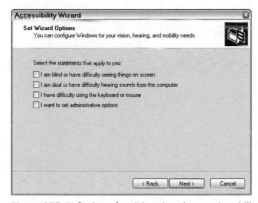

Figure 205-3: Options for vision, hearing, and mobility.

6. Continue going through each dialog, making selections and pressing the Next button. You will do this until you reach the final Accessibility Wizard dialog that will list the major modification items you selected.

7. Click Cancel if you want to quit the wizard. Do this only if you don't want to finish the wizard or if you want to cancel the changes that have been made up to this point. A Save Changes prompt appears.

8. If you didn't choose to cancel, click Finish to complete the changes to Windows XP based on the selections you made.

note

This can become a very long wizard. The end results, however, are that you can do a large number of customizations to Windows XP to make it more accessible.

note

You can make changes to some of the individual settings presented in this wizard by selecting the Control Panel from the Start menu. In the Control Panel, select the Accessibility Options category. Finally, select the Accessibility Options Control Panel icon. This displays a tabbed dialog with many of the Accessibility settings.

note

If you want to throw out all of the changes you have selected, click No. If you want to keep the changes that have already been made based on your selections in the wizard, select Yes.

caution

Once you press the Finish button on the last page, you are committing to the changes you selected.

Task 206

Using and Setting StickyKeys

note

Another Windows XP accessibility option is ToggleKeys. This feature causes a sound to occur if the NumLock, ScrollLock, or CapLock keys are pressed. You can turn this feature on by either using the Accessibility Options dialog (see Steps 1 and 2), or by holding the NumLock key down for five seconds.

Windows XP includes a number of special features that work with keys on the keyboard. StickyKeys make it easier to use a combination of keys. Specifically, it allows you to press Shift, Ctrl, Alt, or the Windows logo key followed by a second key. If StickyKeys is turned on, then even though the two keys are not pressed at the same time, it will treat them as if they were. For example, Ctrl+C is the keyboard shortcut for performing a copy. StickyKeys allows you to press the Ctrl and have it remain selected until you press the C key. It will treat these two key presses as if they happened at the same time.

The following steps show you how to turn StickyKeys on and off, as well as how to set a number of options specific to them:

1. Select the Accessibility Options from the Control Panel on the Start menu.

2. Select the Accessibility Options Control Panel icon. The Accessibility Options dialog window appears (see Figure 206-1). Make sure the Keyboard tab is selected.

Figure 206-1: The Keyboard options in the Accessibility Options dialog window.

3. Check the box next to Use StickyKeys if you want to turn StickyKeys on. Clear this box to turn StickyKeys off.

4. Click Settings. The dialog in Figure 206-2 appears, which contains additional options for StickyKeys.

5. If you want to be able to turn StickyKeys on and off using the shortcut method, then leave the check next to the Use Shortcut Option. The shortcut is to press the Shift key five times. If this option is active, then after pressing the Shift key five times in a row, you will see the message in Figure 206-3 pop up.

   Clicking OK turns StickyKeys on. Clicking Cancel turns StickyKeys off (or cancels the message if StickyKeys is not already turned on). Clicking Settings takes you to the dialog window shown in Figure 206-2.

cross-reference

FilterKeys is another special feature similar to StickyKeys. FilterKeys allows you to ignore brief or repeated keystrokes. Task 207 covers using and setting FilterKeys.

tip

If you have the shortcut option turned on, you can activate (or deactivate) StickyKeys by pressing the Shift key five times in a row.

Figure 206-2: The StickyKeys options dialog window.

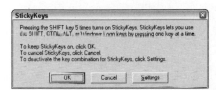

Figure 206-3: The StickyKeys shortcut message window.

6. Set the options in the Settings for StickyKeys dialog window. Select Press Modifier Key Twice to Lock if you want to be able to lock a key. For example, to type in all uppercase letters, you can lock the Shift key. You can also select Turn StickyKeys Off If Two Keys Are Pressed at Once.

7. Set the notification options. Select Make Sounds When Modifier Key Is Pressed if you want an audible notification that a key has been pressed. Check the Show StickyKeys Status on Screen notification option if you want to have a visual representation of any active keys. This representation is done in the notification area of the taskbar. Figure 206-4 shows this notification. Note that the key representation is filled when a key is pressed.

Shift

Windows logo

Control (Ctrl)   Alt

Figure 206-4: The Show StickyKeys Status on Screen notification option.

8. Click OK to save the settings for the StickyKeys options.

9. Click OK on the Accessibility Options dialog window.

10. Close the Control Panel window.

tip

If StickyKeys seems to be turned off at random times, you should check your settings in the StickyKeys options (see Step 6). If Turn StickyKeys Off If Two Keys Are Pressed at Once is active, then StickyKeys will be turned off if you press two keys at once.

note

To see which StickyKeys are currently active (pressed), you should turn on the notification option to show the key status on the screen (see Step 7).

Using and Setting FilterKeys

Windows XP includes a number of special features that work with keys on the keyboard. FilterKeys prevents you from bumping a key multiple times in a row by accident. The FilterKeys feature ignores multiple key presses from the same key within a given period of time. When you hold a key down, it will also repeat itself. The FilterKeys feature determines how often, or how frequently, a key is repeated when you hold it down.

The following steps show you how to turn FilterKeys on and off, as well as how to set a number of options specific to them:

1. Select Accessibility Options from the Control Panel on the Start menu.

2. Select the Accessibility Options Control Panel icon. The Accessibility Options dialog window appears (see Figure 207-1). Make sure the Keyboard tab is selected.

Figure 207-1: The Keyboard options in the Accessibility Options dialog window.

3. Check the box next to Use FilterKeys if you want to turn FilterKeys on. Clear this box to turn FilterKeys off.

4. Click Settings within the FilterKeys area of the dialog window. This presents you with the dialog in Figure 207-2, which contains additional options for FilterKeys.

5. Turn on or off the keyboard shortcut for FilterKeys. If you want to turn the shortcut on, check the box next to Use Shortcut. Clear the box to turn off the shortcut.

6. Set the Filter options.

   If you don't want a key to repeat itself when you hold it down, select Ignore Repeated Keystrokes. Selecting the Settings button next to this option displays a dialog box where you can set the amount of time that is required in between pressing the same key over.

note

Another Windows XP accessibility option is ToggleKeys. This feature causes a sound to occur if the NumLock, ScrollLock, or CapLock keys are pressed. You can turn this feature on by either using the Accessibility Options dialog (see Steps 1 and 2) or by holding the NumLock key down for five seconds.

caution

The SlowKeys option in Figure 207-4 is the amount of time that you must hold down a key before it will be typed. If you don't set this to 0.0 seconds, you will need to hold each key you press for the specified amount of time before it is displayed. This can make typing very slow.

tip

If you have the shortcut option turned on, you can activate (or deactivate) FilterKeys by pressing and holding down the right Shift key for eight seconds.

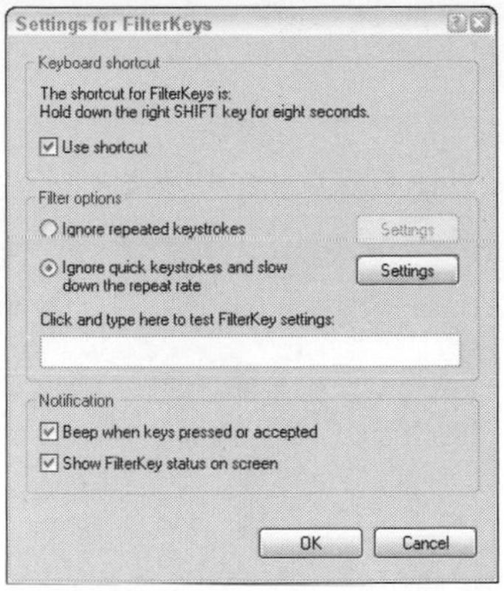

Figure 207-2: The Settings for FilterKeys dialog.

If you want to make sure a key is held down for a period of time before a character is typed, select the Ignore Quick Keystrokes and Slow Down the Repeat Rate. Selecting the Setting button next to this option in the Settings for FilterKeys dialog displays the dialog in Figure 207-3. You can turn off the repeating of a key or you can change how much time is between each repeat when the key is held down.

Figure 207-3: Advanced settings for FilterKeys.

cross-reference

StickyKeys is another special feature similar to FilterKeys. Task 206 covers using and setting StickyKeys.

7. Set the notification options in the Settings for FilterKeys dialog window. Select Beep When Keys Pressed or Accepted if you want an audible notification that a key has been pressed. Select the Show FilterKeys Status on Screen notification option if you want to have a visual representation of any active keys. Figure 207-4 shows the FilterKeys Clock icon in the notification area of the taskbar.

Figure 207-4: The FilterKeys status in the taskbar (represented as a clock).

8. Click OK to save the settings for the FilterKeys options.

Part 16: Working with User Accounts

Task 208: Setting Up a Guest Account

Task 209: Creating New User Accounts

Task 210: Deleting a User Account

Task 211: Changing a User's Account Name

Task 212: Changing the Icon on a User Account

Task 213: Changing a User"s Account Type

Task 214: Adding a Password to a User Account

Task 215: Changing a User Account"s Password

Task 216: Removing a Password from a User Account

Setting Up a Guest Account

Windows XP allows you to set up different accounts for different users. This means that each user can customize an account. You can also set up generic accounts. Windows XP provides one generic account already called the Guest account.

The Guest account can be used when you want to set up an account for people to use who would not normally be logging in to your computer or whom you don't want to give full access. The following steps walk you through turning on as well as turning off the Guest account on your computer. You need to have administrator rights in order to do this task.

1. Select Control Panel from the Start menu.

2. Select User Accounts from the Control Panel categories. The User Accounts dialog window appears (see Figure 208-1). As you can see, this dialog lists the accounts on the computer, including the Guest account.

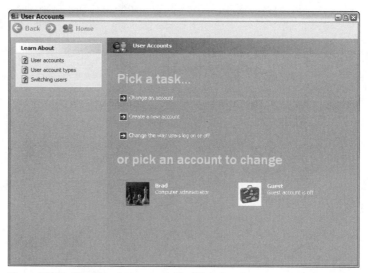

Figure 208-1: The User Accounts Control Panel options.

3. Click the Guest account. If the Guest account has not already been turned on, the window in Figure 208-2 appears. This window asks if you want to turn on the Guest account.

4. Click Turn On the Guest Account. You'll see in the list of accounts that the Guest account has been turned on. You will now find that there is a Guest icon on your Windows Welcome screen.

---

cross-reference

You need to have administrator rights to turn on the Guest account. Task 223 shows you how to set account types such as administrator.

note

Documents, folders, and other files that are password-protected will not be accessible to anyone using the Guest account.

note

The icon for the Guest account will be in grayscale if it is turned off (see Figure 208-1). When turned on, it will be in color.

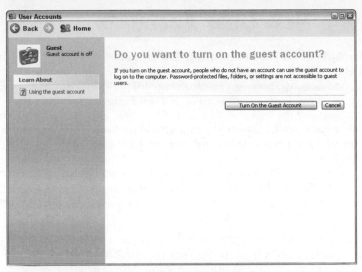

Figure 208-2: The prompt for turning on the Guest account.

5. Close the Control Panel windows. You can now log in to Windows with the Guest account. If you want to turn off the Guest account, continue with the following steps.

6. If you want to turn off the account, first click the Guest Account icon. The Guest account's options appear (see Figure 208-3).

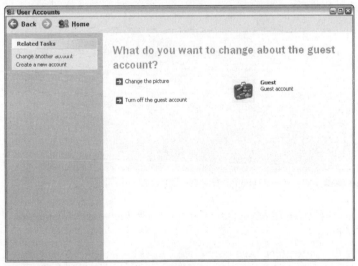

Figure 208-3: Guest account user options.

7. Click Turn Off the Guest Account. This immediately turns off the Guest account and returns you to the User Accounts page.

Task **208**

cross-reference

You can learn how to set up additional accounts other than the Guest account in Task 209.

note

If your computer is part of a network with a domain, you may not be able to set up a Guest account. On standalone computers and computers using workgroups, you can set up a Guest account.

cross-reference

You can change the icon used on a Guest account. Change it the same way graphical icons are changed on other accounts. Task 212 walks you through the steps.

Creating New User Accounts

Windows XP allows you to set up different accounts for yourself or for different users. This means that each user can have an account that he or she can customize. Additionally, it means you can set up different accounts, each one having different settings. Each account can have its own customized look. This includes customizing the background image, the screen saver, and other desktop settings, as well as customizing the Start menu and toolbars. Each user account also gets its own area to store documents and other files, including recently visited Web pages and Favorites.

The following walks you through the basic steps of creating a user account on your computer. You will need to have administrator rights to create an account.

1. Select Control Panel from the Start menu.

2. Select User Accounts from the Control Panel categories. The User Accounts dialog window, as shown in Figure 209-1. As you can see, this dialog lists the accounts on the computer.

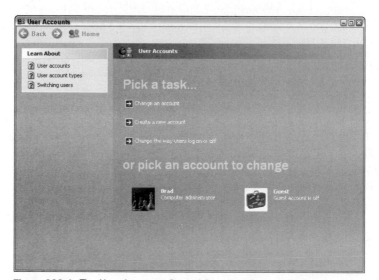

Figure 209-1: The User Accounts Control Panel options.

3. Click the Create a New Account task. The dialog window in Figure 209-2 appears.

4. Enter the name to be used on the account. This name will appear on the Start menu and the Windows Welcome screen.

cross-reference

You need to have administrator rights to create user accounts. Task 213 shows you how to set account types such as an administrator.

note

The name on an account will be displayed on the Windows Welcome screen and the Start menu.

note

You can limit what a person can do on your computer by setting up a limited user account for that user.

cross-reference

You can learn how to set up a Guest account in Task 208. A Guest account can be used as a general account to give limited access to anyone who would normally not use your computer.

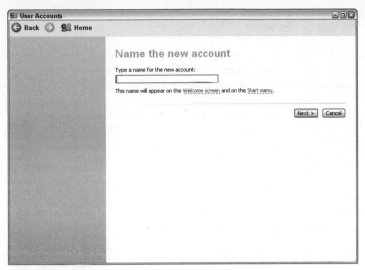

Figure 209-2: Adding user accounts.

5. Click Next. The second dialog window used for creating an account appears (see Figure 209-3).

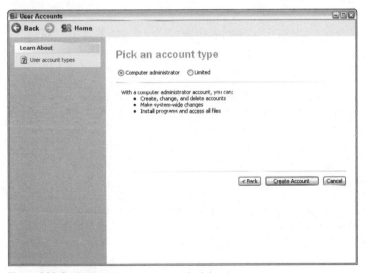

Figure 209-3: Setting the user account's rights.

6. Select either Computer Administrator or Limited Rights. If you don't want someone to have full access to your computer, you will want to select Limited. You can change the access rights later (as shown in Task 213).

7. Click Create Account. The new account is added on the User Account window.

8. Close the Control Panel windows. The new account is now set up on the computer.

note

If your computer is part of a network with a domain, you may not be able to set up a user account. On standalone computers and computers using workgroups, you can set up user accounts.

cross-reference

You can change the icon used on an account. Task 212 walks you through the steps

caution

This account has not had a password assigned. Task 214 shows you how to add, and Task 215 shows you how to change an existing password.

Task 210

Deleting a User Account

When you are through with a user account, or when a person is no longer going to be using your computer, the account can be removed. Removing the account takes the icon off the Windows Welcome screen and removes many of the Windows XP files associated with the account. Some files, such as documents and pictures that the user may have created and saved, will not be removed. To delete an account, use the following steps. You need to have administrator rights to delete an account.

1. Select Control Panel from the Start menu.

2. Select User Accounts from the Control Panel categories. The User Accounts dialog window shown in Figure 210-1 appears. As you can see, this dialog lists the accounts on the computer.

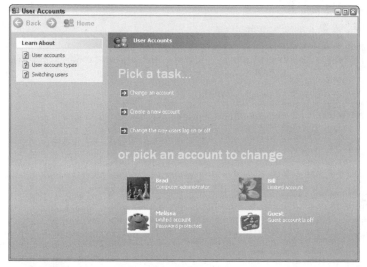

Figure 210-1: The User Accounts Control Panel options.

3. Click the icon or name of the account you want to remove. The User Accounts dialog window appears (see Figure 210-2).

4. Click Delete the Account. If the account you are deleting is logged on, you will see a message. You need to switch to the account being deleted and log it out.

   If the account you are deleting is already logged out, you will be presented with the dialog window in Figure 210-3.

5. Click either Keep Files or Delete Files depending on whether you want to keep or remove the user's files. This copies the values of the My Documents folder from the user's account to your desktop. The files are placed in a folder with the same name as the user's account name. Regardless of which option you select, you are presented with one or more windows before the deletion occurs. Figure 210-4 shows the window if files will be kept.

cross-reference

You need to have administrator rights to delete a user account. Task 213 shows you how to set account types such as administrator.

note

If you are using a limited-access account type, you will not be able to delete a user account — not even your own account.

cross-reference

See Task 4 if you need help switching users.

cross-reference

You can't delete the Guest account. Rather, you simply turn it off as shown in Task 208.

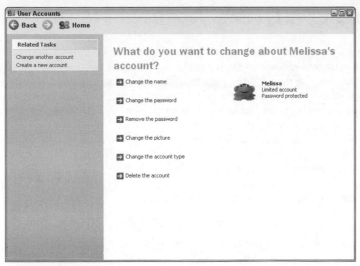

Figure 210-2: The User Accounts options.

Figure 210-3: User Accounts File Options dialog window.

6. Click Delete Account. The account is deleted, and you are returned to the User Accounts dialog window.

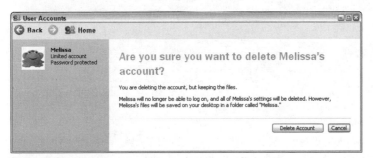

Figure 210-4: Confirmation window for deleting an account.

caution

Email and some other files will be lost if you delete an account — even if you select to keep files. Files in the My Documents folder, including the My Pictures and My Music folders, can be saved.

note

Figure 210-4 shows the dialog window that is displayed if you click the Keep Files button. If you choose to delete the files, you will see a slightly different message displayed; however, you will use the same buttons.

caution

Once you delete an account, it is gone. You can re-create a new account with the same name; however, the original account and its settings are no longer available.

note

If on a network anyone with administrator rights can press Ctrl+Alt+Del, select the Users tab, click the User to disconnect, and click Disconnect to disconnect from the network.

Task 211

Changing a User's Account Name

There are a number of customizations that you can make to your user accounts. You may want to change the name that is on your account. While the account name is generally the name of the person using the account, you can actually make it any name you want. For example, you may want to change your account name to use your nickname rather than a proper name.

You can also set up multiple accounts for yourself. You can name your primary account with your own name. You could have other accounts, such as one for games and one for working. You may decide to call these Games and Work. Later you may decide that you want to rename one of these. For example, you may decide to rename the Games account to Entertainment.

To rename an account, you must be set up and logged in to Windows XP as an administrator. You can rename an account using the following steps:

1. Select Control Panel from the Start menu.

2. Select User Accounts from the Control Panel categories. The User Accounts dialog window appears (see Figure 211-1). As you can see, this dialog lists the accounts on the computer. If you are using a limited account, you will not see this window. Rather, you will see the results shown in Figure 211-2 of Step 3, which follows.

Figure 211-1: The User Accounts Control Panel options.

3. Click the icon or name of the account you want to rename. The User Accounts dialog window appears (see Figure 211-2).

caution

If you don't have administrator rights, you will not see an option to rename your account.

cross-reference

You need to have administrator rights to rename any account. Task 213 shows you how to set account types to act as an administrator.

note

When you rename an account, it will change the name that is displayed on the Start menu and on the Windows Welcome screen.

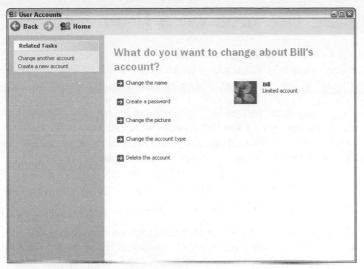

Figure 211-2: The User Accounts options.

4. Click Change the Name. The window shown in Figure 211-3 appears, with the current name of the account highlighted. As you can see, the dialog window asks you to enter a new name for the current account. In the case of Figure 211-3, it is asking you to rename Bill's account.

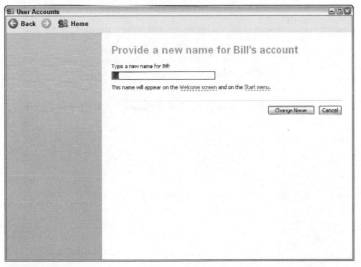

Figure 211-3: Prompt for renaming an account.

5. Enter the new name that you want to give to the account.

6. Click Change Name. You are taken back to the User Account screen for the user you are working with. The username is immediately changed and the messages in the window reflect this.

cross-reference

Once you change a user account name, you can't undo the change. You can rename the account back to the original name; however, you will have to remember what the original name was.

cross-reference

You can't rename the Guest account. Rather, you can simply turn it off as shown in Task 208, and then create a new limited account that you can let people use.

Task 212

Changing the Icon on a User Account

Microsoft Windows XP assigns a somewhat random picture to a user account when it is created. You can customize this picture to use one of several that are included with Windows XP, or you can use a picture of your own.

The steps for changing the picture on your account are slightly different depending on whether you are using a limited account or a computer administrator account. The following steps walk you through changing your picture. Differences between the account types are noted in the steps.

1. Select Control Panel from the Start menu.

2. Select User Accounts from the Control Panel categories.

   - If you are using an administrator account, you are taken to the User Accounts dialog window. You can select the account you want to change by clicking on its icon or the name of the user in the lower half of this dialog window. Once you click on the user, you are shown the options for the selected user in a window similar to 212-1. For an administrator, you will see a few additional options beyond what are shown in this figure.

   - If you are using a limited account, then when you click User Accounts from the Control Panel categories, you are taken directly to the options for your account. These options will be similar to some of the options in Figure 212-1.

caution

Anyone can change the image associated with his or her account with the exception of the Guest account. Someone with an administrator account is the only person who can change a Guest account.

cross-reference

An administrator can change the picture on anyone's account. Task 213 presents information on user account types.

cross-reference

You can get pictures from a number of places to use with your account. This can be pictures you copy from a digital camera (see Task 61), ones you scan into your computer, that you create in a program like Microsoft Paint (see Task 65), or that you download or copy off the Internet (see Task 144).

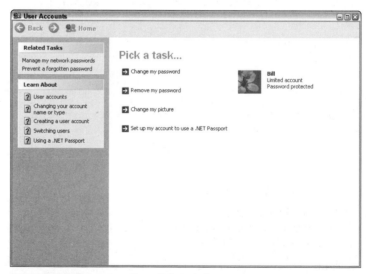

Figure 212-1: The user options dialog window.

3. Click Change My Picture. If you are an administrator changing someone else's account, the link will be Change the Picture. The dialog window for selecting a new picture appears, as shown in Figure 212-2.

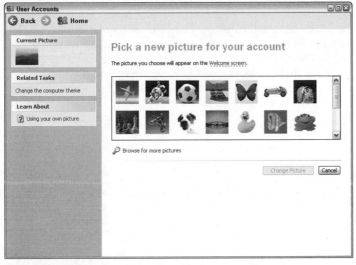

Figure 212-2: The dialog window for selecting a new picture.

4. Select the picture you want to use.

   To use one of the existing, standard pictures, do the following:

   a. Click the image from the choices presented in the middle of the window (see Figure 212-2). You can scroll to additional choices that are not displayed. When selected, a box appears around the image.

   b. Click Change Picture. The picture you selected is applied to the user account.

   If you want to use your own picture instead of one of the provided images, do the following:

   a. Click Browse for More Pictures. A Windows Explorer window opens.

   b. Click the My Pictures folder.

   c. Click Open. The My Pictures folder appears, listing the picture files contained in it. Other pictures you have saved on your computer may also be in this folder.

   d. Click the picture file you want to use.

   e. Click Open. The picture is applied to the user account.

5. Close the User Accounts and Control Panel windows.

note

You can see the user account picture used on the Welcome screen and in the Start menu.

note

Pictures may be stored in a number of places on your computer. By default, pictures are placed in the My Pictures folder. Each user has his or her own My Pictures folder.

cross-reference

To learn how to look for pictures in other locations on your computer, see Task 22, which discusses the Microsoft Windows Explorer.

Changing a User's Account Type

When a user is created for Windows XP, he or she is given an account type. The account type determines the permission that the person has for looking at files on the computer, as well as to perform various activities. There are two standard account types in Windows XP: Computer Administrator, which has full access and full rights to do anything, and the standard account, which has limited access and rights.

Administrators can make changes to other accounts on the machine, as well as to their own account. Additionally, administrators can protect their files so they can't be seen by anyone using a limited account. Conversely, users with limited accounts can be prevented from seeing the documents and other files that an administrator has on the computer. Users with limited accounts can only make changes to their own account, and even then they are limited on what they can change.

To set the account type, use the following steps. You must use an existing administrator account to change another account's type.

1. Select Control Panel from the Start menu.

2. Select User Accounts from the Control Panel categories. The User Accounts window appears. On the bottom half of this window, the user accounts for this computer are listed.

3. Click the account that you want to change. You are taken to the options window for the account, as shown in Figure 213-1.

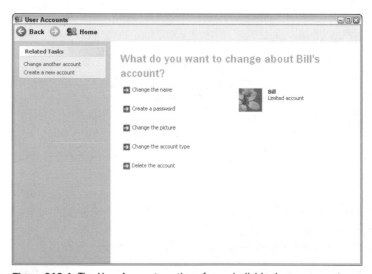

Figure 213-1: The User Accounts options for an individual user account.

4. Click Change the Account Type. If the account you are changing is currently a limited account, you are presented with the dialog window shown in Figure 213-2.

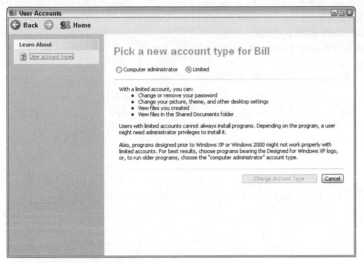

Figure 213-2: The dialog window for changing a limited account.

If the account you are changing is currently an administrator account, then you will see the dialog window shown in Figure 213-3.

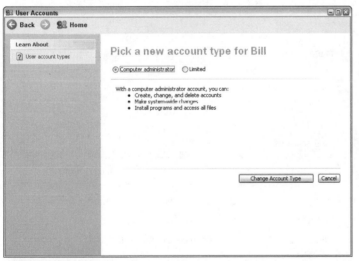

Figure 213-3: The dialog window for changing an administrator account.

5. Click Change Account Type. The account type is changed, and you are returned to the User Accounts dialog window.

6. Close the User Accounts and Control Panel windows.

note

One account must remain as an administrator account. You cannot change the last administrator account to a limited account.

note

The Guest account is also limited. You cannot change the account type of the Guest account.

note

A user with a limited account can change his or her own icon picture, as well as create, change, or remove his or her own password.

note

A computer administrator account can install programs and hardware, make system changes, access and read all files, create user accounts, change user accounts, delete user accounts and account names, and change account types.

Adding a Password to a User Account

Microsoft Windows XP does not force you into using a password; however, if you don't want people to get onto your computer — or more specifically, if you don't want them to use your account — then you will want to add a password. Additionally, if you want to protect your documents or other files, you should add a password to your user account as well.

1. Select Control Panel from the Start menu.

2. Select User Accounts from the Control Panel categories. If you are using an administrator account, a User Accounts window appears. Select the user account that will have the password added. You are taken to the options for the account you selected, as shown in Figure 214-1.

   If you are using a limited account, you are taken directly to the options for the account. This will also be a window similar to Figure 214-1.

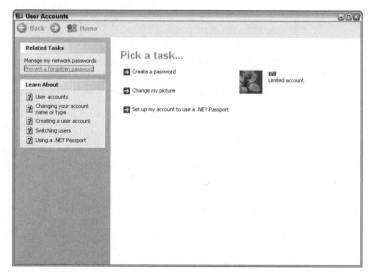

Figure 214-1: The User Accounts options for an individual user account.

3. Click Create a Password to add a password. The dialog window shown in Figure 214-2 appears.

4. Enter the new password into the first entry box.

5. Enter the same password into the second entry box. You must enter the password twice in order to confirm that you entered it correctly.

note

The steps for adding a password will be slightly different depending on whether you are set up with an administrator user account or a standard, limited user account. The steps in this task walk you through adding a password. Differences between the two accounts are noted.

note

A user with a limited account can only add a password to his or her account. An administrator can add a password to any account.

caution

Passwords are case-sensitive. This means that typing in **MyPassword** is not the same as **mypassword**.

note

If you forget your password, you can use the password tip to help you remember. If you still can't remember, you will need to have an administrator remove the password. Alternatively, you can create a password restore disk. To do so, log in to the user account and go to the User Account window as shown in Step 2 of this task. Click Prevent a Forgotten Password on the upper-left side of the window. A wizard will walk you through creating the reset disk.

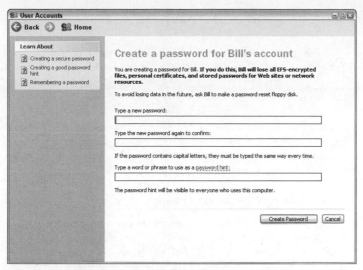

Figure 214-2: Prompts for adding a password.

6. Enter a word or phrase into the third entry box that will help you, or the user of the account, remember the password. If the user forgets his or her password, the user can have this phrase displayed. It is the only hint that will be available to help obtain the password.

7. Click Create Password. If you did not enter the passwords identically in the first two boxes, you are presented with an error message as shown in Figure 214-3. Click OK and reenter the password into the first two boxes again.

Figure 214-3: The error message if you enter the passwords incorrectly.

If you did enter the password the same in both, and if the account that the password has been added to is a limited account, you are returned to the User Account Options dialog window. In this case, you can continue to Step 9.

If the account is an administrator account, you are presented with a window that prompts you to hide your files from other accounts.

8. Click Yes, Make Private if you don't want other people to be able to see the files you have saved on the computer. Select No if you are willing to let people see the files you have on the computer.

9. Close the User Accounts and Control Panel windows.

cross-reference

Task 215 shows you how to change your password, while Task 216 shows you how to remove it.

caution

Remember that anyone using the computer can see your password hint. If your hint is too easy, then someone may be able to guess your password.

tip

A good password includes both characters and numbers.

tip

A good password will not be something obvious like your birthday, a loved one's name, or your pet's name.

Changing a User Account's Password

If your user account has a password on it, you may want to change it. In fact, you should change passwords every now and then just to be safe. Windows XP lets you change your own password. Nobody else can change yours for you unless they know your original password.

The steps for changing a password are slightly different depending on whether you are setting up with an administrator user account or a standard, limited user account. The following steps walk you through changing a password. Differences between the two accounts are noted.

1. Select Control Panel from the Start menu.

2. Select User Accounts from the Control Panel categories. If you are using an administrator account, a User Accounts window appears. Click on the user account that will have the password changed. You are taken to the options window for the account you selected.

   If you are using a limited account, you are taken directly to the options for the account.

3. Click Change the Password to add a password. (If you are changing the password on your own account, this will say Change My Password.) If you are changing your own password or changing an administrator type account's password, you are presented with the dialog window shown in Figure 215-1.

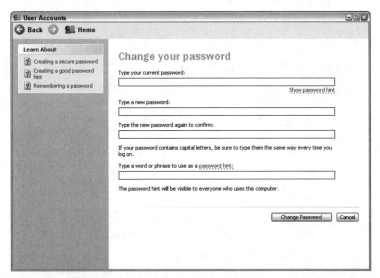

Figure 215-1: Prompts for changing a password on your own account.

If you are an administrator and you are changing the password on a limited-type account, a window similar to Figure 215-2 appears. Notice that, in this window, an administrator doesn't have to enter the original password for a limited account in order to change the password.

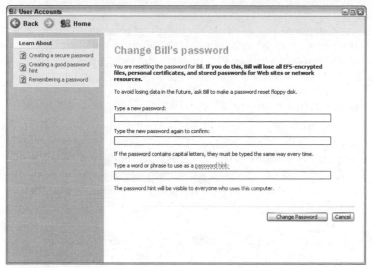

Figure 215-2: Prompts for changing a password on a limited account by an administrator.

4. If you are changing your own password, enter your current password into the first entry box. If you are an administrator changing a limited account's password, you won't have this entry box.

5. Enter the new password into the entry box for the new password.

6. Enter the same password into the second password entry box. You must enter the password twice in order to confirm that you entered it correctly.

7. Enter a word or phrase into the third entry box that will help you, or the user of the account, remember the new password. If the user forgets his or her password, the user can have this phrase displayed. It is the only hint that will be available to help obtain the password.

8. Click Change Password. If you did not enter the passwords identically in the first two boxes, you are presented with an error message. Click OK and reenter the password into the first two boxes again.

If you did enter the same password in both text boxes, you are returned to the User Accounts Options dialog window.

caution

Passwords are case-sensitive. This means that typing in **MyPassword** is not the same as **mypassword**.

note

If you forget your password, you can use the password tip to help you remember. If you still can't remember, you will need to have an administrator change or remove the password.

caution

Remember that anyone using the computer can see your password hint. If your hint is too easy, someone may be able to guess your password.

tip

A good password will not be something obvious like your birthday, a loved one's name, or your pet's name. These are all poor choices for passwords. A good password is also six or more characters in length.

Removing a Password from a User Account

If your user account has a password on it, and you no longer need it, you can remove the password. Windows XP lets you remove your own password as long as you remember what it is. If you have forgotten your password, you need someone with an administrator account to remove your password.

The steps for removing a password are slightly different depending on whether you are set up with an administrator user account or a standard, limited user account. The following steps walk you through changing a password. Differences between the two accounts are noted.

1. Select the Control Panel from the Start menu.

2. Select User Accounts from the Control Panel categories. If you are using an administrator account, a User Accounts window appears. Click the user account that needs the password changed. You are taken to the options window for the account you selected, as shown in Figure 216-1.

   If you are using a limited account, you are taken directly to the options for the account. This window is similar to Figure 216-1; however, fewer options are listed.

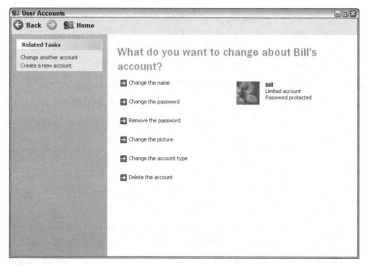

Figure 216-1: The User Accounts options for an individual user account.

3. Click Remove the Password. (If you are removing the password on your own account, this will say Remove My Password.) If you are removing your own password, the dialog window in Figure 216-2 appears.

note

An administrator can remove the password on another account without knowing the original password. Administrators must know the original password of their own account, however, in order to delete it.

tip

If you are an administrator and you forget your password, you can always create a new administrator account and then switch to it. Using the new account, you can change or remove the password in your original account.

caution

While you may be tempted to simply delete a password and then add a new one, you are better off using the Change Password feature instead. Deleting a password may cause the password to be removed from other areas as well.

cross-reference

Task 214 shows you how to add passwords, while Task 215 shows you how to change them.

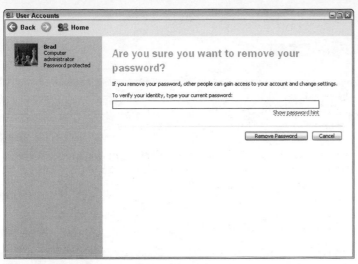

Figure 216-2: The window displayed if you are deleting your own password.

If you are an administrator and you are removing someone else's password, the dialog window in Figure 216-3 appears.

Figure 216-3: The window displayed when an administrator is deleting someone else's password.

4. If you are removing your own password, enter your current password into the password box shown in Figure 216-2. If you are an administrator and you are removing someone else's password, you will not need to enter this value.

5. Click Remove Password. The password is removed and you are returned to the User Accounts window.

6. Close the User Accounts and Control Panel windows.

note

A user with limited account can only delete his or her password. An administrator can remove the password from any account.

caution

Once a password is removed, it is irretrievable.

caution

If your computer is on a network with a domain, you should consult the network administrator before removing the password.

Part 17: Configuring Your Hardware

Task 217: Checking Your Hardware's Status

Task 218: Customizing Speaker Settings

Task 219: Installing a Printer

Task 220: Using a Removable Storage Device

Task 221: Installing a Game Controller

Task 222: Setting Up Two Monitors

Task 223: Uninstalling a Device

Checking Your Hardware's Status

Windows XP includes a feature called the Device Manager. This program allows you to view the hardware installed on your computer, as well as how it is configured. You do updates to the software that helps Windows XP interact with this hardware (software called *device drivers*), as well as do some troubleshooting.

The Device Manager is an advanced feature. As such, you may need to be logged in to Windows XP as an administrator in order to use all of its features. Additionally, you should use caution when making any changes within the Device Manager.

The following steps show you how to open the Device Manager, as well as how to review some of the settings for your hardware:

1. Select Control Panel from the Start menu.

2. Select Performance and Maintenance.

3. Select System. The System Properties dialog window appears.

4. Select the Hardware tab in the System Properties dialog window.

5. Click the Device Manager button in the Device Manager section. A Device Manager window similar to what is shown in Figure 217-1 appears. This dialog lists the different types of hardware that are in the computer.

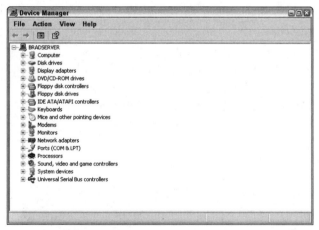

Figure 217-1: The Device Manager.

6. Double-click on a device type or click the plus sign next to the device type. The items for that device type are listed, as shown in Figure 217-2.

cross-reference

You can troubleshoot problems with your hardware using the Device Manager. See Task 249 for more on troubleshooting.

Figure 217-2: An expanded list of devices.

7. Right-click the device and select Properties from the pop-up menu. This displays the properties for the given device. Figure 217-3 shows the Properties dialog for one of the Communications ports on my computer. You should see something similar.

8. Review the information on the General tab. Looking at the Device status section, you can determine if the device is operating properly.

Figure 217-3: The general properties for a device.

tip

You can print reports on a device. Select the device by clicking on it in the Device Manger dialog window (see Figure 217-1). Select Action⇨Print from the menus.

note

If you have a hardware device in your computer that is experiencing problems, you can check in the Device Status of the General tab to see if a problem is indicated.

note

Each device may have additional tabs within their properties dialog windows. These tabs contain additional information and settings for the selected device.

Task 218

Customizing Speaker Settings

How many speakers you connect to your computer is up to you. Whether your computer has a simple built-in speaker (such as in a notebook computer) or high-quality surround sound speakers, you should configure Windows XP to get the best sound from them.

Windows XP lets you customize settings to take advantage of the speaker or headphone setup that is on your system. The following steps walk you through configuring the speakers once you've plugged them into the computer:

1. Select Control Panel from the Start menu.

2. Select Sounds, Speech, and Audio Devices from the categories displayed in the Control Panel window.

3. Select Change the Speaker Settings. The Sounds and Audio Devices Properties window appears (see Figure 218-1).

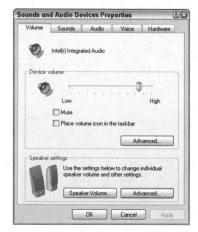

Figure 218-1: The Sounds and Audio Devices Properties window.

4. Select the Advanced button in the Speaker Settings section on the Volume tab. The Advanced Audio Properties dialog appears (see Figure 218-2). As you can see in the figure, the default setup on this computer is with two desktop stereo speakers.

5. Select your speaker configuration from the Speaker Setup drop-down list. You'll see options for a variety of configurations that include No Speaker, Laptop Stereo, and various advanced setups. When you select an option from the list, the picture changes to show the speaker setup.

cross-reference

Windows XP comes with several programs that can take advantage of high-quality speakers. Among the programs that can take advantage of these devices are Windows Media Player (see Part 5), Sound Recorder (see Task 197), and Windows Movie Maker (see Part 6).

note

Most computers sold today include a sound card. There are different qualities of sound cards that your computer can have. Some sound cards may not be able to take advantage of higher-end speakers.

cross-reference

The Sound Recorder requires that you have a microphone plugged into your computer. The Sound Recorder is covered in Task 197.

tip

If you change the speakers on your computer to a different style, you'll want to change the settings as shown in this task.

note

In order to use speakers, your computer must include a sound card or sound card features. If your computer is equipped with these features, there will be one or more plugs that allow you to connect the speakers. If you are using a notebook computer, the speakers may be built into the system.

note

Higher-quality microphones and speakers generally result in better recordings and sound.

Figure 218-2: Advanced Audio Properties window.

6. Click the Performance tab in the Advanced Audio Properties window. The options shown in Figure 218-3 appear.

Figure 218-3: The Advanced Audio Properties window.

7. Click Apply to apply the changes.

8. Adjust the performance settings. The settings can be adjusted to enhance the performance on your system. If you are noticing issues with the sound from you system, you can adjust the settings on this page. Lowering the settings, especially on the Sample Rate setting, can help your system's performance.

9. Click OK. All of your changes are applied and the window is closed.

10. Click OK to close the Sounds and Audio Device Properties window.

note

Most computers can be set up with from one to seven speakers. Alternatively, you can use headphones with your system.

Installing a Printer

When you are installing a new printer, Windows XP will generally do all the work for you. When you connect the printer to your computer, Windows XP should detect the printer and automatically load the software that allows the printer to operate. If the software needed — called a device driver — is not automatically found, you will be asked to insert a disk into the computer with the software.

If you want to use a printer that is on a network or if the automatic process doesn't work, you can still install a printer. You simply have to follow a few manual steps as shown in this task.

1. Select Printers and Fax from the Start menu. A window appears that shows the printers and faxes that your computer is currently set up to use.

2. Select Add a Printer from the Printer Tasks shown on the left side of the window. This starts the Add a Printer Wizard. As you can see in the first page of the wizard, shown in Figure 219-1, Windows XP should automatically find most printers.

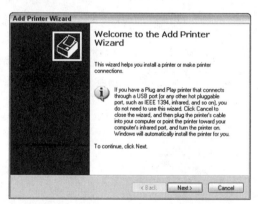

Figure 219-1: The Add Printer Wizard initial page.

3. Click Next to continue.

4. Select either the local or networked printer option. Choose Local Printer Attached to This Computer and check the Automatically Detect and Install My Plug and Play Printer if you are installing a printer connected to your current machine. Select a Network Printer, or a Printer Attached to Another Computer if you are using a shared printer.

5. Click Next. If you are adding a local printer, follow the instructions in the wizard and skip to Step 7. If you are adding a network printer, you are presented with a new dialog for specifying a printer.

6. Select Browse for a Printer and click Next. If you are accessing a networked or shared printer, a dialog similar to Figure 219-2 appears, displaying the computers and printers on your network.

note

Windows XP should be able to install most printers automatically. You should be able to plug them into your computer, and Windows XP should take care of the rest.

note

Like most pieces of computer equipment, if you buy a new printer, it will most likely include a floppy disk or CD. This disk may contain the software needed to make the printer work. The disk may also include additional software or programs that you can use.

note

You will be asked if you want the printer you are installing to be your default printer. The default printer is the one that is selected first when you choose to print from any application.

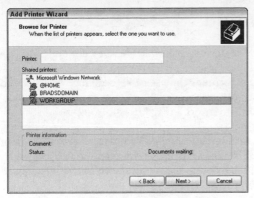

Figure 219-2: Browse for Printer page of the Add Printer Wizard.

7. Select the printer to be added by clicking on it. You may need to double-click on the names in the list to expand them. Double-clicking expands the list and displays the printers on that computer. In Figure 219-3, you can see that the expanded items for the selected computer show a Compaq and an HP printer that can be selected by clicking on their names.

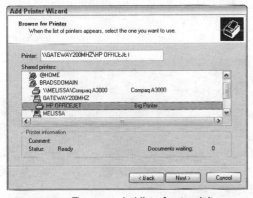

Figure 219-3: The expanded list of network items.

8. Click Next. The wizard continues.

9. Follow the remaining prompts provided in the wizard.

cross-reference

If you are on a network, you can share printers that are connected to individual machines. For more on networks, see Part 18.

tip

If you are asked for an "INF" file, you need to insert the disk that was provided with the printer. It should contain an appropriate INF file.

note

You can install more than one printer on your computer.

Task 220

Using a Removable Storage Device

A number of removable storage devices are available. Devices built into your computer that allow you to insert a disk or drive into a slot can be used without doing anything special. This includes the use of Zip disks, floppies, and more. There are also external versions of these drives. Using the external versions requires a few extra steps.

The following steps walk you through adding and removing a removable storage device that is designed for a USB plug-and-play connection. If you are using an older device that doesn't use a USB connection, you should consult the installation instructions that came with the device.

1. Plug the device into the computer. Windows notices the new device and displays a message stating that a new piece of hardware has been detected. Windows XP automatically attempts to install the necessary software to use the device.

2. Use the device. See the documentation or help files that came with the device for more information on the specific device. When you are ready to remove the device, continue to Step 3.

3. Right-click the Safely Remove Hardware icon in the notification bar as shown in Figure 220-1. A pop-up item removing devices in your system appears.

Figure 220-1: Windows XP Safely Remove Hardware icon.

4. Click the item you want to remove. You may also be presented with a generic option in this pop-up menu if you have multiple devices installed. The Safely Remove Hardware dialog appears (see Figure 220-2).

Figure 220-2: The Safely Remove Hardware dialog window.

5. Select the item to be removed from the list in the dialog by clicking on it.

6. Click Stop. This may result in an additional window being displayed. For example, in stopping a thumb drive, the extra window in Figure 220-3 is displayed.

Figure 220-3: The Stop a Hardware Device dialog window.

7. Click OK. The device is stopped, and Windows XP prepares for it being removed.

8. Carefully unplug the device from your computer if it is a plug-and-play device. If it is not a plug-and-play device, shut down the computer first.

Installing a Game Controller

There are thousands of games you can play on a computer. While some games work just fine with the keyboard, others are much more fun if you install a game controller.

A number of different types of controllers are available, ranging from standard joysticks to game pads, to throttles and steering wheels. With Windows XP, installing most of these devices is a simple matter of plugging them into your computer and letting Windows XP automatically install them. In some cases, however, you may need to change a setting or manually configure a game controller. The following steps help you to do this:

1. Select Control Panel from the Start menu.

2. Select the Printers and Other Hardware category.

3. Select Game Controllers in the Control Panel's icon area. The Game Controllers dialog window appears (see Figure 221-1).

Figure 221-1: The Game Controllers dialog window.

4. Click Add. The dialog window shown in Figure 221-2 appears.

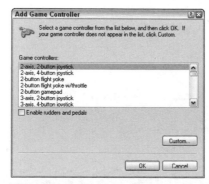

Figure 221-2: The Add Game Controller dialog window.

---

cross-reference

Game controllers are generally used with games. To learn about the proper way to install other software — including games — see Task 19.

note

Game controllers generally install in either a game port (which is a 15-pin connector) or a USB port.

note

A game controller with a USB connection can be plugged into your computer when your computer is turned on.

cross-reference

A joystick or controller may also be used as an accessibility device. See Part 15 for more on accessibility options within Windows XP.

5. Select the type of controller you are adding. If your controller is in the list, skip to Step 8. If your controller is not in the list, select the closest controller to the one you are installing and go to Step 8, or select Customize. The Customize button displays the dialog window in Figure 221-3.

Figure 221-3: The Custom Game Controller dialog window.

6. Fill out the custom information for your game controller. Make sure you give your controller a name. This name is displayed in the Game Controllers List in the Add Game Controllers dialog window.

7. Click OK to return to the Add Game Controller dialog window.

8. Select Enable Rudders and Pedals if your controller has a rudder or pedal.

9. Click OK to return to the Game Controllers dialog window with your new controller added.

10. Click OK to close the window.

caution

You can only assign one controller to any given game port. If your machine only has one game port, you might receive a message stating you need to remove or reassign an existing controller in order to add a new controller.

note

If you no longer have a specific game controller on your computer, you should remove it from the Installed Game Controllers list in the Game Controllers dialog window. Just select the controller and then click Remove. You are then prompted to verify that you want to remove the controller.

note

If your controller came with installation instructions or an installation disk, you should follow the instructions provided with it.

Task **222**

Setting Up Two Monitors

Windows XP Pro can support multiple monitors at the same time. If you have two video cards in your computer, you can connect two separate monitors. You can then set your desktop to use both monitors. You can even have your desktop spread across both. This allows you to display different information onto each. The following steps show you how to configure Windows XP to work with the two monitors.

1. From the Start menu, select Control Panel.

2. Select Appearance and Themes.

3. Select Display. The Display Properties dialog window appears.

4. Select the Settings tab if it isn't already selected. The dialog window in Figure 222-1 appears, which shows the settings for the current monitor. The Display setting as well as the Screen Resolution and Color Quality settings all apply to the first monitor.

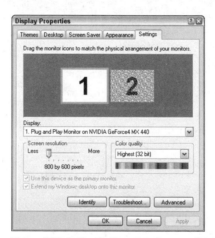

Figure 222-1: The Settings tab for your display's properties.

5. Click the Monitor icon for the second monitor (the white box in the dialog with the number 1). The settings for the second monitor are displayed. If you are not sure which monitor is the first and which is the second, you can click on the Identity button. This displays a number on the monitor that is currently selected, as shown in Figure 222-2.

6. Select the monitor you want to use as the primary monitor. What is considered the default window is determined by this choice. The default window is where most programs will start. It is also where the start screen and other login screens are displayed when you turn on your computer. You make this selection by checking the Use This Device as the Primary Monitor option. If the monitor is already selected as the primary monitor, this selection is disabled.

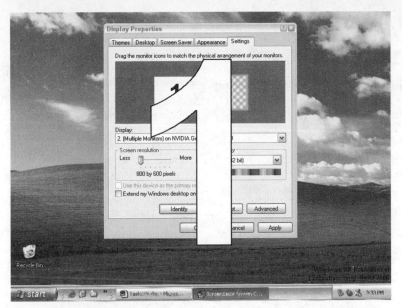

Figure 222-2: Identifying a monitor.

note

If you want the second monitor to be the primary monitor, you can select the option as shown in Step 6 of this task. If you also want this monitor's content to appear to the left of the second monitor's content, you can drag the icon in the Settings tab to the left of the first icon.

7. On the second monitor, select the Extend My Windows Desktop onto This Monitor option. This allows the second monitor to act as a continuation of the first. The option is disabled on the primary monitor's settings but is enabled on the secondary monitor.

8. Position the monitor icons relative to each other. You can drag and drop the icons in the upper area of the Settings tab. Where you place the icons determines how you drag items from one monitor to another. For example, if you want to drag items from one monitor to the other by moving to the left or right side of your screen, place the Monitor icons next to each other as shown in Figure 222-1. If you want to drag items from one monitor to the other by going to the top or bottom of the screen, place the icons above or below each other.

9. Click OK to save the settings you've selected and to close the dialog window.

note

Windows XP supports up to 10 monitors.

Uninstalling a Device

The longer you have your computer, the more likely you will want to upgrade a device. Before taking a device out of your computer, you should make sure you uninstall it. Even if you are planning on replacing the device with a different device of the same type, you should first run through the steps that follow to let Windows XP know that the original device is being removed.

The following steps show you how to open the Device Manager, as well as how to review some of the settings for your hardware:

1. Select Control Panel from the Start menu.

2. Select Performance and Maintenance.

3. Select System. The System Properties dialog window appears.

4. Select the Hardware tab in the System Properties dialog window.

5. Click on the Device Manager button in the Device Manager section. A Device Manager window similar to Figure 223-1 appears. This dialog lists the different types of hardware that are in your computer.

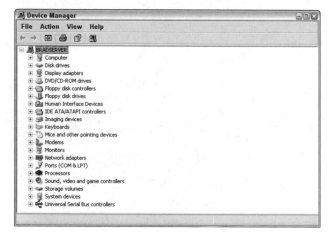

Figure 223-1: The Device Manager.

6. Double-click on a device type or click the plus sign next to the device type. The items for that device type appear, as shown in Figure 223-2.

cross-reference

You should be logged in as an administrator account type in order to remove a device. Task 213 explains how to set account types.

note

You should not remove the hardware device until after you have uninstalled it as shown in this task.

cross-reference

Although it is simple to unplug a USB device, you should still uninstall the device first.

cross-reference

This task shows you how to remove the device. If software was installed with the device, you may want to remove it as well. Task 20 shows you how to remove software from your computer.

cross-reference

See Task 217 for more on using the Device Manager.

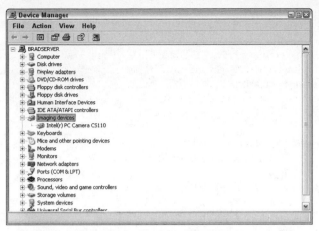

Figure 223-2: An expanded list of devices (imaging devices in this case).

7. Right-click the device and select Uninstall from the pop-up menu. A dialog appears that asked you to confirm you really want to uninstall the selected device. For example, Figure 223-3 shows the dialog that is displayed when removing a digital video camera from the computer.

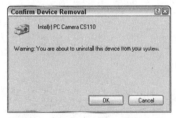

Figure 223-3: A confirmation message for removing a device.

8. Click OK. The device is uninstalled, and you are returned to the Device Manager window. Your hardware has now been uninstalled.

9. Close Device Manager.

10. Remove the device. If the device is a USB plug-and-play device, you can simply remove it at this point. If it is not, you should first turn off your computer before removing the device.

tip

You can also uninstall USB devices by clicking on the Safely Remove Hardware icon in the system tray, selecting the device from the list shown, and following the instructions provided.

Part 18: Creating a Simple Network (LAN)

Task 224: Setting Up Your Own Network

Task 225: Configuring Your Computers for the Network

Task 226: Sharing a Printer

Task 227: Accessing a Shared Printer

Task 228: Sharing Files

Task 229: Accessing Shared Files

Task 230: Assigning a Drive Letter to a Shared Folder

Task 224 Setting Up Your Own Network

With PC prices coming down, the number of homes that have more than one computer is increasing. And if you have more than one computer, it won't be long before you're asking questions like, "Isn't there a way I can get to the file on the other computer's hard drive?" or "How can I print something from this computer on that computer's printer?" The answer to these questions, and many others, is a local area network (LAN). The cost and complexity of creating your own LAN has come down dramatically in recent years, so now almost anyone can do it.

<div class="tip">

tip

Some computers have Ethernet adapters built in when you buy them. Check your computer before you spend the money on a new one.

</div>

<div class="tip">

tip

Another option is to get a switch instead of a hub. You can also find switches that act as a router, allowing you to connect in your cable/DSL modem. Switches are a more sophisticated technology that provide better performance across your network. Their price has come down so that they are competitive with hubs and routers. If you have the extra cash, a switch is the way to go.

</div>

1. Purchase all the items you'll need:

   - An Ethernet adapter (also called a LAN card, network interface card, or NIC) for each computer. These are typically cards that are installed inside your computer's case, although you can buy adapters that plug into your USB port. This is the device that allows your computer to communicate on the network.

   - A network hub, shown in Figure 224-1, acts as the central switching station that all your computers are connected to. This is where all the connections are made.

   - If you have a cable or DSL modem, a router or switch is what you want. A router fills the role of a hub, while at the same time allowing you to hook up your cable/DSL modem to the network and share it with all the machines on the network.

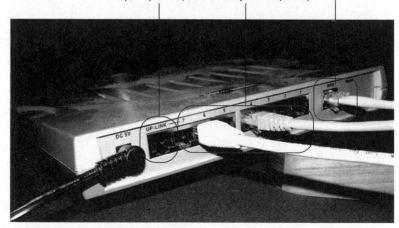

Figure 224-1: A network hub.

   - Ethernet cables (also called Category 5, Cat 5, or RJ-45). The connectors on each end look a lot like a telephone wire connector, but they are wider. You'll need one for each computer. The cables tie everything together.

2. Install the Ethernet adapters in each computer. Follow the instructions included with the adapter when you purchased it.

3. Plug the network hub/router's power cable into an outlet, and place the hub/router in a central location.

4. For each computer, plug an Ethernet cable into the Ethernet adapter (see Figure 224-2). Then run the cable from the computer to the network hub/router. Plug the other end of the cable into one of the numbered ports on your hub/router.

Ethernet Cable,
connected to hub/router   Ethernet adapter

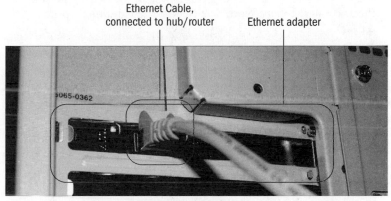

Figure 224-2: Ethernet cable plugged into the Ethernet adapter card, which is installed in a computer.

5. If you have a router and a cable/DSL modem, use an Ethernet cable to connect the cable/DSL modem to the special port on the router labeled WAN or Internet. The final configuration should look something like Figure 224-3.

6. Turn on all your computers. Go to each computer and run the Network Setup Wizard.

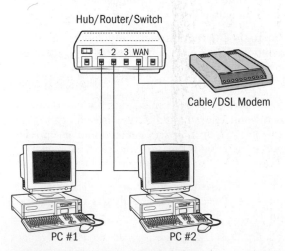

Figure 224-3: Making all the connections.

caution

It doesn't matter which port you plug your Ethernet cable into — except for one case. If one of your ports is labeled Uplink, avoid it. That port is used to connect additional hubs to the network.

cross-reference

To find out how to run the Network Setup Wizard, see Task 225.

Configuring Your Computers for the Network

O nce you have all the hardware set up (as described in Task 224), you're ready to configure each computer on the network so that it works correctly. Fortunately, once again, a Windows XP Wizard makes the task digestible.

1. Choose Start⇨All Programs⇨Accessories⇨Communications⇨ Network Setup Wizard. The opening page of the Network Setup Wizard appears. Click Next. The Before You Continue... page appears.

2. Click Next. The Select a Connection Method page appears (see Figure 225-1).

Figure 225-1: The Select a Connection Method page.

3. If you plan to connect to the Internet with a router connected to a cable/DSL modem, click the second option: This Computer Connects to the Internet through Another Computer on My Network or through a Residential Gateway.

4. If you plan to connect to the Internet through a modem on this computer, click the first option: This Computer Connects Directly to the Internet. The Other Computers on My Network Connect to the Internet through This Computer.

5. Click Next. If you have more than one connection on your computer (for example, a modem connection to the Internet as well as a network connection), the Select Your Internet Connection page appears. Click to select the connection that is the one you use to connect to the Internet. Click Next.

6. The Give This Computer a Description and Name page appears (see Figure 225-2). Chances are your computer already has a name. Type in a description if you like.

note

If you plan to access the Internet through a cable/DSL connection using a router, it doesn't matter in what order you configure the computers on your network. However, if you plan to access the Internet through a modem, you can share that modem connection with other computers on your network. To do that, first be sure that the computer with the modem has its Internet connection set up properly. Then run the Network Setup Wizard on that machine first, before you run it on the rest of the computers.

note

A *residential gateway* is another term for a *router*.

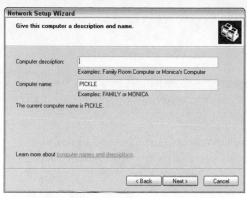

Figure 225-2: The Give This Computer a Description and Name page of the Network Setup Wizard.

7. Click Next. The Name Your Network page appears. Type a name for the workgroup that all your computers will be within.

8. Click Next. The Ready to Apply Network Settings page appears (see Figure 225-3). This page simply summarizes the settings you've chosen. If you wish to change anything, use the Back button to navigate to the appropriate page in the wizard and make the change.

Figure 225-3: The Ready to Apply Network Settings page of the Network Setup Wizard.

9. Click Next. Windows XP applies the settings. When it is done it displays the You're Almost Done... page. Click the last option: Just Finish the Wizard; I Don't Need to Run the Wizard on Other Computers. The final wizard page appears. Click Finish.

10. Repeat this process for each computer on your network.

cross-reference

Once your network is set up and working, you can share files (Task 228) and share a printer (Task 226).

Task 225

Task 226

Sharing a Printer

O ne of the benefits of connecting your computers together is that they can share resources — like a printer. Whether you have a photo-quality color printer or a cheap no-name printer that came with your computer when you bought it, sharing your printer with other computers on your network is pretty easy.

1. Go to the computer that is directly connected to the printer you want to share. Choose Start➪Control Panel. The Control Panel window appears (see Figure 226-1).

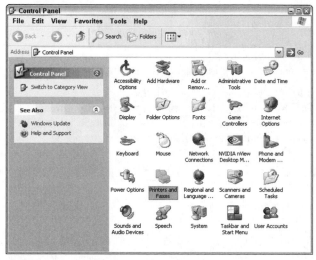

Figure 226-1: The Control Panel.

2. Double-click on the icon labeled Printers and Faxes (the icons are in alphabetical order). The Printers and Faxes window opens (see Figure 226-2). This window may contain a lot of things, including old printers that are no longer connected to your computer. The default printer is the one with a small, white check mark inside a black circle in the upper-right corner of the Printer icon.

cross-reference

Before you do this task, be sure you've run the Network Setup Wizard, described in Task 225.

tip

You may have a link directly to Printers and Faxes on your Start menu. If you do, you can select it directly without accessing the Control Panel.

note

If your Control Panel window doesn't look like Figure 226-1, it's probably because you are in Category view. To switch to Classic view, look at the options along the left side of the window. Under the heading Control Panel, click Switch to Classic View.

Figure 226-2: The Printers and Faxes window.

3. Right-click on the default printer. Choose Sharing... from the pop-up menu. The printer properties dialog appears, showing the Sharing tab (see Figure 226-3).

Figure 226-3: The Sharing tab of the printer properties dialog.

4. Click Share this printer. Enter a descriptive name for the printer. Use only letters and numbers — no spaces or punctuation.

5. Click OK. Your printer is now available to all the other computers on your network for printing.

caution

Keep this name relatively short — around 8 to 10 characters. This name is combined with the name of your computer to create what's called a UNC (Universal Naming Convention) name, which is limited in its length. Your computer name combined with your printer name should be no longer than 28 characters.

cross-reference

To find out how to access the shared printer from another computer on the network, see Task 227.

Task **227**

Accessing a Shared Printer

Once you've made a printer available to other computers on the network, all that's left is to tell the other computers where the printer is and how to use it.

cross-reference

To find out how to make a printer available to other computers on the network, see Task 226.

tip

You may have a link directly to Printers and Faxes on your Start menu. If you do, you can select it directly without accessing the Control Panel.

note

If your Control Panel window doesn't look like Figure 227-1, then it's probably because you are in Category View. To switch to Classic View, look at the options along the left side of the window. Under the heading Control Panel, click Switch to Classic View.

1. Go to the computer that is directly connected to the printer you want to share. Choose Start➪Control Panel. The Control Panel window appears (see Figure 227-1).

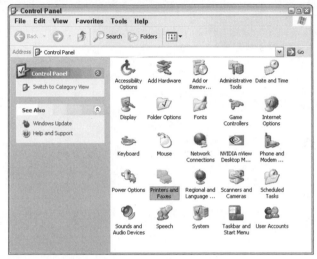

Figure 227-1: The Control Panel.

2. Double-click on the icon labeled Printers and Faxes (the icons are in alphabetical order). The Printers and Faxes window opens (see Figure 227-2).

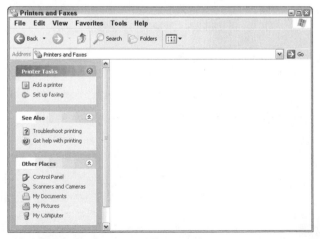

Figure 227-2: The Printers and Faxes window.

3. Along the left side of the window, under the heading Printer Tasks, click the Add a Printer link. The Add a Printer Wizard appears.

4. Click Next. The Local or Network Printer page appears (see Figure 227-3). Click A Network Printer, or a Printer Attached to Another Computer.

Figure 227-3: The Local or Network Printer page of the Add a Printer Wizard.

5. Click Next. The Specify a Printer page appears. Select Browse for a Printer.

6. Click Next. The Browse for Printer page appears (see Figure 227-4). In the Shared Printers list box, find the printer you shared.

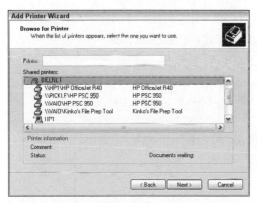

Figure 227-4: The Browse for Printer page of the Add a Printer Wizard.

7. Click Next. The wizard is complete. Click Finish.

note

The printer in the Shared printers list of the Browse for Printer page will appear in this form: \\COMPUTER\PRINTER, where COMPUTER is the name of the computer the printer is attached to, and PRINTER is the name given to the printer, when it is shared.

Sharing Files

In the days before networks were common, if you needed to access some files on a different computer, you got out your trusty floppy disk, copied the files, and brought them back to your computer. It was called *sneakernet*. Today, fortunately, we have networks that are a little more sophisticated and don't require all those annoying steps. In this task, you'll find out how to share a folder full of files so that other computers on the network can access it.

1. Choose Start➪My Computer. Double-click the icon representing your hard drive. Browse through your folders and subfolders to locate the folder you'd like to share with others on the network.

2. Right-click on the folder to share. Choose Sharing and Security from the pop-up menu. The folder Properties window appears (see Figure 228-1).

Figure 228-1: The folder Properties window.

3. Click Share This Folder.

4. In the Share Name text box, type the name you wish to give the folder when other computers access it.

cross-reference

Before you do this task, be sure you've run the Network Setup Wizard, described in Task 225.

tip

You can't share individual files, only folders. Of course, you can always create a new folder and put a single file in it and share that folder.

note

The default value in the Share Name text box is the name of the folder on your hard drive. You might want to give it a more descriptive name for those who access the folder from other computers.

5. If you like, type a comment in the Comment text box.

6. Click Permissions. The Permissions window appears (see Figure 228-2). Decide what permissions you want to give to other users. Your choices are as follows:

   - *Full Control.* They can do anything they want here, just as if they were working with a folder on their own computer.

   - *Change.* They can change files and subfolders, but they can't delete them.

   - *Read.* They can view the files, but they can't change them.

Figure 228-2: The Permissions window.

7. Click OK on the Permissions window.

8. Click OK on the folder Properties window.

Task 229 Accessing Shared Files

When the files are shared, Windows XP makes it pretty easy for you to find and work with them. Just as My Computer allows you to access all the features of the computer in front of you, so My Network Places makes available all the shared resources of the computers on your network.

1. Choose Start⇨My Network Places. The My Network Places window appears (see Figure 229-1).

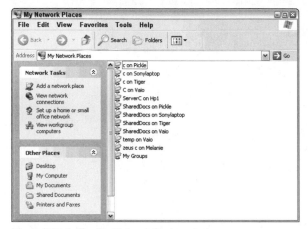

Figure 229-1: The My Network Places window.

2. Look through the folders listed here. If you see the folder you want to access, double-click it.

3. If you don't see the folder in the My Network Places window:

   a. Along the left side of the window, under Network Tasks, click View Workgroup Computers. All the computers in your workgroup appear (see Figure 229-2).

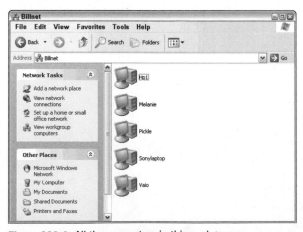

Figure 229-2: All the computers in this workgroup.

b. Double-click on the computer where the folder you want to access is located. All shared resources on that computer are displayed (see Figure 229-3).

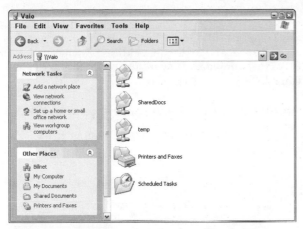

Figure 229-3: All the shared resources on the computer.

c. Double-click on the folder you want to access.

4. If you have permission to access the files in the folder, you see the files in the folder. If not, you may see a logon dialog where you can enter the username and password for a user that has access to the files you want. Or you may simply see an error message (see Figure 229-4).

Figure 229-4: Error message saying that the user does not have permission to access this shared folder.

cross-reference

If you still don't see the folder you want to access, it may not be shared or it may be shared using a name you don't recognize. See Task 228 to find out how to share a folder.

note

To fix this problem, you must change the way the file is shared on the computer where the folder resides. Task 228 shows you how.

Assigning a Drive Letter to a Shared Folder

Your floppy disk drive is usually drive A:. Your hard drive is usually drive C:. Your CD-ROM drive may be drive D:. Letters are assigned to every drive on your computer. You can make a shared folder on another computer look as if it were just another drive on this computer. This ensures that you get easy access to that folder from My Computer whenever you need it.

1. Choose Start⇨My Computer. The My Computer window appears.

2. Choose Tools⇨Map Network Drive from the My Computer window's menus (see Figure 230-1).

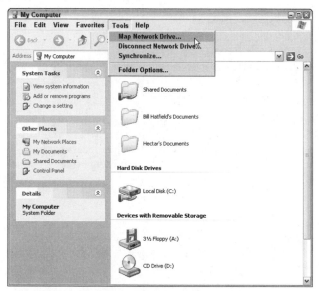

Figure 230-1: Choosing Map Network Drive from the Tools menu of the My Computer window.

3. The Map Network Drive window appears (see Figure 230-2).

Figure 230-2: The Map Network Drive window.

4. Click the Drive drop-down list box. All the available drive letters appear in the list. If any letters are already assigned to other shared folders, you'll see them in the list, along with the folder they are assigned to. Choose a drive letter.

5. Click Browse. The Browse for Folder window appears (see Figure 230-3).

Figure 230-3: The Browse for Folder window.

6. Locate the shared folder you want to map the drive letter to. Click to select it, and click OK. The address for the folder appears in the Folder text box.

7. Be sure Reconnect at Logon is checked.

8. Click Finish. The folder's contents appear in a window (see Figure 230-4). Notice the new drive letter at the top of the window.

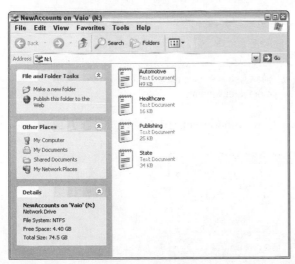

Figure 230-4: The contents of the shared folder, which is now mapped to the drive indicated.

9. Choose Start⇨My Computer. Verify that the new drive appears there.

tip

If you can, choose a drive letter that will remind you of what the shared folder contains. If it contains pictures, you could assign it to drive P:, for example.

cross-reference

If you still don't see the folder you want to access, then it may not be shared or it may be shared using a name you don't recognize. See Task 228 to find out how to share a folder.

note

The address in the Folder text box appears in the form \\COMPUTER\FOLDER, where COMPUTER is the computer's name and FOLDER is the shared folder's name.

Part 19: Taking Windows XP on the Road

Task 231: Conserving Power

Task 232: Putting Your Computer to Sleep: Hibernating

Task 233: Creating Multiple Dial-Up Connections

Task 234: Taking Files with You: Identifying Offline Files

Task 235: Using Offline Files and Resynchronizing

Task 236: Creating and Using a Briefcase

Conserving Power

Battery technology has noticeably lagged behind computing advances over the last 10 years. That's why it's important to do everything you can to squeeze as much power out of your laptop battery as possible. Even if you're on a desktop computer, you'll save money and feel greener about yourself if you tame your computer's appetite for wattage.

note

If your Control Panel window doesn't look like Figure 231-1, it's probably because you are in Category view. To switch to Classic view, look at the options along the left side of the window. Under the heading Control Panel, click "Switch to Classic View."

1. Choose Start➪Control Panel. The Control Panel window appears (see Figure 231-1).

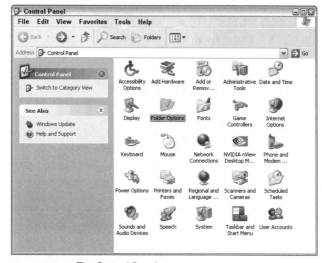

Figure 231-1: The Control Panel.

caution

Your window may look different from the one in Figure 231-2, especially if you are using a laptop. You may see different options for when the computer is plugged in verses when it is using battery power.

2. Double-click on Power Options (the icons are in alphabetical order). The Power Options Properties window appears (see Figure 231-2).

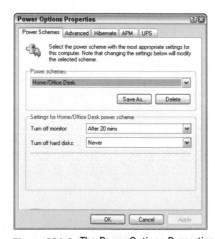

Figure 231-2: The Power Options Properties window.

3. The Power Schemes drop-down list box allows you to choose from several predefined setting schemes. When you choose a scheme, you see the settings below change.

4. If you don't find a scheme that you want, you can create your own scheme:

   a. Change the settings at the bottom of the window so that they are exactly as you want.

   b. Click Save As. The Save Scheme window appears (see Figure 231-3).

Figure 231-3: The Save Scheme window.

   c. Type a name for your scheme. Click OK.

   d. Your new scheme appears in the Power Schemes drop-down list box with the appropriate settings below.

5. To delete a scheme:

   a. Select the scheme you wish to delete from the Power Schemes drop-down list box.

   b. Click Delete.

   c. A window appears asking if you are sure you want to delete the scheme (see Figure 231-4).

Figure 231-4: Confirmation message for deletion of power scheme.

   d. Click Yes. The scheme is deleted.

tip

Often, laptop manufacturers provide their own utilities for viewing your current battery status and managing your power consumption. If your laptop includes such utilities, see your manufacturer's documentation for information on how to use them.

caution

You can sometimes set power management features in the BIOS of your computer. These settings can interfere with your Windows XP power management settings, so it's best to turn them off completely. BIOS settings are accessed when you first turn on or reboot your computer by pressing certain keys at just the right time. Check your computer's user manual to find out how to access these settings on your computer.

cross-reference

Another way you can save power is to put your computer into hibernation when you are not using it. To find out how to do this, see Task 232.

Putting Your Computer to Sleep: Hibernating

You've got five different applications going at once and you're getting lots of work done. Suddenly you hear the announcement: you have to turn off your laptop and prepare for landing. You don't want to lose track of where you are and what you're doing — what do you do? Hibernate! When you ask your computer to go into hibernation, it makes note of what applications you have open, the documents you're editing, and the changes you've made. Then it shuts the computer down. When you turn it on again, Windows XP just puts everything back exactly like it was, and you're ready to pick up where you left off. You can use this feature on your desktop computer, too.

1. Choose Start➪Control Panel. The Control Panel window appears (see Figure 232-1).

note

If your Control Panel window doesn't look like Figure 232-1, then it's probably because you are in Category view. To switch to Classic view, look at the options along the left side of the window. Under the heading Control Panel, click "Switch to Classic View."

Figure 232-1: The Control Panel.

2. Double-click Power Options (the icons are in alphabetical order). The Power Options Properties window appears (see Figure 232-2).

3. Click on the APM tab at the top of the window (see Figure 232-3). Advanced Power Management (APM) is a standard that most newer hardware supports. If your window looks like Figure 232-3, chances are your hardware does support it. Click the Enable Advanced Power Management Support check box.

4. Click the Hibernate tab. Click the Enable Hibernation check box (see Figure 232-4). Click Apply.

5. Click the Power Schemes tab. You should see an option at the bottom labeled System Hibernates. Use this drop-down list box to have your system automatically hibernate when the system is idle for a specified period of time.

caution

Your window may look different from the one in Figure 232-2, especially if you are using a laptop. You may see different options for when the computer is plugged in versus when it is using battery power.

caution

If your computer doesn't support APM, you can't use the hibernation feature.

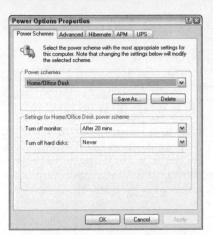

Figure 232-2: The Power Options Properties window.

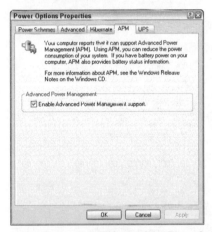

Figure 232-3: The APM tab of the Power Options Properties.

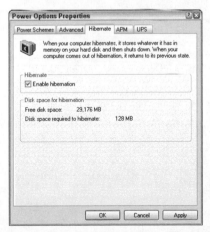

Figure 232-4: The Hibernate tab of the Power Options Properties.

cross-reference

For additional power management settings, see Task 231.

tip

Once hibernation is enabled, you can put your computer into hibernation any time you like by choosing Start➪Turn Off Computer. This displays a dialog that allows you to choose from several options. Click Hibernate.

Creating Multiple Dial-Up Connections

When you're on the road, you are often forced to use a dial-up connection to get to the Internet. The trouble is that you want to use a different, local phone number for each location you visit. So how do you juggle multiple dial-up connections? Windows XP makes it pretty easy.

1. Choose Start⇨Control Panel. The Control Panel window appears (see Figure 233-1).

note

If your Control Panel window doesn't look like Figure 233-1, then it's probably because you are in Category view. To switch to Classic view, look at the options along the left side of the window. Under the heading Control Panel, click "Switch to Classic View."

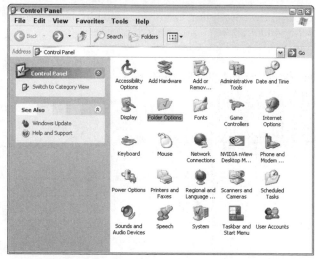

Figure 233-1: The Control Panel.

2. Double-click Network Connections. The Network Connections window appears (see Figure 233-2).

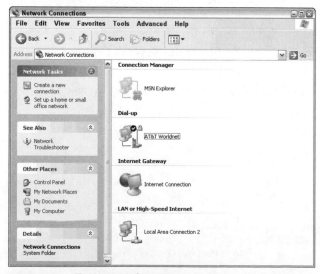

Figure 233-2: The Network Connections window.

Task **233**

3. Along the left side, under the heading Network Tasks, click Create a New Connection. The New Connection Wizard appears.

4. Fill in the appropriate values for your dial-up Internet connection using the wizard. When you have completed the wizard, a new icon representing the new dial-up connection appears in the Network Connections window.

5. Repeat Steps 3 and 4 as many times as you like to create all the new dial-up connections you need.

6. To use one of the connections:

   a. Double-click on the appropriate connection icon in the Network Connections window. The Connect window appears (see Figure 233-3).

Figure 233-3: The Connect window.

   b. Click Dial. Windows XP dials the number and attempts to make the connection.

7. To set one of the connections as the default:

   a. Right-click on the connection in the Network Connections window.

   b. Select Set as Default Connection from the pop-up menu.

cross-reference

For a detailed walkthrough describing how to use the Network Connection Wizard to create a new dial-up connection, see Task 134.

tip

You can drag your connections from the Network Connections window to your desktop. This creates a shortcut, which is easier to access whenever you need it.

tip

You can configure Windows XP to automatically attempt to connect to the Internet with the default connection whenever you launch your browser or email application. Here's how: In the Control Panel, double-click on Internet Options. In the dialog, click the Connection tab. Then select the Always Dial My Default Connection radio button.

Task 234

Taking Files with You: Identifying Offline Files

Whether you're going on a trip across the country or just taking a little work home with you at night, you need to transfer files to and from your laptop. But what if you copy the files to your laptop and then forget to copy them back in the morning? When the responsibility is on you to do the copying, it's really easy for you to lose track of which file is the latest version. It's also easy to accidentally start updating the wrong file.

Windows XP has a feature called Offline Files that helps make this process simpler. It lets you identify files that are on your desktop computer that you want to share with your laptop. Then it copies the files to your laptop and helps you keep the files in sync between the two computers at all times, no matter where they are updated.

cross-reference

If your laptop isn't connected to a network with the machine you want to share files, you can use a Windows XP Briefcase to synchronize files using a floppy disk instead. See Task 236 to find out how.

1. Connect your laptop to the network.

2. Disable Fast User Switching on the laptop:

   a. Select Start➪Control Panel.

   b. Double-click User Accounts. The User Accounts window appears.

   c. Click Change the Way Users Log On or Off.

   d. Click to clear the Use Fast User Switching check box.

   e. Click Apply Options.

3. Turn on the Offline Files feature:

   a. Select Start➪Control Panel.

   b. Double-click Folder Options. The Folder Options dialog appears.

   c. Select the Offline Files tab.

   d. Click to check the Enable Offline Files check box.

   e. Click OK.

note

If the Offline Files Wizard doesn't appear, it's because you (or someone!) has used the Offline Files feature on this computer before. The wizard only appears the first time you do this. If you wish to change the settings after that, follow the Steps 3a through 3c to access the dialog where they can be changed.

4. From your laptop computer, access the folder containing the files on your main computer that you'd like to work with. Right-click the folder and choose Make Available Offline from the pop-up menu. The Offline Files Wizard appears (see Figure 234-1).

5. Click Next. Read the information. Click to check Automatically Synchronize the Offline Files When I Log On and Off My Computer (see Figure 234-2).

Figure 234-1: The Offline Files Wizard.

6. Click Next. Read the information. Make sure both check boxes are checked (see Figure 234-3).

Figure 234-2: The second page of the Offline Files Wizard.

7. Click Finish. The wizard closes and a new icon appears on the desktop — Shortcut to Offline Files.

Figure 234-3: The third page of the Offline Files Wizard.

cross-reference

To find out how to use the Offline Files on your laptop when you are away and then resynchronize when you return, see Task 235.

Using Offline Files and Resynchronizing

cross-reference
Before you can begin using Offline Files, you have to identify what files on your desktop computer should be available to your laptop when you are off the network. See Task 234 to find out how to do that.

note
A conflict occurs if changes are made to a file on the laptop and, at the same time, changes are made to the same file on the desktop computer. When this happens, the computer doesn't know which one it should use, so it asks you with this dialog. You can choose to use the version of the file on the laptop, use the one on the desktop, or save them both. Unless you know exactly what you're doing, save them both and look at them yourself to see what was changed in each.

tip
You can click the View buttons on the Resolve File Conflicts dialog to view the two documents and see what changes were made to each.

Once you've identified the files you want to share between your desktop computer and your laptop, you're ready to begin using the files. Since the files are actually copied to your laptop, working with them is as fast and efficient as working with any files on your laptop's hard drive. And the biggest benefit is that you can now disconnect your laptop from the network and go away from the office to work. When you return, you can resynchronize, and both computers are automatically up-to-date!

1. Log off your laptop and turn it off.

2. Disconnect your laptop from your network. Take it on the plane, take it to a park, or take it home.

3. To work with the Offline Files, simply double-click Shortcut to Offline Files on your desktop. The files and folders inside are all available to you to change as you normally would.

4. When you return to the office, reconnect to the network, turn on your computer, and log on. The files are automatically synchronized with the files on your desktop computer.

5. If there are problems, you may see the Resolve File Conflicts dialog (see Figure 235-1). This dialog appears only when there is a conflict for a particular file. While resynchronizing, it may come up several times if several files have conflicts.

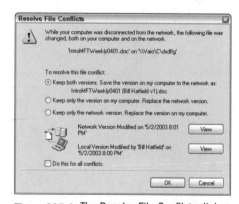

Figure 235-1: The Resolve File Conflicts dialog.

6. Select one of the options on the Resolve File Conflicts dialog and click OK. Do the same for any additional Resolve File Conflicts dialogs.

7. Once the files are synchronized again, you are free to make changes to the files on the laptop or on the desktop.

8. After making a change to an Offline File on the laptop, right-click on the changed file and choose Synchronize (see Figure 235-2). The file is immediately synchronized with the desktop. When you make changes to an Offline File on your laptop while connected to the network, it's a good idea to synchronize often.

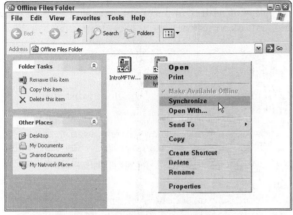

Figure 235-2: Synchronizing an Offline File while connected to the network.

note

If you create a new file in the Offline Files folder, that new file will be added to the desktop computer when you resynchronize. Likewise, if you delete one of the Offline Files, that file will be deleted on the desktop when you resynchronize.

caution

It's important that you try to avoid situations where you make changes on your laptop while offline and someone else makes changes at the same time to the files on your desktop computer. If this happens, you'll see a dialog informing you of the situation the next time you synchronize. You'll have a choice to use the laptop's version of the file, the desktop's version, or save them both using different names.

Task **236**

Creating and Using a Briefcase

If you have files on your desktop computer that you want to take on the road with you or files you just want to take home to work on there, you can do it with Offline Files (described in Tasks 234 and 235). That is, you can do it with Offline Files *if* you can connect your laptop to the same network your desktop computer is connected to. If, for some reason, you can't do that, then there's another method: the Briefcase. The Briefcase is a low-tech approach to keeping files synchronized between two computers. You use a floppy disk to hold the files you want to transfer between your main computer and your laptop. And when you're done, you use a floppy disk to transfer them back. It isn't fancy — but if you need it, it works well!

tip

Of course, the limitation with a floppy disk is that you can't have files bigger than 1.44MB. However, Briefcases aren't limited to floppy disks. You can use a Zip disk, a Jaz disk, or virtually any other removable media.

tip

If you have more files than will fit in one disk, simply repeat Steps 1 through 7 as often as necessary to move all the files you need in several different Briefcases. Be sure to give each Briefcase a unique name.

1. Insert a formatted floppy disk into your disk drive.

2. Choose Start⇨My Computer. Double-click the floppy disk drive. The floppy disk window appears.

3. Right-click inside the window. Choose New⇨Briefcase from the pop-up menu. A new Briefcase appears. Right-click the Briefcase and choose Rename from the pop-up menu. Type an appropriate name. Hit Enter.

4. Double-click on the Briefcase. You see the Welcome to the Windows Briefcase dialog (see Figure 236-1). Read the information provided. When you're done reading, click Finish. The dialog disappears and you see the open, empty Briefcase window.

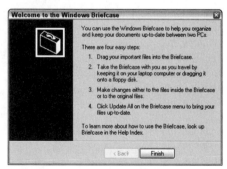

Figure 236-1: The Welcome to the Windows Briefcase dialog.

5. Locate files you want to add to take with you and have available on the laptop. Drag and drop them into the Briefcase. The original file remains where it is, and a copy is made in the Briefcase (see Figure 236-2).

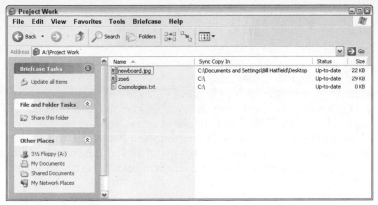

Figure 236-2: A Briefcase with several files in it.

6. When you've finished adding all the files to the Briefcase you want, eject the disk and put the disk in the floppy drive of your laptop. Choose Start⇨My Computer. Double-click the floppy disk drive. The floppy disk window appears.

7. Move the Briefcase to your laptop's hard drive, just as you'd move a folder. Now you can work with and update the files as you see fit.

8. When you return to the office, move the Briefcase back to the floppy disk and put the floppy disk into your desktop computer.

9. Choose Start⇨My Computer. Double-click the floppy disk drive. The floppy disk window appears.

10. Right-click the Briefcase and choose Update All from the pop-up menu. All the files you changed on your laptop are updated on your desktop computer.

cross-reference

To find out how to move a folder, see Task 25.

caution

Don't move the individual files from the floppy to your laptop hard drive. Move the Briefcase, and all the files inside come with it.

Part 20: Maintenance and Optimization

Task 237: Checking Your Hard Drive for Errors

Task 238: Defragmenting Your Hard Drive

Task 239: Cleaning Up Your Hard Drive and Making Room

Task 240: Adding and Removing Windows Components

Task 241: Removing an Application

Task 242: Cleaning Up Your Desktop

Task 243: The Ultimate Undo: System Restore

Task 244: Creating a Restore Point

Task 245: Configuring System Restore

Task 246: Backing Up Your Files

Task 247: Restoring Files from a Backup

Task 248: Updating Your System with the Latest Patches and Add-Ons

Checking Your Hard Drive for Errors

Athunderstorm causes an erratic electrical current to come to your house. Your wife stumbles over your computer cable and knocks it out of the wall. These and many other events can cause your computer's hard drive to lose its place when reading or smear the ink when writing. In short, hard drive errors are a fact of life that's difficult to avoid. But Windows XP includes a utility to look for hard drive errors and either fix them or section off the bad parts so they aren't used anymore.

1. If you have applications open on your computer, close them all.

2. Choose Start⇨My Computer. The My Computer window appears.

3. Right-click on your hard drive icon, and choose Properties from the pop-up menu. The hard drive Properties window appears (see Figure 237-1).

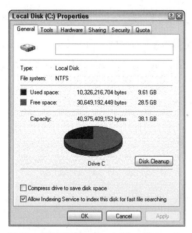

Figure 237-1: The hard drive Properties window.

4. Click the Tools tab (see Figure 237-2).

5. Click Check Now in the Error-Checking section. The Check Disk window appears (see Figure 237-3).

6. Click to check both the Automatically Fix File System Errors check box and the Scan for and Attempt Recovery of Bad Sectors check box.

7. Click Start.

tip

One way to avoid many of the causes of hard drive errors associated with erratic power is to purchase a *line conditioner*. This device helps smooth out the spikes and troughs in the electricity. An even better (but more expensive) solution is a Universal Power Supply (UPS), which does an even better job of smoothing out the power and even acts as a battery if the power goes out, giving you time to shut down your computer normally.

caution

Beware — this process can take time! Be sure you've got an extra 15 to 30 minutes free.

note

It's a good idea to check your disk every now and then. However, if your hard drive is formatted as FAT32, it's more important to do it on a regular basis. FAT32 is more prone to hard drive errors than NTFS. You can find out if you hard drive is FAT32 or NTFS by looking at the General tab of the hard drive Properties dialog (see Figure 237-1). It's at the top, labeled File System.

8. You may see a dialog telling you that it needs exclusive access to some of the files on the hard disk and asking if it can schedule a disk check for the next time you restart (see Figure 237-4). Click Yes and restart your computer.

Figure 237-2: The Tools tab of the hard drive Properties window.

Figure 237-3: The Check Disk window.

cross-reference

It's also a good idea to defragment your hard drive on a regular basis. To find out how to do that, see Task 238.

9. Windows XP walks through five stages in scanning your hard disk: files, indexes, security descriptors, file data, and free space. Any errors are fixed automatically and reported.

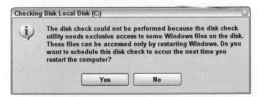

Figure 237-4: Message asking if you want to schedule a disk upon restart.

Task 238

Defragmenting Your Hard Drive

From your perspective, your files may look neat and tidy, organized into folders and subfolders as appropriate. But under the covers, the physical organization of the information on the disk can get jumbled and disorganized as you use your hard disk, save new files, change files, and delete old files over time. The practical upshot of this is that when you open a file, it sometimes takes a lot longer than it should to find where all the pieces are stored on the hard drive surface. This leads to a general slowing down of everything in Windows XP. Fortunately, you can fix this problem by asking Windows XP to *defragment* your hard drive. The defragmenting process is like cleaning out your closet — all those things that were just thrown in there haphazardly are all carefully reorganized and placed where they should go. It's a good idea to defragment your hard drive once a month. That way you can be sure you are keeping your system healthy and fast.

cross-reference

Before you begin this process, it's a good idea to clean up your hard disk (see Task 239) and check your hard disk for errors (see Task 237).

caution

Defragmenting your hard drive can take a very long time. It's probably best to begin it when you leave work for the day or when you go to bed at night. If you do, it might be done by morning.

1. Close all the applications running on your computer. Also disable any virus protection programs you have running in the background.

2. Choose Start⇨My Computer. The My Computer window appears.

3. Right-click on your hard drive icon, and choose Properties from the pop-up menu. The hard drive Properties window appears.

4. Click the Tools tab (see Figure 238-1).

Figure 238-1: The Tools tab of the hard drive Properties window.

5. Click the Defragment Now button. The Disk Defragmenter window appears (see Figure 238-2).

6. Click to select the hard drive you wish to defragment at the top of the window.

tip

It's best not to use your computer for other tasks while Disk Defragmenter is running. However, if you decide you need to use your computer, you can click Pause on the Disk Defragmenter window and click Resume later to continue.

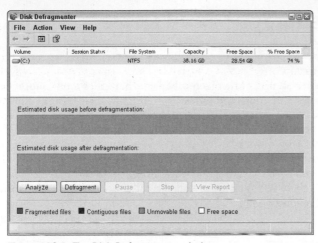

Figure 238-2: The Disk Defragmenter window.

7. Click Analyze. This causes Defragmenter to look at the hard drive and see how messy it is. It then makes a recommendation (see Figure 238-3) whether you should defragment now or not.

Figure 238-3: Recommendation to use Defragmenter.

8. Click Defragment. The recommendation dialog goes away, and Disk Defragmenter begins defragmenting your hard drive (see Figure 238-4). It informs you when it's finished.

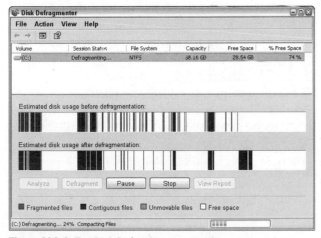

Figure 238-4: The Disk Defragmenter at work.

Cleaning Up Your Hard Drive and Making Room

There are a number of places on your hard drive where files tend to just build up over time, taking up more and more space and not really doing much for you. Microsoft has created Disk Cleanup to help you sweep up the nooks and crannies of your PC's hard drive.

1. Choose Start➪My Computer. The My Computer window appears.

2. Right-click on your hard drive icon and choose Properties from the pop-up menu. The hard disk Properties window appears (see Figure 239-1).

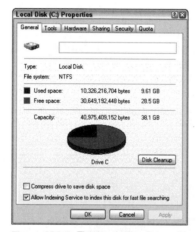

Figure 239-1: The hard drive Properties window.

3. Click Disk Cleanup. A progress window appears while Windows XP examines your system. Finally, the Disk Cleanup dialog appears (see Figure 239-2).

4. Click the check box beside all the items you want to delete. As you do, the Total amount of disk space you gain, right below the list box, increases.

5. Click the More Options tab (Figure 239-3). This tab just provides a convenient place to access other parts of the system that can help you increase the free space on your hard drive.

6. Click the Disk Cleanup tab. Click OK.

tip

You can also access the Disk Cleanup dialog by choosing Start➪All Programs➪ Accessories➪System Tools➪ Disk Cleanup.

tip

Click to select each item in the Files to Delete list box one at a time. When you do, read the text in the Description box at the bottom of the window. It gives you a very good description of what each item refers to. When you click the Recycle Bin, you can click View Files to see the actual files that would be deleted.

Figure 239-2: The Disk Cleanup dialog.

cross-reference

To find out more about adding/removing Windows components, see Task 240. To find out more about uninstalling programs, see Task 241. To find out more about System Restore, see Task 243.

7. A dialog asks you to confirm that you are sure you want to perform these actions. Click Yes.

8. Another progress dialog appears as the files are deleted. When it is done, you are returned to the hard drive Properties dialog. Click OK.

Figure 239-3: The More Options tab.

Task 240

Adding and Removing Windows Components

Windows XP comes with lots of little programs and utilities to make you more productive or to help you accomplish common tasks. But not all of those components are useful to everyone, so there's no point leaving useless programs on your hard drive just taking up space. In this task you'll find out how to remove Windows components you don't need and add in ones you want.

1. Choose Start⇨Control Panel. The Control Panel window appears (see Figure 240-1).

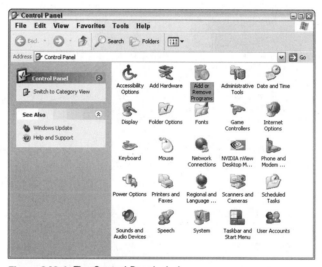

Figure 240-1: The Control Panel window.

2. Double-click Add or Remove Programs (icons are in alphabetical order). The Add or Remove Programs window appears (see Figure 240-2).

3. Along the left side of the window are several icons. Click Add/Remove Windows Components. After a brief pause, the Windows Component Wizard appears (see Figure 240-3). All the components available are listed in the Components list box, along with their size. Those with check marks beside them are already installed. Those that don't have check marks are not.

4. Click to check or clear the check box beside each item as required. As you do, the Total Disk Space Required, below the list box, changes appropriately.

5. If the Details button appears when you select an item in the list box, it means that the item has subitems that you can choose to install or not, individually. To do so, click the Details button. A new window appears with all the subcomponents in it. Click to check or clear the check box beside each item as appropriate.

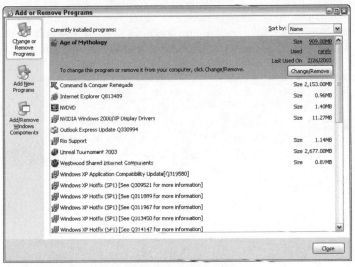

Figure 240-2: The Add or Remove Programs window.

6. Click OK when you are finished.

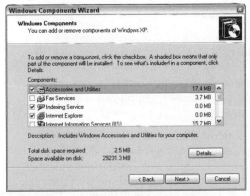

Figure 240-3: The Windows Component Wizard.

7. Click Next. The Configuring Components page appears as the appropriate components are installed or uninstalled. When it is complete, click Finish to close the wizard.

cross-reference

To find other ways to free up hard disk space on your computer, see Tasks 241 and 242.

Removing an Application

When you install an application, it puts files and settings in lots of different places. When you decide you want to remove (uninstall) a program, the best way to ensure you'll get it all removed is to use Windows XP's Add or Remove Programs tool.

1. Choose Start➪Control Panel. The Control Panel window appears (see Figure 241-1).

tip

You can reorganize the list so that the biggest hard drive space hogs are at the top. Just click on the Sort By drop-down list box in the upper-right corner of the window and choose Size. You can also sort by frequency of use and the date you last used the application.

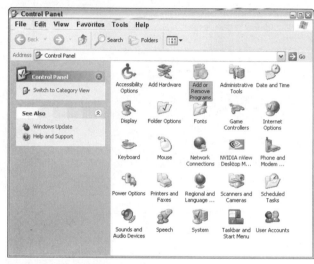

Figure 241-1: The Control Panel window.

2. Double-click Add or Remove Programs (icons are in alphabetical order). The Add or Remove Programs window appears (see Figure 241-2). Each item in the Currently Installed Programs list box represents a different program installed on your computer. For each there is an icon and a name. You also see, along the right, the amount of hard drive space each program takes.

3. Click to select the program you want to remove. If the item has separate Change and Remove buttons, click Remove. Otherwise, click Change/Remove.

4. At this point, the program's own uninstall is run — and each one is different. You will likely be asked to confirm that you do want to remove the program (see Figure 241-3). You may have to select exactly which components you want to remove and/or go through a wizard to answer additional questions. When it removes the program, you'll see a progress indicator as all the files and settings are uninstalled.

note

Some applications in the Currently Installed Programs list box show a link under the name when you click select them. The link says Click Here for Support Information. Clicking this link tells you who created the application and what version it is, and often provides links to the company's Web site.

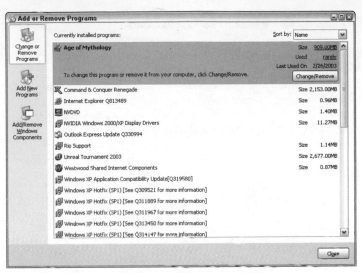

Figure 241-2: The Add or Remove Programs window.

5. When the uninstall is complete, you are returned to the Add or Remove Programs window, and the item representing the program you selected is removed.

Figure 241-3: Confirmation message for application removal.

cross-reference

To find out how to remove Windows components (like Notepad, Calculator, and other included utilities), see Task 240.

Task 242

Cleaning Up Your Desktop

Your Windows XP desktop is intended to be your workspace. Need a place to temporarily put something so you won't lose it? The desktop is there. It's always in front of you, and you can put files or shortcuts anywhere you like. The only trouble is, after a while, your desktop can have a tendency to get cluttered, full of stuff you no longer need. And the clutter makes it hard to find things you do care about. Following are steps to unclutter your desktop:

1. Right-click on a blank part of your desktop. Choose Properties from the pop-up menu. The Display Properties dialog appears.

2. Click the Desktop tab (see Figure 242-1).

tip

Of course, you can always delete any shortcut on your desktop you want by right-clicking and choosing Delete from the pop-up menu.

Figure 242-1: The Desktop tab of the Display Properties dialog.

3. Click Customize Desktop located just below the Background list box. The Desktop Items dialog appears (see Figure 242-2).

Figure 242-2: The Desktop Items dialog.

4. At the top of the dialog are four check boxes indicating whether or not each of these four items should appear on your desktop: My Documents, My Computer, My Network Places, and Internet Explorer. Click to check or clear these check boxes as you like.

5. Click Clean Desktop Now at the bottom of the dialog. The Desktop Cleanup Wizard appears.

6. Click Next. The Shortcuts page appears (see Figure 242-3). Here you'll see a list of all the shortcuts on your desktop that haven't been used in 60 days or more, and a date indicating when they were used. Click to check all those shortcuts you want to delete.

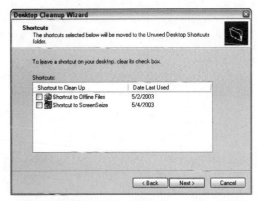

Figure 242-3: The Shortcuts page of the Desktop Cleanup Wizard.

7. Click Next. The wizard is complete. Click Finish.

8. Click OK on the Desktop Items dialog.

9. Click OK on the Display Properties dialog.

note

Remember that all four of these items are available anytime you need them on the Start menu. That's why Microsoft, by default, doesn't clutter your desktop with them.

note

Be aware — you are checking the shortcuts you want to _delete_, not the ones you want to keep!

cross-reference

For more information on customizing and using your desktop, see Tasks 42, 50, 51, 53, and 54.

The Ultimate Undo: System Restore

Have you ever installed something on your computer or messed it up in some way and wished you could just go back in time to yesterday morning or last week when everything was working just fine? Microsoft has granted your wish. No, they haven't invented a time machine, but they've done the next best thing: System Restore.

System Restore is a feature of Windows XP that takes a snapshot of your system on a daily basis. When something goes wrong, you can pick one of those snapshots from the past and Windows XP is reset back to the way it was then. System Restore doesn't mess with the files in your My Documents folder or your email, so you don't lose the work you've done since then. It resets the Windows XP operating system itself. System Restore, by default, sets a restore point (takes a snapshot) every day and every time you install something new. You can also set a restore point yourself, whenever you like.

In this task, you'll find out how to roll your system back to a restore point in the past.

1. Save what you are working on, and close any open applications.

2. Choose Start⇨All Programs⇨Accessories⇨System Tools⇨System Restore. The System Restore window appears (see Figure 243-1).

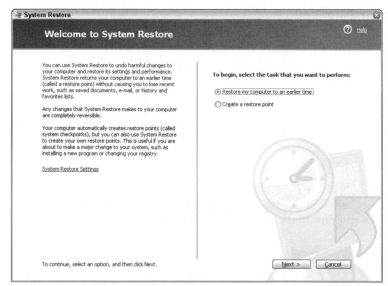

Figure 243-1: The System Restore window.

3. Click Restore my computer to an earlier time.

4. Click Next. The Select a Restore Point page appears (see Figure 243-2). In the calendar on the left, days that have restore points are bolded. Click the day to see the restore points for that day in the box beside the calendar.

cross-reference

To find out how to set a restore point, see Task 244. To find out how to turn off System Restore or change its settings, see Task 245.

caution

Although System Restore can get you out of some tough spots, don't depend on it to save you from a virus. Viruses typically infect files, and System Restore doesn't affect the files in your My Documents folder. You still need good virus protection software.

tip

Another way to access System Restore is to choose Start⇨ Help and Support. Then in the Help and Support Center window, click Undo Changes to Your Computer with System Restore.

tip

Click the < and > buttons at the top of the calendar to jump to a different month. Use the < and > buttons at the top of the box beside the calendar to jump to different days.

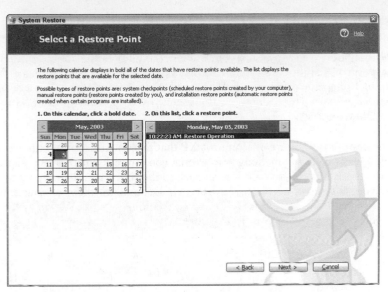

Figure 243-2: The Select a Restore Point window.

5. Click to select the day of the restore point you want to return to. Click to select the restore point in the box beside the calendar.

6. Click Next. The Confirm Restore Point Selection page appears.

7. When you are sure this is what you want to do, click Next. At this point the following events happen:

   • Windows XP is shut down.

   • A progress indicator window appears while the system is being restored.

   • After the system is restored, your computer is restarted.

   • If you normally log on when your computer first starts up, you'll have to log on now.

   • The System Restore Complete window appears, confirming what was just done.

8. Click OK. The system is restored and should work as it did on the date and time of the restore point you selected.

caution

Be aware that if you install new software on your computer and then use System Restore and select a restore point before the software was installed, the software will probably not work correctly. The only option is to reinstall the software.

tip

If the restore didn't produce the results you were hoping for, you can undo the restore and put yourself back where you were. To do this, just open System Restore again and you'll see a third option: Undo My Last Restoration.

Creating a Restore Point

A restore point is a snapshot of your Windows XP operating system configuration. If you are about to do something risky (or foolish), like fiddling with system files or spelunking in the System Registry, it's a good idea to set a restore point first, so that if you really screw things up, you can always put things back to the way they were.

1. Choose Start⇨All Programs⇨Accessories⇨System Tools⇨System Restore. The System Restore window appears (see Figure 244-1).

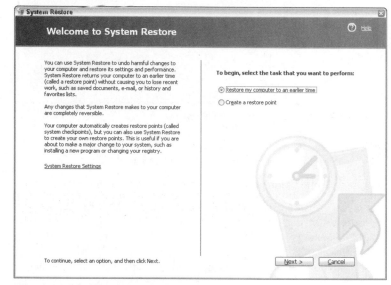

Figure 244-1: The System Restore Welcome window.

2. Click Create a Restore Point.

3. Click Next. The Create a Restore Point page appears (see Figure 244-2).

4. Type a description for your new restore point into the text box.

5. Click Create. The Restore Point Created page appears (see Figure 244-3).

cross-reference

To find out how to return your system to the way it was at a restore point in the past, see Task 243. To find out how to turn off System Restore or change its settings, see Task 245.

tip

Another way to access System Restore is to choose Start⇨ Help and Support. Then in the Help and Support Center window, click Undo Changes to Your Computer with System Restore.

note

Use a descriptive name that you'll be able to recognize when you look back at it later. Don't bother including the date and time — they'll be recorded automatically for you.

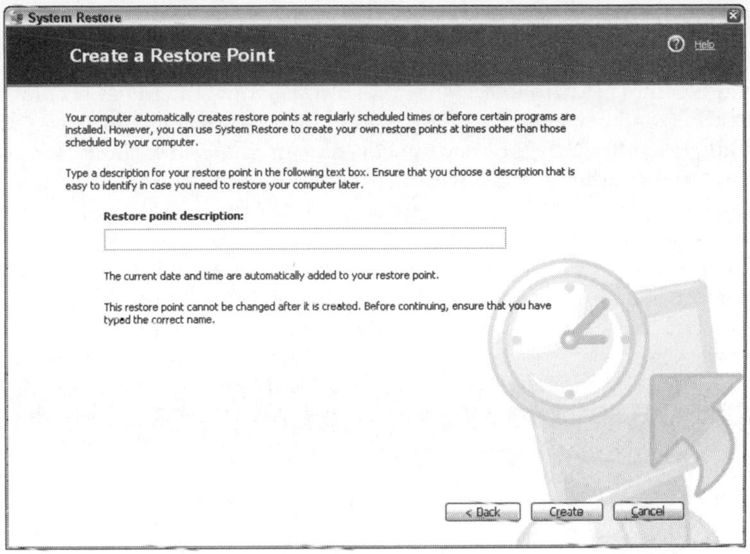

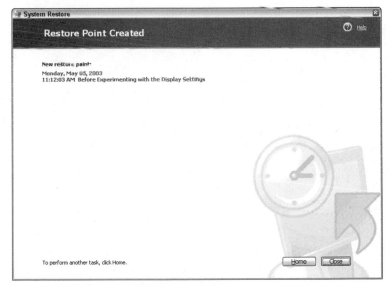

Figure 244-2: The Create a Restore Point page.

6. Click Close.

Figure 244-3: The Restore Point Created page.

note

It's not necessary for you to create a restore point before you install new software, system updates, or drivers. System Restore will automatically create a restore point when one of these events occurs.

Configuring System **Restore**

System Restore is worth its weight in gold when your system has become messed up and you need it to restore it to the way it was in more peaceful times. But remember: All that hocus-pocus, time machine stuff comes at a cost. And that cost is measured in hard drive space. In this task, you find out how you can change the amount of hard drive space System Restore uses and how to turn System Restore off completely.

cross-reference

To find out how to return your system to the way it was at a restore point in the past, see Task 243. To find out how to set a restore point, see Task 244.

tip

Another way to access System Restore is to choose Start⇨ Help and Support. Then in the Help and Support Center window, click Undo Changes to Your Computer with System Restore.

1. Choose Start⇨All Programs⇨Accessories⇨System Tools⇨System Restore. The System Restore window appears (see Figure 245-1).

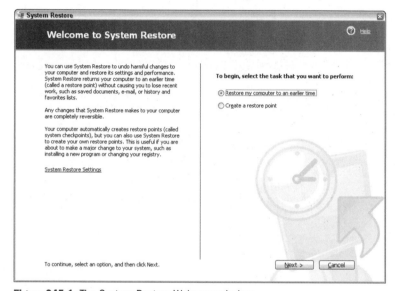

Figure 245-1: The System Restore Welcome window.

2. Click System Restore Settings. The System Properties dialog appears, on the System Restore tab (see Figure 245-2).

3. If you wish to turn off System Restore completely, check Turn Off System Restore.

4. If you only have one hard drive on your system, drag the Disk Space to Use slider to the left or right to change the amount of disk space to use on this drive for System Restore information.

tip

The less space you allocate to System Restore, the fewer restore points it can remember. At a lower setting, for example, the System Restore may only be able to keep the last few days of restore points.

5. If you have more than one drive connected to this computer,

    a. Click to select one of the drives listed in the Available Drives list box.

    b. Click Settings. The Drive Settings dialog appears.

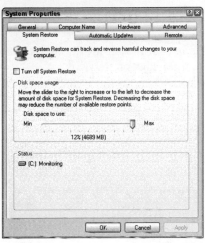

Figure 245-2: The System Restore tab of the System Properties dialog.

c. Drag the Disk Space to Use slider to the left or right to change the amount of disk space to use on this drive for System Restore information.

d. If this drive is not the system drive (where Windows XP is installed), you can turn off System Restore for this drive by clicking the check box at the top of this dialog.

e. When you are happy with the settings, click OK on the Drive Settings dialog.

6. Click OK on the System Properties dialog.

Backing Up Your Files

You've heard the mantra: Always back up your files. It usually comes out of the mouths of those who've had to learn the lesson the hard way — by losing data through accidentally deleting or overwriting a file or through a hard drive going bad. With Windows XP, there's no need to spend extra money on a backup program and no need to spend a lot of time figuring out how it works. Just follow the steps in this task.

1. Choose Start⇨All Programs⇨Accessories⇨System Tools⇨Backup. The Backup or Restore Wizard appears.

2. Click Next. The Backup or Restore page appears. Click Back Up Files and Settings.

3. Click Next. The What to Back Up page appears (see Figure 246-1). Select what information you want to back up.

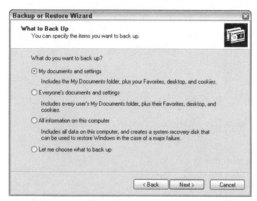

Figure 246-1: The What to Back Up page of the Backup or Restore Wizard.

4. Click Next. The Backup Type, Destination, and Name page appears (see Figure 246-2). Select values for each of the three items:

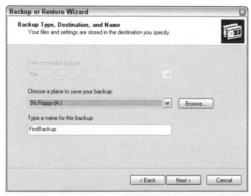

Figure 246-2: The Backup Type, Destination, and Name page of the Backup or Restore Wizard.

- The Select the Backup Type drop-down list box is only available if you have a compatible tape drive attached to your system. Otherwise, your only option is a file backup.

- The Choose a Place to Save Your Backup drop-down list box defaults to your floppy disk. Click Browse to choose the right location.

- The Type a Name for this Backup text box simply allows you to give the backup a name that you'll recognize in the future.

5. Click Next. The wizard is complete.

6. Click Finish. A Selection Information window appears as your system is examined. Then the Backup Progress window appears (see Figure 246-3). As files are copied, you are constantly updated with the progress.

Figure 246-3: The Backup Progress window – Copying files.

7. When the backup is complete, the Backup Progress window changes to give you a summary of the statistics of the backup and let you know whether it was successful (see Figure 246-4). Click the Report button if you want to see additional details.

Figure 246-4: The Backup Progress window when the backup is finished.

8. Click Close.

Task 246

note

If you choose the fourth option in Step 3 (Let Me Choose What to Back Up), you'll take a brief detour at this point to a page called Items to Back Up. Here you'll see check boxes beside every folder on your computer, and you can select exactly what to back up and what to leave behind. When you're done, pick up again at Step 4.

note

Although you can save the backup file to the same hard drive you are backing up, it definitely isn't the best insurance against the drive going bad!

note

You may find that the Backup utility is not installed on your computer. Some computer manufacturers who preinstall Windows XP don't include Backup. Check the Windows XP CD that came with your computer. You can also check with the manufacturer to see if you can get the utility. Or, borrow or buy a copy of Windows XP on CD, and the backup program is on there.

cross-reference

To find out how to restore files from a backup, see Task 247.

Task 247

Restoring Files from a Backup

Backups are no good unless you can restore your files from the backup when you need to. Fortunately, the same wizard that makes quick work of backups also makes restores just as easy.

cross-reference

To find out how to back up your files so that they'll be there for you to restore when things go wrong, see Task 246.

1. Choose Start➪All Programs➪Accessories➪System Tools➪Backup. The Backup or Restore Wizard appears.

2. Click Next. The Backup or Restore page appears. Click Restore files and settings (see Figure 247-1).

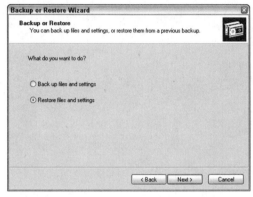

Figure 247-1: The Backup or Restore page.

note

If you have had a major failure and are restoring your files after buying a new hard drive, for example, you probably just want to select everything. However, if you accidentally delete a file that you want to retrieve, you can work through the folders and put a check mark beside just that file.

3. Click Next. The What to Restore page appears. The different backup files that have been created appear on the left. Double-click on each to see what's inside.

4. Click to check those folders you want to restore (see Figure 247-2).

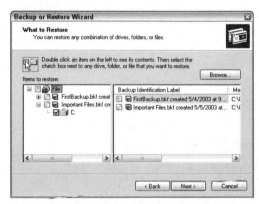

Figure 247-2: The What to Restore page of the Backup or Restore Wizard.

note

If you want to restore a file to a different location than it was when it was backed up, click Advanced on the final page of the wizard.

5. Click Next. The wizard is complete.

6. Click Finish. The Restore Progress window appears (see Figure 247-3).

Figure 247-3: The Restore Progress window – Copying files.

7. When the restore is complete, the Restore Progress window changes to give you a summary of the statistics of the backup and let you know if it was successful (see Figure 247-4). Click Report if you want to see additional details.

Figure 247-4: The Restore Progress window when the restore is finished.

8. Click Close.

Task 248

Updating Your System with the Latest Patches and Add-Ons

In the old days when you wanted to update your software, you went to the store and bought the newest version. Then the Web made it possible to download and install updates yourself. Today software is getting smarter, and Windows XP is smart enough to update itself. All you have to do is tell it which updates you want, and it downloads and installs them for you. It will even download new drivers appropriate for your hardware.

1. Get connected to the Internet, if you aren't already.

2. Choose Start⇨All Programs⇨Windows Update. The Windows Update window appears (see Figure 248-1).

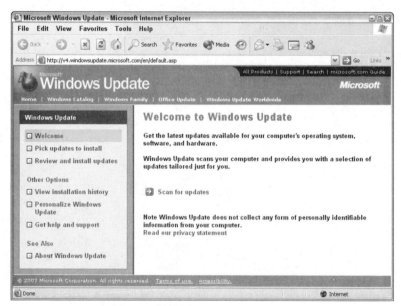

Figure 248-1: The Windows Update window.

3. Click Scan for Updates. After scanning, the header reads Pick Updates to Install.

4. Along the left side of the window under Pick Updates to Install are three options: Critical Updates and Service Packs, Windows XP, and Driver Updates. Click on each of these in turn (see Figure 248-2).

5. Scroll through the list of updates. As you find ones that you want to add to your system, click Add.

6. When you are done picking updates, click Review and Install Updates along the left. You are presented with a list of all the updates you added (see Figure 248-3). You can click Remove if you change your mind about any of them.

note

You may see a dialog asking if it's OK to download controls signed by Microsoft. In order to scan your system Microsoft needs to use software which is downloaded to your computer the first time you come to this page. If you do see such a dialog, click Yes.

note

Windows Update will automatically select critical updates for you to download — you don't have to pick them. If you don't want to download a critical update, click its Remove button.

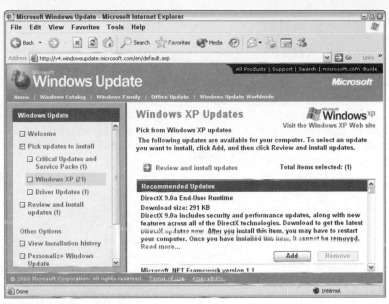

Figure 248-2: Picking updates to install.

7. Click Install Now.

8. The Windows Update dialog appears. Your updates are downloaded and installed. When installation is complete, you are informed. You may be required to restart your system after the updates are installed.

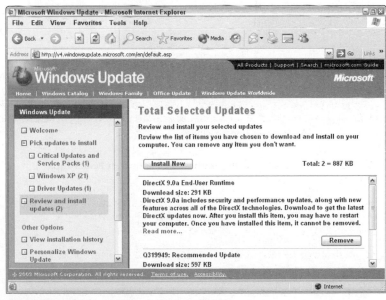

Figure 248-3: Reviewing recommended updates.

note

You may be asked to accept the terms of license agreements, and so on, depending on the updates you picked to download. If so, click Accept.

cross-reference

It's important to keep Windows XP up-to-date, but don't forget about the drivers for your hardware. For example, keeping your video driver up-to-date ensures that you'll be able to run the latest and greatest multimedia and game software. To find out how to do that, see Task 258.

Part 21: Troubleshooting

Task 249: Getting Detailed Information about Your Computer

Task 250: Getting Older Programs to Run in Windows XP

Task 251: Closing a Program That Stops Responding

Task 252: Finding Lost Files

Task 253: Fixing the Screen When It Doesn't Look Right

Task 254: Configuring Your System for Remote Access

Task 255: Using Remote Desktop

Task 256: Asking for Remote Assistance

Task 257: Providing Remote Assistance

Task 258: Updating Your Video Driver

Task 259: Reporting Errors to Microsoft

Task 260: Fine-Tuning Your System's Performance

Task 261: My Computer's Still Too Slow!

Task 249

Getting Detailed Information about Your Computer

What kind of processor do you have? How fast is it? How much memory do you have? How big is your hard drive? How much free space do you have? Whenever you call technical support or your help desk, it's the same thing — an endless barrage of questions that you can't answer. You think, "Look, if I knew all that stuff, what would I need you for?"

Now you can access the answers to any question you or a support person would ever care to ask, right at your fingertips.

note

Sometimes computer manufacturers will customize this help page so that it doesn't look the same. Often the same options are available, but they are just organized differently.

1. Choose Start⇨Help and Support. The Help and Support Center window appears (see Figure 249-1).

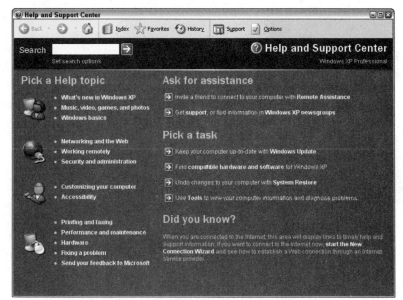

Figure 249-1: The Help and Support Center window.

2. Under the Pick a Task header, click the Use Tools to View Your Computer Information and Diagnose Problems link. Now you see the Tools page.

3. Along the left side of the window, under the heading Tools, click the My Computer Information link. The My Computer Information page appears.

4. Click on the View General System Information about This Computer link. After the information is collected, the My Computer Information — General page appears.

5. Click the Back button in the toolbar at the top of the window.

6. Choose among the other options to access whatever information you need. Here's a summary of what each page provides:

   - *View General System Information About This Computer.* Make and model of your computer and basic statistics like the processor, speed, hard drive size, amount of memory installed, and the version of Windows you're running.

   - *View the Status of My System Hardware and Software.* The hardware you have installed and whether current drivers are installed: video card, network card, sound card, and so on. Also provides your hard disks and memory status.

   - *Find Information about the Hardware Installed on This Computer.* Hard drive capacities and free space. Manufacturer, model, and driver are given for all the installed hardware.

   - *View a List of Microsoft Software Installed on This Computer.* Product ID numbers, programs run at startup, and crash information.

7. On the My Computer Information page, click the View Advanced System Information link. Choose among these options to access whatever information you need. Here's a summary of what each page provides:

   - *View Detailed System Information (Msinfo32.exe).* Runs a separate application that provides extremely detailed information about every aspect of your system.

   - *View Running Services.* The executable name, current status and how it starts up.

   - *View Group Policy Settings Applied.* Security information for the computer and each user.

   - *View the Error Log.* Date/time, application and error reported.

   - *View Information for Another Computer.* Requests the computer name and then opens a new window with these same options for viewing information about that computer.

8. When you are done, close the Help and Support Center window by clicking the red × in the upper-right corner.

tip

If you want to access MSInfo32, you can do it directly by choosing Start⇨Run, typing **MSinfo32.exe** into the Run window, and clicking OK.

cross-reference

For more on getting system information see Task 16.

Task 250

Getting Older Programs to Run in Windows XP

Microsoft put a lot of effort into making sure that older applications would run on Windows XP — and most do. However, some applications are a bit more finicky. For example, some applications expect to have a screen resolution of only 640 by 480 or expect the number of colors to be set to just 256. When the settings are higher than this, the programs may not run or may give an error stating that they are not compatible with the current operating system.

For these and other applications that have compatibility problems, Windows XP provides a feature called *Compatibility Mode*. When you set the Compatibility Mode for an application, Windows XP can simulate the older operating system the application was used to running on, be it Windows 95, Windows 98, or Windows ME. This makes the application more at home in its surroundings and more likely to run correctly. Following are steps to show you how to run a program in Compatibility Mode:

1. Right-click on the troublesome application's shortcut. From the pop-up menu, click Properties. The property dialog appears, on the Shortcut tab (see Figure 250-1).

Figure 250-1: The Shortcut tab.

2. Click the Compatibility tab (see Figure 250-2).

caution

There are some old applications that you shouldn't even try to run in Windows XP, like virus software, hard drive utilities, and troubleshooting tools. Instead, contact the maker of the software and see if they offer upgrade pricing to a Windows XP version.

tip

If you typically open the application through the Start menu, then use the Start menu as you normally would to navigate to the application's folder. When you get to it, instead of clicking it with the left mouse button, click it with the right mouse button. A pop-up menu appears. Choose Properties.

cross-reference

See Task 32 if you need information on locating a program on your hard drive.

Figure 250-2: The Compatibility tab.

3. Click to check the Run This Program in Compatibility Mode For check box. The drop-down list box is enabled.

4. Click the drop-down list box to view the options available:

   - Windows 95

   - Windows 98/Windows ME

   - Windows NT 4.0 (Service Pack 5)

   - Windows 2000

   Pick an operating system that the application is designed for or one that you know it runs well on.

5. If you know the application requires certain display settings, click all the check boxes that apply. The first two options simply switch to the resolution and number of colors specified before running the program. The last option, Disable Visual Themes, is useful if your menus, buttons, or title bars are fouled up when the old program runs because of the theme you selected. These display changes will be in effect only while you run the old program.

6. Click OK.

7. Run the application. If the application doesn't run correctly, repeat this process and choose different settings.

tip

Windows XP also provides a wizard to help you set the compatibility for programs. Run the wizard by selecting Help and Support from the Start menu. Then select the task Find Compatible Hardware and Software for Windows XP.

note

A program must be installed on your hard drive in order for any changes for compatibility to be maintained.

note

Few applications require specific display settings.

cross-reference

See Task 19 for more information on installing programs.

note

Compatibility modes cannot be set on Windows XP programs. While these programs may have a Compatibility tab in their properties pages, the values will all be disabled.

Task **251**

Closing a Program That Stops Responding

Sometimes, in Windows 95, 98, and ME, when an application went bad, everything froze up and you had to restart your computer. In Windows XP, fortunately, those situations are rare. Now an individual application may freeze up, but usually everything else stays on track. But how do you close an application that won't respond?

tip

Another way to access Task Manager is to hit Ctrl+Alt+Delete.

1. Right-click on an empty space in the taskbar, and choose Task Manager from the pop-up menu. The Task Manager window appears (see Figure 251-1). The Application tab shows all the currently running applications and their status.

Figure 251-1: The Task Manager window.

2. Try switching to the application:

   a. Click to select the application in the list.

   b. Click Switch To. The application's window should come forward and Task Manager minimizes itself.

   c. See if you can get the program to respond by clicking on the controls in the window or by entering text from the keyboard.

   d. If the program does not respond, click the Task Manager in the taskbar. The window appears again.

3. If that didn't work, it's probably time to kill the program:

   a. Click to select the application in the list.

   b. Click End Task. The End Program dialog appears (see Figure 251-2).

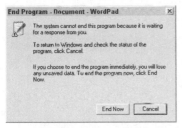

Figure 251-2: The End Program dialog.

   c. Click End Now. The program should be terminated and its entry in the Task Manager list removed.

4. If the program is not terminated, in the Task Manager, select Shut Down⇨Log Off.

5. If you cannot log off, then you are out of options: Hit the reset button on your computer.

note

When an application's status appears as Not Responding in the Task Manager, it's usually a good indication that something is wrong. However, it doesn't necessarily mean that the application is hung up permanently. Sometimes it just means that the application is waiting for input from you or that it is waiting for some other resource. If you just give an application a little time, it will either get what it needs or give up and go on.

cross-reference

One reason a program will stop responding is because it was designed for an older version of Windows. For more information on getting older programs to run in Windows XP, see Task 250.

note

On some computers you must hold the reset or on/off button in for 10 seconds or so for it to take effect.

Task **252**

Finding Lost Files

No matter how well you organize the files into folders on your hard drive, there will come a time when you just can't find what you're looking for. Fortunately there's a little utility in Windows XP called Search Companion that takes a description of your file and then it goes out looking for it. Does it sound like this could be man's best friend? You know it!

tip

If you don't like dogs, you can change your Search Companion Just click the Change Preferences link in the sidebar under the heading You May Also Want To... and then choose With a Different character.

1. Choose Start⇨Search. The Search Results window appears (see Figure 252-1). The Search Companion appears along the left side of the window, in canine form.

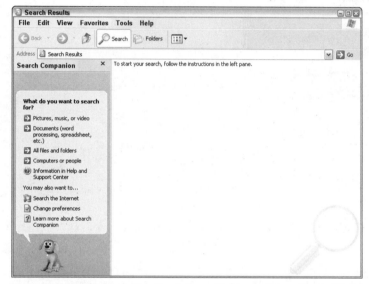

Figure 252-1: The Search Results window with Search Companion (arf!).

2. Click the All Files and Folders link. The window changes to allow you to enter search criteria (see Figure 252-2).

3. If you remember all or part of the file's name, enter that in the first text box.

cross-reference

For more on searching files and folders, see Task 32.

4. If you remember a unique word or phrase within the document, enter that in the second text box.

5. Click the Look In drop-down list box. Pick a place to search.

tip

The more specific you are about where the file is, the faster the search will be.

6. If you want to pick a more specific place to search, choose Browse... from the Look In drop-down list box. The Browse for Folder window appears. Find the folder you want and click to select it. Click OK.

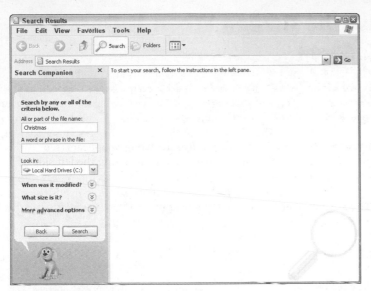

Figure 252-2: Enter your search criteria.

7. If you know when the file was last changed, click When Was It Modified? to give the information. If you have some idea what size the file was, click What Size Is It? to provide that information. Finally, clicking More Advanced allows you to identify what type of file it was, whether hidden or system folders should be searched, and so on.

8. Click Search. The Search Companion begins scratching, sniffing, and searching for your file. The results appear in the window (see Figure 252-3).

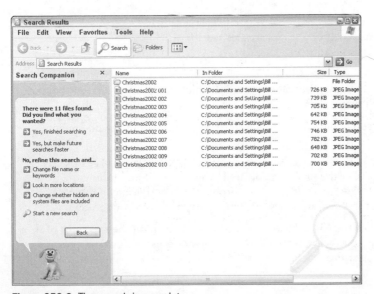

Figure 252-3: The search is complete.

note

If you didn't find what you were looking for, you can revise your search by clicking one of the links to change the filename, location, or the inclusion of hidden/system files. Or just click Start a New Search to start over.

Fixing the Screen When It Doesn't Look Right

Windows XP lets you change the resolution of your screen, as well as the colors you can use. You can customize its look and feel in a number of ways. Because every monitor is different, when you make changes to these settings, you can end up with a window that doesn't look right; it might be scrunched, have rounded sides, not centered, or any of a variety of problems.

Some of these issues can be fixed by using controls on your monitor. Others can be fixed by changing settings within Windows XP. If it simply needs to be expanded or shrunk, then you can use your monitor adjustments. Follow these steps to adjust your screen:

1. Right-click on an open area within the desktop. A pop-up menu appears.

2. Select Properties from the pop-up menu. The Display Properties dialog window appears.

3. Select the Settings tab if it is not already selected (see Figure 253-1).

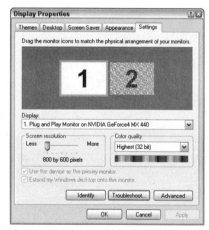

Figure 253-1: The Settings options in the Display Properties dialog window.

4. Select Troubleshoot. The troubleshooting options for the display screen appear, as shown in Figure 253-2. If one of these options matches the problem you are having, select it and follow the instructions on the window. If the problem is that the screen display is not aligned with the physical computer screen, continue to Step 5.

5. Click the Close button — the little × button on the top right of the window — to return to the troubleshooting window and return to the settings tab on the Display Properties dialog window.

cross-reference

Task 41 covered setting the resolution and colors for your monitor. When you change these values, they can cause the screen to be scrunched or not displayed properly. Changing the refresh rate as shown in this task may fix the problem.

note

Most monitors will let you stretch, squash, keystone-correct, and otherwise make minor adjustments to the display settings using buttons or dials on the face of the monitor.

tip

Picking a higher rate to have the screen refresh should result in a screen that flickers less.

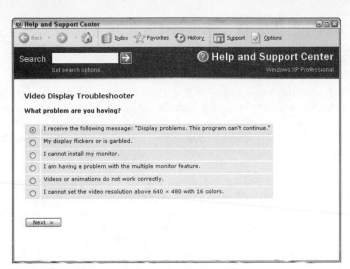

Figure 253-2: The screen setting troubleshooting options.

6. Click Advanced and select the Monitor tab. The dialog window shown in Figure 253-3 appears. As you can see in this dialog, the screen refresh rate is displayed within a drop-down list. Select a refresh rate.

Figure 253-3: The advanced monitor options.

7. Click Apply to set the new refresh rate. The screen may flash and refresh. A message appears, asking if you want to keep the new refresh rate.

8. If the screen looks better, click Yes on the message. If the screen doesn't look better, click No, or wait before you continue to try a new refresh rate. (Return to Step 7.) Keep picking a different refresh setting until you find one that works.

note

Check the box next to Hide Modes That This Monitor Cannot Display to eliminate a number of settings that won't work anyway.

tip

You may not find a refresh rate that is perfect at displaying what is on your screen. You should select the best match and then use any available controls on your monitor to make the final adjustments.

Configuring Your System for Remote Access

Windows XP provides two features that allow remote control of one PC from another PC: Remote Desktop and Remote Assistance.

Remote Desktop allows you to connect to another computer and operate it as if you were sitting in front of it. For example, if you are at home and want to do something on your office computer, you could connect from your home machine to your office machine using Remote Desktop. You could then operate your office computer remotely through your home computer.

On the other hand, if you are having trouble doing something on your computer, you can use Remote Assistance to give control of your computer to a friend or to a help desk support person using a different computer somewhere else. The support person could then operate your computer as if he or she were physically sitting at your keyboard.

To use either of these features requires that you make a couple of settings on your computer.

1. Right-click on My Computer and select Properties from the pop-up menu. If you don't have a My Computer icon on your desktop, you can find it on the Start menu. The System Properties dialog window appears.

2. Select the Remote tab in the Systems Properties dialog. The Remote options shown in Figure 254-1 appear.

Figure 254-1: The Remote options.

---

note

Remote Desktop is not available in Microsoft Windows XP Home Edition.

cross-reference

Task 255 walks through the basic steps of connecting with Remote Desktop.

note

You must be able to connect the two computers via the Internet or a local network in order to use these features.

note

You must be logged on with an administrator account in order to enable the features shown in this task.

3. Check the box in the Remote Assistance area if you want to be able to make requests for remote assistance. Checking this box allows you to give control of your computer to someone else.

4. Configure Remote Assistance settings. Click Advanced to display the Remote Assistance Settings dialog (see Figure 254-2). In this window you determine if remote users can only view — versus control — your computer, as well as determine the maximum length of time someone can be connected to your computer. Click OK when you have completed any changes to these settings.

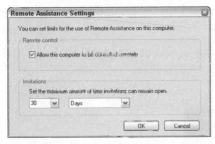

Figure 254-2: The Remote Assistance Settings dialog window.

5. Check the box in the Remote Desktop area of System Properties if you want to allow other users to be able to connect to your computer. For example, if you want to be able to connect to your office computer from home, you would need to check this box on your office computer.

6. Select which users can access this machine using Remote Desktop. Do this by clicking on the Select Remote Users button in the System Properties box and then adding users in the dialog window presented (see Figure 254-3). Users with administrator account types don't need to be added. Users with limited access do need to be added.

Figure 254-3: Adding users for remote access.

7. Click OK to save any changes and to close the System Properties dialog window.

note

To give a user account Remote Desktop access, the account must have a password.

caution

If you are going to allow for remote access to your computer, you should make sure that all the user accounts are using passwords. Task 214 shows you how to set passwords.

Task 255

Using Remote Desktop

I f you are using Microsoft Windows XP Professional, then you have a feature called Remote Desktop. The Remote Desktop allows you to access your computer from another computer. It allows you to connect to another machine and operate it as if you were sitting in front of it. For example, if you are at home and wanted to do something on your office computer, you could connect from your home machine to your office machine using Remote Desktop. You could then operate your office computer remotely through your home computer.

The following steps walk you through the basics of using Remote Desktop:

1. Select Start⇨All Programs⇨Accessories⇨Communications⇨ Remote Desktop Connection. The Remote Desktop Connection dialog window shown in Figure 255-1 appears.

Figure 255-1: The Remote Desktop Connection dialog window.

2. Click Options to expand the current dialog window to include a number of options you will need to complete (see Figure 255-2).

Figure 255-2: The Remote Desktop Connection dialog window options.

3. Enter the name of the computer you want to connect to, along with the user ID and its password in the appropriate fields. This must be a user on the named computer. If you are accessing a computer on a network domain, you'll need to enter the name of the domain as well.

cross-reference

Task 254 shows you how to configure your computer for using Remote Desktop.

note

You can set a number of different options in the Remote Desktop dialog (see Figure 255-2). This includes setting the display resolution and colors, the connection speed, which computer hears sounds, whether local printers are used, and more. You can look through the tabs in the dialog to see the various settings available.

note

Windows XP will remember the information you enter the next time you use Remote Desktop. You can also save the connection settings from the General tab of the Remote Desktop Connection dialog window. By default, the password will not be remembered. You can, however, check the Save My Password box to have it retained as well.

4. Click Connect. Remote Desktop attempts to connect to the computer you specified with the information you entered. If there is a problem, you are given an error message. If there are no problems, then your system connects to the remote machine and your screen changes to show the remote computer's screen. Figure 255-3 shows the results of connecting to a machine called hp400. The taskbar and desktop have changed to the remote machine's.

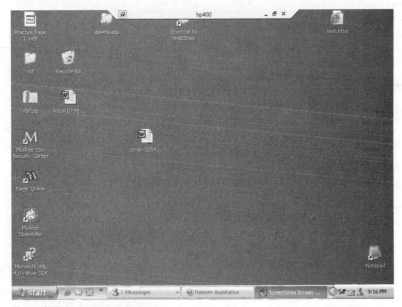

Figure 255-3: A remote desktop.

5. Use or view items on the remote machine.

6. Close the Remote Desktop window to end control. The message shown in Figure 255-4 appears, letting you know you can return to the remote machine later.

Figure 255-4: An exit message when closing the remote desktop.

tip

If you know the connection speed or type of connection that you are using, then you should set this in the Experience tab of the Remote Desktop Connection dialog window (see Figure 255-2).

cross-reference

See Task 16 to get information about a computer, including its name.

tip

You can minimize the Remote Desktop window as well as resize it. This allows you to access your local computer's desktop at the same time.

Asking for Remote Assistance

Have you ever called technical support or a help desk and had to be guided through a complex sequence of windows, mouse clicks, and reboots? Wouldn't it be great if you could just let *them* do it? Windows Messenger makes it possible with Remote Assistance. You can ask anyone in your Windows Messenger contacts list for remote assistance and, as you chat, you can allow them to view your screen or even take control of your computer.

1. If Windows Messenger isn't already open, open it by selecting Start⇨All Programs⇨Windows Messenger. The Windows Messenger window appears.

2. Double-click on the contact you want to request assistance from. The Conversation window appears. Click Ask for Remote Assistance in the I Want To... list in the sidebar along the right side of the Conversation window. Or you can just choose Actions⇨Ask for Remote Assistance from the menu.

3. Wait for the contact to accept your invitation. When he or she does, a dialog appears (see Figure 256-1).

Figure 256-1: Message box asking for your approval to let contact view your screen.

4. Click Yes. A Remote Assistance window appears (see Figure 256-2). In addition, if you had a picture background on your desktop, it disappears.

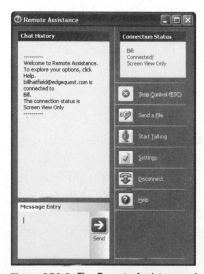

Figure 256-2: The Remote Assistance window.

cross-reference

Task 254 shows you how to configure your computer for using Remote Assistance.

note

Remote assistance works best if you are connecting with your contact over a network or over a high-speed Internet connection. However, if you have a 56K modem, you can still get reasonably good performance.

tip

If you are using a modem, to make things easier for the person helping you, it's best if you set your resolution to 800 by 600 and your colors to 16 bit or less. Do this before you ask for assistance. To find out how to change these settings, see Task 41.

note

Another way of requesting remote assistance is by selecting Start⇨Help and Support. In the Ask for Assistance area, click Invite a Friend to Connect to Your Computer with Remote Assistance. This displays options for remote assistance.

note

If the person you are requesting assistance from is not active, you will get a warning message. However, you can still make the request.

note

The more complicated your desktop is, the more information has to be sent to your contact (and the slower your screen will appear on his or her computer). Your desktop turns white to help reduce the amount of information sent.

5. Use the Remote Assistance window to chat with your contact now (not the Conversation window you opened initially).

6. If you want to communicate via voice using your microphone and speakers, click the Start Talking button.

7. If you like, you can allow your contact to take control of your computer:

   a. The contact must initiate the process. When he or she does, a window appears that informs you and asks if you want to allow it (see Figure 256-3).

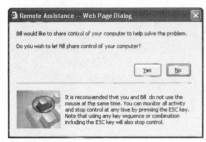

Figure 256-3: Message box asking if you want your contact to control your computer.

   b. Click Yes. The contact can now use his or her mouse and keyboard to control your computer.

   c. When you want control back, just hit the Esc key. Both you and your contact will see a dialog to let you know that the contact is no longer in control anymore.

8. To send a file to your contact:

   a. Click Send a File button. A window (see Figure 256-4) asks for the file's name and path. Click the Browse button. Use the Open dialog to locate the file you want to send and click Open. Click Send File in the window.

Figure 256-4: Sending a file.

   b. Your contact is informed that you are sending a file. Once the contact has selected a location for it, the file is sent. You are notified when the send is complete.

9. Click Disconnect or close the Remote Assistance window to end the remote assistance session.

cross-reference

If you want to take control of a different computer, you should use Remote Desktop as shown in Task 255.

tip

You can also use Remote Assistance to collaborate with someone on a project.

caution

While your mouse and keyboard may work when your contact is in control, it's best if only one of you is manipulating the controls at a time. If you want to do something, hit the Esc key and take control again. Then, if the contact likes, he or she can request control again.

cross-reference

To find out how to provide assistance to someone else, see Task 257.

Task 257 Providing Remote Assistance

Once you've learned your way around and gone through a few difficult experiences of your own, you might very well find yourself moving from student to teacher. When that happens, you may find people asking *you* for remote assistance!

1. If Windows Messenger isn't already open, open it by selecting Start⇨All Programs⇨Windows Messenger. The Windows Messenger window appears.

2. When one of your contacts requests remote assistance and you are not already having a conversation with him or her, you see a small window appear in the lower-right corner of your screen, just above your clock (see Figure 257-1).

Figure 257-1: Message box stating that someone is requesting remote assistance.

3. Click on the text inside the window. This causes a Conversation window to appear.

4. Click the Accept link. After making the connection, the Remote Assistance window appears. Wait a moment while the recipient confirms that he or she wants to allow you to view his or her screen. When the contact does, the contact's screen appears in the Remote Assistance window (see Figure 257-2).

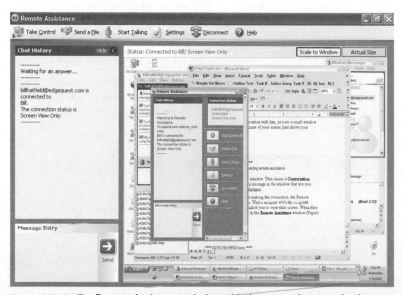

Figure 257-2: The Remote Assistance window with the contact's screen in view.

Task 257

5. Use the left side of the Remote Assistance window to chat with your contact now. Your conversation appears in the Chat History pane, while you type your messages in the lower Message Entry pane.

6. If you want to communicate via voice using your microphone and speakers, click the Start Talking button in the toolbar at the top of the window.

7. If you like, you can take control of your contact's computer:

   a. Click the Take Control button in the toolbar at the top of the window. A window appears on your contact's screen (which *you* can see now!), asking if the contact would like to share control with you.

   b. When the contact clicks Yes, you see a dialog informing you that you're in control (see Figure 257-3).

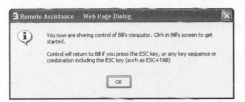

Figure 257-3: You are now in control!

   c. You can now move your mouse around on the contact's computer screen, control the contact's windows, and type text from your keyboard. When you are done, click the Release Control button.

8. If you want to get a closer look at a file, it is sometimes best to just ask your contact to send it to you. To receive a file sent to you:

   a. Ask your contact to start the process by clicking Send File on his or her Remote Assistance window. A window appears on the contact's screen asking for the file's name and path. The contact should click the Browse button, locate the file, and send it.

   b. You see a dialog on your window telling you that your contact is trying to send you a file (see Figure 257-4). Click the Save As button to view a Save As dialog. Here you can pick a location where the new file should be saved.

Figure 257-4: Message box stating that the contact is trying to send you a file.

   c. Once the file is saved, you see another dialog asking if you'd like to open the file now. Click Yes. The file is opened.

tip
You might have a tendency to want to close the big Remote Assistance window on your contact's screen. Don't! If you do, it will close the entire connection. Just minimize it by clicking the minimize button in the upper right corner of the window.

tip
It's best, especially if you are working over a modem connection, to take actions on your contact's computer as if you were moving in slow motion. Your screen will update slowly, but give it a chance to update as you do things to be sure everything is working as you expect.

cross-reference
To find out how to ask for remote assistance from a friend or business associate, see Task 256.

Updating Your Video Driver

A *driver* is software that helps Windows XP communicate with a piece of hardware connected to your computer. The video driver communicates with the video card inside your computer (where your monitor plugs in). This card is responsible for all the beautiful graphics and windows you see on your screen. Typically the driver that came with your computer will work just fine with your video card. But for some graphically intensive applications, like games, it's important to make sure that communication goes as smoothly as possible, so video card manufacturers are always updating their drivers to make them more powerful and more compatible with new games. If you have a game that won't work (or won't work very well) on your system, a good first step is to update your video driver.

1. Choose Start⇨My Computer. Along the left of the My Computer window, under System Tasks, click the View System Information link. The System Properties window appears.

2. Click the Hardware tab (see Figure 258-1).

Figure 258-1: The Hardware tab of the System Properties dialog.

cross-reference

For more information on using the Device Manager, see Task 217.

3. Click the Device Manager button. The Device Manager window appears (see Figure 258-2).

4. Look through the list for an item called Display Adapters. Click on the plus beside this item to open the list below it. You should see one item listed — your video card.

5. Double-click on your video card. The video card properties window appears.

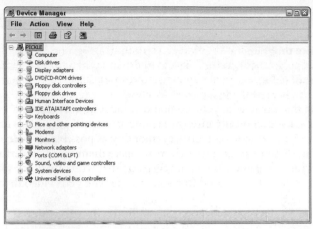

Figure 258-2: The Device Manager window.

6. Click the Driver tab (see Figure 258-3). Write down the name of the card at the top, the provider, the driver date, and the version information.

Figure 258-3: The Driver tab of the video card Properties dialog.

7. Connect to the Internet, open Internet Explorer, and locate your video card manufacturer's site. Look for a links to Support or Driver Downloads.

8. Check to see what the version of the latest driver for your video card is. If it is a number higher than the one you wrote down, you should download the new driver.

9. Follow the instructions on the Web site to download the driver to your hard drive and then install it on your computer.

---

tip

If you don't know the URL of the site, use Google or another popular search engine.

---

tip

Here are some Web sites for common video card manufacturers: nVIDIA: www.nVIDIA. com; ATI Technologies: www. ATITech.ca; SonicBLUE and Diamond Multimedia: www.s3.com; Matrox: www.Matrox.com; SiS: www.SiS.com, Trident Microsystems: www. tridentmicro.com; Cirrus Logic: www.Cirrus.com; Creative Labs: www.Creaf. com. If you need help finding your manufacturer's Web site, check out www. driverzone.com/ video.html.

---

note

If a new video driver still doesn't do the trick, check into upgrading to a new video card. You can usually get one that will run any game out there for a pretty reasonable price. Adding memory to your computer can also help.

Task 259

Reporting Errors to Microsoft

By default, when a program, or Windows XP itself, stops responding or reports an unexpected error, Windows XP asks if you'd like to send an error report to Microsoft detailing the problem. This information is collected and used to help fix errors as they are found and provides continuous feedback to Microsoft about what people are having trouble with in Windows XP. Of course, that doesn't help you with your immediate problem, but it does help Microsoft make future updates to Windows better. But participation in this error reporting is completely voluntary. In this task you'll discover how to turn error reporting on or off for certain applications or for all applications.

1. Choose Start⇨My Computer. Along the left of the My Computer window, under System Tasks, click the View System Information link. The System Properties window appears.

2. Click the Advanced tab (see Figure 259-1).

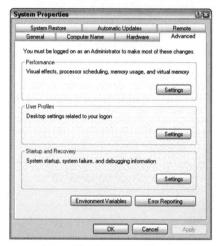

Figure 259-1: The Advanced tab of the System Properties dialog.

3. Click Error Reporting near the bottom of the dialog. The Error Reporting dialog appears (see Figure 259-2).

cross-reference

If you have a program that is not responding, see Task 251 to find out how to close it down.

cross-reference

If you do report errors to Microsoft, be sure you take advantage of the benefits of that by keeping Windows XP up-to-date. To find out how, see Task 248.

note

By default, the Enable Error Reporting option is chosen and both the Windows operating system and Program check boxes are checked. This means that whenever there's an error in either Windows itself or one of your other applications, Windows XP will prompt you to send an error report to Microsoft.

Figure 259-2: The Error Reporting dialog.

4. Click Choose Programs. The Choose Programs dialog appears (see Figure 259-3). Here you can choose to enable error reporting for all programs or just the ones you specify. You can use the list box at the bottom of the dialog, with its Add and Remove buttons, to identify specific applications where you want to stop error reporting.

Figure 259-3: The Choose Programs dialog.

5. Click OK.

6. If you wish to disable error reporting completely, click the Disable Error Reporting option shown in 259-2.

7. Click OK on the Error Reporting dialog. Click OK on the System Properties dialog.

Fine-Tuning Your System's Performance

In computers, performance refers to how fast Windows XP and your applications respond to your mouse clicks and keystrokes. There are a lot of things that can impact performance, and, usually, it's a balancing act. Sometimes fancy new features end up slowing things down. You have to decide if those new features are worth the trade-off. In this task, we show you how to adjust Windows XP so that it works the way you want.

1. Choose Start⇨My Computer. Along the left of the My Computer window, under System Tasks, click the View System Information link. The System Properties window appears.

2. Click the Advanced tab (see Figure 260-1).

Figure 260-1: The Advanced tab of the System Properties dialog.

note

In the list box that fills the lower half of the Performance Options dialog are a whole bunch of cool visual effects that add pizzazz to the Windows XP look and feel as you work with menus, buttons, and drop-down lists. However, each of these features slows your system down — some a little bit, some more.

tip

If you don't have a strong preference, your best option is probably Let Windows Choose What's Best for My Computer.

3. In the Performance section at the top of the dialog, click Settings. The Performance Options dialog appears (see Figure 260-2).

4. Click to select the option at the top of the dialog that best fits what you want to do:

   - *Let Windows Choose What's Best for My Computer.* Windows XP will look at how fast your computer is and then decide which features would slow it down too much and which ones wouldn't.

   - *Adjust for Best Appearance.* Choose this one if you don't care how slow your system crawls, as long as it looks good.

   - *Adjust for Best Performance.* If you're more interested in getting things done fast than seeing flashy effects, choose this one.

   - *Custom.* Choose this option if you'd like to use the check boxes in the list box to pick and choose which options to turn on and off.

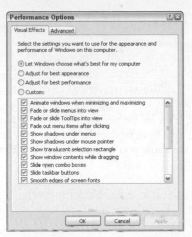

Figure 260-2: The Performance Options dialog.

5. Click Apply.

6. Click the Advanced tab (see Figure 260-3). These options are advanced settings that you won't typically have to change. If this is your primary computer, your settings for Processor Scheduling and Memory Usage should both be Programs. Only if this machine is a server would you change those options.

   The Virtual Memory section is used to decide how much hard drive space is set aside for Windows XP to use as "scratch paper" when it runs out of memory. Usually the default setting is fine.

cross-reference

If you're looking for more options for speeding up your computer, see Task 261.

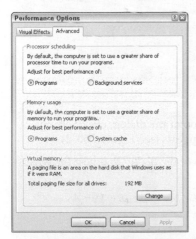

Figure 260-3: The Advanced tab of the Performance Options dialog.

7. Click OK on the Performance Options dialog. Click OK on the System Properties dialog.

Task 261

My Computer's Still Too Slow!

So your computer is running too slow. Is it time to buy a new one? Maybe. But before you break out the wallet, consider these tips for speeding things up at something short of the cost of a whole new computer:

1. Check your Performance Options as described in Task 260. Choose the Adjust for Best Performance option (see Figure 261-1).

Figure 261-1: The Performance Options dialog – Put the pedal to the floor.

2. Defragment your hard drive as described in Task 238 (see Figure 261-2).

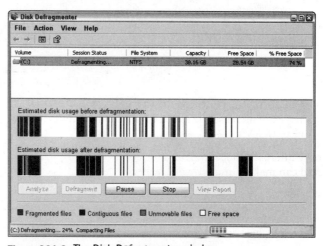

Figure 261-2: The Disk Defragmenter window.

caution

Disk Defragmenter can have a big impact on performance, but it can also take a long time. So set it going when you finish up at night. It might be done by morning!

3. Free up some space on your hard drive. Lots of useless clutter can slow you down — especially if it means your system drive (the one where Windows XP is installed) is almost full.

   - See Task 241 to find out how to remove programs from your hard drive you no longer use with the Add or Remove Programs window.

   - See Task 239 to find out how to use the Windows XP Disk Cleanup program (see Figure 261-3).

Figure 261-3: The Disk Cleanup program.

   - See Task 240 to find out how to remove Windows XP components and utilities that you don't need using the Windows Component Wizard.

4. If you use your computer mostly to surf the Web and get email, then it's not so much the speed of your computer that you need to worry about — it's the speed of your Internet connection. If you are using a dial-up modem, check into getting a cable or DSL connection.

5. If you're still not getting the performance you want, one of the cheapest ways to really increase the speed of your computer is to buy additional memory (RAM).

6. If your primary interest in speeding up your computer is for games, a new video card can make a dramatic difference.

cross-reference

To find out how to get connected to the Internet with cable or DSL, see Task 135.

caution

There are lots of different kinds of memory, and different computers have different requirements on exactly what kind to use and how much you can add. See your computer's user guide for that information.

tip

You don't have to buy a top-of-the-line video card to get much better performance from your games than you get with the video card that came with your computer. Usually you can get an excellent card that will work with virtually all new games for around a hundred dollars.

Index

A

accessibility
FilterKeys, 442–443
keyboard, On-Screen, 432–433
selecting layout, 434–435
Magnifier, 428–429
Narrator, 430–431
StickyKeys, 440–441
system font size, changing, 426–427
Utility Manager, 436–437
Accessibility Options (Control Panel)
FilterKeys, 442
StickyKeys, 440
Accessibility Wizard, usability features, selecting, 438–439
accessories
Calculator program, 408–409
scientific calculator view (Calculator program), 410–411
Sound Recorder, 420–421
mixing with, 422–423
Accessories, WordPad, launching, 252
activation, 6–7
Add or Remove Programs (Control Panel)
fax configuration, 416–417
installing software, 38–39
software, uninstalling, 520–521
uninstalling software, 41
Windows components, adding/removing, 518–519
Address bar, Internet Explorer, turning off, 326
address book. See contacts (Messenger); contacts (Outlook Express)
addresses. See also URLs (Universal Resource Locators)
email, adding contacts to Messenger, 293
Adjust for Best Performance option, 562
Advanced Attributes dialog, 68–69
Align to Grid (desktop icons), 106
alignment, WordPad, 264–265
always on top option, taskbar, 99
animated
mouse pointers, filename extensions, 116
Web graphics, 308

annotations, Picture and Fax Viewer, 148–149
Appearance and Themes (Control Panel)
desktop appearance, changing, 92–93
desktop background, selecting, 88–89
standard desktop icons, adding, 110–111
themes
creating, 96–97
selecting, 84–85
Web pages, adding to desktop, 112–113
applications. See software
Artist list (Windows Media Player), 171
attachments
email
file size considerations, 346
opening, 340–341
saving, 341
sending, 346–347
sending Web pages, 303
vCards, 364–365
Messenger
receiving files, 400–401
sending files, 398–399
newsgroup messages, 376
attributes, files, setting, 69
audio. See also music
Messenger, configuring in, 402–403
movies, adding to, 222–223
recording, 420–421
mixing, 422–423
sounds, assigning to events, 94–95
speakers, configuring, 468–469
streamed, defined, 180
system sounds, themes, 84
volume, setting, 14–15
Auto Arrange desktop icons, 106
auto-hiding, taskbar, 99
Automatic Updates, enabling, 34–35
AutoRun feature, installing software, 38

B

background
changing in Paint drawings, 137
desktop, replacing with image, 138
icons, troubleshooting creation problems, 134
selecting, 88–89
Backup or Restore Wizard
backing up files, 530–531
restoring files, 532–533
backups
creating, 530–531
restoring, 532–533
battery. See also power schemes, creating/deleting
conserving, 498–499
notebook computers, 5
turning hard drive off, 16
turning monitor off, 16–17
binary numbers, converting to (Calculator program), 414–415
bitmap files, 150
Black and White Picture or Text option, uses for, 130
blank home page, setting, 322
blocking contacts (Messenger), 397
BMP files, suitability of, 133
Briefcase, creating, 508–509
broadband Internet access, 286–287
browsers, Internet Explorer, setting as default, 325
browsing, Web sites with Internet Explorer, 296–297
Brush tool (Paint), 137
burning music CDs, 184–185
business cards (electronic)
address book, adding to, 366–367
creating, 362–363
sending, 364–365

C

Calculator program
scientific calculator view, 410–411
numbers, converting base systems, 414–415
statistical calculations, 412–413
trigonometric routines, 411
using, 408–409

camcorder, capturing video from, 204–205

Camera and Scanner Wizard, capturing photos from scanner, 130–131

CD Writing Wizard, 73

CD-ROMs, installing software from, 39

CD-RWs
    music CDs
        creating, 184–185
        duplicating, 186–187
    writing to, 72–73

CDs (music)
    copying to hard drive, 166–167
        legal issues, 167
    creating, 184–185
    duplicating, 186–187
    identification information, 168–169
    Windows Media Player, 164–165

Center option, desktop background, 89

chatting (Messenger), 394–395
    audio and video setup, 402–403
    display name, changing, 396
    files, sending, 398–399
    status, changing, 396

Classic Folders, setting in Folder Options dialog, 58

ClickLock (mouse), enabling/disabling, 114

clipboard, Print Screen key and, 132–133

clips
    deleting from movies, 203
    splicing into movies, 202
    splitting and combining, 210–211
    transitions between, 214–215
    trimming, 212–213
    Video Effects, adding, 216–217

clock
    displaying, 99
    setting, 10–11
    setting automatically, 12–13

closing, My Computer, 45

code. See programming code, saved Web pages

codecs, obtaining for DVD playback, 194–195

collaboration, Remote Assistance as conduit for, 553

collating copies, printing, 261

collections (Windows Movie Maker)
    clips
        splitting and combining, 210–211
        transitions between, 214–215
    deleting, 199
    importing files into, 200–201
    items, playback of, 201
    organizing, 198–199
    pictures, capturing from video, 206–207
    sound, adding to movies, 222–223
    still photos, adding to movies, 220–221
    Video Effects, adding, 216–217

color
    fonts, changing in WordPad, 263
    image annotations, 148–149
    Messenger fonts, changing, 397

Color Box (Paint), 137

color depth
    adjusting, 86–87
    defined, 86
    DVD playback errors and, 194–195
    icons, creating in Paint, 134

color schemes, selecting, 92

Common areas (Windows Explorer), displaying, 61

compression
    files, 74–75
    Zip files, 76–77
        adding to, 78–79

connections
    dial-up, creating multiple, 502–503
    small networks, configuring, 484–485

contacts (Messenger)
    adding, 392–393
    blocking, 397

contacts (Outlook Express)
    adding, 360
    addressing email with, 361
    creating, 360–361
    deleting, 361

Content Advisor, settings, 332–333

Control Panel
    Accessibility Options, 439
    Accessibility Options, FilterKeys, turning on, 442
    Accessibility Options, StickyKeys, turning on, 440

Add or Remove Programs, 38–39, 40–41

Automatic Updates, enabling, 34–35

color depth and resolution, adjusting, 86–87

Date and Time
    adjusting, 10–11
    setting automatically, 12–13

desktop appearance, changing, 92–93

desktop background, selecting, 88–89

Device Manager, opening, 466

dial-up connections, creating multiple, 502–503

Display Properties dialog, 16

game controllers, installing, 474–475

Guest accounts, creating, 446–447

keyboard options, setting, 118–119

monitors, multiple, configuring, 474–475

mouse
    customizing, 114–15
    customizing pointers, 116–117

notebook battery power, conserving, 498–499

notebook computers, hibernation, 500–501

regional settings, changing, 122–123

selecting themes, 84–85

sound schemes, selecting, 94–95

Sounds, Speech, and Audio Devices, 14

speakers, configuring, 468–469

standard desktop icons, adding, 110–111

themes, creating, 96–97

User Accounts
    adding passwords, 458–459
    changing icon for, 454–455
    changing passwords, 460–461
    changing type, 456–457
    creating, 448–449
    deleting, 450–451
    fast switching, 8–9
    locking computer, 18–19

removing passwords, 460–461
renaming, 452–453
Web pages, adding to desktop, 112–113
Windows components, adding/removing, 518–519
Windows Update, 36–37
cookies
blocking, effect of, 329
deleting, 320–321
Internet Explorer privacy settings, 328–329
Copy Options dialog, copying music CDs, 167
CPU, viewing information about, 33
Create Shortcut Wizard, 104–105
cropping, pictures, 146–147
currency, formatting, changing, 124–125
cursor blink rate, setting, 119
customizing
Details view, 56–57
files, 56–57
folders, 56–57
Help and Support Center, 24–25
Help and Support Center, Search Options, 26–27
Links bar (Internet Explorer), 314–315
mouse, 114–115
mouse pointers, 116–117
quick launch (taskbar), 100–101
Standard Buttons bar (Internet Explorer), 327
Standard toolbar (Windows Explorer), 60–61
Start menu, 102–103
taskbar, 98–99

D

Date and Time Properties dialog, displaying, 12
Date, Time, Language, and Regional Options (Control Panel), regional settings, changing, 122–123
day, setting, 10
decoders, obtaining for DVD playback, 194–195
defragmenting hard drive, 562
maintenance operation, 514–515
troubleshooting operation, 562

Deleted Items folder (Outlook Express), 355
emptying, 357
desktop
appearance, changing, 92–93
background, selecting, 88–89
file shortcuts, creating, 70–71
hiding all items, 107
icons, organizing, 106–107
images, replacing background with, 138
organizing, 522–523
shortcuts, adding, 104–105
Show Desktop icon, 105
standard icons, adding, 110–111
taskbar, customizing, 98–99
themes, selecting, 84–85
Web pages, adding, 112–113
Desktop Cleanup Wizard, 523
Details view
customizing, 56–57
files and folders, 55
pictures, 141
Device Manager
displaying, 33
hardware, uninstalling, 478–479
hardware status, checking, 466–467
video drivers, updating, 556–557
dial-up connections, creating multiple, 502–503
DIB files, 150
Did You Know section, Help and Support Center, 30
digital cameras, setting up, 128–129
directories. *See* folders
Disk Cleanup, hard drive maintenance, 516–517
display. *See also* monitor
adjusting problems with, 546–547
background, selecting, 88–89
themes, modifications to, 84
troubleshooting video driver problems, 556–557
Display Properties dialog
adjusting screen settings, 546–547
desktop, organizing, 522–523
displaying, 16
screen saver
locking computer, 20–21
selecting, 90
setting properties, 91

system fonts, changing size, 426–427
themes, selecting from, 84–85
Do Not Move Files to the Recycle Bin option, 65
documents
naming considerations, 254
Notepad
creating, 232–233
printing, 242–243
saving, 234–235
organizing, 235
pictures, inserting into (WordPad), 268–269
WordPad
adding objects, 268–269
changing object properties, 272–273
creating, 252–253
emailing, 276–277
formatting fonts in, 263
saving, 254–255
double-click speed (mouse), setting, 114
downloading
dangers of, 307
email stationery, 349
files from Web, 306–307
image editing software, 136
images from Web sites, 308–309
legal considerations, 307
music, 178–179
newsgroup attachments, 382–383
skins (Windows Media Player), 189
song lyrics, 175
sound effects, 222
Windows Media Player, 162
Windows Movie Maker, 192
drawing, pictures in Paint, 136–137
drive letters, assigning to shared folders, 494–495
DSL Internet access, 286–287
DVD, movies, playing, 194–195

E

editing, summary information (files), 69
effects (display), setting, 93
electronic business cards
address book, adding to, 366–367
creating, 362–363
sending, 364–365

Ellipse tool (Paint), 137
email
    addresses, adding contacts to
        Messenger, 293
    attachments
        opening, 340–341
        saving, 341
        sending, 346–347
    creating, 342–343
    forwarding, 344–345
    message rules, 368–369
    messages
        deleting, 355
        retrieving and viewing,
            338–339
    movies, sending, 228–229
    newsgroup posts, sending as
        email, 381
    Outlook Express, setup,
        336–337
    printing messages, 355
    replying to, 345
    sending, 343
    signatures, 352–353
    stationery, 348–349
        creating, 350–351
    Web pages, sending, 302–303
    Zip files, viruses and, 81
emoticons, 395
Enhanced Keyboard (On-Screen
    Keyboard), 434
envelopes, printing in
    WordPad, 259
Eraser tool (Paint), 137
Error Reporting feature, 558–559
events, assigning sounds to, 94–95
Explorer. *See* Internet Explorer;
    Windows Explorer
extensions. *See* filename extensions
extracting Zipped files, 78–79

F

fast switching
    locking computer and, 18
    user accounts, 8–9
FAT32 filesystem, compared to
    NTFS, 512
Favorites
    Help and Support Center
        adding Knowledge Base
            articles, 30
        creating list of, 28–29
        deleting items from, 28
        displaying, 24
        renaming items, 29

Internet Explorer, 310–311
    organizing, 312–313
faxes
    annotating with Picture and Fax
        Viewer, 148–149
    Fax Console, configuring,
        416–417
    sending, 418–419
filename extensions
    icons, 111, 135
    importance of, 48
    length of, 49
    mouse pointers, 116
    wave files, 94
    zip files, 77
filenames, printing, Notepad, 238
files
    accessing over networks,
        492–493
    attributes, 68
    backing up, 530–531
    compressing, 74–75
    copying, 50–51
    creating with Windows
        Explorer, 48–49
    deleting, 49
    Details view, customizing,
        56–57
    displaying in My Computer,
        44–45
    displaying in Windows
        Explorer, 46–47
    documents, organizing, 235
    downloading from Web,
        306–307
    email attachments, sending as,
        346–347
    Favorites, organizing, 312–313
    filename extensions
        icons, 111, 135
        importance of, 48
        length of, 49
        mouse pointers, 116
        wave files, 94
        zip files, 77
    formats, WordPad
        compatibility, 252
    global viewing options, setting,
        58–59
    hard drive defragmentation and,
        514–515
    icons, locations for, 111
    image file types
        converting, 150–151
        suitability for, 133

Messenger
    receiving, 400–401
    sending in, 398–399
moving, 52–53
music, searching for, 172–173
music format, Windows Media
    Player support, 182
Notepad, compatibility, 232
pictures
    organizing, 138–139
    reducing file size, 151
    preserving when deleting user
        accounts, 450–451
    printing to in WordPad, 261
    properties, displaying, 68
    Recycle Bin, recovering from,
        62–63
    renaming with Windows
        Explorer, 49
    restoring from backup, 532–533
    Search Companion, 544–545
    searching for, 66–67
    selecting multiple, 50
    sharing over networks, 490–491
    shortcuts, creating, 70–71
    temporary, Internet Explorer,
        deleting, 320–321
    timestamp, 11
    video, playing, 196–197
    viewing options, 54–55
    writing to CD-RW, 72–73
    zip
        adding to, 78–79
        creating, 76–77
        deleting, 78–79
        extracting, 78–79
        extracting all items, 80–81
        password protecting, 79
Filmstrip view
    files and folders, 55
    organizing image files, 138–139
filtering (Internet Explorer),
    objectionable material, 332–333
FilterKeys, using, 442–443
finding, email messages (Outlook
    Express), 358–359
firewalls
    automatic time and date
        setting, 13
    Messenger and, 399
first party (Internet privacy), 329
flag indicator (Outlook Express),
    usefulness of, 355
Folder Options dialog, global
    viewing options, setting, 58–59

Folder Properties window, pictures and, 139
folders
    assigning drive letters to, 494–495
    copying, 50–51
    creating with Windows Explorer, 48
    Deleted Items (Outlook Express), 355
    deleting, 49
    Details view, customizing, 56–57
    displaying in My Computer, 44–45
    displaying in Windows Explorer, 46–47
    document names and, 234
    documents, organizing, 235
    email messages (Outlook Express), 356–357
    Favorites, organizing files, 312–313
    global viewing options, setting, 58–59
    Internet Explorer Favorites, 310–311
    moving, 52–53
    picture files, organizing, 138–139
    Quick Launch, 101
    Recycle Bin, recovering from, 62–63
    renaming with Windows Explorer, 49
    saved Web pages, 300
    searching for, 66–67
    selecting multiple, 50
    Startup, 120–121
    viewing options, 54–55
    Web page behavior, enabling, 59
fonts
    changing system font size, 426–427
    display, setting size, 93
    email stationery, readability considerations, 350
    image annotations, 149
    Messenger, changing, 397
    Notepad
        changing, 240–241
        restrictions on, 233
    selecting, Help and Support Center, 24
    special characters, 263

using in Paint, 137
WordPad
    changing characteristics, 262–263
    compared to Notepad, 252
footers, creating, Notepad, 238–239
formatting, paragraphs in WordPad, 264–265
forwarding email, 344–345, 353
full mode, Windows Media Player, switching to skin mode, 195

G
game controllers, installing, 474–475
games, media files, adding to Media Library, 173
Genre list (Windows Media Player), 170
GIF files, 151
Go To menu (Windows Explorer), using, 47
Guest account, setting up, 446–447

H
hard drive. *See also* removable storage devices, adding and removing
    compressing, 74–75
    contents
        displaying in My Computer, 44–45
        displaying in Windows Explorer, 46–47
    defragmenting, 514–515, 562
    Disk Cleanup, 516–517
    errors, checking for, 512–513
    letters assigned to, 32
    line conditioner, 512
    movies, saving to, 226–227
    music CDs, copying to, 166–167
    Recycle Bin, settings for, 64–65
    space requirements for CD-RW writing, 73
    System Restore and multiple, 528
    turning off, 16
    UPS (Universal Power Supply), 512
hardware
    Device Manager, displaying, 33
    mouse, customizing, 114–117
    My Computer, 44–45
    small networks, installing, 482–483

status, checking, 466–467
    uninstalling, 478–479
    viewing in My Computer, 32
headers, creating, Notepad, 238–239
help, compared to troubleshooting, 23
Help and Support Center, 22–23
    customizing, 24–25
    Did You Know section, 30
    Favorites list, creating, 28–29
    Knowledge Base, accessing, 30–31
    Search Options, customizing, 26–27
    system information, obtaining, 538–539
    System Restore, accessing, 526
    troubleshooting options for display, 547
hexadecimal numbers, converting to (Calculator program), 414–415
Hibernate option, 5
hibernation (notebook computers), 500–501
hidden attribute (files), setting, 68
Hide Modes That This Monitor Cannot Display option, 547
Highlight Words on the Results Page, Search Companion (Internet Explorer), 298–299
hijacking, home pages by malicious Web sites, 323
History, Help and Support Center, displaying, 24
history (Internet Explorer)
    clearing, 318–319
    deleting items, 316
    displaying, 316
    number of days tracked, changing, 318–319
    sorting, 317
home page
    MSN as, 294–295
    setting, 322–323
    unauthorized changes to, 323
HTTP protocol, Outlook Express setup, 336–337
hyperlinks. *See* links

I
ICO files, creating in Paint, 134–135
icons. *See also* shortcuts
    creating in Paint, 134–135
    file locations, 111

icons. *See also* shortcuts *(continued)*
    filename extensions, 111
    selecting for application
        shortcuts, 109
Icons view, files and folders, 55
image editing software, Web
    sites, 136
images
    annotating with Picture and Fax
        Viewer, 148–149
    copying in Paint, 147
    as desktop background, 88, 138
    email stationery, creating,
        350–351
    file size, reducing, 151
    file types
        converting, 150–151
        suitability, 133
    icons, creating in Paint,
        134–135
    organizing, 138–139
    printing, 152–153
    resizing in Paint, 144–145
    saving from Web sites, 308–309
    scanning, 130–131
    viewing, 142–143
    Web, saving as backgrounds, 309
importing
    address books into Outlook
        Express, 360
    files into Windows Movie
        Maker collections, 200–201
    still photos into movies, 221
Inbox (Outlook Express)
    flag indicator, 355
    messages
        deleting, 355
        sorting, 355
    pane sizes, adjusting, 354
installation
    AutoRun feature, 38
    game controllers, 474–475
    printers, 470–471
    small network hardware,
        482–483
    software, 38–39
    Windows components,
        adding/removing, 518–519
    Windows Movie Maker,
        192–193
international settings, changing
    regional settings, 122–123
Internet
    accessing through broadband or
        DSL, 285–287

accessing with ISP account,
    284–285
clock, setting automatically, 13
connection speed
    considerations, 563
downloading music, 178–179
downloading pages, 306–307
Help and Support Center
    Did You Know section, 30
    Microsoft Knowledge
        Base, 26
LAN connections, 288–289
MSN accounts, creating,
    282–283
newsgroups
    connecting to, 372–373
    downloading attachments,
        382–383
    downloading multipart
        attachments, 384–384
    posting to, 378–379
    reading messages, 376–377
    replying to messages,
        380–381
    searching for messages,
        386–387
    subscribing to, 374–375
picture printing service,
    154–155
radio, 180–181
searching, 298–299
security, Windows Update
    and, 35
themes, obtaining, 85
video drivers, updating, 557
VPN, accessing through,
    290–291
Web pages, adding to
    desktop, 113
Internet Connection Wizard,
    Outlook Express, setup, 336–337
Internet Explorer
    browsing Web sites, 296–297
    default browser, setting as, 325
    desktop icon, displaying,
        110–111
    downloading Web pages,
        306–307
    Favorites
        organizing, 312–313
        saving, 310–311
    history
        changing number of days
            tracked, 318–319
        clearing, 318–319

displaying, 316
        sorting, 317
    home page, setting, 322–323
    launching, 294
    Links bar, customizing, 314–315
    My Current Web Page,
        displaying on desktop, 113
    objectionable material,
        blocking, 332–333
    privacy settings, 328–329
    searching in, 298–299
    security settings, 330–331
    support programs, changing
        settings, 324–325
    temporary files, deleting,
        320–321
    tools and toolbars, turning off,
        326–327
    URLs, 296
    user accounts and, 294
    Windows Media Player,
        updating, 162–163
    Windows Movie Maker,
        updating, 192
Internet Options dialog
    Content Advisor, settings,
        332–333
    home page, setting, 322
    privacy settings, 328–329
    security settings, 330–331
    support programs, changing
        settings, 324–325
    temporary files, deleting,
        320–321
ISP (Internet service provider),
    Internet access through, 284–285

J

JFIF files, 151
JPE files, 151
JPEG files, 151
JPG files, 133, 145, 151
junk mail (spam), killing with
    message rules, 368–369
justification, WordPad, 264

K

keyboard
    focus of, following with
        Magnifier, 429
    languages, adding support for
        other, 123
    On-Screen, 432–433
        selecting layout, 434–435

options, setting, 118–119
zooming picture view with, 142
Knowledge Base, Help and Support
Center, accessing from, 30–31

L

LAN (local area network). *See*
networks
languages, support, adding
additional, 123
laptop computers. *See* notebook
computers
layout, printing pictures, 152–153
legacy applications, running in XP,
540–541
legal considerations
copying music CDs, 167
downloading files, 307
licensing agreement, Windows
Media Player, 162–163
line conditioners, 512
Line tool (Paint), 137
links
defined, 299
emailing, 302
Links bar (Internet Explorer),
customizing, 314–315
Links folder, 311
List view, files and folders, 55
lists, WordPad, adding to
documents, 266–267
live video, capturing, 208–209
locking
ClickLock (mouse), 114
computer, 18–19
with screen saver, 20–21
taskbar, 99
toolbars, 60
toolbars, Internet Explorer, 327
log files, Notepad, creating with,
246–247
logging off, 4–5
fast switching and, 9
login screen, 2–3
logos, scanning black and
white, 130

M

Magnifier, accessibility features,
428–429
maintenance. *See* system
maintenance
Managed Web Sites list, removing
items, 329

margins (Page Setup)
Notepad, 236–237
printing in WordPad, 256
math calculations, Calculator
program, 408–409
Measurement Units (WordPad),
setting, 276–277
Media Guide, downloading music
files, 178–179
Media Library
playlists, creating, 176–177
song lyrics, adding, 174–175
Windows Media Player,
170–171
memory. *See also* RAM
video, effect on screen
resolution and color, 87
Messenger
audio and video, configuring,
402–403
chatting, 394–395
contacts
adding, 392–393
blocking, 397
display name, changing, 396
files
receiving, 400–401
sending, 398–399
fonts, changing, 397
Passport account, creating,
390–391
password, creating, 390
Remote Assistance, 552–553
status, changing, 396
voice and video communication,
404–405
Microsoft Knowledge Base. *See*
Knowledge Base, Help and
Support Center, accessing from
Microsoft Picture It!, 207
Microsoft Plus! pack, themes, 85
mixing sound (Sound Recorder),
422–423
mobile computing. *See* notebook
computers
modems, Internet access, MSN
accounts, 282–283
monitor
adjusting display problems,
546–547
multiple
backgrounds and, 89
configuring, 474–475
turning off, automatically,
16–17

monitored newsgroups, 379
month, setting, 10
mouse
customizing, 114–115
pointer, following with
Magnifier, 429
pointers
customizing, 116–117
themes, 84
Movie Maker. *See* Windows Movie
Maker
movies
creating, 202–203
playing, DVD, 194–195
saving to hard drive, 226–227
Windows Movie Maker,
updating, 192–193
MP3 players, copying music to,
182–183
MSinfo32.exe, accessing, 539
MSN.com
accounts, creating, 282–283
as home page, 294–295
MSN Groups, 156–157
multimedia
audio, setting volume level,
14–15
camcorder, capturing video
from, 204–205
clips
splitting and combining,
210–211
transitions between, 214–215
trimming, 212–213
collections
importing files into, 198–199
organizing, 198–199
DVD movies, playing, 194–195
live video, capturing, 208–209
movies
creating, 202–203
emailing, 228–229
saving, 226–227
narration, adding to movies,
224–225
pictures, capturing from video,
206–207
sound, adding to movies,
222–223
stills photos, adding to movies,
220–221
titles and credits, adding to
movies, 218–219
Video Effects, adding, 216–217

multimedia *(continued)*
　video files, playing, 196–197
　Windows Movie Maker,
　　updating, 192–193
multipart attachments,
　downloading from newsgroups,
　384–385
multiple monitors, backgrounds, 89
music
　CDs
　　creating, 184–185
　　duplicating, 186–187
　　identification information,
　　　168–169
　　copying CDs, 166–167
　　legal issues, 167
　　downloading, 178–179
　　playing with Windows Media
　　　Player, 164–165
　　portable players, 182–183
　　searching computer for,
　　　172–173
muting audio, 14
My Computer, 32–33
　accessing, 44–45
　desktop icon, displaying,
　　110–111
　remote access setup, 548–549
My Current Home Page option,
　desktop, 112
My Documents
　desktop icon, displaying,
　　110–111
　file and folder viewing options,
　　54–55
My Network Places, desktop icon,
　displaying, 110–111
My Picture Slide Show, screen
　saver options, 91
My Pictures
　Filmstrip view, 55
　images, printing, 152–153
　online picture printing service,
　　154–155
　Photo Album view, 138–139
　scanned images, 131
　user account icons, 455

N

narration, movies, adding to,
　224–225
Narrator, using, 430–431
navigation, files and folders in
　Windows Explorer, 46–47

networks
　Automatic Updates and, 35
　configuring, 484–485
　files
　　accessing shared, 492–493
　　sharing over, 490–491
　folders, assigning drive letters
　　to, 494–495
　Guest accounts and, 447
　hardware installation, 482–483
　Internet connections through,
　　288–289
　logging in, 2
　printers
　　accessing shared, 488–489
　　sharing, 486–487
　user accounts, creating, 449
newsgroups
　attachments
　　downloading, 382–383
　　downloading multipart,
　　　384–385
　connecting to, 372–373
　file attachments, 376
　messages
　　reading, 376–377
　　replying to, 380–381
　　searching for, 386–387
　monitored, 379
　posting to, 378–379
　searching for/subscribing to,
　　374–375
nonresponsive applications, closing,
　542–543
notebook computers
　battery power, conserving, 5,
　　498–499
　Briefcase, 508–509
　dial-up connections, creating
　　multiple, 502–503
　hibernation, 500–501
　Offline Files, 504–505
　synchronizing, 506–507
Notepad
　documents
　　creating, 232–233
　　printing, 242–243
　　saving, 234–235
　file size limits, 232
　filename, printing, 238
　fonts
　　changing, 240–241
　　restrictions, 233
　headers and footers, creating,
　　238–239

　log files, creating with, 246–247
　page setup, changing, 236–237
　searching and replacing text,
　　244–245
　special characters, 239
　tabs, 233
　Web pages, creating with,
　　248–249
notification area (taskbar),
　hiding/showing icons in, 98
Notification icon (Windows
　activation), 6
NTFS, verifying, 74
NTFS filesystem, compared to
　FAT32, 512
numbers
　converting to non-decimal
　　format (Calculator program),
　　414–415
　formatting, changing, 124–125

O

objectionable content, blocking in
　Internet Explorer, 332–333
octal numbers, converting to
　(Calculator program), 414–415
Offline Files
　configuring, 504–505
　synchronizing, 506–507
On-Screen Keyboard
　selecting layout, 434–435
　using, 432–433
Open With option, viewing
　pictures, 142
optimizing performance, 560–563
orientation (Page Setup)
　Notepad, 236
　printing in WordPad, 256
Outbox (Outlook Express), sending
　email, 343
Outlook Express
　attachments
　　opening, 340–341
　　saving, 341
　　sending, 346–347
　contacts, 360–361
　email
　　creating, 342–343
　　sending, 343
　flag indicator, 355
　folders, creating for messages,
　　356–357
　forwarding email, 344–345
　Inbox, organizing, 354–355
　message rules, 368–369

messages
 deleting, 355
 printing, 354
 retrieving and viewing,
  338–339
 searching for, 358–359
 sorting, 355
newsgroups
 connecting to, 372–373
 downloading attachments,
  382–383
 downloading multipart
  attachments, 384–384
 posting to, 378–379
 reading messages, 376–377
 replying to messages,
  380–381
 searching for messages,
  386–387
 subscribing to, 374–375
passwords, remembering, 337
replying to email, 345
setup, 336–337
signatures, 352–353
stationery, 348–349
 creating, 350–351
vCards
 adding to address book,
  366–367
 creating, 362–363
 sending, 364–365

P

page setup (Notepad)
 changing, 236–237
 headers and footers, 238–239
Page Setup options, WordPad,
 256–257
Paint
 copying images, file type
  limitations, 147
 icons, creating, 134–135
 images
  cropping, 146–147
  resizing, 144–145
 pictures, drawing, 136–137
 screen captures and, 132–133
 zooming, 146
paper, selecting characteristics in
 WordPad, 256
paragraph formatting, WordPad,
 264–265
Passport, requirement for (online
 picture publishing), 156–157

Passport account, creating,
 390–391
passwords
 Content Advisor, 332–333
 creating
  advice for, 459
  locking computer, 18
 login screen, 2–3
 Outlook Express, remembering
  in, 337
 recovering forgotten, 3
 remote access considerations, 549
 screen savers and, 20–21
 user accounts
  adding to, 458–459
  changing, 460–461
  removing from, 460–461
 Windows Messenger, 390
 Zip files, protecting with, 79
patches
 defined, 34
 system updating with, 534–535
Pencil tool (Paint), 137
Per Site Privacy Actions dialog,
 changing settings, 329
performance
 Adjust for Best Performance
  option, 562
 downloading files, factors
  effecting, 307
 hard drive, defragmenting, 562
 Internet connection speed
  considerations, 563
 optimizing, 560–561
 RAM amount, 32
Performance and Maintenance
 (Control Panel), Automatic
 Updates, enabling, 34–35
personal information
 Web privacy and, 329
 Web security and, 330
Photo Album view (My Pictures
 folder), 138–139
photo-editing software, Microsoft
 Picture It!, 207
photo quality paper, printing,
 advantages of, 152
photos. See pictures
Picture and Fax Viewer, 142–143
 annotating images, 148–149
pictures. See also images
 capturing from video, 206–207
 capturing photos from scanner,
  130–131
 cropping, 146–147

deleting from Picture and Fax
 Viewer, 143
Details view, displaying
 summary information, 141
digital camera setup, 128–129
email attachments, sending as,
 346–347
JPG file type, suitability of, 145
Messenger, sending in, 398–399
online printing service, 154–155
organizing, 138–139
Paint, creating in, 136–137
printing, 152–153
publishing to Web site, 156–157
resizing in Paint, 144–145
rotating view, 143
screen savers, creating, 158–159
summary information, creating,
 140–141
user accounts, changing for, 455
viewing, 142–143
Web sites, saving from, 308–309
WordPad, inserting into,
 268–269
Pin from Start menu option, 103
playback
 DVD movies, 194–195
 music CDs, 164–165
players, portable music, 182–183
playlists (Windows Media Player),
 creating, 176–177
plus sign, Windows Explorer,
 46–47
PNG files, 151
pointer (mouse)
 customizing, 116–117
 options, setting, 114–115
portable music players, copying
 music to, 182–183
Power Options dialog, turning
 monitor off, 16
power schemes, creating/
 deleting, 17
preview
 printing Web pages, 304
 screen saver, 91
 video effects in Windows Movie
  Maker, 216
 WordPad print preview,
  258–259
Print Preview
 printing Web pages, 304
 WordPad, 258–259
Print Screen key, screen captures,
 132–133

printers
  accessing over networks,
    488–489
  installing, 470–471
  Page Setup (WordPad), 256
  searching for, 243, 305
  sharing over networks, 486–487
Printers and Other Hardware
  (Control Panel)
  keyboard options, setting,
    118–119
  mouse
    customizing, 114–115
    customizing pointers,
      116–117
printing
  collating copies, 261
  email messages, 355
  to file, 261
  filenames, Notepad, 238
  images, 152–153
  Notepad, changing Page setup,
    236–237
  Notepad documents, 242–243
  options in My Pictures
    folder, 153
  photo quality paper, 152
  pictures, online services,
    154–155
  screen captures, 133
  Web pages, 304–305
  WordPad, 260–261
    envelopes, 259
    print preview, 258–259
privacy. *See also* security
  Internet Explorer settings,
    328–329
  turning monitor off, 17
  Windows Media Player,
    downloading and, 162
processor. *See* CPU
Program events, assigning sounds
  to, 94–95
programming code, saved Web
  pages, 301
programs. *See also* software
  launching at computer startup,
    120–121
projects, Windows Movie
  Maker, 202
properties
  files and folders, displaying, 68
  hard drive, checking for errors,
    512–513
  pictures, creating summary
    information, 140–141

program shortcuts, selecting,
  108–109
shortcuts, 71
Start menu, customizing,
  102–103
taskbar, 98–99
publishing, pictures to Web site,
  156–157

Q
quick launch (taskbar)
  customizing, 100–101
  displaying, 99

R
radio (Internet)
  listening to online, 180–181
  video radio stations, 181
RAM
  computer performance and, 563
  requirements, 33
  viewing information about,
    33, 45
read-only attribute (files),
  defined, 68
rebooting. *See* restarting
  Windows XP
recording, audio, 420–421
Rectangle tool (Paint), 137
Recycle Bin
  bypassing, 49, 65
  icons, setting, 111
  options, setting, 64–65
  recovering items from, 62–63
regional settings, changing,
  122–123
registering Windows XP, 7
  viewing registration
    information, 32–33
registry, cautions about
  accessing, 121
remote access, setting up for,
  548–549
Remote Assistance
  obtaining, 552–553
  providing, 554–555
  setup, 548–549
Remote Desktop
  setup, 548–549
  using, 550–551
removable storage devices, adding
  and removing, 472–473
repeat delay (keyboard), setting,
  118–119
repeat playback (Windows Media
  Player), 165

replying to email, 345, 353
resolution
  adjusting, 86–87
  defined, 86
  DVD playback errors and,
    194–195
  Remote Assistance
    recommendations for, 552
  standard sizes, 86
restarting Windows XP, 5
  after software installation,
    38–39
  after updating, 36
Restore Points, creating, 526–527
restoring files from backup,
  532–533
Review and Install Updates list,
  updating Windows XP, 36
ripping CDs, music CDs, 166–167
rotating, pictures, 143
Rounded Rectangle tool
  (Paint), 137
RTF files, document formatting
  and, 255
rules (Outlook Express), 368–369
Run Desktop Cleanup Wizard
  option, 107

S
scanner
  capturing photographs, 130–131
  selecting part of image to scan,
    130
Scanner and Camera Wizard,
  copying pictures to disk, 128–129
scientific calculator view
  (Calculator program), 410–411
  numbers, converting base
    systems, 414–415
  statistical calculations, 411
  trigonometric calculations, 411
screen captures, Print Screen key,
  132–133
screen savers
  creating, your pictures, 158–159
  locking computer with, 20–21
  reasons to use, 20
  selecting/changing, 90
  setting properties of, 91
  turning off, 90
screen size. *See* resolution
search and replace, Notepad,
  244–245
search and replace (WordPad),
  268–269

Search Companion
    files, locating lost, 544–545
    Internet Explorer, 298
    Windows Explorer,
        displaying, 67
searching
    computer for music files,
        172–173
    email messages (Outlook
        Express), 358–359
    Help and Support Center
        Search Options, 26–27
        tips, 23
    for Messenger contacts, 293
    Microsoft Knowledge Base,
        30–31
    music Media Library files, 171
    for newsgroup messages,
        386–387
    for newsgroups, 374–375
    options for, setting, 66–67
    for printers, 243, 305
    Search Companion, 544–545
    the Web, 298–299
    Web pages, within, 299
security. See also privacy
    automatic time and date
        setting, 13
    firewalls, Messenger and, 399
    Internet Explorer settings,
        330–331
    locking computer, 18–19
        screen saver, 20–21
    Windows Update and, 35
separator bars
    adding to toolbars, 61
    Standard Buttons bar, adding
        to, 327
service releases, defined, 34
shortcuts. See also icons
    deleting, 71
    desktop, adding to, 104–105
    files, creating for, 70–71
    program icons, selecting,
        108–109
    properties, viewing, 71
    Start menu, clearing from, 102
Show Desktop icon, usefulness
    of, 105
shuffle playback (Windows Media
    Player), 165
signatures (email), creating,
    352–353
skin mode, Windows Media Player,
    switching to full mode, 195

skins (Windows Media Player),
    selecting, 188–189
Slide Show (Picture and Fax
    Viewer), 143
software. See also programs
    image editing, Web sites
        for, 136
    information about, finding, 520
    installing, 38–39
    legacy applications, running,
        540–541
    nonresponsive applications,
        closing, 542–543
    patches, 534–535
    removing applications, 40–41
    shortcut icons, selecting,
        108–109
    uninstalling, 520–521
    updating Windows XP, 34–35
song lyrics
    adding to Windows Media
        Player, 174–175
    Web sites, 175
sorting
    Details view columns (Windows
        Explorer), 57
    email (Outlook Express), 355
    Internet Explorer history, 317
    Links bar items, 315
    playlists in Media Library, 177
sound. See audio
Sound Recorder
    mixing with, 422–423
    using, 420–421
sound schemes, selecting, 94–95
Sounds and Audio Devices
    Properties dialog, 14
Sounds, Speech, and Audio Devices
    (Control Panel)
    sound schemes, selecting, 94–95
    speakers, configuring, 468–469
spam, killing with message rules,
    368–369
speakers
    configuring, 468–469
    volume controls, 14
special characters, Notepad, 239
spell checker (WordPad), 252
splicing, clips into movies, 202
Stand By option, 5
Standard Buttons bar, Internet
    Explorer
    customizing, 327
    turning off, 326

standard icons, desktop, adding to,
    110–111
Standard Keyboard (On-Screen
    Keyboard), 434
Start menu
    Accessibility Wizard, 438–439
    customizing, 102–103
    Disk Cleanup, accessing, 512
    files and folders, searching for,
        66–67
    Help and Support, 22–23
    Magnifier, turning on, 428
    My Computer, 32–33, 44–45
    Narrator, turning on, 430–431
    On-Screen Keyboard, 432–433
    printers, installing, 470–471
    Startup folder, 120–121
    themes and, 84
    Utility Manager, 436–437
    Windows Explorer,
        launching, 46
    WordPad, launching, 252
Startup folder, adding
    programs, 120
stationery (email)
    creating, 350–351
    selecting, 348–349
statistical calculations, performing
    with Calculator program,
    412–413
Statistics box (Calculator
    program), 412
status bar
    Internet Explorer
        padlock icon, 330
        turning off, 326
    Messenger, 394
    Windows Explorer,
        displaying, 61
StickyKeys, setting, 440–441
still pictures, capturing from video,
    206–207
Storyboard, clips, splicing into
    movies, 202
streamed audio, defined, 180
Stretch option, desktop
    background, 89
subfolders
    contents, displaying, 46–47
    saving Favorite Web sites
        to, 311
    searching through, 67
subscribing to newsgroups,
    374–375

summary information
   creating/editing, 69
   pictures, 140–141
system font size, changing,
   426–427
system information
   finding, 32–33
   My Computer, 44–45
   obtaining, 538–539
system maintenance
   Desktop Cleanup Wizard, 523
   Disk Cleanup, 516–517
   files, backing up, 530–531
   hard drive defragmentation,
     514–515
   hard drive errors, checking for,
     512–513
   patches and add-ons, 534–535
   Restore Points, creating,
     526–527
   System Restore, 524–525
     configuring, 528–529
System Properties dialog
   Error Reporting feature,
     558–559
   performance options, 560–561
   View System Information task,
     32–33
system requirements
   RAM, 33
   small networks, 482
System Restore, 524–525, 528–529

T

tabs, Notepad, 233
Task Manager, nonresponsive
  applications, closing, 542–543
taskbar
   quick launch, customizing,
     100–101
   Remote Desktop appearance,
     551
   resizing, 99
Taskbar and Start Menu Properties
  dialog, taskbar, customizing,
  98–99
taskbar (desktop)
   customizing, 98–99
   location, changing, 98–99
   notification area,
     hiding/showing, 98
   toolbars, displaying, 99
technical support, Remote
  Assistance, 552–553
temporary files (Internet Explorer),
  deleting, 320–321

text, selecting in WordPad, 262
Text tool (Paint), 137
themes
   copying/renaming, 84
   creating, 96–87
   custom, creating, 84
   defines, 96
   deleting, 85
   mouse settings, 114
   screen savers and, 91
   selecting, 84–85
third party (Internet privacy), 329
Thumbnail view, files and
  folders, 54
thumbnails, pictures, displaying as
  in folders, 139
TIF files
   annotating with Picture and Fax
     Viewer, 148–149
   suitability for, 133
Tile option, desktop
  background, 89
Tiles view, files and folders, 54–55
tiling images, email stationery, 350
time, setting, 11
time zone, setting, 11
Timeline (Windows Movie Maker),
  viewing, 203
timestamp, files, 11
Tip of the Day (Windows
  Explorer), turning on/off, 61
titles and credits, adding to movies,
  218–219
ToggleKeys, 440
toolbars
   History Explorer bar, 61
   Internet Explorer
     moving/resizing, 327
     turning off, 326
   quick launch, customizing,
     100–101
   taskbar, displaying on, 99
   Windows Explorer,
     customizing, 60–61
   WordPad, displaying, 277
transitions (video clips), 214–215
transmission speeds, online radio
  stations, 180
trash can. *See* Recycle Bin
trigonometry calculations,
  performing with Calculator
  program, 411
troubleshooting
   compared to help, 23
   legacy applications, 540–541

monitor, adjusting display
   problems, 546–547
nonresponsive applications,
   closing, 542–543
Remote Assistance and,
   552–555
reporting problems to
   Microsoft, 558–559
system information, obtaining,
   538–539
video drivers, updating,
   556–557
TrueType (TT) fonts, 241
trusted sites (Internet Explorer),
  adding, 331
TT (TrueType) fonts, 241
turning computer off, 4–5
TXT files, document formatting
  and, 255
typing, messages in Messenger, 394

U

undoing, copying files and folders,
  51
uninstalling
   applications, 40–41
   devices, 478–479
   software, 520–521
Unpin from Start menu option, 103
unrecoverable files, Recycle Bin
  and, 63
unsubscribing to newsgroups, 375
updating
   Automatic Updates, enabling,
     34–35
   patches and add-ons, 534–535
   software patches, 34
   video drivers, 556–557
   Windows Media Player,
     162–163
   Windows Movie Maker,
     192–193
   Windows Update, 36–37
   Zip files, 79
uploading, defined, 306
UPS (Universal Power
  Supply), 512
URLs (Universal Resource
  Locators)
   defined, 296
   email subject lines, 303
   extensions, 297
   makeup of, 297
usability features
   Accessibility Manager, 438–439
   Utility Manager, 436–437

Use Windows Classic Folders. *See* Classic Folders
user accounts, 2–3
    creating, 448–449
    deleting, 450–451
    fast switching among, 8–9
    Guest account, setting up, 446–447
    icon for, changing, 454–455
    Internet Explorer and, 294
    locking computer, 18–19
    passwords
        adding to, 458–459
        changing, 460–461
        removing from, 460–461
    renaming, 452–453
    type, changing, 456–457
user profiles, 3
Utility Manager, using, 436–437

V

vCards (Outlook Express)
    address book, adding to, 366–367
    creating, 362–363
    sending, 364–365
version (Windows), viewing, 32
video
    camcorder, capturing from, 204–205
    clips
        splitting and combining, 210–211
        transitions between, 214–215
        trimming, 212–213
    emailing, 228–229
    live, capturing, 208–209
    Messenger, configuring in, 402–403
    movies, saving, 226–227
    narration, adding, 224–225
    pictures, capturing from, 206–207
    playback size, setting, 194, 196–197
    playing files, 196–197
    quality, storage space considerations, 205
    sound, adding to, 222–223
    stills photos, adding, 220–221
    titles and credits, adding, 218–219
    Video Effects, adding, 216–217
Video and Visualization pane (Windows Media Player), 165

video drivers, updating, 556–557
video radio stations, 181
Video Visualization pane (Windows Media Player), 164
videophone-type communication in Messenger, 404–405
View Installation History list, updating Windows XP, 37
View system information (My Computer), 45
View System Information task (System Properties dialog), 32–33
views
    file and folder viewing options, 54–55
    global options, setting, 58–59
viruses
    downloading files and, 307
    Zip files and, 81
volume, setting, 14–15
Volume Control dialog, 15
VPN (Virtual Private Network), Internet access through, 290–291

W

wallpaper. *See* background
wave files, defined, 94
Web addresses. *See* URLs (Universal Resource Locators)
Web page behavior, setting for folder display, 59
Web pages
    creating from saved pages, 301
    desktop
        adding to, 112–113
        deleting from, 113
    emailing, 302–303
    JPG image file type, 145
    Notepad, creating with, 248–249
    printing, 304–305
    saving, 300–301
Web sites
    browsing with Internet Explorer, 296–297
    defined, 297
    DVD codecs, 194–195
    email stationery, 349
    image editing software, 136
    images, saving, 308–309
    Microsoft Knowledge Base, 30–31
    MSN Groups, 156–157
    privacy settings for, 329
    publishing pictures to, 156–157

    saving as Favorites, 310–311
    song lyrics, 175
    sound effects, 222
    Windows Media Player, 162
welcome screen, 2
windows, themes and, 84
Windows Classic desktop style, selecting, 92
Windows Classic theme, description, 85
Windows components, adding/removing, 518–519
Windows Explorer
    CD-RW, writing files to, 72–73
    Common areas, displaying, 61
    Details view, customizing, 56–57
    displaying files and folders, 46–47
    file and folder operations in, 48–49
    file and folder viewing options, 54–55
    global viewing options, setting, 58–59
    Go To menu, 47
    left pane views, changing, 47
    navigation buttons in, 47
    Open Each Folder options, 59
    Search Companion, displaying, 67
    Standard toolbar customization, 60–61
    status bar, displaying, 61
    Tip of the Day, enabling/disabling, 61
    Zip files, creating, 77
Windows Media Player
    CD identification information, entering, 168–169
    DVD movies, 194–195
    Media Library, 170–171
    music CDs
        creating, 184–185
        duplicating, 186–187
        playing, 164–165
    playlists, creating, 176–177
    portable music players, copying music to, 182–183
    radio tuner function, 180–181
    searching computer for music files, 172–173
    skin mode, switching to full mode, 195
    skins, selecting, 188–189

Windows Media Player *(continued)*
   song lyrics, adding, 174–175
   updating, 162–163
   video files, playing, 196–197
Windows Messenger. *See*
  Messenger
Windows Movie Maker
   camcorder, capturing video
     from, 204–205
   clips
     deleting from movies, 203
     splicing into movies, 202
     splitting and combining,
      210–211
     transitions between, 214–215
     trimming, 212–213
   collections
     deleting, 199
     importing files into, 200–201
     organizing, 198–199
     playing items from, 201
   live video, capturing, 208–209
   movies
     creating, 202–203
     emailing, 228–229
     saving, 226–227
   narration, 224–225
   pictures, capturing from video,
     206–207
   projects, 202
   sound, adding to movies,
     222–223

   stills photos, adding, 220–221
   Timeline, viewing, 203
   titles and credits, adding,
     218–219
   updating, 192–193
   Video Effects, adding, 216–217
Windows Picture and Fax Viewer,
  142–143
   annotating images, 148–149
Windows Update
   implementing, 36–37
   system maintenance and,
     534–535
Windows XP desktop style,
  selecting, 92
Windows XP theme, description, 85
word wrap option (WordPad),
  setting, 277
WordPad
   configuration options, setting,
     276–277
   documents
     creating, 252–253
     emailing, 276–277
     naming considerations, 254
     saving, 254–255
   envelopes, printing, 259
   fonts, changing characteristics
     of, 262–263
   lists, adding to documents,
     266–267

   objects
     adding, 268–269
     changing properties,
      270–271
   Page Setup options, 256–257
   paragraph formatting, 264–265
   pictures. inserting into, 268–269
   print preview, 258–259
   printing, 260–261
   search and replace, 268–269
   spell checker, 252
   toolbars, selecting, 277
   Word for Windows
     compatibility, 255

Y

year, setting, 10

Z

Zip files
   adding to, 78–79
   creating, 76–77
   dangers associated with, 81
   deleting content from, 78–79
   extracting, 78–79
   extracting all items, 80–81
   password protecting, 79
zooming
   in Paint, 146
   pictures, viewing, 142
   WordPad print preview, 259